"Lochnerism": p.197(a)

556   EP notes: p.88 email

CONSTITUTIONAL LAW

IN A NUTSHELL

Sixth Edition

By

JEROME A. BARRON
Harold H. Greene Professor of Law
George Washington University Law School

C. THOMAS DIENES
Lyle T. Alverson Professor of Law
George Washington University Law School

THOMSON

™

WEST

Mat #40332534

Nutshell Series, In a Nutshell, the Nutshell Logo and West Group are trademarks registered in the U.S. Patent and Trademark Office.

COPYRIGHT © 1986, 1991, 1995 WEST PUBLISHING CO.
© West, a Thomson business, 1999, 2003
© 2005 Thomson/West
      610 Opperman Drive
      P.O. Box 64526
      St. Paul, MN 55164–0526
      1–800–328–9352
Printed in the United States of America

ISBN 0–314–15880–4

*TEXT IS PRINTED ON 10% POST
CONSUMER RECYCLED PAPER*

For Kim
And
For Jonathan, David, and Jennifer

*

FOREWORD TO THE SIXTH EDITION

We submitted the manuscript for the fifth edition of this book in September 2002—nearly three years ago. In that interval, the Court has come down with a substantial number of cases which warrant this new edition. Although close to fifty new cases are discussed in this new sixth edition, we have, of course, given particular attention to the major ones. Some of the most important of these are described below.

In the Commerce Clause area, *Gonzales v. Raich* (2005), the medical marijuana case, was a significant development. A California law exempting from criminal prosecution the production and use of marijuana for medicinal purposes was trumped by the federal Controlled Substances Act. The latter statute was held to be within congressional commerce power. As we point out, *Raich* was a surprisingly strong re-affirmation of the affectation doctrine as well as its cumulative effects corollary. Another important case was *Granholm v. Heald* (2005), the so-called "wine" case. There the Court held that the Twenty-First Amendment did not authorize, and that the Dormant Commerce Clause precluded, the states from discriminating against direct sales by out-of-state wineries.

In the Takings area, we report the long-awaited decision in *Kelo v. City of New London* (2005) where the Court upheld, 5–4, a city's economic development plan even though it involved the taking by the city of the property of private home owners. Economic development was held to be a legitimate public purpose and thus a valid "public use" under the Takings Clause. The protest of the dissenters that all real property in the country was now susceptible to the risks of condemnation is summarized.

This volume also chronicles one of the more significant due process cases in recent years, *Lawrence v. Texas* (2003). There the Court struck down a Texas statute making it a crime for two persons of the same sex to engage in sodomy. Justice Kennedy's influential elaboration of the meaning of the liberty in the Fourteenth Amendment and the protection it extends to individual autonomy is extensively discussed. So is the passionate dissent of Justice Scalia. In the area of procedural due process, the due process rights of citizen enemy combatants are highlighted as outlined by the Court in *Hamdi v. Rumsfeld* (2004).

In equal protection, the major developments were the affirmative action cases coming from the University of Michigan, *Grutter v. Bollinger* (2003) and *Gratz v. Bollinger* (2003). The rationale for upholding the law school program in *Grutter* while at the same time invalidating the college program in *Gratz* is discussed. The holding that educational diversity in public higher education can be a compelling governmental interest satisfying the strict scrutiny standard is traced from its roots in Justice Powell's opinion in *Bakke*. But attention is also given to the Court's ruling that the narrow tailoring requirement of that standard demands individualized consideration for each applicant.

As has usually been the case in recent years, the Court's First Amendment decisions have comprised a substantial part of the Court's work product and, therefore, of each new edition of this book. In that respect, this sixth edition is typical of its predecessors. We give more extended discussion to the most important of these First Amendment decisions. For example, in *Virginia v. Black* (2003), the Court's discussion of true threats as an unprotected category of speech is examined. The focus is on the Court's holding that cross-burnings done with an intent to intimidate are unprotected true threats. Other First Amendment decisions include *United States v. American Library Association* (2003) which upheld the Child Internet Protection Act [CIPA] against a First Amendment challenge. That Act provided that public libraries could not receive grants of federal funds to provide Internet access unless they installed software blocking images containing obscenity or child pornography. In its decision upholding CIPA, the Court's reliance on *Rust v. Sullivan* (1991) and its ruling that public funds can only be spent for the purposes for which Congress has designated them is pointed out.

Several new cases involving speech in the electoral process are included in this book. Clearly the most significant is *McConnell v. Federal Election Commission* (2003). In that case, the Court upheld the most important elements of the Bipartisan Campaign Finance Reform Act of 2002, popularly known as the McCain-Feingold law. The way in which the new law restricts the use of "soft-money" is tracked. We try to summarize the unusually lengthy opinions in a manner which captures the essence of the over-all holding of the Court but which does so in a concise and understandable way.

Another essential part of our First Amendment law concerns freedom of religion. We report several new cases in that field. The Court's two decisions on the Ten Commandments received more national attention than any other religion case during this period. Superficially, the decisions appear to contradict each other since the display of the Ten Commandments in two Kentucky courthouses was deemed a violation of the Establishment Clause while a huge monument on the Texas State Capitol grounds inscribed with the Ten Commandments was held not to violate the Establishment Clause. We point out that the opinions of eight of the Justices in the two cases were in fact in the main consistent. The vote of Justice Breyer was the critical one since he voted differently in the two cases. We try to explain why.

As always our objective is to provide a reader with a short summary of contemporary constitutional law which is long enough to be helpful and short enough to be useful. Generally, in important cases we have tried to indicate which Justice authored the opinion of the Court. Similarly, we often discuss the dissents in such cases and indicate the Justices who authored them. Space, of course, does not permit engaging in this practice on a uniform basis. In this edition, in order to make room for the new, we have had to excise from this new edition some cases which for us were old friends. Our effort in this edition as in its predecessors is to try to be as clear and concise as we can be without making the law clearer than it is. We also have attempted to show divisions on the Court but we have sought to do so with fairness and accuracy. Whether we have succeeded we leave to you our readers.

JEROME A. BARRON
C. THOMAS DIENES

Washington, D.C.
September 2005

*

OUTLINE

OUTLINE

PART TWO. INDIVIDUAL RIGHTS AND LIBERTIES

Page

*

TABLE OF CASES

References are to Pages

TABLE OF CASES

TABLE OF CASES

TABLE OF CASES

TABLE OF CASES

TABLE OF CASES

TABLE OF CASES

*

THE CONSTITUTION OF THE UNITED STATES

1787

Preamble

We the People of the United States, in Order to form a more perfect Union, establish Justice, insure domestic Tranquility, provide for the common defence, promote the general Welfare, and secure the Blessings of Liberty to ourselves and our Posterity, do ordain and establish this Constitution for the United States of America.

Article I

Section 1. All legislative Powers herein granted shall be vested in a Congress of the United States, which shall consist of a Senate and House of Representatives.

Section 2. [1] The House of Representatives shall be composed of Members chosen every second Year by the People of the several States, and the Electors in each State shall have the Qualifications requisite for Electors of the most numerous Branch of the State Legislature.

[2] No Person shall be a Representative who shall not have attained to the Age of twenty five Years,

and been seven Years a Citizen of the United States, and who shall not, when elected, be an Inhabitant of that State in which he shall be chosen.

[3] [Representatives and direct Taxes shall be apportioned among the several States which may be included within this Union, according to their respective Numbers, which shall be determined by adding to the whole Number of free Persons, including those bound to Service for a Term of Years, and excluding Indians not taxed, three fifths of all other Persons.] The actual Enumeration shall be made within three Years after the first Meeting of the Congress of the United States, and within every subsequent Term of ten Years, in such Manner as they shall by Law direct. The Number of Representatives shall not exceed one for every thirty Thousand, but each State shall have at Least one Representative; and until such enumeration shall be made, the State of New Hampshire shall be entitled to chuse three, Massachusetts eight, Rhode Island and Providence Plantations one, Connecticut five, New York six, New Jersey four, Pennsylvania eight, Delaware one, Maryland six, Virginia ten, North Carolina five, South Carolina five, and Georgia three.

[4] When vacancies happen in the Representation from any State, the Executive Authority thereof shall issue Writs of Election to fill such Vacancies.

[5] The House of Representatives shall chuse their Speaker and other Officers; and shall have the sole Power of Impeachment.

Section 3. [1] [The Senate of the United States shall be composed of two Senators from each State, chosen by the Legislature thereof, for six Years; and each Senator shall have one Vote.]

[2] Immediately after they shall be assembled in Consequence of the first Election, they shall be divided as equally as may be into three Classes. The Seats of the Senators of the first Class shall be vacated at the Expiration of the Second Year, of the second Class at the Expiration of the fourth Year, and of the third Class at the Expiration of the sixth Year, so that one third may be chosen every second Year; [and if Vacancies happen by Resignation, or otherwise, during the Recess of the Legislature of any State, the Executive thereof may make temporary Appointments until the next Meeting of the Legislature, which shall then fill such Vacancies.]

[3] No Person shall be a Senator who shall not have attained to the Age of thirty Years, and been nine Years a Citizen of the United States, and who shall not, when elected, be an Inhabitant of that State for which he shall be chosen.

[4] The Vice President of the United States shall be President of the Senate, but shall have no Vote, unless they be equally divided.

[5] The Senate shall chuse their other Officers, and also a President pro tempore, in the Absence of the Vice President, or when he shall exercise the Office of President of the United States.

[6] The Senate shall have the sole Power to try all Impeachments. When sitting for that Purpose, they shall be on Oath or Affirmation. When the President of the United States is tried, the Chief Justice shall preside: And no Person shall be convicted without the Concurrence of two thirds of the Members present.

[7] Judgment in Cases of Impeachment shall not extend further than to removal from Office, and disqualification to hold and enjoy any Office of honor, Trust, or Profit under the United States: but the Party convicted shall nevertheless be liable and subject to Indictment, Trial, Judgment, and Punishment, according to Law.

Section 4. [1] The Times, Places and Manner of holding Elections for Senators and Representatives, shall be prescribed in each State by the Legislature thereof; but the Congress may at any time by Law make or alter such Regulations, except as to the Places of chusing Senators.

[2] The Congress shall assemble at least once in every Year, and such Meeting shall be on the first Monday in December, unless they shall by Law appoint a different Day.

Section 5. [1] Each House shall be the Judge of the Elections, Returns, and Qualifications of its own Members, and a Majority of each shall constitute a Quorum to do Business; but a smaller Number may adjourn from day to day, and may be authorized to compel the Attendance of absent Members, in such

Manner, and under such Penalties as each House may provide.

[2] Each House may determine the Rules of its Proceedings, punish its Members for disorderly Behavior, and, with the Concurrence of two thirds, expel a Member.

[3] Each House shall keep a Journal of its Proceedings, and from time to time publish the same, excepting such Parts as may in their Judgment require Secrecy; and the Yeas and Nays of the Members of either House on any question shall, at the Desire of one fifth of those Present, be entered on the Journal.

[4] Neither House, during the Session of Congress, shall, without the Consent of the other, adjourn for more than three days, nor to any other Place than that in which the two Houses shall be sitting.

Section 6. [1] The Senators and Representatives shall receive a Compensation for their Services, to be ascertained by Law, and paid out of the Treasury of the United States. They shall in all Cases, except Treason, Felony and Breach of the Peace, be privileged from Arrest during their Attendance at the Session of their respective Houses, and in going to and returning from the same; and for any Speech or Debate in either House, they shall not be questioned in any other Place.

[2] No Senator or Representative shall, during the Time for which he was elected, be appointed to any civil Office under the Authority of the United States, which shall have been created, or the Emoluments whereof shall have been increased during such time; and no Person holding any Office under the United States, shall be a member of either House during his Continuance in Office.

Section 7. [1] All Bills for raising Revenue shall originate in the House of Representatives; but the Senate may propose or concur with Amendments as on other Bills.

[2] Every Bill which shall have passed the House of Representatives and the Senate, shall, before it become a Law, be presented to the President of the United States; If he approve he shall sign it, but if not he shall return it, with his Objections to the House in which it shall have originated, who shall enter the Objections at large on their Journal, and proceed to reconsider it. If after such Reconsideration two thirds of that House shall agree to pass the Bill, it shall be sent together with the Objections, to the other House, by which it shall likewise be reconsidered, and if approved by two thirds of that House, it shall become a Law. But in all such Cases the Votes of both Houses shall be determined by Yeas and Nays, and the Names of the Persons voting for and against the Bill shall be entered on the Journal of each House respectively. If any Bill shall not be returned by the President within ten Days (Sundays

excepted) after it shall have been presented to him, the Same shall be a Law, in like Manner as if he had signed it, unless the Congress by their Adjournment prevent its Return in which Case it shall not be a Law.

[3] Every Order, Resolution, or Vote, to Which the Concurrence of the Senate and House of Representatives may be necessary (except on a question of Adjournment) shall be presented to the President of the United States; and before the Same shall take Effect, shall be approved by him, or being disapproved by him, shall be repassed by two thirds of the Senate and House of Representatives, according to the Rules and Limitations prescribed in the Case of a Bill.

Section 8. [1] The Congress shall have Power to lay and collect Taxes, Duties, Imposts and Excises, to pay the Debts and provide for the common Defence and general Welfare of the United States; but all Duties, Imposts and Excises shall be uniform throughout the United States;

[2] To borrow money on the credit of the United States;

[3] To regulate Commerce with foreign Nations, and among the several States, and with the Indian Tribes;

[4] To establish an uniform Rule of Naturalization, and uniform Laws on the subject of Bankruptcies throughout the United States;

[5] To coin Money, regulate the Value thereof, and of foreign Coin, and fix the Standard of Weights and Measures;

[6] To provide for the Punishment of counterfeiting the Securities and current Coin of the United States;

[7] To Establish Post Offices and Post Roads;

[8] To promote the Progress of Science and useful Arts, by securing for limited Times to Authors and Inventors the exclusive Right to their respective Writings and Discoveries;

[9] To constitute Tribunals inferior to the supreme Court;

[10] To define and punish Piracies and Felonies committed on the high Seas, and Offenses against the Law of Nations;

[11] To declare War, grant Letters of Marque and Reprisal, and make Rules concerning Captures on Land and Water;

[12] To raise and support Armies, but no Appropriation of Money to that Use shall be for a longer Term than two Years;

[13] To provide and maintain a Navy;

[14] To make Rules for the Government and Regulation of the land and naval Forces;

[15] To provide for calling forth the Militia to execute the Laws of the Union, suppress Insurrections and repel Invasions;

[16] To provide for organizing, arming, and disciplining, the Militia, and for governing such Part of them as may be employed in the Service of the United States, reserving to the States respectively, the Appointment of the Officers, and the Authority of training the Militia according to the discipline prescribed by Congress;

[17] To exercise exclusive Legislation in all Cases whatsoever, over such District (not exceeding ten Miles square) as may, by Cession of particular States and the Acceptance of Congress, become the Seat of the Government of the United States, and to exercise like Authority over all Places purchased by the Consent of the Legislature of the State in which the Same shall be, for the Erection of Forts, Magazines, Arsenals, dock-Yards, and other needful Buildings;—And

[18] To make all Laws which shall be necessary and proper for carrying into Execution the foregoing Powers, and all other Powers vested by this Constitution in the Government of the United States, or in any Department or Officer thereof.

Section 9. [1] The Migration or Importation of Such Persons as any of the States now existing shall think proper to admit, shall not be prohibited by the Congress prior to the Year one thousand eight hundred and eight, but a Tax or duty may be imposed on such Importation, not exceeding ten dollars for each Person.

[2] The privilege of the Writ of Habeas Corpus shall not be suspended, unless when in Cases of Rebellion or Invasion the public Safety may require it.

[3] No Bill of Attainder or ex post facto Law shall be passed.

[4] No Capitation, or other direct, Tax shall be laid, unless in Proportion to the census or Enumeration herein before directed to be taken.

[5] No Tax or Duty shall be laid on Articles exported from any State.

[6] No Preference shall be given by any Regulation of Commerce or Revenue to the Ports of one State over those of another: nor shall Vessels bound to, or from, one State be obliged to enter, clear, or pay Duties in another.

[7] No money shall be drawn from the Treasury, but in Consequence of Appropriations made by Law; and a regular Statement and Account of the Receipts and Expenditures of all public Money shall be published from time to time.

[8] No Title of Nobility shall be granted by the United States: And no Person holding any Office of Profit or Trust under them, shall, without the Consent of the Congress, accept of any present, Emolument, Office, or Title, of any kind whatever, from any King, Prince, or foreign State.

Section 10. [1] No State shall enter into any Treaty, Alliance, or Confederation; grant Letters of

Marque and Reprisal; coin Money; emit Bills of Credit; make any Thing but gold and silver Coin a Tender in Payment of Debts; pass any Bill of Attainder, ex post facto Law, or Law impairing the Obligation of Contracts, or grant any Title of Nobility.

[2] No State shall, without the Consent of the Congress, lay any Imposts or Duties on Imports or Exports, except what may be absolutely necessary for executing its inspection Laws: and the net Produce of all Duties and Imposts, laid by any State on Imports or Exports, shall be for the Use of the Treasury of the United States; and all such Laws shall be subject to the Revision and Controul of the Congress.

[3] No State shall, without the Consent of Congress, lay any Duty of Tonnage, keep Troops, or Ships of War in time of Peace, enter into any Agreement or Compact with another State, or with a foreign Power or engage in War, unless actually invaded, or in such imminent Danger as will not admit of delay.

Article II

Section 1. [1] The executive Power shall be vested in a President of the United States of America. He shall hold his Office during the Term of four Years, and, together with the Vice President, chosen for the same Term, be elected, as follows:

[2] Each State shall appoint, in such Manner as the Legislature thereof may direct, a Number of

Electors, equal to the whole Number of Senators and Representatives to which the State may be entitled in the Congress; but no Senator or Representative, or Person holding an Office of Trust or Profit under the United States, shall be appointed an Elector.

[3] The Electors shall meet in their respective States, and vote by Ballot for two Persons, of whom one at least shall not be an Inhabitant of the same State with themselves. And they shall make a List of all the Persons voted for, and of the Number of Votes for each; which List they shall sign and certify, and transmit sealed to the Seat of the Government of the United States, directed to the President of the Senate. The President of the Senate shall, in the Presence of the Senate and House of Representatives, open all the Certificates, and the Votes shall then be counted. The Person having the greatest Number of Votes shall be the President, if such Number be a Majority of the whole Number of Electors appointed; and if there be more than one who have such Majority, and have an equal Number of Votes, then the House of Representatives shall immediately chuse by Ballot one of them for President; and if no Person have a Majority, then from the five highest on the List the said House shall in like Manner chuse the President. But in chusing the President, the Votes shall be taken by States, the Representation from each State having one Vote; A quorum for this Purpose shall consist of a

Member or Members from two thirds of the States, and a Majority of all the States shall be necessary to a Choice. In every Case, after the Choice of the President, the Person having the greater Number of Votes of the Electors shall be the Vice President. But if there should remain two or more who have equal Votes, the Senate shall chuse from them by Ballot the Vice President.

[4] The Congress may determine the Time of chusing the Electors, and the Day on which they shall give their Votes; which Day shall be the same throughout the United States.

[5] No person except a natural born Citizen, or a Citizen of the United States, at the time of the Adoption of this Constitution, shall be eligible to the Office of President; neither shall any Person be eligible to that Office who shall not have attained to the Age of thirty five Years, and been fourteen Years a Resident within the United States.

[6] In case of the removal of the President from Office, or of his Death, Resignation or Inability to discharge the Powers and Duties of the said Office, the Same shall devolve on the Vice President and the Congress may by Law provide for the Case of Removal, Death, Resignation or Inability, both of the President and Vice President, declaring what Officer shall then act as President, and such Officer shall act accordingly, until the Disability be removed, or a President shall be elected.

[7] The President shall, at stated Times, receive for his Services, a Compensation, which shall neither be increased nor diminished during the Period for which he shall have been elected, and he shall not receive within that Period any other Emolument from the United States, or any of them.

[8] Before he enter on the Execution of his Office, he shall take the following Oath or Affirmation: "I do solemnly swear (or affirm) that I will faithfully execute the Office of President of the United States, and will to the best of my Ability, preserve, protect and defend the Constitution of the United States."

Section 2. [1] The President shall be Commander in Chief of the Army and Navy of the United States, and of the militia of the several States, when called into the actual Services of the United States; he may require the Opinion, in writing, of the principal Officer in each of the Executive Departments, upon any Subject relating to the Duties of their respective Offices and he shall have Power to grant Reprieves and Pardons for Offenses against the United States, except in Cases of Impeachment.

[2] He shall have Power, by and with the Advice and Consent of the Senate, to make Treaties, provided two thirds of the Senators present concur; and he shall nominate, and by and with the Advice and Consent of the Senate, shall appoint Ambassadors, other public Ministers and Consuls, Judges of the supreme Court, and all other Officers of the United States, whose Appointments are not herein other-

wise provided for, and which shall be established by Law; but the Congress may by Law vest the Appointment of such inferior Officers, as they think proper, in the President alone, in the Courts of Law, or in the Heads of Departments.

[3] The President shall have Power to fill up all Vacancies that may happen during the Recess of the Senate, by granting Commissions which shall expire at the End of their next Session.

Section 3. He shall from time to time give to the Congress Information of the State of the Union, and recommend to their Consideration such Measures as he shall judge necessary and expedient; he may, on extraordinary Occasions, convene both Houses, or either of them, and in Case of Disagreement between them, with Respect to the Time of Adjournment, he may adjourn them to such Time as he shall think proper; he shall receive Ambassadors and other public Ministers; he shall take Care that the Laws be faithfully executed, and shall Commission all the Officers of the United States.

Section 4. The President, Vice President and all civil Officers of the United States, shall be removed from Office on Impeachment for, and Conviction of, Treason, Bribery, or other high Crimes and Misdemeanors.

Article III

Section 1. The judicial Power of the United States, shall be vested in one supreme Court, and in such inferior Courts as the Congress may from time to time ordain and establish. The Judges, both of the supreme and inferior Courts, shall hold their Offices during good Behaviour, and shall, at stated Times, receive for their Services a Compensation, which shall not be diminished during their Continuance in Office.

Section 2. [1] The judicial Power shall extend to all Cases, in Law and Equity, arising under this Constitution, the Laws of the United States, and Treaties made, or which shall be made, under their Authority;—to all Cases affecting Ambassadors, other public Ministers and Consuls;—to all Cases of admiralty and maritime Jurisdiction;—to Controversies to which the United States shall be a Party;—to Controversies between two or more States;—between a State and Citizens of another State;—between Citizens of different States;—between Citizens of the same State claiming Lands under the Grants of different States, and between a State, or the Citizens thereof, and foreign States, Citizens or Subjects.

[2] In all Cases affecting Ambassadors, other public Ministers and Consuls, and those in which a State shall be a Party, the supreme Court shall have original Jurisdiction. In all the other Cases before mentioned, the supreme Court shall have appellate Jurisdiction, both as to Law and Fact, with such Exceptions, and under such Regulations as the Congress shall make.

[3] The trial of all Crimes, except in Cases of Impeachment, shall be by Jury; and such Trial shall be held in the State where the said Crimes shall have been committed; but when not committed within any State, the Trial shall be at such Place or Places as the Congress may by Law have directed.

Section 3. [1] Treason against the United States, shall consist only in levying War against them, or, in adhering to their Enemies, giving them Aid and Comfort. No Person shall be convicted of Treason unless on the Testimony of two Witnesses to the same overt Act, or on Confession in open Court.

[2] The Congress shall have Power to declare the Punishment of Treason, but no Attainder of Treason shall work Corruption of Blood, or Forfeiture except during the Life of the Person attainted.

Article IV

Section 1. Full Faith and Credit shall be given in each State to the public Acts, Records, and judicial Proceedings of every other State. And the Congress may by general Laws prescribe the Manner in which such Acts, Records and Proceedings shall be proved, and the Effect thereof.

Section 2. [1] The Citizens of each State shall be entitled to all Privileges and Immunities of Citizens in the several States.

[2] A Person charged in any State with Treason, Felony, or other Crime, who shall flee from Justice,

and be found in another State, shall on demand of the executive Authority of the State from which he fled, be delivered up, to be removed to the State having Jurisdiction of the Crime.

[3] No Person held to Service or Labour in one State, under the Laws thereof, escaping into another, shall, in Consequence of any Law or Regulation therein, be discharged from such Service or Labour, but shall be delivered up on Claim of the Party to whom such Service or Labour may be due.

Section 3. [1] New States may be admitted by the Congress into this Union; but no new State shall be formed or erected with the Jurisdiction of any other State; nor any State be formed by the Junction of two or more States, or Parts of States, without the Consent of the Legislatures of the States concerned as well as of the Congress.

[2] The Congress shall have Power to dispose of and make all needful Rules and Regulations respecting the Territory or other Property belonging to the United States; and nothing in this Constitution shall be so construed as to Prejudice any Claims of the United States, or of any particular State.

Section 4. The United States shall guarantee to every State in this Union a Republican Form of Government, and shall protect each of them against Invasion; and on Application of the Legislature, or of the Executive (when the Legislature cannot be convened) against domestic Violence.

Article V

The Congress, whenever two thirds of both Houses shall deem it necessary, shall propose Amendments to this Constitution, or, on the Application of the Legislatures of two thirds of the several States, shall call a Convention for proposing Amendments, which, in either Case, shall be valid to all Intents and Purposes, as part of this Constitution, when ratified by the Legislatures of three fourths of the several States, or by Conventions in three fourths thereof, as the one or the other Mode of Ratification may be proposed by the Congress; Provided that no Amendment which may be made prior to the Year One thousand eight hundred and eight shall in any Manner affect the first and fourth Clauses in the Ninth Section of the first Article; and that no State, without its consent, shall be deprived of its equal Suffrage in the Senate.

Article VI

[1] All Debts contracted and Engagements entered into, before the Adoption of this Constitution, shall be as valid against the United States under this Constitution, as under the Confederation.

[2] This Constitution, and the Laws of the United States which shall be made in Pursuance thereof; and all treaties made, or which shall be made, under the Authority of the United States, shall be the supreme Law of the Land; and the Judges in every

State shall be bound thereby, any Thing in the Constitution or Laws of any State to the Contrary notwithstanding.

[3] The Senators and Representatives before mentioned, and the Members of the several State Legislatures, and all executive and judicial Officers, both of the United States and of the several States, shall be bound by Oath or Affirmation, to support this Constitution; but no religious Test shall ever be required as a Qualification to any Office or public Trust under the United States.

Article VII

The Ratification of the Conventions of nine States shall be sufficient for the Establishment of this Constitution between the States so ratifying the Same.

DONE in Convention by the Unanimous Consent of the States present the Seventeenth Day of September in the Year of Our Lord one thousand seven hundred and Eighty seven and of the Independence of the United States of America the Twelfth.   In WITNESS whereof We have hereunto subscribed our Names,

> Go. WASHINGTON—
> *Presidt. and deputy
> from Virginia*

New Hampshire

JOHN LANGDON   NICHOLAS GILMAN

Massachusetts

NATHANIEL GORHAM   RUFUS KING

Connecticut

WM. SAML. JOHNSON   ROGER SHERMAN

New York

ALEXANDER HAMILTON

New Jersey

WIL: LIVINGSTON   WM. PATERSON
DAVID BREARLEY   JONA: DAYTON

Pennsylvania

B. FRANKLIN   THOS. FITZSIMONS
THOMAS MIFFLIN   JARED INGERSOLL
ROBT. MORRIS   JAMES WILSON
GEO. CLYMER   GOUV MORRIS

Delaware

GEO: READ   RICHARD BASSETT
GUNNING BEDFORD jun   JACO: BROOM
JOHN DICKINSON

Maryland

JAMES MCHENRY   DANL. CARROLL
DAN OF ST. THOS. JENIFER

Virginia

JOHN BLAIR   JAMES MADISON, JR.

North Carolina

WM. BLOUNT   HU WILLIAMSON
RICHD. DOBBS SPAIGHT

South Carolina

J. RUTLEDGE   CHARLES PINCKNEY
CHARLES COTESWORTH PINCKNEY   PIERCE BUTLER

Georgia

WILLIAM FEW   ABR BALDWIN
Attest   WILLIAM JACKSON
                                     Secretary

ARTICLES IN ADDITION TO, AND AMEND-
MENT OF, THE CONSTITUTION OF THE
UNITED STATES OF AMERICA, PROPOSED
BY CONGRESS, AND RATIFIED BY THE LEG-

ISLATURES OF THE SEVERAL STATES PUR-
SUANT TO THE FIFTH ARTICLE OF THE
ORIGINAL CONSTITUTION.

Amendment I [1791]

Congress shall make no law respecting an establishment of religion, or prohibiting the free exercise
thereof; or abridging the freedom of speech, or of the
press; or the right of the people peaceably to assemble, and to petition the Government for a redress of
grievances.

Amendment II [1791]

A well regulated Militia, being necessary to the
security of a free State, the right of the people to
keep and bear Arms, shall not be infringed.

Amendment III [1791]

No Soldier shall, in time of peace be quartered in any
house, without the consent of the Owner, nor in time
of war, but in a manner to be prescribed by law.

Amendment IV [1791]

The right of the people to be secure in their persons, houses, papers, and effects, against unreasonable searches and seizures, shall not be violated, and
no Warrants shall issue, but upon probable cause,
supported by Oath or affirmation, and particularly
describing the place to be searched, and the persons
or things to be seized.

Amendment V [1791]

No person shall be held to answer for a capital, or otherwise infamous crime, unless on a presentment or indictment of a Grand Jury, except in cases arising in the land or naval forces, or in the Militia, when in actual service in time of War or public danger; nor shall any person be subject for the same offence to be twice put in jeopardy of life or limb; nor shall be compelled in any criminal case to be a witness against himself, nor be deprived of life, liberty, or property, without due process of law; nor shall private property be taken for public use, without just compensation.

Amendment VI [1791]

In all criminal prosecutions, the accused shall enjoy the right to a speedy and public trial, by an impartial jury of the State and district wherein the crime shall have been committed, which district shall have been previously ascertained by law, and to be informed of the nature and cause of the accusation; to be confronted with the witnesses against him; to have compulsory process for obtaining witnesses in his favor, and to have the Assistance of Counsel for his defence.

Amendment VII [1791]

In Suits at common law, where the value in controversy shall exceed twenty dollars, the right of trial by jury shall be preserved, and no fact tried by jury, shall be otherwise re-examined in any Court of the United States, than according to the rules of the common law.

Amendment VIII [1791]

Excessive bail shall not be required, nor excessive fines imposed, nor cruel and unusual punishments inflicted.

Amendment IX [1791]

The enumeration in the Constitution, of certain rights, shall not be construed to deny or disparage others retained by the people.

Amendment X [1791]

The powers not delegated to the United States by the Constitution, nor prohibited by it to the States, are reserved to the States respectively, or to the people.

Amendment XI [1798]

The Judicial power of the United States shall not be construed to extend to any suit in law or equity, commenced or prosecuted against one of the United States by Citizens of another State, or by Citizens or Subjects of any Foreign State.

Amendment XII [1804]

The Electors shall meet in their respective states and vote by ballot for President and Vice President, one of whom, at least, shall not be an inhabitant of the same state with themselves; they shall name in their ballots the person voted for as President, and in distinct ballots the person voted for as Vice President, and they shall make distinct lists of all persons voted for as President, and of all persons voted for as Vice President, and of the number of votes for each, which lists they shall sign and certify, and transmit sealed to the seat of the government of the United States, directed to the President of the Senate;—The President of the Senate shall, in the presence of the Senate and House of Representatives, open all the certificates and the votes shall then be counted;—The person having the greatest number of votes for President, shall be the President, if such number be a majority of the whole number of Electors appointed; and if no person have such majority, then from the persons having the highest numbers not exceeding three on the list of those voted for as President, the House of Representatives shall choose immediately, by ballot, the President. But in choosing the President, the votes shall be taken by states, the representation from each state having one vote; a quorum for this purpose shall consist of a member or members from two-thirds of the states, and a majority of all the states shall be necessary to a choice. And if the House of Representatives shall not choose a President whenever the right of choice shall devolve upon them before the fourth day of March next following, then the Vice President shall act as President, as in the case of the death or other constitutional disability of the President.—The person having the greatest number of votes as Vice President, shall be the Vice President, if such number be a majority of the whole number of Electors appointed, and if no person have a majority, then from the two highest numbers on the list, the Senate shall choose the Vice President; a quorum for the purpose shall consist of two-thirds of the whole number of Senators, and a majority of the whole number shall be necessary to a choice. But no person constitutionally ineligible to the office of President shall be eligible to that of Vice President of the United States.

Amendment XIII [1865]

Section 1. Neither slavery nor involuntary servitude, except as a punishment for crime whereof the party shall have been duly convicted, shall exist within the United States, or any place subject to their jurisdiction.

Section 2. Congress shall have power to enforce this article by appropriate legislation.

Amendment XIV [1868]

Section 1. All persons born or naturalized in the United States, and subject to the jurisdiction thereof, are citizens of the United States and of the State wherein they reside. No State shall make or enforce any law which shall abridge the privileges or immunities of citizens of the United States; nor shall any State deprive any person of life, liberty, or property, without due process of law; nor deny to any person within its jurisdiction the equal protection of the laws.

Section 2. Representatives shall be apportioned among the several States according to their respective numbers, counting the whole number of persons in each State, excluding Indians not taxed. But when the right to vote at any election for the choice of electors for President and Vice President of the United States, Representatives in Congress, the Executive and Judicial officers of a State, or the members of the Legislature thereof, is denied to any of the male inhabitants of such State, being twenty-one years of age, and citizens of the United States, or in any way abridged, except for participation in rebellion, or other crime, the basis of representation therein shall be reduced in the proportion which the number of such male citizens shall bear to the whole number of male citizens twenty-one years of age in such State.

Section 3. No person shall be a Senator or Representative in Congress, or elector of President and Vice President, or hold any office, civil or military, under the United States, or under any State, who having previously taken an oath, as a member of Congress, or as an officer of the United States, or as a member of any State legislature, or as an executive or judicial officer of any State, to support the

Constitution of the United States, shall have engaged in insurrection or rebellion against the same, or given aid or comfort to the enemies thereof. But Congress may by a vote of two-thirds of each House, remove such disability.

Section 4. The validity of the public debt of the United States, authorized by law, including debts incurred for payment of pensions and bounties for services in suppressing insurrection or rebellion, shall not be questioned. But neither the United States nor any State shall assume or pay any debt or obligation incurred in aid of insurrection or rebellion against the United States, or any claim for the loss or emancipation of any slave; but all such debts, obligations and claims shall be held illegal and void.

Section 5. The Congress shall have power to enforce, by appropriate legislation, the provisions of this article.

Amendment XV [1870]

Section 1. The right of citizens of the United States to vote shall not be denied or abridged by the United States or by any State on account of race, color, or previous condition of servitude.

Section 2. The Congress shall have power to enforce this article by appropriate legislation.

Amendment XVI [1913]

The Congress shall have power to lay and collect taxes on incomes, from whatever source derived, without apportionment among the several States, and without regard to any census or enumeration.

Amendment XVII [1913]

[1] The Senate of the United States shall be composed of two Senators from each State, elected by the people thereof, for six years; and each Senator shall have one vote. The electors in each State shall have the qualifications requisite for electors of the most numerous branch of the State legislatures.

[2] When vacancies happen in the representation of any State in the Senate, the executive authority of such State shall issue writs of election to fill such vacancies: *Provided,* that the legislature of any State may empower the executive thereof to make temporary appointments until the people fill the vacancies by election as the legislature may direct.

[3] This amendment shall not be so construed as to affect the election or term of any Senator chosen before it becomes valid as part of the Constitution.

Amendment XVIII [1919]

Section 1. After one year from the ratification of this article the manufacture, sale, or transportation of intoxicating liquors within, the importation thereof into, or the exportation thereof from the United

States and all territory subject to the jurisdiction thereof for beverage purposes is hereby prohibited.

Section 2. The Congress and the several States shall have concurrent power to enforce this article by appropriate legislation.

Section 3. This article shall be inoperative unless it shall have been ratified as an amendment to the Constitution by the legislatures of the several States, as provided in the Constitution, within seven years from the date of the submission hereof to the States by the Congress.

Amendment XIX [1920]

[1] The right of citizens of the United States to vote shall not be denied or abridged by the United States or by any State on account of sex.

[2] Congress shall have power to enforce this article by appropriate legislation.

Amendment XX [1933]

Section 1. The terms of the President and Vice President shall end at noon on the 20th day of January, and the terms of Senators and Representatives at noon on the 3d day of January, of the years in which such terms would have ended if this article had not been ratified; and the terms of their successors shall then begin.

Section 2. The Congress shall assemble at least once in every year, and such meeting shall begin at noon on the 3d day of January, unless they shall by law appoint a different day.

Section 3. If, at the time fixed for the beginning of the term of the President, the President elect shall have died, the Vice President elect shall become President. If the President shall not have been chosen before the time fixed for the beginning of his term, or if the President elect shall have failed to qualify, then the Vice President elect shall act as President until a President shall have qualified; and the Congress may by law provide for the case wherein neither a President elect nor a Vice President elect shall have qualified, declaring who shall then act as President, or the manner in which one who is to act shall be selected, and such person shall act accordingly until a President or Vice President shall have qualified.

Section 4. The Congress may by law provide for the case of the death of any of the persons from whom the House of Representatives may choose a President whenever the right of choice shall have devolved upon them, and for the case of the death of any of the persons from whom the Senate may choose a Vice President whenever the right of choice shall have devolved upon them.

Section 5. Sections 1 and 2 shall take effect on the 15th day of October following the ratification of this article.

Section 6. This article shall be inoperative unless it shall have been ratified as an amendment to the Constitution by the legislatures of three-fourths of the several States within seven years from the date of its submission.

Amendment XXI [1933]

Section 1. The eighteenth article of amendment to the Constitution of the United States is hereby repealed.

Section 2. The transportation or importation into any State, Territory, or possession of the United States for delivery or use therein of intoxicating liquors, in violation of the laws thereof, is hereby prohibited.

Section 3. This article shall be inoperative unless it shall have been ratified as an amendment to the Constitution by conventions in the several States, as provided in the Constitution, within seven years from the date of the submission hereof to the States by the Congress.

Amendment XXII [1951]

Section 1. No person shall be elected to the office of the President more than twice, and no person who has held the office of President, or acted as President, for more than two years of a term to which some other person was elected President shall be elected to the office of President more than once. But this Article shall not apply to any person holding the office of President when this Article was proposed by the Congress, and shall not prevent any person who may be holding the office of President, or acting as President, during the term within which this Article becomes operative from holding the office of President or acting as President during the remainder of such term.

Section 2. This article shall be inoperative unless it shall have been ratified as an amendment to the Constitution by the legislatures of three-fourths of the several States within seven years from the date of its submission to the States by the Congress.

Amendment XXIII [1961]

Section 1. The District constituting the seat of Government of the United States shall appoint in such manner as the Congress may direct:

A number of electors of President and Vice President equal to the whole number of Senators and Representatives in Congress to which the District would be entitled if it were a State, but in no event more than the least populous state; they shall be in addition to those appointed by the states, but they shall be considered, for the purposes of the election of President and Vice President, to be electors appointed by a state; and they shall meet in the District and perform such duties as provided by the twelfth article of amendment.

Section 2. The Congress shall have power to enforce this article by appropriate legislation.

Amendment XXIV [1964]

Section 1. The right of citizens of the United States to vote in any primary or other election for President or Vice President, for electors for President or Vice President, or for Senator or Representative in Congress, shall not be denied or abridged by the United States or any State by reason of failure to pay any poll tax or other tax.

Section 2. The Congress shall have power to enforce this article by appropriate legislation.

Amendment XXV [1967]

Section 1. In the case of the removal of the President from office or of his death or resignation, the Vice President shall become President.

Section 2. Whenever there is a vacancy in the office of the Vice President, the President shall nominate a Vice President who shall take office upon confirmation by a majority vote of both Houses of Congress.

Section 3. Whenever the President transmits to the President pro tempore of the Senate and the Speaker of the House of Representatives his written declaration that he is unable to discharge the powers and duties of his office, and until he transmits to them a written declaration to the contrary, such powers and duties shall be discharged by the Vice President as Acting President.

Section 4. Whenever the Vice President and a majority of either the principal officers of the executive departments or of such other body as Congress may by law provide, transmit to the President pro tempore of the Senate and the Speaker of the House of Representatives, their written declaration that the President is unable to discharge the powers and duties of his office, the Vice President shall immediately assume the powers and duties of the office as Acting President.

Thereafter, when the President transmits to the President pro tempore of the Senate and the Speaker of the House of Representatives his written declaration that no inability exists, he shall resume the powers and duties of his office unless the Vice President and a majority of either the principal officers of the executive department or of such other body as Congress may by law provide, transmit within four days to the President pro tempore of the Senate and the Speaker of the House of Representatives their written declaration that the President is unable to discharge the powers and duties of his office. Thereupon Congress shall decide the issue, assembling within forty-eight hours for that purpose if not in session. If the Congress, within twenty-one days after receipt of the latter written declaration, or, if Congress is not in session, within twenty-one days after Congress is required to assemble, determines by two-thirds vote of both Houses that the President is unable to discharge the powers and duties of his office, the Vice President shall continue to discharge the same as Acting President; otherwise, the President shall resume the powers and duties of his office.

Amendment XXVI [1971]

Section 1. The right of citizens of the United States, who are eighteen years of age or older, to vote shall not be denied or abridged by the United States or by any State on account of age.

Section 2. The Congress shall have power to enforce this article by appropriate legislation.

Amendment XXVII [1992]

No Law, varying the compensation for the services of the Senators and Representatives, shall take effect, until an election of Representatives shall have intervened.

CONSTITUTIONAL LAW

IN A NUTSHELL

Sixth Edition

*

INTRODUCTION:

CONSTITUTIONAL PRINCIPLES

Constitutional law texts are generally divided into two parts. The first part is devoted to a study of the allocation of powers. This entails two basic principles of American constitutionalism–separation of powers and division of powers.

Separation of powers discusses the interaction among the three constituent elements of the national government. Thus, Art. I of the Constitution is devoted to the powers of the legislative arm of the federal government, the Congress. Art. I sets forth the powers of the Executive and Art. III delineates and circumscribes the jurisdiction of the federal courts. But while these powers are institutionally separated, their exercise often overlaps. Thus, there emerges the need for recognition of another vital feature of American constitutional law, the principle of checks and balances. Although Congress can legislate, the President can veto. Similarly, while the President makes treaties, the Senate must give its advice and consent to make them effective. While the federal courts exercise a power of judicial review, it is the Congress which endows the those courts with such jurisdiction as it chooses within the given parameters of Art. III.

1

Checks and balances are not limited to the national arena. The principle finds expression in the division of powers between the national and state governments. Federalism embodies an effort to achieve national unity while preserving some degree of local autonomy. It strives at once to provide a structure for national government and to provide some protection for regional diversity. But a continuing question is the extent to which the values of federalism are to found in the constitutional allocating of powers in the actual workings of the political process.

From these principles is derived still another foundation of American constitutionalism, the concept of limited government. Government must be afforded the means to operate efficiently and yet its powers must be sufficiently demarcated in order to preserve individual liberty. It is a basic tenet of Madisonian democracy that concentration of power poses a threat to individual autonomy and freedom. Therefore, to the eighteenth century mind, the mind at least of Jefferson and Madison, the objectives of federalism and separation of powers served the cause of liberty. Both limit and diffuse governmental power. Indeed, in the American system, the totality of power is denied to either the national or the state governments or to any component part of our federalism. In the demarcation of national power, the Executive, the Congress, and the federal judiciary are alike denied national absolute power.

Preservation of liberty in the American constitutional scheme is, however, not entirely dependent on the allocation of governmental powers. Limited government finds expression in the specification of rights and liberties for the individual. This is the focus of the second part of the constitutional law course. Some of these guarantees were included in the original Constitution. For example, Art.I Sec. 9 prohibits suspension of the Great Writ, the writ of habeas corpus, except in cases of rebellion and insurrection. Similarly, bills of attainder and *ex post facto* laws are proscribed for both the national and state governments under Art. I, Secs. 9 and 10. But this was insufficient for many of the democrats of the eighteenth century. The First Congress undertook to draft a Bill of Rights, the first ten amendments to the Constitution. These serve as a constant reminder that the newly created federal government must always wield its power in the light of these basic guarantees of individual liberty. This principle has been re-affirmed in most of the subsequent seventeen amendments (with apologies for the Eighteenth or Prohibition Amendment) to the Constitution. Of these later amendments, it must be said that the post-Civil War Amendments, the 13th, the 14th, and 15th Amendments, have been most significant in limiting governmental power in favor of individual liberty. But the amendment process set forth in Art. V is a continuing one as recent proposals for an anti-flag burning amendment illustrate.

PART ONE

THE ALLOCATION
OF POWERS

CHAPTER I

JUDICIAL REVIEW AND
ITS LIMITS

A. FOUNDATIONS OF
JUDICIAL REVIEW

The common law tradition that the lawyers, political theorists, and statesmen who drafted the American Constitution knew was rooted in the concept of Parliamentary supremacy. But there was always an undercurrent in the thinking of those men, trained as they were on John Locke's notion of inalienable rights, that certain actions were denied even to the Legislature. Indeed, in the seventeenth century, Lord Coke in *Dr. Bonham's* case (1610) had written that "the common law will control Acts of Parliament, and sometimes adjudge them to be utterly void." The United States Constitution proclaimed itself to be a product of "We, the people"—a concept of popular rather than Parliamentary supremacy.

4

The unique contribution of the United States to political theory is the doctrine of judicial review. Under this doctrine, the courts have the power to invalidate governmental action as repugnant to the Constitution. It extends to the acts of the national executive and Congress as well as the activities of state governments.

1. REVIEW OF FEDERAL ACTIONS

The seminal document in the life of this doctrine of judicial review is the case of *Marbury v. Madison* (1803). In *Marbury,* Marshall emphasized the fact that the Constitution was the expression of the popular will and, therefore, properly controlled the exercise of all governmental power including the Congress. The Constitution is thus supreme over ordinary law and laws in defiance of the Constitution are null and void.

In *Marbury,* Sec. 13 of the Judiciary Act of 1789, which was read, perhaps improperly, to give original jurisdiction in mandamus actions to the Supreme Court of the United States, was held unconstitutional on the ground that the original jurisdiction of the Supreme Court was set forth with precision in Art. III and did not include mandamus jurisdiction. Therefore, utilizing the canon of construction *expressio unius, exclusio alterius* (the expression of one is the exclusion of all others), Marshall declared that Sec. 13 constituted a transgression of Art. III.

But the real question is who decides that a law is repugnant to the Constitution. For Marshall, the answer was simple. It is emphatically the province and duty of the judicial department to say what the law is. The Constitution is not moral advice; it has the force of law. Indeed, it is fundamental law. But is interpretation of the Constitution equivalent to an interpretation of ordinary law? Congress may correct an erroneous judicial interpretation of a law but only constitutional amendment can revise judicial interpretation of the Constitution. Further, it can be argued that judicial delineation of vague concepts such as equal protection or due process partakes more of a policy or legislative decision than typical judicial interpretation of statute.

There is in fact no explicit textual authority for the doctrine of judicial review in the United States Constitution. While Art. III vests the "Judicial Power," including cases arising under the Constitution, in the federal courts, it nowhere specifies that this judicial power includes the prerogative of invalidating the acts of a co-equal branch of government. Art. VI does establish that "this Constitution and the Laws of the United States which shall be made in Pursuance thereof shall be the supreme Law of the Land," and binds judges of state courts to apply federal law to "anything in the Constitution or Laws of any State to the contrary notwithstanding." But does this language authorize the courts to determine when laws are in pursuance of the Constitution? It could be argued that the judgment that an action or law conforms to the Constitution already has been made by the popularly elected branches, the Congress and the President. In this view, the courts would be bound by the decision of the legislature that the law is constitutional.

Apart from arguments based on the constitutional text, the question of who should decide whether a law is contrary to the Constitution may be approached historically or functionally. As usual, the historical evidence as to the Framers' intent is indecisive although some form of review appears to have been contemplated. We might simply ask: Who is better able to make the judgment of constitutionality? It has been argued that the courts possess the insulation and expertise to exercise a "sober second thought" and thereby give expression to our most basic values. On the other hand, this very alleged insularity can be said to argue against vesting final authority on the meaning of the Constitution in an unelected body of nine judges holding tenure for life.

While *Marbury v. Madison* might have been read narrowly as holding only that the judiciary could act to protect its own jurisdiction against congressional action, it has not been so limited. Rather, the Court has unanimously declared that it stands for the following proposition: "[*Marbury v. Madison*] declared the basic principle that the federal judiciary is supreme in the exposition of the law of the Constitution, and that principle has ever since been respected by this Court and the Country as a permanent and indispensable feature of our Constitutional system." *Cooper v. Aaron* (1958). Thus, the Supreme Court can review and invalidate acts of the President and other executive officials as well as the Congress. While the Court in *United States v. Nixon* (1974) acknowledged a constitutionally based executive privilege of confidentiality, at the same time it affirmed the judicial prerogative of determining the proper exercise of that privilege: "Notwithstanding the deference that each branch must accord the others, the 'Judicial Power of the United States' can no more be shared with the Executive Branch than the Chief Executive, for example, can share with the Judiciary the veto power."

Recently, in the aftermath of the World Trade Center bombing on September 11, 2001 and the subsequent U.S. military action in Afghanistan, questions arose whether enemy combatant detainees could avail themselves of the writ of habeas corpus. In connection with an application for habeas corpus by a citizen enemy combatant detained in a military prison in the United States, the Court held detainees could petition for writs of habeas corpus. *Hamdi v. Rumsfeld* (2004) The proper respondent with respect to the writ of habeas corpus petition is "the person who has custody over the petitioner" and jurisdiction of the issuance of the writ lies with the federal district court that has jurisdiction over the respondent named in the habeas petition. *Rumsfeld v. Padilla* (2004) With respect to enemy combatant detainees held in the U.S. military prison in Guantanamo Bay, Cuba, the Court held that the prison in Guantanamo Bay was a territory where the U.S. exercised exclusive jurisdiction and that federal district courts had jurisdiction to hear applications for habeas corpus from detainees held there. *Rasul v. Bush* (2004).

2. REVIEW OF STATE ACTIONS

Judicial review is not limited solely to review of federal actions and laws. It extends as well to state action. As early as 1810, the Supreme Court in *Fletcher v. Peck* had struck down a state statute as unconstitutional on grounds that the statute offended the Contract Clause of Art. I, Sec. 10. And, in *Martin v. Hunter's Lessee* (1816), the Court established its prerogative of reviewing the judgment on constitutional questions of the highest courts of a state.

The issue in *Martin v. Hunter's Lessee* was the validity of Sec. 25 of the Judiciary Act of 1789 which endowed the Supreme Court with appellate jurisdiction over the state supreme courts. It was contended that Art. III should be read to give the Supreme Court jurisdiction only in cases coming from the lower federal courts. In a decision which has been the linchpin ever since of Supreme Court jurisdiction over the state courts, Mr. Justice Story, speaking for the Court in *Martin,* rejected this contention: "It is the case, and not the court, that gives the jurisdiction."

Under the Supremacy Clause of Art. VI, state judges are bound by the United States Constitution notwithstanding contrary state law. This has been read to confer upon state court judges the power of judicial review even over federal laws. The Art. III subject matter jurisdiction of the Supreme Court includes cases arising under the Constitution. Since the state court has decided the constitutional question originally, the Supreme Court has power to review the issue by way of appellate jurisdiction.

Coupled with this argument based on the constitutional text, Story added a policy justification based on the need for uniformity in federal constitutional interpretation. The Constitution must not mean 50 different things in 50 different jurisdictions. This thesis was later echoed by Holmes when he argued that the Union would not be imperiled if the Court lost its power of judicial review over federal action but would be endangered if it had no such power over state action.

B. FOUNDATIONS OF FEDERAL JURISDICTION

1. THE CONSTITUTIONAL BASIS OF FEDERAL JURISDICTION

Under Art. III, the "federal judicial power" is vested in a Supreme Court and such inferior courts (including the circuit courts of appeals and the federal district courts) as Congress "may" create. Only the existence of the Supreme Court is constitutionally guaranteed. These Art. III courts, as distinguished from courts created by Congress under Art. I, must function within the carefully specified jurisdictional boundaries of Art. III. If a case or controversy does not fall within one of the specified categories of Art. III, Congress cannot constitutionally give the federal courts jurisdiction to entertain the matter and the court must dismiss for lack of jurisdiction. It is very important for the student to realize that Art. III describes the ultimate extent of the jurisdiction of federal courts created under it. Some of the more important examples of Art. III subject matter jurisdiction are cases arising under the Constitution, laws and treaties of the United States (federal question jurisdiction) and cases involving citizens of different states (diversity jurisdiction).

Thus, the jurisdiction of the federal courts, including the twin fountainheads of jurisdiction in the federal courts, federal question jurisdiction and diversity jurisdiction, like the federal judicial power itself, owes its very existence to the Constitution. But the exercise of jurisdiction within these Art. III parameters is at least, in broad principle, at the pleasure of Congress. While it is the Constitution that provides the fuel, it is Congress that must step on the gas.

2.   BASES OF FEDERAL COURT JURISDICTION

Art. III vests *original* jurisdiction in the Supreme Court in all cases affecting ambassadors, other public ministers and consuls and those in which a state shall be a party. As *Marbury* so memorably illustrated, Congress may not enlarge upon this constitutional delineation of the Supreme Court's original jurisdiction. Congress has, however, provided that some of this original jurisdiction should be exercised concurrently with the federal district courts. 28 U.S.C.A. § 1251.

Art. III provides, further, that in all other cases to which the federal judicial power extends, the Supreme Court shall have *appellate* jurisdiction "with such Exceptions, and under such Regulations as the Congress shall make." Pursuant to this "Exceptions" provision, Congress must confer, and may withdraw, subjects from the Supreme Court's appellate jurisdiction. The failure of Congress to confer full power within the confines of Art. III is viewed as an implicit exception by Congress to the grant of federal judicial power and, even after the appellate jurisdiction has been conferred, it may be withdrawn. Thus, in *Ex parte McCardle* (1869), the Supreme Court upheld a congressional statute withdrawing Supreme Court appellate jurisdiction to issue writs of habeas corpus even after the case had been orally argued to the Supreme Court. Was the congressional act of repeal in *McCardle* one of those "Exceptions" contemplated by Art. III or was it an impermissible infringement on the separation of powers principle? The Court held that it was an example of an "Exception."

The potential for mischief presented by *McCardle* has been both serious and enduring. *McCardle* has been the basis for recurrent efforts to legitimize erosion of the domain of the federal courts, including that of the Supreme Court, in controversial areas (to select only some of the more contemporary examples) like school busing, school prayer, abortion, internal security, and reapportionment.

Could congress preclude judicial review of habeas corpus claims in the federal courts with respect to lawful permanent resident aliens? A federal statute authorized the Attorney General to detain without bail certain permanent lawful resident aliens during deportation hearings. These aliens were designated to be deportable since they had been convicted for specified crimes. The statute precluded judicial review of the Attorney General's decision to detain such aliens. But did the statute bar habeas corpus review, a right guaranteed in the Constitution? The Court ruled that it did not. Congressional intent must be clear when it seeks to preclude judicial review of constitutional claims. The "clear text" of the statute disclosed no such intention. Moreover, preclusion of judicial review of habeas claims requires a particularly clear statement of congressional intent to bar habeas review. This was lacking in the statute here. The Court did not pass on the question whether congress could preclude habeas review without violating the text of Art. I., sec. 9, cl. 2 that the writ of habeas corpus shall not be suspended unless rebellion or invasion requires it. *Demore v. Hyung Joon Kim* (2003).

McCardle, however, has had many detractors. For one thing, even on its facts, its precedential value is less impressive than appears. *McCardle* did not end all routes to Supreme Court *habeas corpus* jurisdiction but only one (as *Ex parte Yerger* (1868) proved). The significance of the fact that some *habeas corpus* jurisdiction still remains even though Congress may have eliminated a particular statutory source of *habeas corpus* jurisdiction has been reaffirmed. When Congress withdrew Supreme Court jurisdiction over second or successive *habeas corpus* petitions filed in the federal courts, it was charged that Congress had unconstitutionally ousted the Supreme Court of its appellate jurisdiction in violation of Art. III, Sec. 2. But the withdrawal of jurisdiction was upheld since the Supreme Court still retained jurisdiction over original *habeas corpus* petitions. *Felker v. Turpin* (1996).

McCardle was not a massive blow to an essential function of federal court jurisdiction, such as the power of the Supreme Court to review state court constitutional decisions, which preserves the unity of federal law. Since *McCardle* could be read to involve only a minor exception to Supreme Court jurisdiction, or more narrowly to remove only one remedy, it should not be read to support a radical revision of the contemporary role of the federal judiciary in the American system. Further, even a recognition of a broad congressional power to "except" certain subjects from the federal judicial power does not address possible constitutional limitations on the exercise of that power. For example, would Congress violate the due process guarantee by withdrawing the ability of federal courts to review, on constitutional matters, criminal convictions? Could the equal protection guarantee embodied in Fifth Amendment due process be vitiated by withdrawing from federal courts the power to order the only effective remedies available to vindicate the right (*e.g.*, the power to require busing)?

In short, Mr. Justice Douglas's observations in *Glidden Co. v. Zdanok* (1962), although made in the context of a dissent, has great force: "There is a serious question whether the *McCardle* case could command a majority view today." On the other hand, more literal readers of Art. III may be persuaded by Justice Frankfurter's brutal observation on the fragility of Supreme Court jurisdiction in *National Mutual Insurance Co. v. Tidewater Transfer Co.* (1949): "Congress need not give this Court any appellate power; it may withdraw appellate jurisdiction once conferred and it may do so even while a case is *sub judice*." Under such a view, it was the intent of the Framers to leave it to Congress to decide whether federal courts, at least those inferior to the Supreme Court, were needed at all and also to decide the occasions when the federal judicial power should be exercised.

Nevertheless, there are separation of powers limits on Congressional power over the federal judiciary. For example, after the Supreme Court ruled that certain securities cases were barred by the statute of limitations, an attempt by Congress to then retroactively extend the statute of limitations and reopen these previously decided cases was held unconstitutional. This retroactive modification of the law violated both separation of powers and the doctrine of *Marbury v. Madison* that it is for the courts to determine what the law is. The federal judiciary, not Congress, has the "power not merely to rule on cases, but to *decide* them." *Plaut v. Spendthrift Farm, Inc.* (1995).

3.   STATUTORY FORMS OF REVIEW

In 1988 Congress made a major change in the statutes setting forth the basis for Supreme Court jurisdiction. The old distinction between appeal, technically a matter of right, and certiorari, involving the exercise of discretion, is now largely a matter of history. The principal route now for obtaining Supreme Court review of lower court decisions is by means of certiorari. See 28 U.S.C.A. §§ 1254 and 1257. The certiorari jurisdiction is a discretionary one. Therefore, this means that the Supreme Court has almost complete control over whether or not it will take a case. Jurisdiction by appeal, technically a matter of right, still is available in the limited number of cases where a three judge federal court must be convened. See 28 U.S.C.A. § 1253. But the fundamental point is that the great bulk of cases decided by the Supreme Court come to it by certiorari.

There are a number of grounds for granting certiorari. Perhaps, the clearest case for certiorari arises when federal courts of appeal are in conflict. But the Court has also noted that certiorari is appropriate when lower courts have decided significant novel federal constitutional questions or where a state court has decided a constitutional question in a way which is probably in conflict with prior Supreme Court decisions. The student should note that only four justices have to agree to grant the writ of certiorari. This means that a majority may subsequently decide that the writ was improvidently granted. A denial of certiorari is not a disposition on the merits and does not indicate approval or disapproval of the decision below.

C. CONSTITUTIONAL AND POLICY LIMITATIONS ON JUDICIAL REVIEW

Even if a case appears to fall within the confines of the federal jurisdiction outlined in Art. III, there is no assurance that a federal court will decide the case on the merits. There are a number of doctrines whereby an Art. III court can avoid disposition of the constitutional issue and dismiss the case. These doctrines emanate from two principal sources. First, the doctrine may be grounded in the constitutional text itself. For example, the Eleventh Amendment prohibits, on its face at least, federal courts from entertaining specified cases brought against a state without its consent. Another such textual limitation on judicial review is the requirement of Art. III that the jurisdiction of courts created thereunder be limited to "cases and controversies." The second principal source of limitation is born of the Court's own sense of self-restraint in the exercise of its judicial review powers. *Rescue Army v. Municipal Court of Los Angeles* (1947).

1. CONSTITUTIONAL LIMITATIONS

a. The Bar of the Eleventh Amendment

In defining the subject matter of the federal courts, Art. III, Sec. 2 indicates a number of instances where a federal court can hear a suit brought against a state. There are indications, however, that it was widely believed that the doctrine of sovereign immunity would prevent any such actions against the state without its consent. But in *Chisholm v. Georgia* (1793), the Supreme Court permitted a citizen of one state to sue another state in a federal court. The notion that the new federal courts could entertain suits against a state which the state as sovereign would not tolerate in its own courts was shocking. As a result, popular reaction to *Chisholm v. Georgia* led to the first new amendment after the Bill of Rights. The Eleventh Amendment rejected *Chisholm* by providing: "The judicial power of the United States shall not be construed to extend to any suit in law or equity commenced or prosecuted against one of the United States by Citizens of another State, or by Citizens or by Subjects of any Foreign State." Judicial interpretation utilizing the doctrine of sovereign immunity extended the bar to suits by a citizen against his own state, *Hans v. Louisiana* (1890), and also suits against the state by citizens of a foreign country.

The Eleventh Amendment, however, has not been the bar to federal judicial review of state action that a literal reading of its text might suggest. First, it is a bar to suit only against the state or its agencies and not local governments and their agencies. *Lake Country Estates, Inc. v. Tahoe Regional Planning Agency* (1979) [Eleventh Amendment held not to bar suit against the Tahoe Regional Planning Agency since its activities make it more analogous to a county or municipal agency rather than a state agency].

Second, a state may consent to be sued in federal court. This exception does create a logical problem since the Eleventh Amendment purports to preclude "the Judicial power" in a suit against the state. How can a state grant jurisdiction to a federal court when the Constitution says the judicial power shall not extend to that case? The courts have treated the Eleventh Amendment as granting personal immunity founded on the doctrine of sovereign immunity. This personal immunity can be waived. Although this reasoning has satisfied later courts, it is less satisfying to the logical faculty.

Third, and most important, is the principle that when an official acts unconstitutionally the action is not state action at least for the purposes of the Eleventh Amendment. This precept, the doctrine of *Ex parte Young* (1908), is a kind of American analogue to the English common law precept that the King Can Do No Wrong. Under this doctrine, a state can never act unconstitutionally because the Eleventh Amendment provides sovereign immunity from constitutional review. State officials, however, in their individual capacity, can commit constitutional wrongs and in such a case, the Eleventh Amendment provides no refuge from federal jurisdiction. The need to vindicate federal constitutional rights prevails. Thus, the Eleventh Amendment was held not to bar a suit against named state officials for their alleged unconstitutional acts resulting in the death of students at Kent State University. *Scheuer v. Rhodes* (1974). However, the Eleventh Amendment has been interpreted as a bar against a federal court order requiring state officials to conform to state law since, under these circumstances, the state is the real party in interest and there is no need to vindicate federal rights. *Pennhurst State School & Hosp. v. Halderman* (1984). The task of a court seeking to determine whether state officials can be sued under the doctrine of *Ex Parte Young* is simply to conduct a straightforward inquiry into whether the complaint involves an ongoing violation of federal law and seeks the type of relief which can fairly be characterized as prospective in nature. *Verizon Maryland Inc. v. Public Service Commission of Maryland* (2002).

The *Ex parte Young* exception to the Eleventh Amendment bar has proven of critical importance in the growth of American constitutional law. In the absence of the *Ex parte Young* doctrine, unruly states would have been less easily subjected to the single rule of federal constitutional law. For example, the problem of state legislative malapportionment could not have secured redress in the federal courts against the wishes of recalcitrant states. In short, without *Ex parte Young,* the reapportionment decisions would not have been possible. The mandates of the Fourteenth Amendment would have fallen on the shoals of the Eleventh Amendment. But invocation of the doctrine does raise a logical dilemma. How can the acts of a state official constitute "state action" for purposes of establishing a violation of the Fourteenth Amendment but not constitute state action sufficient to invoke the bar of the Eleventh Amendment? The answer to this question haunts Justice Peckham's decision in *Ex parte Young* but it is a ghost he failed to exorcise. Later federal courts have not worried much about the problem either. Some commentators have suggested that all that is necessary to say by way of explanation is that the Fourteenth Amendment qualifies *pro tanto* the Eleventh Amendment.

Where the relief requested would in fact constitute a retroactive charge against the state treasury, indistinguishable from an award of damages against the state itself, however, the Eleventh Amendment will bar the action. *Edelman v. Jordan* (1974). The *Edelman* exception to the *Ex parte Young* doctrine does not bar prospective remedies, even if they involve expenditures by the state in order to comply with a court order. By way of illustration, in *Hutto v. Finney* (1978), the Court held that the award of attorneys' fees against state prison officials for their bad faith unconstitutional actions would not involve an Eleventh Amendment violation even though the award constituted monies that would be paid by the state. Similarly, judicially imposed state expenditures to implement desegregation orders are treated as ancillary and do not violate the Eleventh Amendment. *Milliken v. Bradley* (1977) (*Milliken II*).

A final exception to Eleventh Amendment immunity arises from congressional power to legislate under the Thirteenth Amendment, Sec. 2, the Fourteenth Amendment, Sec. 5, and the Fifteenth Amendment, Sec. 2. The Civil War Amendments were enacted subsequent to the Eleventh Amendment and imposed specific prohibitions against state action. Pursuant to Congress's textually granted power to enforce these guarantees by appropriate legislation, it may legislate remedies even if they run against the state. *Fitzpatrick v. Bitzer* (1976).

Congressional power to abrogate the states' Eleventh Amendment immunity and to render a state liable for money damages was extended to legislation enacted under the Commerce Clause. *Pennsylvania v. Union Gas Co.* (1989). But the sovereign immunity principle of the Eleventh Amendment was soon resurrected and *Union Gas* was reversed. A federal statute, enacted under Art.I, Sec. 8, cl. 3 which grants Congress power "To regulate Commerce ... with the Indian Tribes," authorized certain money damage suits by Indian tribes against states to be brought in federal court. The statute was struck down. While excepting legislation enacted under Section 5 of the Fourteenth Amendment cases, the Court held, 5–4, per Chief Justice Rehnquist, that Congress in legislating under the Commerce Clause cannot abrogate state Eleventh Amendment immunity. *Seminole Tribe of Florida v. Florida* (1996).

Legislation enacted by Congress under the Spending Power is unaffected by *Seminole*. When

Congress provides funds to the states under the Spending Power contingent on their consent to certain conditions, the Eleventh Amendment does not render the state immune from suit in federal court for violation of those conditions provided state Eleventh Amendment immunity is made "unmistakably clear in the language of the statute." *Atascadero State Hospital v. Scanlon* (1985). The state itself can intentionally waive its Eleventh Amendment immunity. But such waiver must be done expressly: "Thus, in order for a state statute or constitutional provisions to constitute a waiver of eleventh amendment immunity, it must specify the State's intention to subject itself to suit in federal court." Accordingly, a state's receipt of funds under the federal Rehabilitation Act of 1973 did not without more waive its Eleventh Amendment immunity. *Atascadero State Hospital v. Scanlon* (1985). By contrast, the Port Authority of New York and New Jersey was held to have waived Eleventh Amendment immunity when it agreed (1) to the consent to suit provisions in the statutory bi-state compact which created the Port Authority and (2) to a venue provision in the bi-state compact which referred to judicial districts established by the United States. *Port Authority Trans–Hudson Corp. v. Feeney* (1990). But a state waives its Eleventh Amendment immunity when it removes a case against it from state court to federal court. *Lapides v. Board of Regents of the University System of Georgia* (2002).

The *Atascadero* case was the occasion for a major but unsuccessful effort by Justice Brennan to limit the scope of the Eleventh Amendment. Justice Brennan in a lengthy and passionate dissent, joined by Marshall, Blackmun and Stevens, contended that the Eleventh Amendment as a matter of both text and history intended only to bar diversity suits against state governments in federal courts, *i.e.,* suits by a citizen of State B against State A. In 1890, *Hans v. Louisiana* put a gloss on the Eleventh Amendment which also barred suits by a citizen of State A against State A in federal courts. In Brennan's view, the gloss *Hans* imposed on the Eleventh Amendment was wrong and should be reversed. Justice Powell for the Court rebuffed this assault on *Hans* declaring that the Eleventh Amendment exemplified a principle of state sovereign immunity which was rooted in a justified concern for state sovereignty. However, if a suit filed in a state court raises a federal issue, the Eleventh Amendment will not bar Supreme Court review even though the Eleventh Amendment would have barred instituting suit in the federal court in the first place. This result is based on the need for a uniform federal law. *McKesson Corp. v. Division of Alcoholic Beverages* (1990). Finally, state sovereign immunity precludes federal administrative agencies from assuming jurisdiction over a private party's complaint against a nonconsenting state whether the suit is for money damages or other relief. *Federal Maritime Commission v. South Carolina State Ports Authority* (2002).

b. The "Case or Controversy" Requirement

In defining the subject matter jurisdiction of federal courts, Art. III speaks in terms of cases and controversies. The Court has said that this language requires that litigation be presented to the federal courts in an adversary form and context capable of judicial resolution and that its resolution not violate separation of powers principles limiting the occasions for judicial review. *Flast v. Cohen* (1968). Thus, the Supreme Court will not give advisory opinions on federal constitutional questions—it will decide only "flesh and blood" controversies. Art. III federal courts cannot reach out to resolve even vital constitutional questions, even at the behest of Congress and the President. Congress, therefore, cannot make the United States a defendant in a federal court unless the United States truly has an interest adverse to the plaintiff. *Muskrat v. United States* (1911). Moreover, parties who are interested in securing resolution of a constitutional issue from a federal court cannot by their own agreement confer jurisdiction on the court. If the parties are merely curious about a matter but there is no real adversity between them, the bar of the Constitution—the case and controversy requirement—will require dismissal of the suit.

The "flesh and blood" controversy principle embodied in the ban on advisory opinions indicates one of the great paradoxes of American constitutionalism. The Court has undertaken to fashion broad principles transcending the immediate parties to a controversy but nevertheless insists that such principles be sown from the matrix of an actual dispute between adverse parties. This reflects the Court's commitment to the adversarial system. It also bears witness to reliance on practical empiricism as the wisest means of passing on constitutional issues even when they involve the most fundamental questions. The assumption appears to be that insistence on actual controversy limits and tempers the Court's undoubted power to generate new constitutional doctrine. If the case or controversy requirement is thus analyzed, it becomes apparent that it also serves the ends of the separation of powers principle. The price paid for assuring adversity and restraint in the use of judicial power is that the Court often postpones or indeed sometimes forgoes the exercise of its peculiar competence. Further, the harm done by the operation of an unconstitutional law while we await a case and controversy to move from embryo to reality may never be fully undone by a later decision even if it is forthcoming. Thus, when Chief Justice John Jay refused to give general legal advice on behalf of the Court to Secretary of State Jefferson on treaty questions, more was involved than a mere unwillingness on the part of the Court to do legal research for the Executive.

2. POLICY LIMITATIONS

Closely related to the constitutional restraints flowing from the case and controversy language of Art. III are a variety of policy limitations developed by the federal courts whereby they avoid disposition of constitutional issues on the merits. Thus, in *Ashwander v. Tennessee Valley Authority* (1936), the Supreme Court indicated that it would avoid deciding a constitutional issue raised in friendly non-adversary proceedings. Similarly, a federal court, according to the orthodox canon, will not decide a constitutional issue until it is absolutely necessary. This mode of avoiding decision is often accomplished by relying on alternative non-constitutional grounds for decision, if available, or by construing a statute in such a way as to avoid a constitutional problem. Further, a federal court will presume that legislation is constitutional, imposing on the challenging party the burden of demonstrating its invalidity.

All of these principles reflect the Court's commitment to self-restraint in the exercise of judicial review by the federal judiciary. Many times the Court has been admonished that the only limitation on the Court's power is its own sense of self-restraint. An inventory of factors justifying this policy of self-restraint would include: (1) the delicacy of the judicial function in constitutional cases; (2) the comparative finality of decisions resting on constitutional grounds; (3) the need for appropriate consideration by "other repositories of constitutional power"; (4) the need to preserve the constitutional allocation of powers, including that of the courts; and (5) "the inherent limitations of the judicial process." *Rescue Army v. Municipal Court of Los Angeles* (1947). In respecting such a limitation on the use of judicial power, the Court has asserted that it is providing a firmer foundation for private rights than if it were to involve itself actively in the political process.

Careful consideration of the policy occasions for avoiding unnecessary constitutional decision indicate that they generally overlap with the limitations which flow from the case and controversy requirement in Art. III. This suggests a critical problem underlying most of the discussion which follows. In cases where the Court avoids a decision on the merits, it is often difficult to determine whether the barrier to decision arises from the Constitution or from the Court's self-imposed sense of restraint. Yet the distinction is critical. A policy barrier to decision can be avoided if there are important factors counseling the need for decision. While Congress cannot override a limitation on judicial review which has its origin in the Art. III delineation of "the Judicial Power" (*i.e.,* federal court jurisdiction), the Congress can, by enacting legislation, allow the federal courts to entertain suits where the courts might otherwise refuse to adjudicate on the basis of policy or (as they are now often called) "prudential considerations."

D. SPECIFIC DOCTRINES LIMITING JUDICIAL REVIEW

The case and controversy mandate of Art. III coupled with the closely associated policy considerations have found expression in a number of specific doctrines whereby a federal court dismisses a case without reaching the constitutional merits. These doctrines can be conveniently grouped around three basic questions. First, *WHO* may litigate a constitutional claim (*i.e.,* the question of standing)? Second, *WHEN* may a constitutional question be litigated (the problem of timing, *e.g.,* ripeness, mootness, and abstention)? Third, *WHAT* constitutional questions may be litigated to a federal court (the problem of subject matter, *e.g.,* the political question doctrine)?

1.   WHO MAY LITIGATE?—THE PROBLEM OF STANDING

a.   Constitutional Requirements for Standing

The problem of who can litigate a constitutional question involves both the requirements of the case and controversy provision and the policy considerations underlying judicial self-restraint. Insofar as the Art. III cases and controversy requirement is concerned, the Supreme Court has required that the parties seeking relief allege "such a personal stake in the outcome of a controversy as to assure that concrete adverseness which sharpens the presentation of issues upon which the Court so largely depends for illumination of difficult constitutional questions." *Baker v. Carr* (1962).

In *Lujan v. Defenders of Wildlife* (1992), the Court, per Justice Scalia, elaborated further. Standing has three constitutionally required elements: "*First*, the plaintiff must have suffered an 'injury in fact'—an invasion of a legally—protected interest which is (a) concrete and particularized and (b) an 'actual or imminent, not conjectural or hypothetical.' *Second*, there must be a causal connection between the injury and the conduct complained of—the injury has to be 'fairly trace[able] to the challenged action of the defendant, and not th[e] ... result [of] the independent action of some third party not before the court.' *Third*, it must be 'likely,' as opposed to merely 'speculative,' that the injury will be 'redressed by a favorable decision.' '" [Emphasis supplied.] Further, the litigant must demonstrate that he has standing sufficient to justify the particular relief sought. *Los Angeles v. Lyons* (1983) [litigants' past physical injury resulting from police implementation of a departmental choke hold policy does not afford standing for injunctive relief].

(1) *Injury in Fact.* The personal stake requirement does not necessarily mean legal injury. Rather, the requirement is that the litigant demonstrate some factual injury. This may take the form of economic injury, aesthetic or environmental injury, or even intangible injury, such as the ability to live in an integrated community. A resident of a community in which a nuclear power plant is to be built may be able to show environmental injury in fact sufficient to challenge the constitutionality of a federal statute making construction of the plant possible. *Duke Power Co. v. Carolina Environmental Study Group* (1978). But the Court has attempted to insert more rigor in the injury in fact requirement by declaring that injury in fact is demonstrated by the "invasion of a legally protected interest

which is (a) concrete and particularized and (b) 'actual or imminent not conjectural' or 'hypothetical.' " *Lujan v. Defenders of Wildlife* (1992).

Lujan involved a regulation issued by the Secretary of the Interior under the Endangered Species Act (ESA) which required other federal agencies to consult with him on federally funded projects in the United States and on the high seas which were likely to jeopardize the existence or habitat of endangered species. There was no such consultation requirement with respect to projects abroad and environmental groups challenged this omission in the regulation.

Two members of the these environmental groups pointed specifically to projects in Egypt and Sri Lanka which might adversely affect endangered species. The Court, per Justice Scalia, rejected their challenge on standing grounds. Standing is not an " 'ingenious academic exercise in the conceivable.' " True, a desire to see or to use an animal species in some way can constitute cognizable injury in fact. But individual members of groups challenging the failure of the Secretary to extend the consultation requirement to projects abroad must show that they were personally affected in a concrete manner. Otherwise, their claim is too speculative. Statements that the plaintiffs might some day visit the regions of the world affected were simply too vague: " '[S]ome day' intentions—without any description of concrete plans, or indeed even any specification of *when* the some day will be—do not support a finding of the 'actual or imminent' injury that our cases require." *Lujan*.

A particularly troublesome aspect of *Lujan* was whether it somehow altered the rule that Congress could by statute provide for standing. Congress can by statute, create an interest, the denial of which, is said to constitute injury in fact. *Warth v. Seldin* (1975). The "aggrieved person" provisions in the enabling legislation of federal regulatory agencies permitting those aggrieved by federal administrative action to obtain review in the federal courts typify this kind of statute. The Endangered Species Act, on which the plaintiffs based their claim for standing, contained a provision authorizing "any person" to bring an action to enforce the statute. Statutory creation of standing by Congress was justified on the theory that Congress had by enacting the statute created a legal interest the denial of which constituted injury in fact. Nonetheless, the Court held there was no standing. Generalized grievances about government which cannot be differentiated from that shared by members of the public at large cannot provide a basis for standing. To hold otherwise would permit Congress to transfer the commonly shared interest of the public in the duty of executive officers to comply with the law from the Executive to the Judiciary. The courts would become the monitors of the wisdom of executive action.

Lujan did not contradict, the Court insisted, the principle that the injury in fact which Article III requires for standing may exist "solely by virtue of 'statutes creating legal rights, the invasion which creates standing.' " The broadening by statute of categories of injury that may qualify for standing was distinct from dispensing with the requirement that the plaintiff must herself have suffered injury. In a concurrence, Justice Kennedy, joined by Justice Souter, sought to make clear that the prior law on the right of Congress "to define injuries and articulate chains of causation" was not changed by *Lujan*.

Indeed, subsequently, the ESA citizen suit provision allowing "any person" to bring an action was held to expand the zone of interests to the fullest extent permitted by Article III and thus remove any prudential standing barrier. The Fish and Wildlife Service determined that a proposed federal project might adversely affect two endangered fish species. The Service recommended that minimum water levels be maintained at specified reservoirs. Ranch operators and irrigation districts sued under the citizen suit provision of the ESA. Justice Scalia, speaking for the Court, ruled that since plaintiffs alleged that the amount of available water would be reduced if the Service's suggestion were implemented, it was "easy to presume specific facts under which [the plaintiffs] would be injured—for example, the Bureau's distribution of the reduction pro rata among its customers." The ranchers and irrigation districts were able to show the particularized injury in fact which the plaintiffs in *Lujan* were not able to demonstrate. *Bennett v. Spear* (1997).

A strict application of the *Lujan* approach to the injury in fact requirement was demonstrated by a suit challenging the Line Item Veto Act instituted by some members of Congress. The Court held, per Chief Justice Rehnquist, that the plaintiff members of Congress lacked Article III standing. Their injury was insufficiently particularized. The Congressional plaintiffs claimed that they had lost political power but they had not lost any private right. They had not been deprived of their seats in Congress. Their claim of institutional injury indicated no claim distinct from that of all other members of Congress and was insufficiently concrete. *Raines v. Byrd* (1997).

In *Clinton v. City of New York* (1997), unlike *Raines*, the parties in each case were able to show a "personal stake" in having an actual injury redressed as opposed to the "abstract and widely dispersed" institutional injury alleged in *Raines*. The plaintiffs appeared before the Court with the requisite standing to justify substantive constitutional review—and invalidation—of the Line Item Veto Act. See *infra*, Ch. 4. A provision of the Balanced Budget Act of 1997 was canceled under the Line Item Act resulting in a multi-million dollar liability to the state of N.Y. The state and the city, which would suffer immediately, sustained an immediate concrete injury in fact. A provision of the Tax Relief Act of 1997 that resulted in the loss of tax benefits to certain food refiner and processor sellers was also canceled under the Line Item Veto Act. The Court held that the farmers' cooperatives that purchased from the sellers were intended beneficiaries under the Tax Relief Act. These farmers' cooperatives lost a "bargaining chip" and, therefore, sustained economic injury in fact from the cancellation.

The rigorous approach to the injury in fact requirement set forth in *Lujan* was loosened considerably in *Friends of the Earth, Inc, v. Laidlaw Environmental Services, Inc.* (2000). There the Court, per Justice Ginsburg, permitted plaintiff environmental groups to use a citizen suit provision of the Clean Water Act against a defendant who was illegally discharging several pollutants into a river. Some of the members of these groups lived near the affected river. Even though there was no proof that the river was in fact polluted, the plaintiff groups were held to have standing. The Court said it was entirely reasonable that a company's discharge of pollutants would lead the plaintiff members who lived near the river to forego recreational uses of the river such as swimming or fishing. Moreover, it was reasonable as well that these illegal discharges would cause them economic and aesthetic injury. The Court declared: "The relevant showing for purposes of Article III standing [i]s not injury to the environment but injury to the plaintiff." The Court distinguished *Lujan* on the ground that the plaintiffs who lived along the river had stated they would use the river for recreational purposes if the defendant was not discharging pollutants into it. This was hardly equivalent to the "speculative 'some day' intentions" of the plaintiffs in *Lujan* "to visit endangered specie halfway around the world." A signal that *Friends of the Earth* marked a retreat from the restrictive approach to injury in fact taken in *Lujan* was highlighted by the fact that Justice Scalia, author of the *Lujan* opinion, dissented in *Laidlaw.*

Suppose an injury in fact which plaintiffs complain of is widely shared? This issue arose when ordinary voters challenged the Federal Election Commission's (FEC) refusal to call the American Israel Public Affairs Committee (AIPAC) a "political committee"—a designation which imposed limits on campaign contributions and extensive disclosure obligations. The voters sued under the FECA's "aggrieved person" provision. Since the history of "aggrieved person" provisions demonstrated congressional intent "to cast the standing net broadly," prudential standing requirements were met. Congress had power to authorize federal courts to adjudicate this suit under Article III. The inability of these voters to obtain information which the FECA requires AIPAC to make public and which would aid them in voting for candidates for political office constitutes the injury in fact demanded by the case or controversy requirement of Article III. The FEC responded that this was a "generalized grievance" which was widely shared. The Court held, per Justice Breyer, that a harm can be concrete even though widely shared. *Federal Election Commission v. Akins* (1998).

Ideological opposition to a government policy is insufficient to satisfy the injury in fact requirement. Such injury must rise above a mere "generalized grievance" against the challenged law. For example, the Louisiana legislature created a majority-minority district in order to enhance the voting strength of African Americans. Justice O'Connor, for the Court, described the district as a "Z-shaped creature" which zigzagged throughout the state. White voters who were not resident in the district did not have standing to challenge the constitutionality of the redistricting. Their complaint was merely a generalized grievance against allegedly invalid government conduct. *United States v. Hays* (1995).

By contrast, white voters who were residents of "racially gerrymandered" majority-minority districts had standing to challenge the districting. The resident white voters had more than a generalized political grievance. Such voters been denied "equal treatment" and had suffered special representational harms. *Miller v. Johnson* (1995). Justice Stevens denied there was standing in either case and rejected the "offensive and demeaning" premise that "voters of a particular race 'think alike, share the same political interests, and will prefer the same candidates at the polls.' "

Members of a racial minority or persons of low or moderate income do not have standing to challenge an exclusionary zoning ordinance merely because of their race or income level. They must show some direct or indirect injury to them personally resulting from the law to which they object. Thus, in *Warth v. Seldin* (1975), the litigants were unable to demonstrate that any developer who would build housing suitable to their needs was being excluded by reason of the zoning law. Similarly, the litigants had failed to allege or identify a specific developer with a specific project the furtherance of which had been precluded by the zoning law. On the other hand, in *Village of Arlington Heights v. Metropolitan Housing Development* (1977), a black litigant who desired housing near his employment and who would qualify for the housing that a developer wished to build was held to have standing to challenge the exclusionary official action as racially discriminatory. A non-profit housing developer who was a plaintiff in the same case, who had contracted to purchase land to build racially integrated housing, was also held to have standing since he had suffered economic injury based on financial outlays in connection with the planned housing project. Further, the Court indicated that injury in fact could also be found in the more intangible injury reflected in the "frustration of [the developer's] desire to make suitable low-cost housing available in areas where such housing is scarce."

Note that in these cases standing does not turn on the legal issue being litigated. Instead, standing reflects only the existence of a factual injury.

(2) *The Fairly Traceable Requirement.* In order to have standing, the challenging parties also must demonstrate that the injury in fact is caused by the government action they are challenging. In *Warth v. Seldin* (1975), minority and low income residents of Rochester, New York were held not to have standing to challenge exclusionary zoning by the suburban town of Penfield, New York. These residents were unable to show that a developer who would

build housing there suitable for them was precluded from doing so because of the zoning ordinance. Similarly, developers lacked standing to protest the town's exclusionary zoning since no developer could point to a specific project which was in fact being thwarted by the zoning ordinance. In short, the plaintiffs must "establish that, in fact, the asserted injury was the consequence of the defendant's actions or that prospective relief will remove the harm." *Warth v. Seldin* (1975). They must demonstrate that the alleged injury is fairly traceable to the asserted unlawful government conduct.

Stated in different terms, the plaintiff must demonstrate that there is a "substantial likelihood" that he will personally profit from the requested judicial relief; he must show that the judicial relief requested will redress the alleged injury. This causation requirement has proven to be a significant obstacle where the litigant alleges that the government defendant's action unconstitutionally motivates some third party not before the court to act in a way that produces injury to the litigant. The causation requirement is particularly important since it has been described as a "minimum requirement of Article III." *Warth v. Seldin.*

Candor requires acknowledgement that judicial assessment of the sufficiency of injury in fact or the existence of the requisite causal relationship is susceptible to doctrinal manipulation. Indeed, in dissent in *Warth v. Seldin*, Justice Brennan castigated the Court's approach to injury in fact as explainable "only by an indefensible hostility to the claim on the merits."

Illustrative of the malleability of the causal relationship requirement is *Northeastern Florida Chapter of Associated General Contractors of America v. Jacksonville* (1993). A construction contractors association challenged a city ordinance requiring 10% of the funds spent on city contracts each fiscal year be set aside for Minority Business Enterprises. The contractors association contended that many of its members would have bid on the set aside contracts if permitted to do so. Although the court of appeals had held that the association lacked standing because its members had not demonstrated that but for the set aside program they would have bid successfully for any of the set aside contracts, the Supreme Court, per Justice Thomas, disagreed and held that the association had standing. *Warth* was distinguished because there the plaintiffs had complained about the exclusionary zoning, not that they could not equally compete with others.

In essence, in *Northeastern Florida Chapter*, the Court relaxed the rigor of the causal relation requirement for standing. When a government classification makes it more difficult for members of one group to obtain a benefit than members of another group, the plaintiff is not obliged to show that the benefit would be available absent the government discrimination.

In *Allen v. Wright*, (1984) Justice O'Connor declared to the surprise of many that the causation requirement implemented separation of powers concerns; the requirement served to prevent judicial frustration of administrative policies fashioned by the executive. In *Allen*, the litigants claimed that the IRS's failure to deny tax-exempt status to racially discriminatory private schools diminished the ability of their children to receive a racially desegregated education. The Court, per Justice O'Connor, held 5–3 that the complaint alleged a sufficient claim of injury, but that the injury was not shown to be fairly traceable to the IRS's conduct. Although the litigants had named a number of segregated schools enjoying tax exemptions, it was uncertain how many segregated schools benefitted from tax breaks. Moreover, it was only speculative that withdrawal of tax benefits would cause a segregated school to change its admissions policy—parents and officials would have to respond collectively to produce a significant change in the racial composition of the schools. The causal connection was "attenuated at best." The litigants also contended that the tax breaks to racially discriminatory schools imposed a "stigmatizing injury" on the members of minority groups. This claim was rejected because the litigants had failed to "allege a stigmatic injury" which they had suffered because they had personally been deprived of equal treatment.

But Justice O'Connor was not finished. Prior cases had indicated that the Art. III standing involved solely an inquiry into whether the litigant had sufficient adversity to litigate, and that separation of power concerns over the propriety of judicial intervention were not central to Art. III standing.

Flast v. Cohen (1968). But Justice O'Connor declared: "[T]he law of Art. III standing is built on a single basic idea—the idea of separation of powers." Suits such as that involved in *Allen* would invite litigation challenging "the particular programs agencies establish to carry out their legal obligations." Such litigation was "rarely if ever appropriate, for federal courts are not the proper forum for general complaints about how government does its business." Justice O'Connor specifically accepted the principle that separation of powers' concerns can be used "to interpret the 'fairly traceable' component of the standing requirement." Justice Stevens, dissenting, argued that the injury was "fairly traceable." The very purpose of the tax subsidy is to encourage certain behavior; it follows logically that withdrawal of such subsidies because of particular undesirable conduct would discourage that conduct. Basic economics suggested that if segregated education became more expensive, less would be purchased.

A more generous approach to the causation requirement is found in *Duke Power Co. v. Carolina Environmental Study Group* (1978) which upheld a lower court finding of a causal relation between environmental injury from the operation of nuclear power plants and the federal Price–Anderson Act. The lower court judgment that the injury was "fairly traceable" to the Act's limitation on the potential liability for nuclear accident was not clearly erroneous since the statute made it feasible to construct the plants. While it was possible that the plants

would be built even without the federal statute or
that the government itself might build its own
plants, the Court reasoned that the plaintiff need
not eliminate all alternative possibilities. *Duke Power Co. v. Carolina Environmental Study Group*
(1978).

The Court's treatment of the causal relationship
requirement in *Allen v. Wright* and *Duke Power*
suggests the requirement's lack of precision. Causality is a difficult concept whenever it is encoun-
tered in the law and it is no less so in the constitutional arena. It is certainly possible to argue that
the Court's treatment of the causality issue in *Duke
Power* is partially attributable to its greater willingness to decide important constitutional and policy
issues involving nuclear power. Perhaps, for this
reason *Duke Power* should not be read as involving
too great a relaxation of the causal relation requirement. *Allen v. Wright* indicates the potential for
using causation requirements as a vehicle for infus-
ing separation of powers concerns over the propriety of using judicial power into the law of standing.
While considerations relating to the judicial role are
usually handled as prudential considerations under
the label of justiciability, *Allen* suggests that they
may, in the future, serve as a more formidable
jurisdictional impediment to litigating constitutional claims.

(3) *The Redressability Requirement.* The redressability requirement, discussed by the Court in *Allen
v. Wright* and *Lujan v. Defenders of Wildlife* (1992),
is of increasing importance. In *Steel Co. v. Citizens*

for a Better Environment (1998), Citizens for a Better Environment ("CBE") sued a manufacturer under the Emergency Planning and Community Right-to-Know Act of 1986 ("EPCRA") alleging that the manufacturer had failed to make timely filings of toxic and hazardous chemical inventory forms and toxic chemical release forms as required under EPCRA. The manufacturer responded that its filings were up to date when the suit was brought, that the EPCRA did not allow suits for past violations, and that, therefore, the federal court had no jurisdiction. Justice Scalia ruled that the standing issue must be decided first before proceeding to the merits and that there was no standing. Even assuming that CBE suffered a concrete injury in fact by being denied the information required by the EPCRA, there was no standing because the CBE complaint failed the third requirement of standing, redressability.

Since there was no dispute about the fact that the defendant had violated the EPCRA by filing late reports, declaratory relief would be worthless to the citizen group; indeed, it would be "worthless to all the world." CBE's request that the manufacturer pay civil penalties also failed the redressability requirement since these penalties were payable to the federal government rather than to CBE. Therefore, they could not remedy the injury to CBE. Nor is the redressability component of standing satisfied by the costs associated with bringing suit. Similarly, prospective injunctive relief cannot remedy a past wrong. Relief that does not remedy the injury cannot bootstrap a plaintiff into a federal court. The plaintiff must seek remediation of its own injury. General vindication of the rule of law does not satisfy the redressability requirement. *Friends of the Earth v. Laidlaw* (2000) *supra*, implicitly modified *Steel Co.* by ruling that if the alleged violation is a continuing one, deterrence may satisfy redressability.

b. Federal Taxpayer Standing

Federal taxpayers generally lack a sufficient personal stake in the spending of federal monies to challenge the constitutionality of federal spending measures. Federal taxes become part of the general revenue and lose any separate identity with a particular taxpayer. If a challenge to a federal spending measure were successful, it is highly unlikely that the judicial remedy striking down or enjoining the program would yield any economic benefit to the taxpayer litigant. As the Court said in *Frothingham v. Mellon* (1923): "The party who invokes the [judicial] power must be able to show that he has sustained or is immediately in danger of sustaining some direct injury as the result of the statute's enforcement, and not merely that he suffers in some indefinite way in common with people generally." It was never clear, however, whether the *Frothingham* impediment to a federal taxpayer's standing had its origin in the Art. III case and controversy requirement or was a prudential consideration born out of judicial self-restraint.

While the Court never has completely removed this uncertainty, it is now established that a federal taxpayer can challenge spending measures if two conditions are satisfied. First, the taxpayer litigant must be challenging an exercise of the taxing and spending power rather than any incidental appropriation pursuant to a regulatory measure. For example, a taxpayer would not have standing as a taxpayer to challenge a congressional appropriation to fund an agency to enforce federal pollution laws. Second, the taxpayer must allege that the challenged enactment violates a specific constitutional limitation on the taxing and spending power. Thus, in *Flast v. Cohen* (1968), the Court held that a federal taxpayer had standing to challenge federal spending benefiting parochial schools on the ground that such appropriations violated the Establishment Clause of the First Amendment. One of the historic purposes of the prohibition against Establishment was to prevent the use of government monies for religion.

Remaining unclear after *Flast* was the issue of whether the second nexus in the *Flast* test, *i.e.,* the requirement that there be a connection between the legal claim of the plaintiff and the taxing and spending power, originates in Art. III or is merely a prudential consideration which the Court was free to relax. It is now established, however, that the second nexus, focusing on the litigant's legal claim must be satisfied only when federal taxpayer standing is in question. *Duke Power Co. v. Carolina Environmental Study Group* (1978). With respect to standing contentions which are not predicated on federal taxpayer standing alone, the test would still be whether the government enactment has caused the factual injury.

In *Valley Forge Christian College v. Americans United for Separation of Church & State, Inc.* (1982), the Court dramatically demonstrated the narrowness of the *Flast* recognition of federal taxpayer standing. Respondents had challenged an HEW grant of surplus funds to the college as violated the Establishment Clause. The Court held that the respondents lacked standing as federal taxpayers because they were challenging the actions of an administrative agency rather than Congress. Further, the land transfer was made under the Property Clause of Art. IV, and was not an exercise of the Congressional taxing and spending power.

A state taxpayer who cannot make a showing of "direct injury," such as pecuniary loss, does not have federal standing even though the status of being a state taxpayer may suffice to create standing in the state courts. *Doremus v. Board of Education* (1952). However, where a judgment of a state court causes "direct, specific and concrete" injury to the plaintiff, the Supreme Court may exercise its certiorari jurisdiction. This is so even though the plaintiff might not have been able to meet federal standing requirements when the original action was commenced. *ASARCO Inc. v. Kadish* (1989).

c. Citizen Standing

In the absence of congressional legislation, a citizen lacks standing to challenge federal actions as unconstitutional. The citizen *qua* citizen is said to have only a generalized grievance which cannot be differentiated from that of other citizens. When a complaint is made that a federal agency, for example, is acting contrary to a specific clause of the Constitution, the claim will fail for lack of standing. Thus, a citizen lacks standing to challenge a federal statute which permits the director of the CIA merely to certify expenditures as a violation of Art. I, Sec. 9, cl. 7, requiring a regular accounting of public funds. The assertion that citizens need such information in order to vote intelligently was held to be only a generalized grievance rather than an allegation of particularized injury. *United States v. Richardson* (1974). See *Schlesinger v. Reservists Comm. to Stop the War* (1974) [no citizen standing to challenge practice of members of Congress serving in Armed Forces Reserve as violation of Art. I, Sec. 6, Cl. 2, prohibiting House members from holding any office under the United States].

Nor does the fact that the challenge to federal action is based on the Establishment Clause provide a basis for citizen standing. In *Valley Forge,* the Court of Appeals had held that the Establishment Clause created a personal, but shared, constitutional right in citizens distinguishable from other claims of citizen standing. The Supreme Court, per Justice Rehnquist, rejected this effort to have citizen standing vary with the constitutional claim being asserted. A claim that the Constitution has been violated, without more, does not establish the personal injury in fact required by Art. III. The fact that no one would have standing, said Justice Rehnquist, "is not a reason to find standing." To the extent that the impediment to citizen standing is based on Art. III, the ability of Congress to confer standing by statute is limited. But note that Congress may, by statute, create a legal interest in a person. It can be argued that if such a statutory interest is violated, the personal injury in fact required for Art. III standing is present. See *Gladstone Realtors v. Village of Bellwood* (1979) [violation of rights conferred under 1968 Civil Rights Act held sufficient to confer standing].

d. Third Party Standing

Third party standing or, as the courts often call it, *jus tertii,* is as a generality easy to state: A is normally not considered to have standing to raise the legal rights of B. Even if A has sufficient injury in fact to assert his own legal claims, this standing is still insufficient to permit him to assert the legal claims of B. The basis for the rule is grounded in a "best plaintiff" concept. In the normal course of events, B is deemed the most appropriate person to litigate with respect to claims affecting him. The person most directly affected also will be the most likely to insure that the case is adequately presented. The rule has obvious connections with the adversity requirement associated with the case and controversy rule but it also reflects the Court's desire to avoid constitutional questions until decision is necessary (*i.e.,* strict necessity of decision).

In fact, it is now established that the third party standing rule is a prudential doctrine. Indeed, this area of the law of standing is now characterized by exceptions that almost negate the rule. If A can offer sufficient reason for allowing him to litigate B's legal claims, he may be permitted to do so. Some of the most frequently cited reasons for allowing standing in third party situations, despite the *jus tertii* rule, are as follows. If it would be difficult if not impossible for B to assert his own legal rights, then A may be allowed to litigate B's claims (assuming A has Art. III standing). If there is a close personal relationship between A and B, the Court is once again likely to relax the third party standing impediment. Thus, a physician has been permitted to raise the privacy rights of his patients in challenging the constitutionality of restrictive abortion laws. The physician-patient relationship is close and personal. Further, it would be difficult for the patient to assert her own rights since she might be chilled from litigating her claim by a desire to avoid publicity. *Singleton v. Wulff* (1976). Since laws discriminating between males and females in their ability to purchase beer impairs the relationship between sellers and potential buyers, the seller will have standing to raise the equal protection challenge to the laws. *Craig v. Boren* (1976).

But standing was denied when an atheist father sued in federal court as "next friend" for his daughter, a public school student, contending that the phrase "under God" in the Pledge of Allegiance, required to be recited by public school students on a daily basis, constituted a violation of the Establishment Clause because it was an unconstitutional endorsement of religion. The Ninth Circuit held that the phrase "under God" in the Pledge was unconstitutional. The father and mother of the student were in a custody dispute but the mother had legal custody. The mother intervened in the federal action to object to the father's purported representation of their daughter's interests. Moreover, a California state court ordered the father not to undertake representation of his daughter or to bring suit as her "next friend." The Ninth Circuit held, however, that even a non-custodial parent had Article III standing to object to government action affecting his child.

The Supreme Court, 5–3, reversed the Ninth Circuit. The Court, per Justice Stevens, held that where state law had deprived a father who had been deprived by state law of the right to bring suit on behalf of his child, he lacked prudential standing. There are prudential limitations on the powers of an unelected and unrepresentative judiciary. The obligation to exercise jurisdiction had to be weighed against the "deeply rooted" commitment not to decide constitutional question unless necessary. In the area of domestic relations, it was particularly appropriate for the federal courts to decline jurisdiction. Although the father's rights here flowed from his relationship with his daughter, he still lacked the right to litigate as her "next friend." The father and daughter's interests were not only not parallel, they were potentially in conflict. The father was free to inform his daughter on his views about religion but he had "no right to dictate to others what they may or may not say to his child respecting religion." Since the father had been deprived under California law of the right to sue as "next friend" for his daughter, it would not be proper for the federal courts to permit suit by a plaintiff whose standing to sue was predicated on family law rights that were in dispute.

Chief Justice Rehnquist, joined by Justices O'Connor and Thomas, concurred in the result but dissented with respect to standing. Relying on the father's assertion that the "[S]chool District's pledge ceremony infringes his right under California law to expose his daughter to his religious views," Chief Justice Rehnquist reasoned that the daughter was not the *"source"* of the father's standing but instead it was their relationship that provided the basis for his standing. On the merits, the dissenters contended that the phrase "under God" was not a religious exercise but "simply a recognition of the role of religion in the country's history." *Elk Grove Unified School District v. Newdow* (2004).

Organizations can raise the legal rights of their members if the following conditions are met: (1) the members themselves must have injury in fact for Art. III standing, (2) the interests involved in the litigation must be relevant to the organization's purposes, (3) the claims asserted and the relief requested do not require the participation of the individual members. *Hunt v. Washington State Apple Advertising Com'n* (1977). Since the third *Hunt* condition requires individual participation, associational standing is usually denied when an organization seeks damages. But, unlike the first two *Hunt* conditions, the third condition is prudential and Congress can grant such standing. *United Food & Commercial Workers Union Local 751 v. Brown Group, Inc.* (1996).

In sum, organizational standing continues to be one of the liveliest examples of the exception to the *jus tertii* rule.

2.   WHEN CAN CONSTITUTIONAL LITIGATION BE BROUGHT? THE PROBLEM OF TIMING

a.   Rule Against Mootness

When a judicial decision cannot have any practical legal effect because the issues that generated it either have been resolved or disappeared, it is said that the case has become moot. In federal constitutional law, mootness obviously serves what are called prudential considerations in limiting the occasions for judicial review. But there is a constitutional dimension to the mootness doctrine which should be understood. A case or controversy requires a *present* flesh and blood dispute that the courts can resolve. Nevertheless, it should be emphasized that the mootness cases in the Supreme Court are not easily rationalized. Many of the recent mootness decisions suggest that mootness is being used in a tactical way by the Court in order to find refuge from resolving controversial constitutional questions where no one point of view has captured a majority of the justices.

When Marco De Funis challenged the University of Washington Law School's affirmative action admission program, De Funis was in his third year of law school. The University indicated that if he successfully completed the program, he would graduate regardless of the Court's decision. These facts, the Court ruled in *De Funis v. Odegaard* (1974), rendered the case moot. Even if the highly speculative possibility that De Funis were to fail in his exams were realized, he would still not have to face again the initial admissions requirements. The Supreme Court is bound by Art. III requirements even though the state courts of Washington were not; they indeed, had not found mootness to be a barrier to decision.

While the mootness doctrine may be grounded in Art. III, this has not prevented the federal courts from fashioning exceptions to the mootness doctrine which do not entirely cohere with the mootness rationale. For example, if a case is found to be "capable of repetition and yet evading review," a federal court may take review even though the particular fact pattern might otherwise fall under the mootness doctrine. But how does the repetitious quality of the issue diminish the Art. III problem? In short, how is the requirement of present adversity satisfied?

The exemplar of the recurring issue case is the famous abortion decision, *Roe v. Wade* (1973). By the time the case reached the Supreme Court, nine months had long since passed and the case was technically moot. But the Supreme Court said this was a classic example of a case "capable of repetition yet evading review." Even if Ms. Roe were not to become pregnant again—and she might—all that would be required is that some member of her class be capable of becoming pregnant. Marco De Funis, on the other hand, had not filed a class action. For him, the question of the constitutionality of the law school's admission program would not recur. There was no reason to believe that the issue would again "evade review." If a suit is not filed as a class action, the recurring issue exception applies only if the issue is "capable of repetition" for the litigating party. *First National Bank v. Bellotti* (1978).

Another example of the "capable of repetition yet evading review" exception arose under the federal Education of the Handicapped Act. An emotionally disturbed student sought injunctive relief against school officials who had suspended him for violent and disruptive behavior relating to his handicap. The student involved was 20 but had not yet finished high school. The student was still eligible for educational services under the Act and, given his disability, was still likely to be in need of them. The school officials for their part were still insistent that they had authority to exclude disabled children for violent and disruptive conduct. In the circumstances, the Court held the case was not moot since it was reasonably likely that the action of the school officials which the student complained of was capable of being repeated. On the other hand, a similar challenge by a student no longer eligible because of his age for the benefits of the Act was held to be moot. *Honig v. Doe* (1988).

A second exception to the mootness doctrine which was asserted but also found unavailing in *De Funis* is the principle that the "voluntary cessation of unlawful activities" will not render a case moot at least where there is a reasonable likelihood that the wrong will be resumed. The reason for this exception is that a contrary rule would allow exploitation of the mootness doctrine because a wrongdoer could momentarily halt his mischief to escape judicial review. In *Friends of the Earth v. Laidlaw Environmental Services, Inc.* (2000), an alleged polluter shut down its offending plant and contended that the case brought against it was therefore moot. But the critical factor in the voluntary cessation exception to the mootness doctrine is whether the wrongful behavior can reasonably be expected to be repeated. On this point, the Court declared the defendant has the "formidable burden of showing that it is absolutely clear the allegedly wrongful behavior could not reasonably be expected to recur."

Suppose the defendant changes its conduct after suit is brought? Is the case now moot? In *Northeastern Florida Chapter of Associated General Contractors of America v. Jacksonville* (1993), the city changed its affirmative action program after the

Court granted certiorari to consider an equal protection challenge to an earlier affirmative action program. Under the old program, 10% of city contracts were set aside for members of seven different minority groups. Under the new program, participation goals of 5% to 16% were established but the new program applied solely to women and blacks. Five alternative methods for achieving the participation goals were set forth, only one of which was a set aside program. The city contended that the change in programs rendered the case moot. The Court invoked the voluntary cessation exception to the mootness doctrine and rejected this contention. In this case, there was not just a risk that the city would revert to its allegedly illegal conduct, it had in fact done so. The basis of the contractors' complaint was that the city's affirmative action program disadvantaged their ability to secure city contracts. That was still the case. There is no requirement that "it is only the possibility that the *selfsame* statute will be enacted that prevents a case from being moot."

A third exception arises in those infrequent cases where there are important unsettled collateral consequences that remain unresolved. Thus, a criminal conviction or a finding of insanity can impact on an individual even after he has been released from confinement. A wrongful criminal conviction is presumed to have collateral consequences but the presumption of collateral consequences does not extend to parole revocation. A parole revocation cannot be assumed to have the same collateral consequences as a criminal conviction. To overcome the mootness determination in such circumstances the existence of collateral consequences must be demonstrated if the case or controversy requirement of Article III is to be met. *Spencer v. Kemna* (1998).

b. Ripeness, Prematurity, and Abstractness

A federal court will not hear a case unless there is present injury or significant threat of imminent injury. Something adverse must be happening to the individual now or in the immediate future. The constitutional underpinnings of the precept that an issue be ripe for judicial resolution is once again the case or controversy requirement of Art. III. The ripeness doctrine was used as a bar to review in *United Public Workers of America v. Mitchell* (1947), where the Hatch Act banning political activities by government employees was challenged. While one employee who had violated the Act and was being threatened with removal was allowed to challenge (albeit unsuccessfully), other employees who merely wished to engage in political activities but had not yet done so were barred from challenging the act. As to them, the Court said it would be required to speculate as to the nature of the political activity and the probable response of the government to it. For example, for all the Court knew, the government might not choose to act. It is doubtful, however, that a government employee would be required to engage in political activity to the point of inviting job dismissal to raise the constitutional issue—imminent harm is sufficient.

National Park Hospitality Association v. Department of the Interior (2003) re-affirmed once again the point that delay in judicial resolution of an uncertain legal issue does not constitute the hardship necessary to render a case ripe for review. An association of park concessioners challenged a National Park Service regulation rendering the Contract Disputes Act (CDA) inapplicable to concession contracts. Denying that the regulation caused real hardship to the concessioners, Justice Thomas declared that the regulation was a statement of policy and did not have the force of law. Indeed, the National Park Service was not even delegated rulemaking authority under the CDA nor was it given any power to administer the law. The primary conduct of the concessioners was unaffected. They were still free to do business as they wished. Indeed, they were still free to follow the procedures set forth in the law once a dispute over a concession contract arose. The concessioners had as yet suffered no practical harm. If uncertainty about the validity of a legal rule established sufficient hardship to be ripe for review, an inundation of requests for "what essentially would be advisory opinions" would follow. The issue here "should await a concrete dispute about a particular concession contract."

Once again, however, Art. III requirements shade into prudential considerations. Even where the issue may be technically ripe, the Court has found the issues to be excessively premature or abstract. In *Socialist Labor Party v. Gilligan* (1972), the Court dismissed an appeal from an unsuccessful challenge by a minor political party to a state loyalty oath citing the lack of clarity and specificity of harm provided by the pleadings. Even if the technical requirements of standing and ripeness were met, the constitutional issues were not presented in a "clean-cut and concrete form." For example, the Socialist Labor Party had not pleaded that it would not sign the loyalty oath. It was entirely possible that the Party intended to sign the oath and would appear on the ballot.

A case based on contingent events in the future is not ripe for review. The case either may not arise as anticipated or, indeed, may not arise at all. The Texas Education Code provided for sanctions for school districts failing to meet state mandated educational achievement levels. Texas asked the United States Attorney General whether any of the sanctions provided in the Code affected voting and thus required a preclearance under Section 5 of the Federal Voting Rights Act of 1965. The Attorney General responded that under certain circumstances imposition of some sanctions might require preclearance. Texas then sought a declaratory judgment to the contrary. The Court, per Justice Scalia, held that the matter was not ripe for review. First, a problem that may not need to be solved is not fit for adjudication. Second, the hardship to Texas was not substantial. The Texas claim of immediate harm due to a "threat to federalism" was rejected as an abstraction. *Texas v. United States* (1998).

Similarly, a Sierra Club challenge to a Forest Service plan, not yet approved or implemented, which allegedly permitted too much logging and clearcutting, was rejected. The Court, per Justice Breyer, unanimously held the suit was not ripe for judicial review. First, it was not clear that delayed review would cause hardship to the plaintiffs. Second, premature judicial intervention might inappropriately interfere with administrative action. Third, the Court might benefit from further factual development of relevant issues. The Forest Service might make changes in the plan now challenged. The case presented the kind of abstract quarrel over administrative policy which it is the very purpose of the ripeness doctrine to avoid. *Ohio Forestry Association v. Sierra Club* (1998).

3.   WHAT CAN BE LITIGATED? THE POLITICAL QUESTION DOCTRINE

As early as 1803, in *Marbury v. Madison,* Chief Justice Marshall indicated that there is a class of constitutional cases which federal courts cannot review because "the subjects are political." On the other hand, in 1821 in *Cohens v. Virginia,* Chief Justice Marshall stated: "We have no more right to decline the exercise of jurisdiction which is given, than to usurp that which is not given." Further, it has become clear that jurisdiction is not to be declined merely because the case involves either political values or the political process.

What then is the key to the "non-justiciability" of political questions or, to put it another way, to those situations where the political question doctrine is a barrier to review of a case by the federal courts? In *Baker v. Carr* (1962), precursor to a powerful line of cases resolving the problem of state malapportionment, Justice Brennan provided an authoritative examination of the foundations and the characteristics of the political question doctrine. Beginning from the premise that "[t]he non-justiciability of the political question is primarily a function of the separation of powers," Justice Brennan noted that, in part, the doctrine required federal courts to determine whether a question had been committed by the Constitution to another branch of the national government. Further, the doctrine of non-justiciability necessitated an inquiry into whether "the duty asserted can be judicially identified and its reach judicially determined, and whether protection for the right asserted can be judicially molded." While the political question doctrine suggests roots in Art. III, it is primarily based on what the Court calls, in the standing context, prudential considerations.

In a much-quoted passage in *Baker v. Carr,* Justice Brennan set forth criteria, reflecting classic, functional and prudential considerations, for identifying a political question case. First, invoking a *classic* concern, Justice Brennan said that a case should be held non-justiciable if there is "a textually demonstrable constitutional commitment of the issue to a coordinate political department." It has been suggested that only such a constitutional commitment of an issue to the autonomous discretion of another branch of the national government would justify a federal court in declining the exercise of its Art. III jurisdiction. Other commentators have raised the question whether there is any issue that is totally committed to another branch of government in the sense that the judiciary could not, if it chose, review the matter. In support of this view is Justice Brennan's statement in *Baker v. Carr* describing the Supreme Court as the "ultimate interpreter of the Constitution." Perhaps, the most appropriate resolution of this issue is to recognize that under the classical approach there are subjects which are charged primarily to the discretion of either the executive or the Congress, but that the identification of the subjects so charged and the constitutionality of the exercise of the discretion given remains subject to judicial review.

Other criteria mentioned by Justice Brennan in *Baker* reflect *functional* considerations relating to the capabilities of the judicial department. Thus, Justice Brennan would have federal courts ask whether there is "a lack of judicially discoverable and manageable standards for resolving (the question)" or would have them consider "the impossibility of deciding without an initial policy determination of a kind clearly for non-judicial discretion." Professor Scharpf, in his article *Judicial Review and the Political Question: A Functional Analysis,* 75 Yale L.J. 517 (1966), cites such considerations as the difficulty of acquiring accurate information and the need for uniformity of decision of the respective branches of government as bearing on the justiciability of a particular question.

Stalin asked, "How many divisions has the Pope?" Andrew Jackson, according to an apocryphal story, said: "John Marshall has made his decision. Now let him enforce it." In a similar vein, it was concern that the Supreme Court and the federal courts would fail if they sought to resolve the "mathematical quagmire of reapportionment" that influenced Justice Frankfurter's strong and anguished dissent in *Baker*. As Frankfurter put it, "There is not under our Constitution a judicial remedy for every political mischief, for every undesirable exercise of legislative power." But for the Court, the equal protection challenge to malapportionment involved well developed and familiar Fourteenth Amendment standards. The courts were fully capable of identifying and implementing the constitutional mandate.

Prudential considerations are reflected in Justice Brennan's references to "the impossibility of a court's undertaking independent resolution without expressing lack of the respect due coordinate branches of government" or "an unusual need for unquestioning adherence to a political decision already made" or "the potentiality of embarrassment for multifarious pronouncements by various departments on one question." The late Professor Alexander Bickel carried this theme even further, arguing that an issue should be deemed non-justiciable because of its strangeness, momentousness, or its "intractability to principled decision-making," anxi-

ety concerning the consequences of judicial involvement, or the "self-doubt of an institution lacking
electoral responsibility or enforcement capability."
Justice Frankfurter, haunted by the South's "massive resistance" to compliance in *Brown v. Board of
Education* (1954) reflected these same concerns in
dissent in *Baker* and warned that judicial involvement in political reapportionment threatened the
Court's authority even in its established terrain:
"The Court's authority possessed of neither the
purse nor the sword ultimately rests on sustained
public confidence in its moral sanction." Frankfurter implored the Court to exercise complete detach-
ment from political entanglements involving the
clash of political forces in order not to jeopardize
this public confidence. For him, the forum for such
struggles was the electoral and not the judicial
process.

Baker v. Carr was a watershed in the evolution of
the political question doctrine. The Court in *Baker*
made it clear that the federal judiciary would resolve equal protection challenges to malapportionment despite Justice Frankfurter's admonitions
that the courts would become enmeshed in a "political thicket".

In another political question case, *Powell v.
McCormack* (1969), the Court held that congressional exclusion of an elected representative is justi-
ciable. A specific provision of the constitutional text,
Art. I, Sec. 5, making each house "the Judge of the
Qualifications of its own members" was not commitment of all questions relating to an elected per-

son's qualifications to take his seat. Instead, it was a limited reference to the qualifications for membership specified in the Constitution, *i.e.,* age, citizenship, and state residence. In *United States v. Nixon* (1974), the Court held the President could be required to respond to judicial process. The fact that the President was a defendant did not render non-justiciable the question of privilege for confidential communications. A plurality of the Court in *Goldwater v. Carter* (1979), reflecting the traditional reluctance to become involved in the foreign affairs sphere, held that the unilateral termination of a treaty by a President was a matter which the overtly political branches of government were quite capable of resolving. Finally, in a pre-*Baker* case concerning the propriety of judicial supervision of the Article V amendment process, the Court invoked the political question doctrine and, by declining to resolve the matter, left problems of ratification to Congress. *Coleman v. Miller* (1939).

The criteria for defining a political question set forth by Justice Brennan in *Baker* have continuing importance. Yet it must be recognized that these criteria are not in themselves always applied in a uniform or predictable way. Some cases, of course, do present issues beyond the competence of the federal judiciary. A federal judge had been impeached by the House of Representatives. Was a Senate rule which allowed a committee of Senators to hear evidence and to report that evidence to the full Senate consistent with the Impeachment Trial Clause, Art. I, Sec. 3, cl. 6, which states that the

"Senate shall have the sole Power to try all Impeachments"? The Court held that the question presented was a non-justiciable political question. *Nixon v. United States* (1993). The word "sole" means that the power was "reposed in the Senate and nowhere else." The Senate's power to try impeachments was subject to the specific requirements of Art. I., Sec. 3, and the other limitations set forth in the Constitution. In light of the specificity of these requirements, the Court was disinclined to add to them and rule "that the Framers used the word 'try' as an implied limitation on the method by which the Senate might proceed in trying impeachments." The word "try" in the Impeachment Trial Clause was too imprecise to provide any judicially manageable standards of review.

In summary, the political question doctrine is most likely to be invoked in areas of traditional presidential or congressional competence. The foreign affairs area, the national security context, questions about the exercise of the war power and the amendment process are not the traditional fare of the courts but today comprise the hard core definition of the political question doctrine.

CHAPTER II

NATIONAL LEGISLATIVE POWERS

A. SCOPE OF CONGRESSIONAL POWER

In *McCulloch v. Maryland* (1819), Chief Justice John Marshall stated: "This government is acknowledged by all to be one of enumerated powers." It follows from this principle that there is in American constitutionalism no doctrine of inherent legislative powers, at least in the domestic arena. Whenever the constitutionality of congressional legislation is at issue, some relationship to a specifically enumerated power in the constitutional text must be shown. Candidly, relationships are sometimes "found" which might not be obvious to the average reasonable person. Indeed, the lack of an inherent powers doctrine and the formal allegiance to an enumerated powers approach is less important in the end result than might appear.

Under our Constitution, all powers not delegated to the national government under the Tenth Amendment are retained by the states and the people. This is a basic premise of the division of powers, "Our Federalism." But it remains to be

68

determined how the scope of the delegated powers
should be delineated.

In *McCulloch v. Maryland* (1819), the Court considered whether the constitutional delegation of
powers to Congress included a power to incorporate
a national bank. Chief Justice Marshall conceded
that there was no *express* provision granting such
power to Congress and that incorporation was normally a prerogative of the states. There were, however, express powers in Art. I, Sec. 8, to lay and
collect taxes, to borrow money, to regulate commerce, to declare and conduct wars, and to raise
and support armed forces. Did these powers of
sword and purse include a power to incorporate a
national bank? Certainly there was nothing in the
Constitution expressly prohibiting Congress from
enacting such legislation. But John Marshall had
emphasized the need for an affirmative grant of
power.

Beginning with the great premise, "It is a Constitution we are expounding," Marshall argued for a
doctrine of implied powers. A Constitution must be
read broadly to provide government with all of the
means to effectuate the powers granted in the basic
instrument, subject, of course, to the restrictions
contained therein. But Marshall did not rely solely
on this logical and practical argument (which found
support in the Federalist Papers), regarding the
nature of the Constitution. Instead, he found specific authorization for implied powers in the Constitution itself. The Necessary and Proper Clause, Art. I,
Sec. 8, Cl. 18, provides that Congress shall have

power "To make all Laws which shall be necessary and proper for carrying into Execution the foregoing Powers, and all other Powers vested by this Constitution in the Government of the United States, or in any Department or Officer thereof."

Counsel for Maryland, which was seeking to tax the national bank, argued that the Necessary and Proper Clause should be interpreted restrictively by limiting it to those means which are indispensable to the execution of the granted power. But for John Marshall, "Necessary and Proper" didn't necessarily mean necessary. Our Constitution was "intended to endure for ages to come." The inclusion of the word "proper" with the word "necessary," the placement of the Necessary and Proper Clause among the powers of Congress in Art. I, Sec. 8, rather than in the Art. I, Sec. 9 limitations on congressional powers as well as the language of the Clause itself all led to a single conclusion—the express powers set forth in the Constitution were not to be read narrowly but were to be read broadly in order to accomplish the goal of making this new federal government work.

Marshall himself provided a broad interpretive guide to federal legislative power in *McCulloch* which is still being quoted and used in our courts: "Let the end be legitimate, let it be within the scope of the Constitution, and all means which are appropriate, which are plainly adapted to that end, which are not prohibited, but which consist with the letter and spirit of the Constitution, are constitutional." Applying this principle, the incorporation of a national bank was clearly "a convenient, a useful, and essential instrument" in carrying on the national government's fiscal operations.

The Chief Justice did include one limitation on his broad approach to congressional power. In what has come to be known as the Pretext Principle, Marshall reasoned that if Congress enacted legislation, "for the accomplishment of objects not entrusted to the government," it would become the duty of the courts to declare the law unconstitutional even though Congress purported to be executing its granted powers. While this principle was used in the early part of the twentieth century to overturn congressional legislation allegedly invading the residual powers of the states, unlike the Constitution, this principle has not endured for the ages.

A rare reference in contemporary Supreme Court cases to both Marshall's pretext theory and the Necessary and Proper Clause occurred in *Jinks v. Richland County* (2003). A federal law extending state statutes of limitations for supplemental jurisdiction claims dismissed by the federal courts was unsuccessfully challenged as an improper exercise of the Necessary and Proper Clause. Justice Scalia for the Court declared that *McCulloch* had long ago rejected the idea that an Act of Congress be "absolutely necessary" in order to exercise an enumerated power. Congress had implied power to enact the law which was necessary and "plainly adapted" to the power of Congress to "constitute inferior tribunals inferior to the Supreme Court," Art. I, sec. 8, cl. 9, and to provide for the "fair and efficient" exercise of federal judicial power under Art. III, Sec. 1. The parties did not contend that the law was being used as a pretext to accomplish ends not entrusted to the federal government. Nor was the law an impermissible trespass upon state sovereignty. State law limitation periods did not fall into the category of state procedure "immune from congressional regulation."

B.   THE COMMERCE POWER

1.   ESTABLISHING THE FOUNDATIONS

The most important of the express domestic powers of Congress set forth in Art. I, Sec. 8, is the commerce power: "Congress shall have power to regulate commerce among the several states." This clause received its initial interpretation in the great case of *Gibbons v. Ogden* (1824). New York had given an exclusive navigation license to one party. Congress had conferred a license to traverse the same waters to another party. In this case of conflict, which power, state or federal, should prevail?

Chief Justice Marshall had little difficulty in including navigation within the term "commerce" given the Framers' concern with ending trade wars between the states. A greater problem was presented by the phrase "among the several states". Employing what Felix Frankfurter called an organic theory of commerce, Marshall read these words to mean "that commerce which concerns more states than one." Only that commerce which is exclusively internal to a state, which does not affect other states, would be precluded from the reach of the Commerce Clause under this interpretation. And Marshall chose not to extend the congressional power to this internal commerce only because "[s]uch a power would be inconvenient and is certainly unnecessary."

Had Marshall's organic interpretation of the Commerce Clause prevailed, much of subsequent commerce power history might have been different. Limitations placed on the Commerce Clause to frustrate the national economic recovery during the New Deal era, for example, would have been far more difficult. However, the Court gradually developed a territorial approach to the Commerce Clause limiting its reach to interstate commerce, *i.e.,* commerce crossing a state line. Today, through express reliance on the Commerce Clause and the doctrine of implied powers, there has been a return to that broad conception of the commerce power envisioned by Marshall.

Finally, Chief Justice Marshall turned to the meaning of the power "to regulate Commerce." And once again he employed his broad vision of the constitutional grant of federal powers: "This power, like all others vested in Congress, is complete in itself, may be exercised to its utmost extent, and acknowledges no limitation, other than are prescribed in the Constitution." In short, the power to regulate commerce is "plenary" with respect to the objects of the power. The principal restraint on the exercise of this regulatory power is found in the wisdom and discretion of the Congress where, ironically, after a convoluted constitutional history, it remains today. It is the people exercising their power through the political process that safeguards constitutionally granted legislative powers from abuse.

2. USING THE COMMERCE CLAUSE FOR POLICE POWER ENDS

The Framers of the Constitution considered but rejected a proposal to vest a national police power in the Congress. But the question remained whether Congress, through the exercise of its delegated powers, could regulate to achieve police power objectives. Classically, these police powers concerned health, morals, and well-being. With the rise of the positive state in the twentieth century, such legislation often takes the form of social welfare laws. But John Marshall's Pretext Principle in *McCulloch v. Maryland* appeared to repudiate any effort to use the federal legislative power for social welfare ends. This more limited view of the commerce power is illustrated by *Hammer v. Dagenhart* (1918), in which a federal law restricting the interstate shipping of goods produced by child labor was held unconstitutional as invasive of the reserved powers of the states. For the Court, the congressional regulatory power over interstate commerce, while "ample," was limited by the Tenth Amendment. In this view, the powers reserved to the states served to limit the powers granted to the national government. This was the doctrine of dual federalism.

But even in the heyday of the Pretext Principle, the doctrine was not always followed. For example, in the case of *Champion v. Ames* (The Lottery Case) (1903), fifteen years before *Hammer,* the Court validated federal anti-lottery legislation, clearly a police power measure. The first Justice Harlan, speaking for the Court in *Champion,* said Congress has the power to protect the people of the United States against the pollution of the channels of interstate commerce. In *Hammer,* the *Lottery Case* was distinguished on the ground that the evil being legislated against followed rather than preceded the interstate transaction. For Justice Holmes, dissenting in *Hammer,* this distinction was a casuistry which was hardly persuasive. Justice Holmes concluded that the plenary regulatory power of Congress included the power to prohibit the movement of interstate commerce when it was being used to encourage what Congress in its judgment concluded is a moral evil: "It may carry out its views of public policy whatever indirect effect they may have upon the activities of the states."

The restrictive view of the commerce power adopted in *Hammer* as well as the Pretext Principle itself were conclusively rejected in *United States v. Darby* (1941). In upholding a provision of the Fair Labor Standards Act prohibiting the shipment of goods in interstate commerce which had been produced by employees working for substandard wages or excessive hours as defined by the Act, Chief Justice Stone in *Darby* returned to the Protective Principle fashioned in *Champion:* "Congress, following its own conception of public policy concerning the restrictions which may appropriately be imposed on interstate commerce, is free to exclude from the commerce articles whose use in the states for which they are destined it may conceive to be injurious to the public health, morals, or welfare, even though the state has not sought to regulate their use." It is for Congress to define the conditions for using the channels of interstate commerce.

The function of the Court, reasoned Stone, was not to probe the purpose or motive of Congress in regulating interstate commerce since these are "matters for the legislative judgment upon the exercise of which the Constitution places no restriction and over which the courts are given no control." Nor did the reserved powers of the states limit an otherwise constitutional exercise of the commerce power: "Our conclusion is unaffected by the Tenth Amendment. The Amendment states but a truism that all is retained which has not been surrendered." The dual federalism doctrine set forth in *Hammer* which so long and so effectively limited the reach of the federal commerce power was rejected. *Hammer* was overruled; implicitly, the Holmes dissent in *Hammer* was now the law. Congress could use the commerce power for social welfare purposes.

3.   THE STREAM OF COMMERCE

Can Congress, using its commerce power, regulate the wages and hours of workers at the Chicago stockyards? Under the classic view, activity at the stockyards might be viewed as an entirely local transaction which would normally fall within the purview of the state police power. Nevertheless, in *Stafford v. Wallace* (1922), the Court upheld such federal legislation reasoning that "[t]he stockyards are but a throat through which the current [of interstate commerce] flows, and the transactions which occur therein are only incident to this current." The seemingly local activity at the stockyards was in fact part of the stream of interstate commerce subject to federal control.

But note that the *Stafford* Court addressed itself only to local activities at the "throat" of interstate commerce. It did not undertake to approve federal regulatory power over activities, such as agricultural production and mining, which arguably are antecedent to interstate commerce. Nor did it say that Congress could regulate activities, such as the sale and consumption of goods, solely on the ground that the goods had once traveled in interstate commerce. However, whether or not the "stream of interstate commerce" in fact extends to these activities has not proven critical. Even if such activities are not *in* interstate commerce, Congress can reach them under the Affectation Doctrine. Since the Affectation Doctrine brings a wider range of activity under the scope of federal regulation, it has virtually displaced the "stream of commerce" doctrine.

4.   THE AFFECTATION DOCTRINE

In *McCulloch v. Maryland* (1819), Chief Justice Marshall had made it clear that congressional power is not limited to the express grants of Art. I, Sec. 8, but includes such power as is necessary and proper to the effectuation of the express powers. Using the broad interpretive approach to implied powers adopted by John Marshall, it can be said that the commerce power encompasses federal regulation of local activity when such regulation is reasonably appropriate to the effective regulation of interstate commerce.

In the pre-New Deal era, the Court translated this principle to mean that Congress can regulate local activities which "directly" affect interstate commerce but not those local activities where the effect was only "indirect." This conceptualistic approach had the practical effect of precluding any inquiry into the magnitude of the impact of local transactions on interstate commerce and the need for federal regulation for our national economy. But beginning with *NLRB v. Jones & Laughlin Steel Corp.* (1937), the Court increasingly began to inquire into the extent of the burden on the free movement of interstate commerce.

The era of the modern affectation doctrine was launched with the case of *Wickard v. Filburn* (1942), upholding federal legislation regulating the most local of all activities—production of wheat for personal consumption on the family farm. Justice Jackson, for the Court, stated the controlling principle: "[E]ven if [the farmer's] activity be local, and though it may not be regarded as commerce, it may still, whatever its nature, be reached by Congress, if it exerts a substantial economic effect on interstate commerce, and this irrespective of whether such effect is what might at some earlier time have been defined as 'direct' or 'indirect'."

In defining whether the farmer's activities had a substantial adverse effect, the Court introduced the cumulative effects principle. In a context like *Wickard,* the effect must be considered in the light of the farmer's "contribution taken together with that of many others similarly situated." It is the aggregate or cumulative impact of all the individual producers that provided the predicate for congressional regulation.

Applying these principles to the marketing restrictions before them, the Court, in *Wickard,* concluded that Congress could reasonably have found that home consumed wheat would have substantial influence on price and market conditions. First, such wheat would overhang the market and thus introduce an uncontrolled variable on supply and demand. Second, even if never marketed, the wheat would satisfy the needs of the grower thus withdrawing him from the market. A wag of the time, parodying Cardozo's style, said of the hapless farmer in *Wickard:* "Grow it he can, but eat it he cannot."

The modern Affectation Doctrine fashioned in *Wickard* controls Commerce Clause analysis to the present day. Its broad sweep is indicated by the fact that since the New Deal congressional legislation grounded in the commerce power has been held unconstitutional for want of federal legislative power only recently. See *United States v. Lopez* (1995), *infra; United States v. Morrison (2000).*

The breadth of the congressional commerce power thus recognized is indicated by two cases upholding the public accommodations provisions of the 1964 Federal Civil Rights Act which was based principally on the federal commerce power. In *Heart of Atlanta Motel v. United States* (1964), the Court held that Congress had power to prohibit racial discrimination in hotels and motels serving interstate travelers. Even though the motel's racial discrimination occurred locally, by discouraging blacks from traveling the discrimination burdened interstate commerce. Justice Clark, for the Court in *Heart of Atlanta* observed: "How obstructions in commerce may be removed—What means are to be employed—is within the sound and exclusive discretion of the Congress. It is subject to only one caveat—that the means chosen by it must be reasonably adapted to the end permitted by the Constitution. We cannot say that its choice here was not so adapted. The Constitution requires no more." The contention that since Congress was legislating against "moral wrongs" the use of the Commerce Clause was improper was similarly rejected in *Heart of Atlanta.* Given the burdensome effect of racial discrimination on commerce, Congress could act. The *Heart of Atlanta* case, therefore, made it clear,

if any doubt remained, that a police or social welfare motivation would not in itself render a congressional exercise of the commerce power invalid.

In the companion case, *Katzenbach v. McClung*
(1964), the commerce power provided the foundation for the extension of the public accommodations
provisions of the Civil Rights Act to Ollie's Barbecue, a small restaurant catering to a local trade.
Only forty-six percent of the food purchased by
Ollie's Barbecue came through the channels of interstate commerce. But this was sufficient since
Congress could rationally conclude that restaurants
practicing racial discrimination sold less interstate
goods, that interstate travel was obstructed, and
that business in general suffered. While the volume
of food purchased by Ollie's from interstate sources
might be insignificant, the cumulative effects doctrine dictated that Congress might consider the
aggregate impact in determining the burden on the
free flow of commerce: "[W]here we find that the
legislators, in light of the facts and testimony before
them, have a rational basis for finding a chosen
regulatory scheme necessary to the protection of
commerce, [the Supreme Court's] investigation is at
an end." Together with *Heart of Atlanta, Katzenbach v. McClung* demonstrates that the judiciary
will extend great deference to a congressional assertion that it is acting under the Commerce Clause.
Nevertheless, the Court does not abandon all investigation into the matter. At least a nominal inquiry
into the regulated conduct's effect on interstate
commerce is conducted.

ectation Doctrine also has provided a vehi-
e federalization of criminal law, a traditional bastion of the local police power. For example, in *Perez v. United States* (1971), the Court
upheld Title II of the Consumer Credit Protection
Act, the criminal sanctions of which were applied to
a local loan-sharking situation. Justice Douglas said
that Congress could reasonably conclude that local
loan-sharking was one of the most lucrative sources
of revenue or organized interstate crime.

But had *Perez* any tie-in to interstate criminal
organization? In response, Justice Douglas appeared
to say that none was needed. He apparently invoked
the cumulative effects doctrine: "Where *the class* of
activities is regulated, and that *class* is within the
reach of federal power, the courts have no power 'to
excise, as trivial, individual instances' of the class."
But there remained a problem. There was no indication that *Perez* was a member of the class of loan
sharks having ties to interstate crime. Justice Stewart observed in a bitter dissent: "[U]nder the statute before us, a man can be convicted without any
proof of interstate movement, of the use of the
facilities of interstate commerce, or of facts showing
that his conduct affected interstate commerce."

In *United States v. Lopez* (1995), for the first time
since the New Deal, the commerce power was held
inadequate to sustain a law. The Court held 5–4
that the Gun–Free School Zones Act, prohibiting
knowing possession of firearms in a school zone, is
unconstitutional. There were three categories of
activity which Congress could regulate under the

Commerce Clause. First, Congress could regulate
the channels of interstate commerce. Second, Congress could regulate the instrumentalities of interstate commerce. Third, Congress could regulate
those activities which have a substantial effect on
interstate commerce. If Congress had authority to
legislate in this area, it had to be under the third
category, *i.e.*, that the activity being regulated substantially affected commerce. Chief Justice Rehnquist rejected the Government's Affectation Doctrine argument. Four factors were critical to the
analysis in *Lopez*. First, the Act did not have a
jurisdictional nexus requiring that the firearms or
the defendant have some connection with interstate
commerce. Second, *Lopez* placed a new emphasis on
the necessity that the activity being regulated have
a commercial character. The Gun–Free School
Zones Act was not limited to "commercial transactions" which in the aggregate, substantially affect
interstate commerce. Third, Congress had made no
findings that school violence had a substantial commercial effect on interstate commerce. While findings are not required, their absence makes it more
difficult to conclude that such a substantial effect
exists. Fourth, the regulated act had only a remote,
attenuated effect on interstate commerce. The fact
that the federal law at issue regulates activities
historically allocated to the states like education,
family law or criminal law bears on whether a
particular use by Congress of the federal commerce
power is an appropriate one. The Government argued that the use of guns in schools affects the

national economy because of the substantial cost of violent crime, the impediment violence places on travel and the less productive citizenry produced by a handicapped educational process. Chief Justice Rehnquist responded that accepting such arguments would allow federal regulation of any activity, even in areas such as family law where the states have traditionally been sovereign. Justice Kennedy, joined by Justice O'Connor, concurred, arguing that the Act is unconstitutional, given its significant interference with state sovereignty, "[a]bsent a stronger connection or identification with commercial concerns that are central to the Commerce Clause."

Justice Breyer, joined by Justices Stevens, Souter and Ginsburg, dissenting, stressed that the specific question was whether Congress could have "a rational basis" for concluding that the regulated act has a "significant" effect on interstate commerce. The absence of findings only deprives the statute of some extra leeway beyond the deference required. Congress could rationally conclude that gun related violence near the schools, through its effect on education, has a significant effect on economic activity. Violence around the schools "is a commercial, as well as a human, problem."

In sum, *Lopez* signifies there are limits to the power of Congress to legislate under the Commerce Clause.

Lopez has proved not to be a flash in the pan but instead the harbinger of a new and limiting approach to the Commerce Clause. In *United States v. Morrison* (2000), a 5–4 decision, the Court, per Justice Rehnquist, held that a provision of the Violence Against Women Act affording a civil remedy for victims of gender-motivated violence was not authorized by the Commerce Clause and was, therefore, unconstitutional. The Government based its Commerce Clause authority for the Violence Against Women Act under the third *Lopez* category, *i.e.*, that the regulated activity substantially affected commerce. Using analysis set forth in *Lopez*, the Court disagreed. First, the regulated activity was not commercial in character but instead involved violent criminal conduct. Second, the statute contained no express jurisdictional element which would limit its reach or establish that the regulation was in pursuance of Congressional power over interstate commerce. On the contrary, the statute regulated a broad area of "purely intrastate" violent crime. Third, although unlike *Lopez*, the law in *Morrison* was supported by findings that gender-based violence substantially affected commerce, such findings were not dispositive. Whether activities substantially affected commerce sufficiently to be within the scope of the federal commerce power ultimately was a matter for independent judicial determination. This constituted a change from, or at least an implicit challenge to, the deferential rational basis standard of review used in Commerce Clause cases since *United States v. Darby* (1941). Further, the force of Congressional findings supporting the Violence Against Women Act were weakened because the fact that the aggregate effect of non-economic activity had some effect on interstate commerce could not justify a use of the federal commerce power. Such an approach would "obliterate the Constitution's distinction between national and local authority." While the Court was not "adopting a categorical rule against aggregating non-economic activity" in federal commerce power cases, the Court said that its past cases had upheld federal commerce power regulation only where the activity at issue was economic in character.

Justice Souter, writing for the dissenters, said that the Violence Against Women Act would have been upheld during the entire period from *Wickard v. Filburn* (1942) to *United States v. Lopez* (1995). The Court was now clearly giving lesser weight to "obviously substantial, cumulative effects on commerce." Past Commerce Clause cases remained "nominally undisturbed." But rational basis review was now being supplanted by a new and more stringent "criterion of review" which asserted a "unique judicial competence" to review Congressional legislation challenged under the Commerce Clause. The Court's new demand that the activity being regulated under the federal commerce power be commercial in nature was not an economic conception but instead was designed to serve a certain conception of federalism. But this was simply a replay of the idea rejected in *United States v. Darby* (1941) that if Congress regulated in an area of "traditional state concern," that fact was somehow a limitation on the federal commerce power. The "federalism of some earlier time" was simply inadequate to cope with the realities of today's integrated national economy.

The integrated nature of the national economy has in fact served to limit the reach of *Lopez* and *Morrison*. For example, the Federal Safety Highway Act requires states to identify dangerous sections of state highways in order to apply for funds to repair them. Congress amended the Act to authorize the states to keep this information protected from discovery in civil trials. The Supreme Court of the state of Washington held, *inter alia*, that Congress lacked authority under the Commerce Clause to enact such an amendment because it was not an integral part of the regulation of the federal highway system. In a unanimous opinion, per Justice Thomas, the Supreme Court reversed. Congress could reasonably conclude that protecting the material at issue would result in more diligent collection and more candid information about hazardous locations. In the long run, this would lead to greater safety on the nation's roads. Commerce Clause legislative authority includes laws "aimed at improving safety in the channels of commerce and increasing protection for the instrumentalities of interstate commerce." *Pierce County v. Guillen* (2003).

Where "concededly economic activity" was concerned, *United States v. Lopez* did not purport to set forth a new rule. In *Citizens Bank v. Alafabco, Inc.* (2003) the issue presented was whether commercial lending between an Alabama-based bank and an

Alabama-based construction company had a sufficient effect on interstate commerce to come under the Federal Arbitration Act. The Supreme Court of Alabama, relying on *United States v. Lopez*, ruled that there had been no showing " 'that any portion of the restructured debt was actually attributable to interstate transactions; that the funds comprising the debt originated out-of-state; or that the restructured debt was inseparable from any out-of-state projects.' " Rejecting the Alabama court's "cramped view" of the Commerce Clause, the Supreme Court held that congressional power under the Commerce Clause could be exercised in individual cases without having to show some specific effect upon interstate commerce. However, the economic activity in the aggregate had to constitute ' "a general practice subject to federal control.' " Futhermore, the general practice had to bear on interstate commerce in a substantial manner. The intrastate commercial lending affected interstate commerce since Alafabco used the loans to engage in interstate business, the loans were secured by goods assembled using interstate materials and commercial lending has a broad impact on the national economy.

In 1996 California enacted a law which created an exemption from criminal prosecution for doctors, patients and primary caregivers who possess or grow marijuana for medicinal purposes under the direction of a doctor. Nonetheless, federal Drug Enforcement Administration agents seized and destroyed cannabis plants grown for personal use by two Californians with serious medical conditions.

Doctors had recommended the use of marijuana to these individuals. The DEA agents were enforcing the federal Controlled Substances Act (CSA) which prohibits the cultivation and use of marijuana. The issue presented was whether congressional commerce power extended to the prohibition of the local cultivation and use of marijuana. The Court, 6–3, ruled that the federal law was a valid exercise of congressional Commerce Clause authority. Using the affectation doctrine, the Court relied on *Perez v. United States* (1971) to the effect that Congress has power to regulate purely local activities which form part of an economic class of activities which have a substantial effect on interstate commerce. The cumulative effects corollary to the affectation doctrine set forth in *Wickard v. Filburn* (1942) was brought into service. *Lopez* had cited *Perez* with apparent approval. Yet the concern expressed in *Lopez* and *Morrison* about unjustified over-extensions of the affectation doctrine cast some doubt about the future of *Perez* and *Wickard*-type analysis. But *Perez* was now front and center. Similarly, *Wickard*, regarded even in its day as an extreme application of the affectation doctrine, was accorded a resounding revival. *Gonzales v. Raich* (2005).

The Court in *Gonzales* declared that the similarities between the wheat grown for home consumption in *Wickard* and the marijuana grown for home consumption here was striking. Furthermore, the rational basis standard of review for evaluating legislation challenged under the Commerce Clause was also re-affirmed. The Court did not need to determine whether "activities, taken in the aggregate, substantially affect interstate commerce in fact, but only whether a 'rational basis' exists for so concluding." *Lopez* and *Morrison* were distinguished on the ground that those cases dealt with matters that were clearly non-economic and, therefore, outside congressional commerce power altogether. Here the area being regulated was clearly economic. The CSA regulated "the production, distribution and consumption of commodities for which there is an established and lucrative interstate market." The CSA was a federal law which was a valid exercise of the Commerce Clause; therefore, the CSA trumped the California law on the basis of the Supremacy Clause. Justice Scalia, concurring, stressed the propriety of the use of Necessary and Proper Clause to reach non-economic activity which in fact constitutes part of a larger economic market. Justice O'Connor, joined by Chief Justice Rehnquist and Justice Thomas, dissenting, mourned this federal trespass on state sovereignty and its adverse impact on the use of the states as laboratories for the resolution of difficult social problems. The dissenters complained that the Court's "definition of economic activity is breathtaking." The Court had taken far too anemic a view of *Lopez*. But the teaching of the majority in *Gonzales* was clear: Where economic activity affecting a larger interstate market is concerned, the affectation doctrine is very much alive even in the era of post-*Lopez* and *Morrison* Commerce Clause jurisprudence.

The Court sometimes avoids deciding the issue of whether Congress has exceeded its commerce clause powers by choosing statutory interpretation rather than constitutional interpretation to resolve the case. In *Jones v. United States* (2000), the Court, per Justice Ginsburg, declined to view a private residence as a building "currently involved in interstate commerce" in interpreting the federal arson statute. The government had contended that a house was involved in interstate commerce because it was financed by national companies and serviced by utilities doing business in interstate commerce. The Court rejected this interpretation because it would mean that every building in the country with the possible exception of a hermit's cabin would, therefore, be in interstate commerce. It was doubtful this was the Congressional intent. Moreover, such an interpretation would raise serious questions under *Lopez*.

In *Solid Waste Agency of Northern Cook County v. United States Army Corps of Engineers* (2001), the Court once again took refuge from *Lopez-Morrison*-type problems by relying on statutory interpretation. The Court held, 5–4, per Chief Justice Rehnquist, that the interpretation by the Army Corps of Engineers of a provision of the Clean Water Act which extended federal authority to an abandoned sand and gravel pit that served as a habitat for migratory birds exceeded the power granted to the Corps by Congress. The Court pointed out that Congress had not made a clear statement that the provision was intended to extend to an abandoned sand and gravel pit containing non-navigable waters. Additionally, if the statute were read to permit federal jurisdiction, the consequence would be a significant incursion into the traditional and primary power of the States with respect to land and water use. Chief Justice Rehnquist observed: "[W]here an otherwise acceptable construction of statute would raise serious constitutional problems, the Court will construe the statute to avoid such problems unless such construction is plainly contrary to the intent of Congress."

C. THE TAXING POWER

Congress can use taxation as a necessary and proper means for effectuating its delegated powers. Additionally, Art. I, Sec. 8, provides that Congress shall have an independent power to lay and collect taxes. At least in form, this is a fiscal power, not a regulatory power. In the earlier part of this century, the Court struck down nominal taxing powers when it determined that the law in fact imposed a regulatory "penalty." In *Bailey v. Drexel Furniture Co.* (1922), the Court held unconstitutional the federal child labor tax on grounds that "its prohibitory and regulatory effect and purpose [were] palpable." The penalties of the Act were triggered by the guilty knowledge of the employer. Chief Justice Taft observed acidly: "Scienters are associated with penalties not with taxes."

But in modern times the "penalty" doctrine has given way to the doctrine of objective constitutionality. As the Court explained in *United States v.*

Kahriger (1953), upholding an occupational tax on gamblers: "Unless there are provisions, extraneous to any tax need, courts are without authority to limit the exercise of the taxing power." As long as the federal law is revenue producing on its face, the Court will not probe to discover hidden regulatory motives and will not be overmuch concerned with whether the effects of the law trespass on the traditional state police power domain.

D. THE SPENDING POWER

While Congress has no express power to legislate for the general welfare, Art. I, Sec. 8, authorizes Congress to use federal monies to provide for the common defense and the general welfare. Federal spending is not simply a means for accomplishing Congress's delegated powers; it is an independent source of federal power. In *United States v. Butler* (1936), Justice Roberts professed to choose Hamilton's construction of the spending power (a power separate and distinct from the other enumerated powers) over Madison's construction (the spending power was only a means for furthering the enumerated power). As the Court said in *Butler,* "the power of Congress to authorize expenditure of public monies for public purposes is not limited by the direct grants of legislative power found in the Constitution."

Once again, spending is a fiscal not a regulatory power. During the New Deal era, this conception of the spending power as fiscal in nature was used to invalidate federal economic recovery legislation. In *United States v. Butler,* the Agricultural Adjustment Act of 1933, which sought to use the taxing and spending power to increase farm prices by controlling farm production, was invalidated as an intrusion on the regulatory powers of the state. Since the power to regulate agricultural production belonged to the states, Congress could not use taxing and spending as a constitutionally permissible means for achieving a non-delegated end. The tax and the federal spending were "but means to an unconstitutional end." Although Hamilton may have prevailed in theory, Madison prevailed in fact.

But this judicially fashioned limitation was not to survive the New Deal. Thus, the Social Security Act of 1935 was upheld against a Tenth Amendment based challenge in *Chas. C. Steward Machine Co. v. Davis* (1937). Today, Congress is free to spend and impose reasonable conditions on receipt of the federal grants. States and localities remain free to reject the federal monies but if they accept them they are taken subject to the conditions imposed by Congress. In *Fullilove v. Klutznick* (1980), upholding a ten percent set-aside of federal construction contracts for minority business concerns, Chief Justice Burger stated that Congress may "further broad policy objectives by conditioning receipt of federal monies upon compliance by the recipient with federal statutory and administrative directives" and may use its spending power "to induce governments and private parties to cooperate voluntarily with federal policy." Today, the spending power is conceived of in a much more expansive fashion than Madison would ever have contemplated. As Chief Justice Burger said in *Fullilove*: "The reach of the Spending Power within its sphere is at least as broad as the regulatory powers of Congress." Theoretically, a condition imposed by Congress which was completely unrelated to any federal interest in the spending program involved would be illegitimate. In a dissent, Justice O'Connor tried to breathe new life into this idea. See *South Dakota v. Dole* (1987). However, this limitation on the spending power is now of little importance since the reach of federal power is so extensive and the judicial review accorded exercises of the spending power so deferential.

When a federal law made it a crime to offer bribes to state or local officials of entities which received at least $10,000 in federal funds, the statute was unsuccessfully challenged as facially unconstitutional because it did not require a connection between the crime and the federal funding. Under the Spending Clause, Congress can appropriate federal funds to promote the general welfare. Under the Necessary and Proper Clause, Congress has power to see to it that the federal funds which it appropriates are not wasted on graft, that public officials are not corrupt and that those officers properly insist on value for the dollars expended. The Court said it would not "presume the unconstitutionality of federal criminal statutes lacking explicit provision of a jurisdictional hook." No such requirement was necessary where, as here, there was no reason to believe that the enforcement of the federal criminal statute extended beyond legitimate Spending Power interests. Instead, the law was a measure designed to bring federal power to bear on those who would use federal funding as a means for private gain. *Sabri v. United States* (2004).

A caveat, however, should be noted. Mere hortatory language in federal grants will not be interpreted by the courts as conditions unless the language of the grant setting forth the conditions is sufficiently precise. A federal grant is in the nature of a contract and the parties must be clear in their mutual undertaking. In *Pennhurst State School and Hosp. v. Halderman* (1981), language in federal mental disability legislation calling for treatment in "the setting that is least restrictive of personal liberty" was held not to be a condition for receipt of federal monies to the state institutions involved but only a policy objective.

In the Low–Level Radioactive Waste Policy Amendments Act, Congress provided monetary incentives to states which imposed a surcharge on radioactive wastes generated in other states. *New York v. United States* (1992). Unlike *Pennhurst*, the Court, per Justice O'Connor, said the conditions imposed by Congress on the states were unambiguous. The legislation authorized the Secretary of Energy to collect a portion of the surcharge and place it in an escrow account. The funds in this account were then to be used to provide grants to states which complied with federal deadlines for establishing waste disposal sites within the state.

The conditions imposed by the statute were held to be reasonably related to the purpose of the expenditure; they were designed to resolve the difficult question of radioactive waste disposal.

Those challenging the validity of the legislation pointed out that the federal statute (1) required the funds to be collected in a separate escrow account, (2) empowered the Secretary of Energy to hold the funds only as trustee, (3) declared that the funds deposited in the escrow account were not the property of the United States, and (4) noted that the states were largely in control of whether they would pay into the escrow account. Accordingly, it was contended that the legislation did not call for the *spending of federal funds*. The Court rejected this analysis. Congress had power under the spending power to structure federal spending as it had done here. The spending power does not mandate any particular form of accounting: "That the States are able to choose whether they will receive federal funds does not make the resulting expenditures any less federal." Endowing the states with choice is inherent "in any conditional exercise of Congress' spending power." Since the challenged legislation was authorized by the Spending Clause, an affirmative grant of power in the Constitution, the legislation did not violate the Tenth Amendment.

The insistence in *Pennhurst* that Congress must be clear and precise when it sets forth conditions on its grants was relied on in *Gonzaga University v. Doe* (2002). The Family and Educational Rights and Privacy Act (FERPA) conditions grants to state agencies and individuals upon compliance with the Act's requirements regarding the privacy of student records. The Court rejected a claim that FERPA created individual enforceable rights of action by virtue of an implied right of action under FERPA or by way of Sec. 1983 action. Congress must speak with a "clear voice" and manifest an "unambiguous" intent to confer individual rights and it had not done so in FERPA.

E. INTERGOVERNMENTAL IMMUNITIES

There are two dimensions to the intergovernmental immunities problem. One deals with the power of the state or locality to tax or regulate federal activity. The other deals with the power of the federal government to tax or regulate the states. Both of these situations are greatly affected by the Supremacy Clause of Art. VI which enables the federal government to enjoy a greater immunity from state taxation and regulation and a greater power to tax and regulate state activities.

A state may not directly tax or regulate the federal government or its instrumentalities. *McCulloch v. Maryland* (1819). Moreover, a state may not discriminate against the federal government, or those who deal with the federal government, in the absence of a showing that significant differences between the classes warranted the inconsistent treatment. For example, a Michigan state law exempting from taxation all retirement benefits paid by Michigan to its former employees but which taxed pensions paid to federal retirees in Michigan violated the doctrine of intergovernmental immunities. The differences were insufficient to justify the differing treatment of the two classes of retirees. *Davis v. Michigan Department of Treasury* (1989).

To what extent may the federal government regulate the states and localities themselves? In the past, in the heyday of the doctrine of dual federalism, the Tenth Amendment had been interpreted to be an independent limitation on federal power. But this view of the Tenth Amendment was apparently rejected in *United States v. Darby* (1941). In recent times, however, the principle that the existence of the states imposes some limitation on congressional legislative power was revived by the decision in *National League of Cities v. Usery* (1976).

In holding unconstitutional provisions of the federal Fair Labor Standards Act regulating the wages and hours paid by the state to their employees, the Court in *National League of Cities* resurrected state sovereignty as an affirmative limitation on the congressional commerce power. Congress was not merely displacing police power to regulate wages and hours; Congress was regulating the states as states. Justice Rehnquist, for the Court, declared: "We hold that insofar as the [federal provisions] operate to directly displace the States' freedom to structure integral operations in areas of traditional governmental functions, they are not within the authority granted Congress by Art. I, Section 8, cl. 3." The federal law was seen as displacing the considered policy choices of state officials on how they wish to structure delivery of basic governmental services to their citizens. Determination of the wages of those that the state employs to perform such functions was considered an undoubted "attribute of state sovereignty" since it implicated "functions essential to [the states'] separate and independent existence."

For the four dissenting justices, the Court's decision constituted a startling restructuring of our federal system. Justice Brennan speaking for three of the dissenters noted that "there is no restraint based on state sovereignty requiring or permitting judicial enforcement anywhere expressed in the Constitution; our decisions over the last century and a half have explicitly rejected the existence of any such restraint on the commerce power." For the dissent, it was not judicial enforcement of the Tenth Amendment but the political processes that protect state sovereignty.

Justice Blackmun provided the crucial fifth vote in *National League of Cities*. In a concurring opinion, Justice Blackmun expressed his belief that the Court was simply adopting a balancing approach which would allow the federal government to regulate where the federal interest is overriding and the need for state compliance is demonstrable. It was this less than full endorsement of the Court's opinion in *National League of Cities* that led its critics to hope that the decision was not a bellwether of a return to the discarded doctrine of dual federalism.

In subsequent cases, the Court struggled with the nature of the limitation fashioned in *National League*. It declared that a law would be held to violate the doctrine of state sovereignty only if it satisfied each of the following requirements: "First, there must be a showing that the challenged statute regulated 'States as States.' Second, the federal regulation must address matters that are indisputably attributes of state sovereignty. And, third, it must be apparent that the States' compliance with the federal law directly impair their ability to 'structure integral operations in areas of traditional functions.' " Even if these conditions were met, Tenth Amendment concerns could be overridden by a sufficiently compelling national interest. *Hodel v. Virginia Surface Mining and Reclamation Association, Inc.* (1981). In applying these standards to a variety of varying fact contexts, the Court indicated that *National League of Cities* was a unique situation and not an indicator of a new major emphasis on state sovereignty as a limitation on federal legislative power.

In *Garcia v. San Antonio Metropolitan Transit Auth.* (1985), the Supreme Court, 5–4, reversed its position on the limitations on congressional commerce power to enforce wage provisions of the FLSA against the states and overruled *National League of Cities*. Justice Blackmun had switched sides and wrote for the new majority. He had become convinced since *National League* that a determination of state immunity from federal regulation, based on an appraisal by an unelected federal judiciary of what constitutes a traditional or integral governmental function "is not only unworkable but is inconsistent with established principles of federalism."

While accepting in principle that the Constitution's federal structure imposes limitations on the commerce power, he rejected the view that federal courts have a "license to employ free standing conceptions of state sovereignty when measuring congressional power." Rather than focusing on "predetermined notions of sovereign power," as in *National League of Cities,* protection of federalism is to be found in "the built-in restraints that our system provides through state participation in federal governmental action. The political process ensures that laws that unduly burden the states will not be promulgated." The Constitution guarantees a process of decision, not a favorable result for the states. However, the constitutional structure does impose affirmative limits on federal power enforceable by the courts. Justice Blackmun did not explore what such limits on federal incursions into state sovereignty might be other than to assert they "must be tailored to compensate for possible failings in the national political process rather than to dictate a 'sacred province' of state autonomy."

The dissent challenged the assertion that there was no workable standard for the state sovereignty limitation, arguing that the proper approach is a balancing of the respective national and state interests with a sensibility for state autonomy. Political processes, they argued, are inadequate to assure that states would perform their role as an effective counterpoise to overreaching federal power. For example, members of Congress, while locally elected, are still members of the federal government. Most troubling for the dissent was their belief that the Court was implicitly abandoning the teaching of *Marbury* that it is the province of the federal judiciary to say what the law is: "In rejecting the role of the judiciary in protecting the states from federal overreaching, the Court's opinion offers no explanation for ignoring the teaching of the most famous case in our history."

The *Garcia* dissenters expressed hope for a future return to the federalist principles of *National League of Cities*. But in *Garcia* the majority of the Court rejected any significant judicial role in limiting Congress' power to regulate the states as states; such cases generally are the equivalent of political questions, inappropriate for judicial resolution. Coupled with the broad congressional commerce power over private activity, the national regulatory power is sweeping indeed. Absent any violation of some particular constitutional right or liberty, *Garcia* suggested there is minimal judicially enforceable limitation on the exercise of the commerce power. But *cf. Printz v. United States* (1997). And it is difficult to believe that the Court would treat Congress fiscal powers any differently.

In *Gregory v. Ashcroft* (1991), a provision of the Missouri Constitution requiring state judges to retire at age 70 was unsuccessfully challenged as violative of the federal Age Discrimination in Employment Act (ADEA). *Gregory* amplified the idea expressed in *Garcia* that there remains a certain area of state sovereignty which the federal government may not displace. Under *Garcia*, the political process provides the primary protection for the states against an intrusive exercise of the commerce power by Congress. But the principle of an inviolate core of state sovereignty influenced statutory interpretation in *Gregory*. Invoking the "plain statement" rule, the Court held, per Justice O'Connor, that Congress had not made plain an intention to apply the ADEA to state judges. Similarly, in *Jones v. United States* (2000), the Court refused to construe a federal law punishing arson on property used in interstate commerce to apply to private residences. A contrary interpretation would place almost every building in the country within the reach of the federal law. Since arson was a "paradigmatic common-law state crime," this would unnecessarily raise *Lopez*-type issues. Furthermore, Congress has to speak in clear and precise terms before the federal-state balance can be altered.

In *New York v. United States* (1992), the Court, per Justice O'Connor, held that Congress could not compel the states to regulate. The take title provision of the Low Level Radioactive Waste Policy Amendments of 1985 was invalid. The take title provision gave the states an unwelcome and invalid choice between taking title to radioactive waste or regulating according to the direction of Congress: "Either type of regulatory action would 'commandeer' state governments into the service of federal regulatory purposes, and would for this reason be inconsistent with the Constitution's division of authority between federal and state governments." Whether one looked at the take title provision as not authorized by the enumerated powers of Congress or as "infringing upon the core of state sovereignty reserved by the Tenth Amendment," the take title provision was inconsistent with the "federal structure of our government established by the Constitution."

Justice O'Connor distinguished *Garcia* by saying that the legislation in that case subjected a "State to the same legislation applicable to private parties" whereas in *New York v. United States* the federal legislation was directed at the state alone. The rationale for the invalidity of the take title provision was the offense it did to political accountability. When the federal government requires the states to regulate, state officials bear the wrath of the citizenry. Yet the federal officials who designed the offending federal legislation remain "insulated from the electoral ramifications of their decision."

Congress, of course, pursuant to its authorized powers, may regulate directly. Congress could validly authorize states with disposal sites to increase costs or deny access to waste generated in states not complying with federal deadlines for the construction of waste disposal sites. Congress could give the states the choice of regulating in accordance with federal standards or having the state law preempted by federal legislation. But political accountability is undermined "when elected state officials cannot regulate in accordance with the views of the local electorate in matters not preempted by federal regulation." In dissent, Justice White, joined by Justices Blackmun and Stevens, complained that Justice O'Connor had made an end run around *Garcia* on the basis of a distinction without a difference.

The idea in *New York v. United States* that the federal government cannot "commandeer" the states into federal service gathered new force when a provision of the Brady Handgun Violence Prevention Act was invalidated for doing just that. The provision called for a waiting period before a handgun could be sold and required the chief law enforcement officers of each local jurisdiction check whether there was any legal bar to selling the applicant a handgun. In a 5–4 decision, Justice Scalia declared that this provision violated the doctrine that the states and federal government were dual sovereignties. True, there was nothing in the Constitution which addressed whether Congress could compel state officers to execute federal law. Yet, on the basis of historical understanding and practice, the structure of the constitution and the Court's own case law, the provision was unconstitutional. Relying on Madison in *The Federalist No.39*, Justice Scalia declared that the states retained " 'a residuary and inviolable sovereignty.' " *Printz v. United States* (1997).

The division of power between two spheres of sovereignty—state and federal—is one of the ways the structure of the Constitution protects liberty:

"The power of the Federal Government would be augmented immeasurably if it were able to impress into its service—and at no cost to itself—the police officers of the 50 States." Besides dual sovereignty, liberty is protected by the separation of powers among the three branches of the federal government. The Brady Bill impermissibly transfers executive power to the States. Executive power could easily be diminished if Congress could require the states rather than the President to execute its laws. In *Garcia*, Justice Blackmun had relied on the structure of the Constitution to defeat the idea that state sovereignty was a limitation on the delegated powers of Congress: since the states were represented in the Congress, the very enactment of federal legislation signified state participation and consent. Although *Printz* did not address this contention directly, it is clearly in conflict with it. Justice Scalia denied that the Brady Act provision was "necessary and proper" to the execution of Congressional Commerce Clause power to regulate handgun sales. He called attention to the word "proper" in the Necessary and Proper Clause. If a federal statute trespassed on state sovereignty, it was not a "proper" law for carrying out the delegated powers of Congress within the meaning of the Necessary and Proper Clause.

Finally, *New York v. United States* was not distinguishable because the Brady Act did not require state officials to make policy but merely to assist in the implementation of federal law. To attempt to draw a line between what constituted policymaking and what did not would be an impossible task. Furthermore, the challenged provision obscured the accountability of state and federal officials. Congress could take credit for addressing a problem but the financial burden of implementation was imposed on the states. In any event, since the state officials had to implement the law, the public would associate them with its success or failure. Contrary to the dissent, it did not matter that the invalidated provision in *New York v. United States* was addressed to the states and the Brady Act provision was directed to individuals. These "individuals" were given federal directions in their official capacities as state and local officials. Nor was the provision redeemed because the burden imposed by it was temporary or minimal. A balancing of the competing interests is not appropriate when a federal law jeopardizes "the structural framework of dual sovereignty." Congress cannot mandate the states to enact or implement a federal regulatory program.

In a strong dissent, Justice Stevens contended that the Commerce Clause, buttressed by the Necessary and Proper Clause authorized the challenged provision. Further, the Tenth Amendment imposed "no restriction on the exercise of delegated powers." State sovereignty is not mentioned in the constitutional text and is not a limitation on the Necessary and Proper Clause. To do so runs counter to the principle in *McCulloch* that the Necessary and Proper Clause enlarges rather than diminishes the powers of the federal government. The structure of the federal system protects the interests of the states through their representatives in the Congress. Finally, if the federal government may not use state officials for federal purposes, the result will be the expansion not the diminution of the federal bureaucracy.

In sum, although *Garcia* has not been reversed, *Printz* illustrates that a majority of the Rehnquist Court believes that state sovereignty limits federal regulatory power as applied to the states. *Printz*, therefore, marks a new and less hierarchical direction in the relationship of the federal government to the states. Nonetheless, the *New York* and *Printz* cases have limits. Relying on *New York* and *Printz*, South Carolina challenged a federal law restricting the release by state departments of motor vehicles of personal information about licensed drivers arguing that the law invalidly captured state regulatory machinery. The Court, per Chief Justice Rehnquist, upheld the Act and distinguished *New York* and *Printz* on the ground that the Act regulated "state activities" and did not seek "to control or influence the manner in which States regulate private parties." *Reno v. Condon* (2000).

CHAPTER III

STATE POWER IN AMERICAN FEDERALISM

States have broad police powers to legislate for the health, morals, and well-being of their citizens. But, like the national government, state action is subject to constitutional limitations arising either from specific guarantees or from the constitutional division of powers between the federal and state governments. It is with the working out of the parameters of "Our Federalism" that the present chapter is concerned.

Some constitutional powers are exclusively national in character; they do not admit of concurrent exercise by both the federal and state governments. For example, the war power and the power over foreign affairs are vested in the national government to the point that state regulation in the same area is essentially precluded. Other powers such as the power to raise revenues through taxation and the spending power are concurrent powers.

An issue that often arises in federal-state constitutional conflicts is the extent of the power of the states. Do the states have all powers that the Constitution does not withhold from them? Do the reserved powers of the states under the Tenth

Amendment refer only to those powers the states had prior to ratification of the Constitution? Does the source for the authority of the constitution derive from the consent of the states? From the consent of the people of each state? Or, as Marshall so memorably declared in *McCulloch v. Maryland* (1819), from the consent of the undifferentiated people of the Nation as a whole?

These issues received new consideration in the *Term Limits* case. An amendment to the Arkansas Constitution limiting ballot access for Congressional candidates who had already served a specified number of terms was struck down, 5–4, by the Supreme Court. Justice Stevens for the Court held that constitutional text, history and structure combined to implicitly divest the States of power to add or to alter the qualifications for Congress set forth in Art. I, Secs. 2 and 3. The very structure of the Constitution proclaimed the democratic idea that the people of the United States are free choose their own representatives. Although the Constitution is admittedly silent on the issue of term limits, the power to add qualifications was not within the "original powers" of the States and thus was not a reserved power of the states under the Tenth Amendment. Even if the States had some original power on this matter, the Framers intended Congress to be the exclusive source of qualifications for members of Congress. Election of representatives to the national legislature was a new right and thus could hardly be a reserved power of the states since prior to the adoption of the Constitution no such right existed. *U.S. Term Limits v. Thornton* (1995).

In a concurring opinion, Justice Kennedy said that the Constitution created a federal right of citizenship—"a relationship between the people of the Nation and their National Government, with which the States may not interfere." When the states added terms limits to the Constitutionally ordained qualifications for Congress, they trespassed on "this federal domain."

In a learned and vigorous dissent, Justice Thomas turned the silence of the Constitution on the issue of term limits into an argument *for* terms limits. True, the Constitution set qualifications for the members of Congress but these were only minimal qualifications. Nothing in the Constitution prevented the states from adding to those qualifications. Justice Thomas contended that the federal government and the states operated under different default rules: "[W]here the Constitution is silent about the exercise of a particular power—that is, where the Constitution does not speak either expressly or by necessary implication—the Federal Government lacks that power and the States enjoy it." Indeed, the Constitution derives its authority not from the undifferentiated people of the Nation as whole but from the consent of the people of each of the states. Where the Constitution is silent, either the states or the people may act. Therefore, if the states wished to set term limit qualifications for their representatives in Congress, they could do so. The views of Justice Thomas did not prevail but what is interesting is that they fell short of ascendancy only by one vote. The *Term Limits* case was a serious challenge to the understanding of the powers of the states *vis-a-vis* the federal government established as long ago as *McCulloch v. Maryland* (1819).

A. STATE POWER TO REGULATE COMMERCE

1. THE NATURE OF THE POWER

In *Gibbons v. Ogden* (1824), the Court examined the question whether the commerce power is exclusive or concurrent. While John Marshall found "great force" in the argument for exclusivity, it was unnecessary to finally resolve the issue since the state law conflicted with the congressional act. Under the Supremacy Clause of Art. VI, the state law yielded to the federal enactment. In addressing the nature of the commerce power, Marshall considered the basis upon which the states were allowed to enact inspection laws which would appear to constitute regulations of interstate commerce. His conclusion was that such state regulation was an exercise of the police power, not an exercise of the national power over interstate commerce. This distinction would accommodate states' need to regulate the subjects of interstate commerce as part of their effort to protect the health, morals and well-being of their citizens. However, this distinction really avoided the basic issue of the extent to which states could exercise their powers when interstate commerce is affected. Whether a state regulation is called a police power or an exercise of the commerce power, the critical question remains how the state law comports with the national commerce power.

2. THE SUBJECT OF THE REGULATION: THE *COOLEY* DOCTRINE

Cooley v. Board of Wardens (1851), upheld a Pennsylvania statute requiring vessels entering or leaving Philadelphia to have local pilots. Justice Curtis began from the premise that the law did constitute a regulation of interstate commerce but that the regulation of interstate commerce was a concurrent power. Indeed, the *Cooley* approach may be described as setting forth a doctrine of "selective exclusiveness"—whether the dormant Commerce Clause, *i.e.,* Congress had not legislated, itself precluded state regulation was to be determined on a selective basis by looking to the subject of the regulation.

The Court fashioned what now has come to be known as the *Cooley* Doctrine: "Whatever subjects of this [commerce] power are in their nature national, or admit only of one uniform system, or plan of regulation, may justly be said to be of such a nature as to require exclusive legislation by Congress." Applying this standard to the facts, the *Cooley* Court determined that the regulation of pilotage is best provided for by diverse regulation accommodated to local needs.

But if the *Cooley* Doctrine means that the Court should focus only on the subject matter of the state regulation and not the nature of the regulation, its adequacy as a test of the negative implications of the dormant Commerce Clause is questionable. If the Commerce power is unexercised by Congress—if it is dormant—a critical question still remains: What is the effect of the state law on interstate commerce? This cannot be answered solely by looking to the subject matter of the state law. For one thing, such an approach is likely to end up as a jurisprudence of labels.

3. THE MODERN APPROACH: THE BALANCING OF INTERESTS

The modern approach to commerce power litigation recognizes that the "dormant" Commerce Clause does have "negative implications" limiting state power to regulate. This power is to be determined by the nature of the state regulation, using the following standard:

Where the statute regulates even-handedly to effectuate a legitimate local public interest, and its effects on interstate commerce, are only incidental, it will be upheld unless the burden imposed on such commerce is clearly excessive in relation to the putative local benefits. If a legitimate local purpose is found, then the question becomes one of degree. And the extent of the burden that will be tolerated will of course depend on the nature of the local interest involved, and on whether it could be promoted as well with a lesser impact on interstate activities. *Pike v. Bruce Church, Inc.* (1970).

This avowed balancing approach replaced the earlier nominalistic test which made the validity of a state law turn upon whether the effect on interstate commerce was deemed to be "indirect" or "direct." Instead, the balancing approach forces a court into a fact-gathering inquiry to determine (1) whether the state law is an even-handed regulation pursuant to a legitimate state objective or is discriminatory against interstate commerce interests; and, (2) if the law is non-discriminatory, whether the state interest in the regulation overrides the adverse effect on interstate commerce. The overriding questions are whether balancing of interests is appropriate for the courts and whether courts are capable of weighing non-legal factors such as economic data and considerations.

a. Discrimination: Purpose, Means, Effects

The modern Dormant Commerce Clause doctrine mandates that the courts initially determine whether a state has a legitimate police power interest in regulating. If the sole objective of the state is to favor local as against out-of-state interests, such discriminatory legislation almost certainly violates the Commerce Clause. The historic purpose of the Commerce Clause was to prevent parochial state legislation which inevitably stimulates reprisals by other states. Further, out-of-state interests which are adversely affected by such discrimination are said to lack recourse to the ordinary legislative means for correcting wrongs—they have no representation in the discriminating state's legislature (the political rationale). It follows that purposeful protectionist regulation is virtually *per se* impermissible.

In *Baldwin v. G.A.F. Seelig, Inc.* (1935), the Court struck down a New York law which prohibited the sale of milk bought out of state at a price lower than the sale price of in-state milk. The Court reasoned that "when the avowed purpose of the obstruction, as well as its necessary tendency, is to suppress or mitigate the consequences of competition between the states, the Commerce Clause is offended." The ultimate principle is "that one state in its dealings with another may not place itself in a position of economic isolation." Even if the state has critical social welfare purposes at stake, it cannot erect trade barriers to the free flow of interstate competition consistent with the Common Market philosophy underlying the Commerce Clause: "The Constitution was framed under the dominion of a political philosophy less parochial in range. It was framed upon the theory that the people of the several states must sink or swim together and that in the long run prosperity and salvation are in union not division."

Even if a state law is designed to serve a legitimate police power objective, that does not mean that it is not discriminatory. As was said in *City of Philadelphia v. New Jersey* (1978), "the evil of protectionism can reside in legislative means as well

as legislative ends." In *City of Philadelphia,* the
Court held unconstitutional a New Jersey law prohibiting the importation into the state of out-of-
state solid or liquid waste. To put the question
bluntly, could New Jersey refuse to be a garbage
dump for Philadelphia? The Court answered, "No."
New Jersey might refuse to allow the dumping of
any more solid or liquid waste within its borders,
but it could not set up a barrier solely against out-
of-state waste. "[W]hatever New Jersey's ultimate
purpose, it may not be accomplished by discriminating against articles of commerce coming from outside the state unless there is some reason apart
from their origin to treat them differently." In
short, when a state law imposes burdens on the face
of its regulation on out-of-state interests which it
does not impose on in-state interests, such burdens
are likely to be categorized as facially discriminatory means which should be subjected to more searching judicial review.

The non-discrimination principle of *City of Philadelphia* was invoked in *Hughes v. Oklahoma* (1979).
An Oklahoma statute prohibiting the out-of-state
sale of free swimming minnows, even though in-
state sales were permitted, was struck down. Such
facially discriminatory legislation, stated Justice
Brennan, "invokes the strictest scrutiny of any purported legitimate local purpose and of the absence
of non-discriminatory alternatives." Even assuming
that the statute served Oklahoma's ecological and
environmental concerns, "the means selected were
the most discriminatory available." Conservation

was achieved by placing the entire burden on out-of-state interests.

The heightened scrutiny test for judging state legislation using facially discriminatory means has been applied in a variety of other contexts. Thus, the test was used to invalidate a state statute requiring utility companies to give a preference to in-state customers for hydroelectric power. The statute employed facially protectionist means, and hence, was invalid. *New England Power Co. v. New Hampshire* (1982).

In some circumstances, however, a state discriminatory means regulation can survive a Dormant Commerce Clause challenge. A Maine prohibition on the importation of live-baitfish for fear of parasites not common to Maine fisheries was upheld. A state may use discriminatory means to serve a legitimate state police power interest, *i.e.*, protection of local fisheries, if no less restrictive means are available. *Maine v. Taylor* (1986). But a "plain discrimination against products of out-of-state manufacture" will be struck down. Thus, an Ohio tax credit against its fuel sales tax for each gallon of ethanol sold as a component of gasohol, but only if the ethanol was produced in Ohio or in a state that granted similar tax advantages to Ohio ethanol, was violative of the Dormant Commerce Clause. The reciprocity provisions didn't save the legislation since, if anything, they enhanced the discrimination by seeking more favorable treatment for Ohio ethanol elsewhere. The facial disadvantage imposed on out-of-state sellers was not justified by the speculative health and commerce interests advanced by the state. *New Energy Co. v. Limbach* (1988).

Recently, state and local regulation of solid waste has foundered on the shoals of the Dormant Commerce Clause. The Court has been unmoved by appeals to validate such regulation on the ground of local health and safety considerations if the regulation presents barriers to the free flow of interstate commerce. In *Chemical Waste Management, Inc. v. Hunt* (1992), an Alabama statute which imposed an additional fee on out-of-state hazardous waste disposed of inside the state was invalidated. Although local safety and health interests might be legitimate, "only rhetoric, and not explanation" had been offered to explain why Alabama had only targeted interstate hazardous waste to meet these concerns. Furthermore, there were less discriminatory alternatives available. These included a generally applicable additional fee on all hazardous waste disposed of within the state, a per-mile tax on all vehicles transporting hazardous waste on state roads, or an even-handed cap on total tonnage in state landfills.

In *Fort Gratiot Sanitary Landfill, Inc. v. Michigan Dept. of Nat'l Resources* (1992), a Michigan law stating that solid waste generated in another county, state, or country cannot be accepted for disposal unless explicitly authorized in the receiving county's 20 year waste disposal plan was invalidated. The law was impermissibly protectionist. The fact that the law treated waste generated in other Michigan counties no differently from out of state waste did not save the law: "[A] State (or one of its political subdivisions) may not avoid the strictures of the Commerce Clause by curtailing the movement of articles of commerce through subdivisions of the State, rather than through the State itself."

Novel state schemes to banish out-of-state waste from their borders continue to be checkmated. An Oregon statute that imposed a $2.25 per ton surcharge on in-state disposal of waste generated out-of-state but only a $0.85 per ton surcharge on the disposal of waste generated in-state was held to be facially discriminatory. *Oregon Waste Systems, Inc. v. Department of Environmental Quality of the State of Oregon* (1994). Although *Chemical Waste Management* suggested that "a differential surcharge might be valid if based on the costs of disposing of waste from other states," Oregon had failed to provide a legitimate reason for subjecting out–state waste to a discriminatory surcharge three times higher than that imposed on in-state waste. No intrastate tax burden had been identified which would justify the differential in the surcharges.

Nor could the surcharge on out-of-state waste be justified because the state wished to spread the cost of the in-state disposal of Oregon waste to all state citizens. State conferral of a cost advantage on handlers of local waste was invalid economic protectionism. Oregon's argument that its surcharge on out-of-state waste constituted resource—not economic—protectionism was rejected because a state cannot prefer its citizens over out-of-state consumers in providing access to natural resources located within the state.

The invalidity of resource protectionism is illustrated by the invalidation of an Oklahoma law requiring that the state's coal-fired electric generating plants producing power for sale in the state burn a mixture of coal which contain at least 10% Oklahoma coal. The Oklahoma law "on its face and in practical effect discriminates against interstate commerce." *Wyoming v. Oklahoma* (1992). The law's stated preference for coal from domestic sources was "protectionist and discriminatory." The state contention that efforts to sustain the state "coal-mining industry would diminish state reliance on a single source of coal delivered over a single rail line" was rejected. Legitimate goals cannot be secured "by the illegitimate means of isolating the State from the national economy."

The Dormant Commerce Clause applies to charitable or non-profit entities as well as to profit-making ones. A Maine property tax provided for tax exemptions for Maine charitable corporations operated principally for the benefit of Maine residents but not to the same extent for those benefitting mostly nonresidents. A Maine non-profit corporation summer camp benefitting mostly nonresident children which was denied a full tax exemption brought suit. The tax was held, 5–4, to be discriminatory on its face. The Court, per Justice Stevens, ruled that the Dormant Commerce Clause applied to nonprofit entities as well as to profit-making ones. Both entities were significant participants in interstate markets. Nor was the Maine statute redeemed even if viewed as an indirect subsidy catering to local needs. A direct subsidy to non-profits benefitting Maine residents would be valid but the Court's cases did not warrant a similar conclusion for a tax exemption. Justice Scalia, dissenting, argued, for the acceptance of a domestic charity exception to the Dormant Commerce Clause. *Camps Newfound/Owatonna, Inc. v. Town of Harrison* (1997).

If a state law operates to regulate activities outside the state, it is likely to be found discriminatory and subjected to more stringent judicial review. For example, a New York law which required liquor distillers to sell to wholesalers in New York at a price that was no higher than the lowest prices charged wholesalers in other states constituted an impermissible extraterritorial regulation in violation of the Commerce Clause. A state may seek lower prices for its consumers but it can not require that producers or consumers in other states surrender competitive advantages they might otherwise have: "Economic protectionism is not limited to attempts to convey advantages to local merchants; it may include attempts to give local consumers an advantage over consumers in other states." *Brown–Forman Distillers Corp. v. New York State Liquor Authority* (1986).

A clash between the Twenty-first Amendment and the Dormant Commerce Clause was the occasion once again for the Court to strike down state laws which "by their own terms" discriminate against interstate commerce. Laws in Michigan and New York permitted in-state wineries to sell directly to their own residents but prohibited or severely restricted direct sales by out-state wineries. The out-of-state wineries contended that the challenged legislation was discriminatory in that its purpose was to "grant in-state wineries a competitive advantage over wineries located beyond the State's borders." Michigan and New York responded that the Twenty-first Amendment authorized the states to discriminate against out-of-state alcoholic products.

The Court, 5–4, held that the challenged Michigan and New York laws violated the Dormant Commerce Clause. The Court rejected the Twenty-first Amendment defense of the states:"[S]tate laws that violate other provisions of the Constitution are not saved by the Twenty-first Amendment." Justice Kennedy, for the Court, reasoned that while federal legislation as well as Section 2 of the Twenty-first Amendment gives the states broad authority to control and regulate the transportation, importation and use of alcoholic beverages, neither federal legislation nor the Twenty-first Amendment authorized the states to pass laws that discriminate against out-state goods. "[T]ime and again," the Court has struck down state laws which seek to treat in-state and out-state interests differently in order to advantage the former and disadvantage the latter. Indeed, state laws that discriminate against interstate commerce are subject to a " 'a virtually *per se* rule of invalidity.' "

A question remained: Could the laws at issue be saved because they promoted legitimate local purposes that could not otherwise be accomplished by reasonable nondiscriminatory alternatives? The states pointed to the need to prevent drinking by minors and the need to facilitate tax collections on in-state sales by out-of-state wineries. But evidence was lacking that there was any relationship between the incidence of underage drinking and a ban on direct shipping of wine to state residents by out-of-state wineries. If ordering wine by mail by minors from out-of-state wineries was a problem, less burdensome alternatives were available to the states than an outright ban. Similarly, tax evasion by out-of-state wineries was not shown to present such a threat to state treasuries to justify this explicit discrimination against out-of-state commerce. The requisite showing that no less discriminatory alternative was available had not been made. *Granholm v. Heald* (2005).

Justice Thomas, joined by Chief Justice Rehnquist and Justices Stevens and O'Connor, argued in *Granholm* that federal legislation legitimated what might otherwise have constituted a Dormant Commerce Clause problem. Because this was so, they did not think it necessary to reach the Twenty-first Amendment issue. As to that issue, however, they believed that the Twenty-first Amendment "displaced the negative Commerce Clause as applied to regulation of liquor imports into a State."

Even if a statute is facially non-discriminatory and is designed to serve a legitimate social welfare objective, the law still may be discriminatory in its impact on interstate commerce. In *Hunt v. Washington State Apple Advertising Comm'n* (1977), a North Carolina statute requiring that all closed containers of apples sold in the state bear only the U.S. grade was held unconstitutional. While the law on its face appeared to be non-discriminatory in that it applied equally to out-of-state and in-state sellers alike, in fact this was not the case. Application of the North Carolina requirements to the Washington sellers in fact denied the latter the competitive advantage of being able to utilize the state's superior grading system. When a law is found to have a discriminatory impact, "the burden falls on the State to justify it both in terms of the local benefits flowing from the statute and the unavailability of non-discriminatory alternatives adequate to preserve the local interests at stake. *Dean Milk Co. v. Madison*."

The North Carolina law purported to be a consumer protection measure but it was not. The apple growing state of Washington had developed a more refined system of grading for its apples than the U.S. Department of Agriculture grading systems. The application to the State of Washington's apples of the U.S. grade, therefore, deprived consumers of information which they previously had. There were other, non-discriminatory alternatives available, *e.g.*, banning state grades inferior to the USDA standards.

A town flow control ordinance requiring that all solid waste be processed at a designated transfer station was deemed to have an invalid discriminatory effect even though, like the state law in *Hunt*, it did not facially discriminate on the basis of geographic origin. *C & A Carbone, Inc. v. Clarkstown* (1994). Unlike the statute in *Philadelphia v. New Jersey*, the town contended that its ordinance posed no barrier to the import or export of solid waste but merely required that the waste be channeled through a designated facility. But the article of commerce, the Court declared, was not the solid waste "but rather the processing and disposing of it."

The ordinance had an impermissible discriminatory effect on the processing and disposing of solid waste in interstate commerce. First, the ordinance's requirement that all waste be channeled through a designated facility drove up the costs of waste generated from outside the town. Second, the ordinance barred all but a single favored local facility from processing waste within the town. The ordinance thus prevented out-of-state competitors from competing in the local processing market. The fact that the flow control ordinance was a means of financing the waste disposal transfer facility was irrelevant: "[R]evenue generation is not a local interest that can justify discrimination against interstate commerce." Less discriminatory means such as uniform safety regulations were available to accomplish the town's health and safety objectives.

Another law which did not facially discriminate on the basis of geographical origin but which still had a discriminatory effect was a Massachusetts pricing order imposing an assessment on all fluid milk sold by dealers to Massachusetts retailers. The proceeds were then placed in a fund which was distributed to Massachusetts dairy farmers as a subsidy. The Court, per Justice Stevens, held that the purpose and effect of the pricing order was "to enable higher cost Massachusetts dairy farmers to compete with lower cost dairy farmers in other States." The assessment acted as a tax which served to make out-of-state milk more expensive. Furthermore, although the tax applied to milk produced in Massachusetts, the consequences of the tax as to milk produced in-state were entirely offset because of the subsidy which went only to Massachusetts dairy farmers. Although a "pure subsidy" funded out of general revenue "ordinarily imposes no burden on interstate commerce," the subsidy in this case was funded chiefly from the sale of out-of-state milk: "By conjoining a tax and a subsidy, Massachusetts has created a program more dangerous to interstate commerce than either part alone." In short, the Massachusetts pricing order was unconstitutional because, like a tariff, it neutralized advantages which belonged to the place of origin, *i.e.*, the lower costs of out-of-state dairy farmers. *West Lynn Creamery v. Healy* (1994).

The 2000 Maine Rx Program which made discounted prescription drugs available to Maine residents was upheld against a Dormant Commerce Clause challenge. The state negotiated rebates with drug manufacturers. The fund created from the rebates made it possible to offer reduced prices for prescription drugs sold to Maine Rx participants.

An association of nonresident drug manufacturers contended that, as was the case in *West Lynn Creamery, Inc. v. Healy* (1994), the program impermissibly discriminated against interstate commerce in order to subsidize in-state retail sales. The Court, per Justice Stevens, rejected this contention and held that this program was different from that considered in *West Lynn Creamery*. Payments to local pharmacists under the Maine plan provided "no special benefit to competitors of rebate-paying manufacturers." An out-of-state drug manufacturer would not be freed of its rebate obligation "by operating production facilities in Maine." Even if the out-of-state manufacturer were to take that step it would receive no advantage from the rebates. Nor did the Maine program constitute extraterritorial regulation. Maine neither facially nor in effect regulated the price of out-of-state transactions. The program did not mandate a set price under which manufacturers were to sell to wholesalers. Finally, the program did not tie the price of Maine products to out-of-state prices. *Pharmaceutical Research and Manufacturers of America v. Walsh* (2003).

Of course, it is not always easy to identify a law which has a discriminatory impact on interstate commerce. *Exxon Corp. v. Governor of Maryland* (1978), involved the validity of a state law prohibiting gasoline producers or refiners from operating gasoline retail service stations within Maryland. In upholding the law, the Court rejected the claim that the law was discriminatory, even though Maryland essentially had no local producers or refiners and thus interstate companies would bear the burden of divestiture. The Court reasoned that the Maryland law "creates no barriers whatsoever against interstate independent dealers; it does not prohibit the flow of interstate goods, place added costs upon them, or distinguish between in-state and out-of-state companies in the retail market." The structural character of the market rather than the interstate character of the company determined the law's applicability.

What is the difference between an ad hoc balancing test and a heightened scrutiny test used in these discrimination cases? The state laws which were challenged in the cases set forth above might well have survived an *ad hoc* balancing test. Certainly, the state interests being asserted were of substantial weight. For example, in *Carbone*, Justice Souter in dissent, joined by Chief Justice Rehnquist and Justice Blackmun, applied the *Pike* balancing test and concluded that the town ordinance was valid. The ordinance was free from discriminatory purpose or effect. While it created a local monopoly, local monopolies were subject to challenge under the Sherman Act not the Dormant Commerce Clause. In this view, the town ordinance was valid under *Pike* since the burdens it imposed fell on local residents not on interstate commerce. *Carbone* thus illustrates the difference in result that may obtain in Dormant Commerce Clause cases depending on whether the heightened scrutiny test or the *Pike* balancing test is used. The majority in *Carbone* had applied the heightened scrutiny test and invalidated the ordinance.

The heightened strict scrutiny test dictates the result in a way the balancing test does not. The heavy burden that the state must meet to justify a facially discriminatory statute if the heightened scrutiny test is used (especially the demand that the state show the absence of any less burdensome alternative means) largely dooms the law.

b. Undue Burdens—Ad Hoc Balancing

Even if a law is not discriminatory that does not necessarily mean that it passes Commerce Clause muster. Although a law may be even-handed, it still can run afoul of the Dormant Commerce Clause if it imposes an excessive burden on interstate commerce. How is an "excessive" or undue burden on interstate commerce determined? It is determined by an inquiry into whether the regulatory interests of the state justify or outweigh the law's impediment to the free movement of interstate commerce. Courts employ an *ad hoc* balancing test probing the nature and functions of the regulation, the character of the business involved, and the actual effect of the law on the flow of interstate commerce.

A growing number of Justices, such as Chief Justice Rehnquist and Justice Scalia, believe that judicial balancing of interests in this context is inappropriate. In their view, if the state law is non-discriminatory, then judicial intervention should be foreclosed; a balancing of interests test when discrimination is absent give courts an improper mandate to legislate. In their view, if the problem is a serious one, Congress is available to correct it. Nor is it only the conservatives on the Court who question judicial invalidation of state laws in the absence of discrimination. Justice Brennan, and more recently, Justice Blackmun, took a deferential view of state regulation in this area since they believed regulation of the economy is not the focus of judicial review. Justice Souter, as indicated by his deferential attitude toward local regulation in his dissent in *Carbone*, may be moving toward this position.

When using the balancing approach, the courts accord great weight to traditional state police power concerns such as public health and safety, prevention of consumer fraud and the regulation of public highways. But even in these areas of local prerogative, the burden on the free movement of interstate commerce may override the state concern. Protection of the environment and conservation of depletable natural resources are interests not only of the regulating state but also of the Nation. Not surprisingly, then, state conservation and environmental protection laws receive marked judicial deference. In *Minnesota v. Clover Leaf Creamery Co.* (1981), the Court upheld a Minnesota law prohibiting the use of plastic milk containers. While the law imposed a more severe burden on the out-of-state plastic industry than on the Minnesota pulpwood industry, the Court did not deem the law either discriminatory or excessively burdensome. All milk retailers, interstate and local, were subject to the ban on plastic containers. The minimal costs of using non-plastic containers in Minnesota was justified by the substantial state interest in conservation of natural resources and reducing the problem of solid waste disposal.

Another state law which survived a challenge as unduly burdensome concerned an Indiana statute. The law provided that when an entity or person acquired controlling stock of an Indiana corporation which had a substantial number of Indiana stockholders, the acquiring party received no voting rights unless the stockholders agreed to give voting rights. The Indiana statute was held not to violate the Commerce Clause. The law was not discriminatory; it applied to all tender offers whether or not the offeror was an Indiana resident. The law applied only to Indiana corporations; therefore, there was no danger that business would be subjected to inconsistent state regulation. The Indiana statute did not impose an undue burden on interstate commerce since the statute was limited to Indiana corporations and was concerned with protecting the stockholders of Indiana corporations, including residents of Indiana, from takeovers. The state legislation was concerned with preventing the corporate form from being used as a shield for unfair business practices. *CTS Corp. v. Dynamics Corp. of America* (1987).

The Supreme Court has long declared that state highway regulation is in a special category justifying a greater presumption of validity than is the case with the general run of state law. Indeed, at times the Court has suggested that the usual balancing-of-interest approach should not be applied to state highway legislation. The standard used should be the deferential rationality approach. This deference is due to the historic and necessarily unique role of local prerogative in this area. While state regulation of the railways is deemed to be more intrusive on the free flow of national commerce [*Southern Pacific Co. v. Arizona* (1945)], state regulation of the highways implicates predominantly local concerns—at least this is the theory.

In fact, state highway laws are judged under the Dormant Commerce Clause. The Court has regularly struck down state regulations where the local interests in highway management have been deemed insufficient to outweigh the burden on interstate commerce. This is especially true when the state legislation grants exceptions or other favorable conditions only to local business or where the particular state law is markedly out of step with the laws of other states governing the same activities.

Kassel v. Consolidated Freightways Corp. (1981), struck down an Iowa law which generally prohibited use of sixty-five foot double-trailer trucks within the state. Even though the state had offered substantial safety evidence to support the law in the trial court, the state's safety interest was characterized as illusory. *Kassel* ruled that the state law significantly impaired the federal interest in efficient and safe interstate transportation. Empirical evidence was closely scrutinized. The Iowa law required the use of a greater number of smaller trucks to be driven through Iowa and forced larger trucks to drive greater distances to bypass Iowa. Various provisions in the law benefitted only Iowa residents and imposed added burdens on neighboring states.

In summary, *Kassel* illustrates that the Court is still wedded to an *ad hoc* balancing approach even when the state interest is very strong, as is the case with state highways. Three justices, it should be noted, dissented in *Kassel*. There continues to be a vocal minority on the Court which insists on the abandonment of the balancing approach at least in highway cases and, perhaps more broadly, for all non-discriminatory state laws. As Justice Rehnquist said in dissent in *Kassel,* the Court's present balancing approach "arrogate(s) to this Court functions of forming public policy, functions which, in the absence of congressional action were left by the Framers of the Constitution to state legislatures."

4. STATE AS MARKET PARTICIPANT

There is one context, however, when the Dormant Commerce Clause does not apply. When the state is not acting in a regulatory capacity, but is, instead, itself participating in the marketplace as a buyer or a seller, it may regulate free of restrictions flowing from the Dormant Commerce Clause. *Hughes v. Alexandria Scrap Corp.* (1976). The Dormant Commerce Clause does not preclude a state from discriminating in favor of its own citizens in the form of subsidies or through market transactions entered into by the state. However, this market participant exception to the Dormant Commerce Clause may not extend to state discrimination with respect to natural resources which the state has not had time to develop. However, the Court has not yet made an explicit statement to this effect. The lead case in this area did not involve natural resources. Thus, in *Reeves, Inc. v. Stake* (1980), the Court held that the Commerce Clause did not prevent the State of South Dakota from discriminating in favor of its residents with respect to sales from a state-owned cement factory despite the fact that Wyoming businesses had long relied on the output of the factory.

In *Reeves*, the Court, per Justice Blackmun, stated: "The Commerce Clause responds principally to state taxes and regulatory measures impeding free private trade in the national marketplace. There is no indication of a constitutional plan to limit the ability of the states themselves to operate freely in the free market." In addition to this historical basis, support for the market participant principle was found in concern for state sovereignty (*i.e.,* the ability of a state to provide public benefits to its citizens), the ability of an enterprise to choose its customers, the fact that private traders are not subject to Commerce Clause constraints, and the complexity of adjusting competing interests when the state engages in proprietary action. The Court did, however, emphasize that the state's business in this instance involved an extensive undertaking on its part and left open the possibility that restrictions placed on the use of the state's natural resources might be subject to the Dormant Commerce Clause.

A significant problem generated by *Reeves* lies in identifying those occasions when the state is acting as a participant rather than as a regulator. In *White v. Massachusetts Council of Const. Employers* (1983), the Dormant Commerce Clause doctrine was held not to apply to an executive order requiring that all city construction projects be performed by a work force at least half of which were city residents. While the dissent noted that "the economic choices the city restricts in favor of its residents are the choices of private entities engaged in interstate commerce," the Court, per Justice Rehnquist, reasoned that "[i]mpact on out-of-state residents figures in the equation only after it is decided that the city is regulating the market rather than participating in it." Since the city had expended only its *own* funds in entering into construction contracts for *public* projects, it was acting as a market participant. But see *South–Central Timber Dev., Inc. v. Wunnicke* (1984) [plurality expresses view that an Alaskan requirement that timber taken from state lands be processed in Alaska was subject to the Dormant Commerce Clause doctrine. Alaska participated in the timber-selling market but regulated the timber processing market. The state used its leverage in the timber-selling market to exert a regulatory effect in the processing market].

The student should note also that the Court has held that such resident preferences in hiring might violate the Privileges and Immunities Clause of Art.

IV, Sec. 2. See *United Bldg. & Const. Trades Council v. Mayor and Council of Camden* (1984).

What is the current status of the market participant doctrine? Some members of the present Court are clearly supporters of the doctrine. In *Oregon Waste Systems*, Chief Justice Rehnquist, joined by Justice Blackmun, dissented and criticized the Court for making no "distinction between publicly and privately owned landfills". They noted that *Philadelphia v. New Jersey* had "specifically left unanswered the question whether a state or local government could regulate disposal of out-of-state solid waste landfills owned by the government."

In dissent in *Carbone*, Justice Souter, joined by Chief Justice Rehnquist and Justice Blackmun, said that the ordinance there did not extend a benefit to local private actors "but instead directly aids the government in satisfying a traditional governmental function." Although the majority in *Carbone* viewed the processing facility as privately operated, Justice Souter contended that functionally it was a municipal facility and that it should be obvious that "favoring state-sponsored facilities differs from discriminating among private economic actors, and is much less likely to be protectionist."

In sum, the Court has not relied on the market participant exception to the Dormant Commerce Clause since the early 1980's. Yet it has not disavowed the doctrine either and it remains available as a doctrinal escape hatch for the states and localities from the rigors of the Dormant Commerce Clause.

5. INTERSTATE PRIVILEGES AND IMMUNITIES

In constitutional law particularly, the same fact pattern may be approached under a number of overlapping constitutional alternatives. Thus, facts that could be resolved through a Commerce Clause analysis may be equally responsive to resolution under the Interstate Privileges and Immunities Clause of Art. IV, Sec. 2. Unfortunately, there is no particular geiger counter which can predict when the courts will use one clause rather than the other or, possibly, use both clauses.

The Privileges and Immunities Clause of Art. IV, Sec. 2, should be distinguished from the Privileges and Immunities Clause set forth in the Fourteenth Amendment, Sec. 1. Art. IV protects out-of-state citizens from unreasonable discrimination in regard to their fundamental national interests—interests which concern the Nation's vitality as single entity. While the Clause does not necessarily guarantee any particular right or privilege, it does require that, when a state confers a benefit on its own citizens, it cannot deny that same benefit to out-of-state citizens unless it demonstrates substantial justification. Substantial justification generally means that a state must establish that non-residents are a particular source of the problem that the state is seeking to remedy and that the law bears a substantial relationship to the eradication of the problem. *Hicklin v. Orbeck* (1978) [Alaska-hire law requiring preferential treatment to be given to state residents in employment held unconstitutional].

It is important to note that Art. IV, Sec. 2, requires that there be fundamental national interests at stake. The crucial question is whether the activity at issue is so "fundamental" to the well-being of the Nation as to be within the privileges and immunities protected by Art. IV, sec. 2. Thus, the Clause has been held to be inapplicable to a Montana statute which discriminated against non-residents in regard to license fees for elk hunting. *Baldwin v. Fish & Game Com'n* (1978). The Court concluded that Art. IV, Sec. 2, was designed only to reach that discrimination which would "hinder the formation, the purpose or the development of a single union of States." Simply, hunting for elk "is not basic to the maintenance or well-being of the Union." *Hicklin v. Orbeck* (1978). Compare *Supreme Court of New Hampshire v. Piper* (1985) [state supreme court rule limiting bar admission to state residents is violation of "National fundamental right" protected under "privileges and immunities" because of the important part which lawyers play in commercial intercourse and the national economy which the Clause was intended to protect.] Relying on *Piper*, the Court struck down as violative of the privileges and immunities clause a Virginia Supreme Court rule requiring out-of-state lawyers to become permanent residents of Virginia in order to become admitted to the Virginia bar without taking the Virginia bar examination: "[L]awyers who are admitted in other States are [not] less likely to respect the bar and further its interests solely because they are nonresidents." *Supreme Court of Virginia v. Friedman* (1988).

Similarly, local court rules of the District Court of the Virgin Islands which required that applicants for admission to the bar live on the Virgin Islands for one year and declare an intent to reside and practice law there following admission were struck down. On the basis of *Piper*, these requirements were held violative of the privileges and immunities clause of Art. IV, Sec. 2. Less restrictive means were available to meet the demands of legal practice in the Virgin Islands. For example, even if a nonresident lawyer was not able to make a court appearance, no showing had been made as to why the government interest could not be met by substituting a local lawyer for the nonresident lawyer. *Barnard v. Thorstenn* (1989).

The substantial justification test used in the bar admission cases is used as well in Privilege and Immunities Clause challenges to state tax laws. A New York law allowing New York residents to deduct alimony expenses but barring nonresidents from deducting alimony expenses from their New York taxable income was challenged under the Privileges and Immunities Clause. The New York Court of Appeals ruled that since New York residents are subject to the burden of taxation on all of their income regardless of its source, New York residents should be entitled to the benefit of full deduction of expenses but nonresident personal expenses such as alimony were more properly allocated to the taxpayer's state of residence. The Supreme Court reversed, holding 6–3, per Justice O'Connor, that New York failed to show a substantial justification for the different treatment accorded to nonresidents. The Privilege and Immunities Clause requires a rule of substantial equality for resident and nonresident taxpayers. The Clause secures the right of citizens to engage in business in another state without being subjected to taxes more burdensome than those imposed on in-state citizens.

Concern for the integrity of the Privileges and Immunities Clause is implemented through a standard of review substantially more rigorous than that applied, for example, to state tax distinctions on different trades and professions. New York must show a substantial justification for its different treatment of nonresidents as well as how that justification relates to the discrimination. New York contended that there was a distinction between business expenses related to the business income a nonresident earns in New York versus expenses linked entirely to personal activities outside New York. Justice O'Connor ruled that the New York law prohibiting nonresidents from deducting any alimony expenses even if the alimony expense related to New York constituted an "unwarranted denial to citizens of other States of the privileges and immunities enjoyed by citizens of New York." *Lunding v. New York Tax Appeals Tribunal* (1998).

In *United Building & Const. Trades Council v. Mayor and Council of Camden* (1984), the Court held that a city's imposition of a 40% resident hiring requirement upon all contractors working on city-funded public works construction projects must satisfy Art. IV, Sec. 2, analysis. The Court rejected the argument that municipalities are not bound by Art. IV, Sec. 2, and that conditioning the exercise of the privilege upon municipal rather than state citizenship or residency removed the ordinance from the Clause's reach. The privilege in question is "an out-of-state resident's interest in employment on public-work contracts in another state." Such employment is " 'sufficiently basic to the livelihood of the Nation' " as to fall within the scope of Art. IV, Sec. 2. However, because there was insufficient fact finding at the trial level, the Court did not decide whether Camden's ordinance satisfied the second part of the Privileges and Immunities Clause test. The Court did indicate, however, that if Camden could establish that out-of-state citizens were a particular source of the socioeconomic evils at which the ordinance was aimed and if the ordinance was narrowly tailored to eradicate this evil, Art. IV, Sec. 2, would be satisfied.

The Supreme Court held unanimously that an Art. IV. sec. 2 claim is not precluded because the challenged state regulation does not discriminate on its face against out-of-state citizens. While not every state differential between in-staters and out-of-staters is in violation of Art. IV, sec. 2, the Court declined to decide whether the Clause barred any classifications which had the practical effect of discriminating against out-of-state citizens. *Hillside Dairy, Inc. v. Lyons* (2003).

B. WHEN CONGRESS SPEAKS

Our prior analysis has been focused on situations when Congress has not legislated in the area in which a state seeks to regulate. In such situations, the restriction on state regulatory power flows from the negative implications of the Dormant Commerce Clause. But what happens when Congress enacts valid legislation in areas where the states also have regulated? Obviously, if Congress says it intends to occupy the field to preclude state action, the Supremacy Clause of Art. VI makes it clear that the valid federal regulatory scheme will prevail. But sometimes Congress legislates in areas where the state also has legislated without declaring its intent. Questions then abound: Did Congress intend its scheme to function concurrently with the state scheme or did Congress intend to occupy the field? Can any inferences be drawn from the congressional silence?

1. PREEMPTION

If the state law "stands as an obstacle to the accomplishment and execution of the full purposes and objectives of Congress" [*Jones v. Rath Packing Co.* (1977)], under the Art. VI Supremacy Clause, the state law is preempted. Even if the state law is generally compatible with the objectives of the federal legislation, a court may determine that Congress intended to foreclose state action. Unfortunately, there is little by way of general doctrine controlling when preemption will be found. Each case tends to turn on its particular facts.

The Court has provided factors to be considered in determining whether Congress intended to preempt non-conflicting state law. If the area requires uniformity of regulation rather than diversity, preemption is more likely. The pervasiveness of the federal law—whether it appears that Congress sought to regulate all the critical aspects of the subject—will often be of controlling importance. If the subject area is one that historically has been dominated by the state government, the Court is more likely to reject preemption absent some clear indication by the Congress to the contrary. If administration of both the federal and the state law is likely to produce conflict, the courts are more likely to find a congressional intent to exclude the states. Finally, under what is sometimes referred to as the one-master theory, congressional creation of an agency to provide regular superintendence over a regulatory area suggests that continued state action is precluded.

Application of these principles is found in *English v. General Electric Co.* (1990), where a unanimous Court held that an action for intentional infliction of emotional distress based on state law was not preempted by the Federal Energy Reorganization Act which prohibited employers from discharging nuclear plant employees who reported safety violations. Although the federal statute provided a federal remedy for unlawful discharge of whistleblowers, Congress had not explicitly precluded state tort recovery in the federal statute nor did the federal remedy establish a Congressional intent to occupy the field. Concededly, the threat of state tort actions might influence some nuclear safety policy decisions. Yet this consequence was insufficiently direct or substantial to justify a conclusion that the state tort claim fell into the federally preempted field of nuclear safety. Furthermore, there was no "actual conflict" between the state tort claim and the prohibitions of the federal act.

2. LEGITIMIZATION

While Congress may speak to preempt state regulation, Congress alternatively can legislate to legitimize state regulation which might otherwise fail to satisfy the demands of the dormant Commerce Clause. The Court has recognized that the congressional power over interstate commerce is plenary and that Congress in the exercise of this plenary power might choose to leave an area, over which it could otherwise legislate, to state legislation. Even if the Supreme Court has invalidated state legislation on the ground that it conflicts with the negative implications of the Commerce Clause, the Congress may rescue such legislation simply by authorizing it. *Prudential Insurance Co. v. Benjamin* (1946) [state discriminatory taxation of out-of-state insurance companies held valid given federal law authorizing state control].

While the Congress has authority to legitimize state regulations that discriminate or burden interstate interstate commerce, the legitimization of such burdens or discrimination must be explicit. For example, the Federal Agricultural Improvement and Reform Act stated that it should not be construed to preempt or limit California from regulating either (1) the percentage of milk solids, solids or fats in fluid milk products sold in California, or (2) the labeling of such products. California unsuccessfully contended that this law served to immunize California pricing and pooling regulations of fluid milk products from Dormant Commerce Clause challenges. The federal law at issue here did not clearly express an intent on the part of Congress to immunize pricing and pooling laws from Commerce Clause challenges. *Hillside Dairy Inc. v. Lyons* (2003).

CHAPTER IV

CONGRESS AND THE EXECUTIVE POWER

Under the Articles of Confederation, executive functions were performed by congressional committees. But the Framers of the Constitution provided in Art. II, Sec. 1: "The Executive Power shall be vested in a President of the United States of America." Was this Vestiture Clause simply a short-hand reference to all of the express executive powers provided in Art. II, or perhaps simply a reference to the choice of a single rather than a plural Executive? Or was it a separate grant of power for the President to perform all functions which are "executive" in character (sometimes called "inherent" executive power). While Presidents have regularly claimed inherent executive power (usually citing the Vestiture Clause), and the claim has received some favorable reaction from the Supreme Court [*United States v. Midwest Oil Co.* (1915); *In re Debs* (1895); *In re Neagle* (1890)] reliance on the Vestiture Clause as an independent source of power has never really been necessary to justify executive action. The broad undefined express powers of Art. II have provided ample room for presidential initiatives. See generally, A.S. Miller, *Presidential Power In A Nutshell* (1977).

A reading of the express powers set forth in Art. II would not begin to provide even a flavor of modern executive power. The need for prompt, informed, and effective action in domestic and foreign affairs has meant that power has tended to flow to the Executive. While many of the vague, open-ended executive powers provided in the Constitution are shared with Congress, presidential initiatives have generally produced only congressional acquiescence and the courts have tended to avoid judicial review of executive actions, especially in the area of foreign affairs and national security. Indeed, it has been suggested that separation of powers questions involving the allocation of powers between Congress and the Executive should generally be treated as political questions inappropriate for judicial resolution. J. Choper, *Judicial Review and the National Political Process* 263 (1980).

What emerges from the Constitution's allocation of powers between the Executive and Congress is a system of separation of powers in which there are separate institutions generally exercising shared or blended powers. The actual relationship of the national institutions is determined more by practical realities and by custom and usage than by formal constitutional language.

Most of the executive powers set forth expressly in the text of the Constitution are stated in quite general terms and involve matters where power is

shared with Congress. Unsurprisingly in such circumstances, executive and congressional power
sometimes collide. In the past, the Executive has
usually tended to prevail in the case of conflict.
Congress, however, has increasingly tried to specify
and structure the division of power between it and
the Executive. This legislation is enacted under the
banner of promoting Executive responsibility and
accountability. But in light of the fact that the
Executive and Legislative Branches have been controlled by different political parties during much of
the post-Lyndon Johnson era, it is also clear that
these legislative efforts have their source in parti-
san or political differences.

When Congress attempts to specify Executive
power, does it trespass on Executive power? Does
Congress thereby usurp the powers it shares with
the other Branches? In the main, it has been left for
the Supreme Court to answer these questions. The
Court's answers to these questions have not been
unequivocal. Indeed, the Court may be said to have
given two sets of answers. One approach may be
called a formalist or textually literal approach. This
approach puts great weight on the text of the Constitution and on formal observance of a strict separation of powers. The Court's other approach is a
functional one which highlights the need for checks
and balances and the interdependence of the
Branches. In this view, the Branches of government
cannot be approached as air-tight compartments;
the constitutional text and the lines between the
Branches must on occasion be subordinated to flexi-

bility and function. In the contest between these two approaches—the functional versus the formalist—the functional approach, aided by its formidable spokesman, Chief Justice Rehnquist, has been employed in *Morrison v. Olson* (1988) and *Mistretta v. United States* (1989). On the other hand, the formalist approach has found its voice in cases such as *Bowsher v. Synar* (1986), *INS v. Chadha* (1983), and *Clinton v. City of New York* (1998).

A. THE DOMESTIC ARENA

1. EXECUTIVE LAWMAKING

Art. I provides that the legislative power is vested in the Congress. The President's formal constitutional power in lawmaking is found primarily in his power to recommend legislation and in the veto power, and even this negative power to refuse to assent to legislation can be overridden by a two-thirds vote of both houses. Art. I, Sec. 7. But again, the Constitution only hints at the lawmaking role of the President. Using the Executive Office to frame legislation and influence legislative deliberations, the President has truly become the Legislator–in–Chief.

The President also "legislates" independent of the formal lawmaking process. Through the issuance of executive orders and proclamations he directs the massive federal bureaucracy. What are the parameters of this executive policy-making? To what extent can the President act independent of (or even contrary to) statutory authorization? Such questions are not readily answered by reference to the Constitution's allocation of powers. Nor have the courts provided much guidance.

Perhaps the most significant judicial effort at providing some answers came in *Youngstown Sheet & Tube Co. v. Sawyer* (The Steel Seizure Case) (1952), in which the Court held unconstitutional President Truman's seizure of the steel mills during the Korean War to prevent a crippling strike. Justice Black, for the Court, noted that Congress had specifically rejected seizure as a method for preventing strikes. But the President wasn't relying on statutory authorization for his action but on the aggregate of his Art. II powers. Focusing on Congress' power to make the laws, Justice Black rejected executive domestic lawmaking: "In the framework of our Constitution, the President's power to see that the laws are faithfully executed refutes the idea that he is to be a lawmaker." The presidential power as Commander–in–Chief (and presumably his foreign affairs powers) could not be extended to mean that the President has "the ultimate power" to seize private property to prevent domestic production stoppages: "This is a job for the Nation's lawmakers, not for its military authorities."

Nevertheless, the *Steel Seizure Case* is as often cited as authority for executive domestic lawmaking as for its rejection of such a presidential prerogative. The reason is that a majority of justices accepted presidential power to take emergency action in the domestic sphere, at least in the absence of a specific congressional negative. Justice Vinson, speaking for three dissenters, cited the Art. II presidential powers to see that the laws are faithfully executed and to act as Commander–in–Chief and a history of executive initiatives lacking statutory authorization, to justify "at least interim action necessary to execute legislative programs essential to the survival of the Nation." Three Justices, while concurring in holding the seizure unconstitutional given the congressional rejection of seizures, nevertheless did not foreclose presidential emergency initiatives. What would constitute an "emergency" was left unanswered.

Justice Jackson's concurring opinion has had an especially enduring value. "Presidential powers," he reasoned, "are not fixed but fluctuate depending upon their disjunction or conjunction with those of Congress." When the President acts with congressional authorization, his constitutional authority is maximized; when he acts contrary to the congressional will, his power is at its lowest ebb. When the President must rely on his own authority, he acts in "a zone of twilight in which he and Congress may have concurrent authority, or in which the distribution is uncertain." In the twilight zone of shared powers, "the imperatives of events and contemporary imponderables rather than abstract thesis of law" determines the meaning of separation of powers.

2.   EXECUTIVE IMPOUNDMENT

Art. I vests the powers of the purse in Congress. Nevertheless, presidents have regularly claimed the prerogative of impoundment, *i.e.*, withholding or delaying the expenditure of congressionally appropriated funds. When legislation vests discretion in the Executive to take such action, the constitutional problems are minimal. But in the 1970s, as the President increasingly used impoundments, it was claimed that constitutional power existed to impound funds even though Congress had mandated that they be spent. The argument was made that the President has a constitutional duty to execute all of the laws, including those imposing budgetary and debt limitations, requiring that he reconcile the competing legislative mandates. Further, inherent executive power was said to include the maintenance of fiscal control. Indeed, it was questioned whether Congress itself had constitutional power to mandate spending when the impoundment involved foreign affairs or national security—areas of traditional executive responsibility.

Critics of impoundment argued in response that the power to execute the laws cannot include the power to set aside the policy choices of Congress. "To contend that the obligation imposed on the President to see the laws faithfully executed implies a power to forbid their execution, is a novel construction of the Constitution and entirely inadmissible." *Kendall v. United States ex rel. Stokes* (1838) [the President could not legally order the Postmaster General to pay less for services than Congress had mandated]. They argue further that inherent executive power, even if accepted, cannot be stretched to include the prerogative of setting aside the congressional power to make the laws. Finally, opponents claim that the practical effect of impoundment allows the President to exercise an item veto which is not authorized by the Constitution.

While lower court decisions generally have rejected the President's constitutional arguments, the Supreme Court has not reached the constitutional question. See *Train v. New York* (1975). In 1974, Congress enacted the Congressional Budget and Impoundment Control Act which requires either congressional approval or failure to disapprove (depending on the nature of the impoundment) of presidential impoundments. The constitutionality of the Act, however, is subject to question. Does it excessively intrude on executive power, especially in the areas of foreign affairs and national security or is it only a reasonable allocation of roles in exercising shared powers? Does it embody a legislative veto proscribed by *Immigration & Naturalization Service v. Chadha* (1983)?

3. DELEGATION, THE LEGISLATIVE VETO, AND THE LINE ITEM VETO

A venerable precept of American constitutionalism with deep roots in the separation of powers principle is the idea that that which has been delegated cannot be redelegated. Obviously, this nondelegation doctrine has not been applied too literally or our modern administrative state would not be possible. Given the complexity of the modern state, the nondelegation doctrine has been interpreted with understandable latitude. Thus, when Congress created the United States Sentencing Commission, placed it in the Judicial Branch and delegated power to the Commission to promulgate Sentencing Guidelines which would be binding on the federal courts, it was held that the nondelegation doctrine was not violated. The nondelegation doctrine is not violated so long as Congress sets forth an intelligible principle to which those exercising the delegated authority are directed to conform. Since the law establishing the Commission set forth policies and principles to govern the substantive formulation of the Sentencing Guidelines, delegation of rulemaking authority to the Commission to promulgate Sentencing Guidelines did not violate the nondelegation doctrine. *Mistretta v. United States* (1989).

Generally, the Court has taken a fairly generous view of what constitutes an intelligible principle. A provision of the Clean Air Act directed the Environmental Protection Agency (EPA) to set primary ambient air quality standards "the attainment and maintenance of which" were required "to protect the public health" with an "adequate margin of safety." The scope of discretion afforded the EPA by the provision was held to meet the intelligible principle standard and was upheld against a nondelegation doctrine challenge. The statutory provision at issue was "well within the outer limits of our nondelegation precedents." Merely because the EPA was obliged by the statute to make judgments of degree was not conclusive and did not mean that it was exercising legislative power in violation of Article 1, Section 1, which places all legislative power in Congress. *Whitman v. American Trucking Associations, Inc.* (2001).

Neither the nondelegation doctrine nor the separation of powers principle were violated when Congress delegated to the President the power to define the aggravating factors that permit imposition of the statutory penalty of death in capital court-martial cases. Art.I, Sec. 8, cl. 14 vesting in Congress the power "To make Rules for the Government and regulation of the land and naval Forces" is not to the contrary. This Clause does not exclude Executive authority. The delegated duty relates to duties already constitutionally assigned to the President. In such circumstances, Congress may give to the President as Commander in Chief "wide discretion and authority." *Loving v. United States* (1996).

Although it has been relatively easy for Congress to delegate legislative authority, it has been more difficult for it to retain control over that which has been delegated. The Legislative Veto has been a major weapon in the congressional arsenal for preserving executive accountability. Congress enacts legislation containing a broad delegation of power to the Executive but then provides for congressional review and veto of executive actions taken pursuant to the grant. In *Immigration & Naturalization Service v. Chadha* (1983), the Court, per Chief Justice Burger, held 7–2, that a one-House veto of executive orders involving deportation of aliens is unconstitutional.

Chadha was an unfortunate case for making the constitutional decision since it didn't involve agency rule-making or executive policy choices, but rather a deportation decision in a particular case. Chadha, an East Indian, admitted that he was deportable for overstaying his student visa. In 1974, he sought and obtained suspension of the Attorney–General's deportation order as permitted under the Immigration and Nationality Act because of the hardship such deportation would involve. However, the same Act authorized either the Senate or the House by resolution to "veto" the executive decision. The House of Representatives passed a resolution vetoing the suspension. In 1976, Chadha was ordered to be deported and he appealed to the courts.

The Supreme Court held the Legislative Veto provision unconstitutional. While the Court might have overturned the congressional action in *Chadha* on narrow grounds that the particular Legislative Veto in question violated the separation of powers, the Court instead chose to attack the Legislative Veto device itself. The Legislative Veto was held to violate the Presentment (Art. I., Sec. 7, cl. 3) and Bicameralism (Art. I, Secs. 1 and 7) Clauses which are "integral parts of the constitutional design for the separation of powers." Chief Justice Burger began from the premise that presentment of legislation to the President for his signature before becoming law and the presidential veto were considered by the Framers as imperative to permit the President to defend himself against Congress. Further, presentment was designed to protect against "oppressive, improvident, or ill-considered" laws and to engraft a "national perspective" on the legislative process. The President's veto power was similarly checked by providing that two-thirds of both Houses could override the President's veto. Like the Presentment Clause, bicameral consideration was intended to assure "that legislation should not be enacted unless it has been carefully and fully considered by the Nation's elected officials." The legislative power "would be exercised only after opportunity for full study and debate in separate settings." Dividing authority between two houses also protected against "legislative despotism," reflected the Framer' fears "that special interests could be favored at the expense of public needs" and responded to the concerns of both the large and small states over congressional representation.

Legislative power, then, must "be exercised in accord with a single, finely wrought and exhaustively considered procedure." But was the House's Veto action an exercise of the "legislative power?" Examining the action of the House in this case indicated that "it was essentially legislative in purpose and effect." The House's actions altered the legal rights, duties and relations of persons. Further, absent the veto, the Attorney General's action rejecting deportation could have been overridden, if at all, only by legislation requiring deportation. Since the House's actions were "legislative," presentment and bicameral consideration were required and the Legislative Veto was unconstitutional. Concluding that the Legislative Veto provision was severable from the rest of the legislation delegating the power to suspend deportation orders to the executive, the Court held that the Attorney General's suspension order was effective.

Justice White, dissenting, stressed the value of the Legislative Veto in overcoming Congress's dilemma,. *i.e.,* either to undertake the hopeless task of writing detailed statutes specifying future action in endless specific circumstances or "to abdicate its lawmaking function to the executive branch and independent agencies." The Veto, he reasoned, "is a necessary check on the unavoidably expanding power of the agencies, both executive and independent, as they engage in exercising authority delegated by Congress." The concerns that underlie Art. I, Sec. 7, simply were not in issue. Neither Art. I nor separation of powers is violated by a mechanism designed to preserve Congress's lawmaking role and make separation of powers effective. The Court's reliance on Art. I in *Chadha* put in jeopardy all of the nearly 200 laws containing Legislative Veto provisions. For example, both the War Powers Resolution and the Impoundment Control Act of 1974, use this device to control Executive action. In *Chadha*, adherence to the formal structure and literal text of the Constitution was deemed more important than the admittedly useful function that the legislative veto served in allowing Congress to maintain control over the legislative process.

The Line Item Veto Act provided still another terrain for the battle between formalism and functionalism. The Line Item Veto Act gave the President the power to "cancel in whole" three categories of provisions in statutes that had been signed into law—"(1) any dollar amount of discretionary budget authority; (2) any item of new direct spending; or (3) any limited tax benefit." Before canceling a provision the President must determine that cancellation will (1) reduce the federal budget deficit; (2) not damage basic government functions; and (3) not harm the national interest. The President must transmit a special message to Congress informing it of a cancellation within 5 calendar days after enactment of the canceled provision. The President complied with these requirements. But did the provisions of the Line Item Veto Act satisfy the requirements of Art. I, Sec. 7?

President Clinton canceled two provisions of duly enacted statutes, a section of the Balanced Budget Act of 1997 and a section of the Taxpayer Relief Act of 1997, thus depriving these sections of any effect. The practical effect of the President's cancellation of these provisions constituted an amendment or repeal by the President of portions of two Acts of Congress. The Court held, 6–3, per Justice Stevens, that the President had no authority to unilaterally enact, amend or repeal statutes. Under the constitutional scheme, if the President disapproves of a bill he "returns" (vetoes) it to Congress which can then override his veto by a two-thirds vote in each House. The veto power set forth in the Constitution, Art. I, Sec. 7, cl. 2, differs from the cancellation authority granted to the President by the Line

Item Veto Act. "The constitutional return takes place *before* the bill becomes law; the statutory cancellation occurs *after* the bill becomes law." Furthermore, the Constitution provides for the return of the entire bill but the statutory cancellation set forth in the Line Item Veto Act concerns only parts of the bill.

Although the Constitution does not expressly prohibit unilateral action by the President repealing or amending only a *part* of a bill, the silence of the text was "equivalent to an express prohibition." Justice Stevens quoted *Chadha* for the principle than the enactment of laws mandated compliance with the "single, finely wrought and exhaustively considered procedure" set forth in Article I. The Court declared that the President must approve all parts of a bill or reject it altogether. The cancellation provisions of the Line Item Veto Act were unconstitutional since they violated Article I, Sec. 7, the Presentment Clause of the Constitution. *Clinton v. City of New York* (1998).

Justice Breyer in dissent said that the Line Item Veto Act was entirely valid and denied that it constituted a repeal or an amendment of a law by the President. The Act merely delegated a power to the President to choose between alternatives: "[T]he delegated power to nullify statutory language was *itself* created and defined by Congress, and included in the statute books on an equal footing with (indeed, as a component part of) the sections that are potentially subject to nullification." Justice Scalia, dissenting and concurring in part, contended that there was not a "dime's worth of difference between Congress's authorizing the President to *cancel* a spending item, and Congress's authorizing money to be spent on a particular item at the President's discretion." Justice Scalia insisted that if the Line Item Veto Act had authorized the President to "decline to spend" a spending item in the Balanced Budget Act of 1997 it would clearly have been constitutional. The vigor of the dissents demonstrates that the functionalist approach has adherents on the Supreme Court although the identity of those adherents may change from case to case. Compare Justice Scalia's dissent in *Morrison v. Olson* (1988), *infra*, with his dissent in the Line Item Veto case. Nonetheless, the Line Item Veto Act case shows that the formalism which carried the day in *Bowsher* and *Chadha* still has sufficient force on the Rehnquist Court to prevail.

4.   APPOINTMENT AND REMOVAL

The checks and balances which characterize the tripartite nature of American government are illustrated in the constitutional provisions for appointment and removal of government officers. The strength of these provisions is in the limits they place on absolute power in any one Branch by dividing authority between Branches; the difficulty with them is in their silence on crucial questions.

Congress may not vest the Appointment Power in persons other than those indicated in Art. II, Sec. 2, cl. 2 which provides: "[The President] shall nominate, and by and with the advice and consent of the Senate, shall appoint Ambassadors, other public Ministers and Consuls, Judges of the Supreme Court, and all other Officers of the United States, whose appointments are not herein otherwise provided for, and which shall be established by law, but the Congress may by law vest the Appointment of such inferior Officers, as they think proper, in the President alone, in the Courts of Law, or in the Heads of Departments." Congress cannot vest the appointment power in persons other than those indicated in the foregoing provision. Thus, a federal statute providing that the voting members of the Federal Election Commission should be appointed by the President pro tem of the Senate and the Speaker of the House was struck down because these Congressional leaders did not come within the terms "Courts of Law" or "Heads of Departments" as mandated by Art. II, Sec. 2, cl. 2. Congress cannot vest the Appointment Power in itself since this would constitute an impermissible usurpation of power. *Buckley v. Valeo* (1976).

A critical question in the Appointment Power context is this—what is the basis for distinguishing a principal officer from an inferior officer? This question is best answered by a functional inquiry into whether the officer is subordinate or independent, the scope and breadth of the officer's jurisdiction and the extent of the duties performed. The importance of this distinction is illustrated by a constitutional challenge to a federal statute, the Ethics in Government Act which vested the appointment of an Independent Counsel in a Special Division of the United States Court of Appeals for the District of Columbia; the Independent Counsel was charged with investigating certain Executive Branch officials. If the Independent Counsel was an inferior officer, this interbranch appointment was permissible unless it impaired the ability of the Executive Branch to perform its functions or was otherwise incongruous. The statute was upheld. The Independent Counsel was declared to be an "inferior officer," subject to removal for good cause by the Attorney General, and possessed of a limited jurisdiction. Chief Justice Rehnquist, emphasized for the Court, that the Independent Counsel performed only limited duties of investigation and prosecution and did not make general policy. Moreover, the office of Independent Counsel under the statute was limited in term to the completion of the specified task. *Morrison v. Olson* (1988).

When does the President have the power to remove Executive Branch officials? In the past, the answer to this question turned on whether an official was categorized as a "purely executive official"—in which case the President's power of removal was seen as "incident to the power of appointment." *Myers v. United States* (1926). However, if the official was categorized as one who exercised "quasi-legislative" or "quasi-judicial" power, then the separation of powers principle precluded placing an "illimitable power of removal" in the President. *Humphrey's Executor v. United States* (1935).

While not rejecting these categories, the Court has criticized reliance on the literal and excessive use of these "rigid categories" because they obscure the "real question"—are the restrictions on removal imposed by Congress "of such a nature that they impede the President's ability to perform his constitutional duty?" Applying this approach in *Morrison*, the Court held that the provision in the Ethics in Government Act that the Attorney General can remove an Independent Counsel only for good cause did not impermissibly burden the President's duty to faithfully execute the laws. Conceding that law enforcement functions belong to the Executive Branch, Chief Justice Rehnquist concluded, nevertheless, that the President's need to control the exercise of discretion of an inferior officer such as the Independent Counsel was not so central to the operation of the Executive Branch "as to require as a matter of constitutional law that the counsel be terminable at will by the President." Congressional limitation of the Attorney General's power to remove the Independent Counsel was "essential" if she was to have the necessary independence to perform her task. Misconduct on the part of the Independent Counsel was still nonetheless a ground for removal. In the circumstances, Congress has not usurped the President's removal power over executive officials.

When Congress can remove officials by means other than impeachment, can Congress also vest executive functions in such officials? This issue was presented by some provisions of the Gramm–Rudman Act, enacted to control the burgeoning federal deficit, which vested in the Comptroller General authority to specify spending reductions binding on the President. The Act gave final authority to the Comptroller General to decide which budget cuts should be made. The Court held that the Act vested executive authority in the Comptroller General since he was placed in the position of interpreting and implementing the legislation. Such action constituted execution of the laws—an executive function. At an earlier time, however, Congress had enacted legislation providing that the Comptroller General could be removed for certain specifically stated, if generally phrased, reasons such as inefficiency and neglect of duty. This rendered the Comptroller General an agent of Congress since he could be removed by Congress for defying its will. Congress had, therefore, impermissibly inserted its own agent over the execution of the Gramm–Rudman Act. Congress had thereby invalidly usurped an executive function in violation of the principle of separation of powers. *Bowsher v. Synar* (1986).

5. SEPARATION OF POWERS GENERALLY

Separation of powers problems will sometimes be analyzed in terms of the general separation of powers principle itself. When this approach is undertaken, the Court examines the extent of the intrusion on the constitutional functions of the other Branch, gauges the extent to which the challenged action aggrandizes in one Branch power that should properly be shared, and balances the competing interests at stake.

In *Morrison v. Olson* (1988), the Court analyzed the Ethics in Government Act from this perspective. From an overall point of view, the Act's appointment of an Independent Counsel to investigate and prosecute high executive officials did not unduly thwart the functioning of the Executive Branch. Nor did Congress wrongfully arrogate to itself any Executive Branch functions. The Attorney General retained sole and unreviewable power to request the appointment of the Independent Counsel and could remove her for good cause. He still retained several means for supervising and controlling the Independent Counsel's prosecutorial powers. Although it was true that the Independent Counsel was freer from executive direction than most federal prosecutors, the Ethics in Government Act still afforded the Executive Branch "sufficient control" to enable the President to perform his constitutionally assigned duties. In the last analysis, that was the dispositive point.

B. THE FOREIGN ARENA

While the Court generally has reacted negatively to assertion of inherent domestic governmental powers, the claim of extra-constitutional national powers in external relations has received a far more sympathetic judicial response. In *United States v. Curtiss–Wright Export Corp.* (1936), the Court upheld a congressional resolution delegating broad power to the President to prohibit arms sales to certain countries. Justice Sutherland, for the Court, indicated that the normal constraints on broad delegation of legislative powers do not apply in the foreign arena since "the investment of the federal government with the powers of external sovereignty did not depend upon the affirmative grants of the Constitution." He reasoned that upon our separation from Great Britain, the powers of external sovereignty passed directly from the Crown to the *Union* of States, since foreign affairs powers are "necessary concomitants of nationality." The Constitution, however, allocates only the powers previously lodged in the *separate* states. While this declaration of inherent foreign affairs powers, operating independently of the Constitution, represents a questionable interpretation of history, it has never been rejected by the Court and has, on occasion, been embraced. See, *e.g., Perez v. Brownell* (1958).

1.   ALLOCATING THE FOREIGN RELATIONS POWER

In *Curtiss–Wright,* Justice Sutherland argued for executive primacy in the exercise of foreign relations powers, both constitutional and extra-constitutional. While this presidential power must be exercised consistent with the Constitution, Justice Sutherland asserted, the President acts "as the sole organ of the Federal Government in the field of international relations." What is the basis for this

assertion of executive prerogative in the foreign
arena? Certainly, the constitutional grants of power
do not indicate an intent to vest the President with
such a dominant position. Rather, the formal constitutional grants of foreign relations power are allocated between the President and Congress. In addition to the general presidential powers, Art. II vests
in the President the powers to recognize and withdraw recognition from foreign governments, to
make treaties, and to serve as Commander–in–
Chief. Further, it is generally accepted that the
President has implied power to represent the Nation in day-to-day negotiations with foreign countries. From these powers and from custom and
usage flows the broad presidential role in the making and execution of foreign policy. But the Congress also has express foreign affairs powers, such
as the power to regulate foreign commerce, to raise
and maintain armies, and to declare war as well as
its general law-making powers, including the critical powers to tax and spend. The Constitution then
appears to envision a sharing of power in the foreign arena. *Curtiss–Wright*'s claim for executive
primacy appears to rest primarily on the respective
capabilities of the branches and the teachings of
history. The President's abilities to acquire information, maintain secrecy and respond quickly to
events was specifically cited by Justice Sutherland
as necessitating executive discretion in foreign affairs independent of congressional authorization.
Certainly, the historical expansion of presidential

foreign affairs powers vis-a-vis Congress cannot be denied.

Nevertheless, it is questionable that these considerations would provide an adequate justification for presidential action in the foreign arena *contrary* to congressional legislation. Perhaps the best explanation of the allocation of foreign affairs powers remains that provided by Justice Jackson in the *Steel Seizure Case*. When the President acts pursuant to authorization from Congress, as he did in *Curtiss–Wright,* his authority is maximized; when he acts contrary to the will of Congress, his power is at its lowest ebb. And when the President acts without any congressional authorization or denial of authority, he acts in a twilight zone where the distribution of powers remains uncertain. Coupled with the fact that courts are more reluctant to intrude into foreign affairs decision-making (*i.e.*, the political question doctrine), the predicate for a free congressional-executive interplay in the foreign affairs arena is apparent.

2.   TREATIES AND EXECUTIVE AGREEMENTS

Art. II, Sec. 2, authorizes the President, with the advice and consent of two-thirds of the Senators present, and subject to any Senate reservations, to make treaties (*i.e.,* the President negotiates and "ratifies" a treaty). There is no constitutional provision dealing with the question of how treaties are to be terminated and the issue whether the President can unilaterally abrogate an existing treaty has been a subject of controversy. See *Goldwater v. Carter* (1979). If a treaty is executory, congressional legislation will be necessary to make the treaty effective domestically. Coupled with the necessary and proper clause, a treaty can provide the constitutional basis for congressional legislation that might otherwise be of doubtful validity. *Missouri v. Holland* (1920).

While the Constitution in Art. II speaks only of treaties, the President, often with congressional participation, today makes more use of international agreements and compacts than formal treaties. In fact, executive agreements can be used to speedily and privately commit the United States to action in the foreign arena without the need for any congressional involvement, *i.e.,* a "pure" executive agreement. Increasing executive reliance on international accords rather than treaties has generated congressional efforts to control and limit their use. While most such efforts have failed, Congress has enacted legislation requiring that Congress at least be notified of the existence of the agreement.

Both treaties and executive agreements enjoy Art. VI supremacy over contrary state law. *United States v. Belmont* (1937); *United States v. Pink* (1942). While the language of Art. VI might appear to make treaties equal with the Constitution, it is now generally accepted that international agreements of all kinds are subject to constitutional limitations. *Reid v. Covert* (1957). The Tenth Amendment reserved powers clause, however, is not such a limit on the federal power. *Missouri v. Holland* (1920). If acts of Congress conflict with treaty provisions, the later in time will be given effect domestically. *Whitney v. Robertson* (1888). Whether an executive agreement made solely on the basis of presidential power, without any congressional involvement, has legal effect when it conflicts with congressional legislation has not been decided by the Supreme Court, although it seems doubtful that the agreement would prevail.

An excellent example of the importance of executive agreements, and of the continuing vitality of Justice Jackson's approach to shared powers in the *Steel Seizure Case,* is provided by *Dames & Moore v. Regan* (1981). Pursuant to an agreement between the governments of the United States and Iran for the release of embassy personnel held hostage in Iran, President Reagan ratified executive orders nullifying certain attachments and ordering the transfer to Iran of Iranian assets held frozen in United States banks. An executive agreement also obligated the United States to terminate all legal proceedings in United States courts against Iran. The Court, per Justice Rehnquist, found specific congressional authorization for the presidential action nullifying attachments and ordering the transfer of assets. The order therefore enjoyed "the strongest of presumptions and the widest latitude of judicial interpretation." The challenger failed to satisfy its heavy burden to prove that "the federal government as a whole lacked the power exercised by the President." While the Court found no similar specific congressional authorization for presidential suspension of pending court claims, a history of congressional acquiescence in independent presidential action in emergencies indicated an intent to accord the President broad discretion, at least in the absence of any contrary expression of congressional intent. Congressional acquiescence in the use of executive agreements to settle foreign claims, the character of existing federal legislation in the area of claims settlement, and the judicial acceptance of the legality of executive agreements, led the Court to uphold this particular presidential action as a necessary incident to resolving a major foreign policy dispute.

In *American Insurance Association v. Garamendi* (2003), the Court struck down, 5–4, per Justice Souter, the California Holocaust Victims Relief Insurance Act which basically required European insurance companies to disclose information about insurance policies they had issued to Holocaust victims or else lose their license to do business in California. The insurance companies successfully contended that the California law was preempted by executive agreements with Germany, Austria and France. The Supreme Court ruled that executive agreements which affected claims against corporations rather than foreign governments still preempted state law. Nor did it matter either that the executive agreements here did not include explicit preemption clauses. Vindicating the interests of victims injured by enemy corporations in wartime is a subject where national interests override state policy. Moreover, there was a clear conflict between state and national policy. Justice Ginsburg, for the dissenters, contended that courts should not rule that state laws have been preempted when "they rely on no legislative or even executive text, but only on inference and implication."

3. ALLOCATING THE WAR POWER

Art. II declares that the President is Commander–in–Chief of the armed forces. But Congress has the power to declare war and to maintain the armed forces. To what extent can the President acting pursuant to his role as Commander–in–Chief and his other executive powers commit the armed might of the Nation in foreign ventures without congressional authorization? While the question is of critical importance, neither the Constitution nor the Court has provided very much by way of an answer. Indeed, the Court regularly avoided review of challenges to the validity of the military actions that might have provided guidelines for the exercise of the shared war power.

The debate over presidential-congressional roles in using the war powers frequently focuses on the War Powers Resolution which restricts presidential commitment of the armed forces absent congressional authorization. 50 U.S.C.A. §§ 1541–48. The Resolution contains consultation and reporting requirements for presidential involvement in hostilities and provides for termination of the use of the armed forces 60 days after reporting absent congressional action. For some, the Act is an unconstitutional intrusion on the Executive's war powers; for others, the Resolution is a proper use of Congress's implied powers to define the proper use of the shared war power.

Aside from presidential interaction with Congress concerning the war power, what is the nature of the President's war power itself? Advocates of a broad reading of the presidential war power tend to stress custom and usage. It does seem clear that the President has power to repel an invasion. *The Prize Cases.* There is also ample historical evidence, which is fortified by custom and usage, that the President can act unilaterally to preserve our neutrality and to protect American citizens abroad and possesses an ill-defined power to act in an "emergency." Finally, presidential initiatives are frequently defended by invoking collective security agreements or congressional actions such as the Gulf of Tonkin Resolution. Those seeking to limit presidential war powers emphasize that the original intent of the Framers was to make the President "top general and top admiral," *The Federalist* No. 69 (A. Hamilton). "[G]enerals and admirals even when they are 'first' do not determine the practical purpose for which troops are to be used; they command them in the execution of policy made by others." L. Henkin, *Foreign Affairs and the Constitution* 50–51 (1972).

C. PROMOTING EXECUTIVE RESPONSIBILITY

1. EXECUTIVE PRIVILEGE

While there is no provision in the Constitution establishing an executive privilege to withhold information from a judicial forum, a unanimous Supreme Court in *United States v. Nixon* (1974), found "constitutional underpinnings" for a conditional privilege relating to confidential communications between the President and his advisers on domestic matters. President Nixon, an unindicted co-conspirator, had asserted a claim of privilege in refusing to turn over tapes and other memoranda to a special grand jury investigating the Watergate break-in. The Court accepted the existence of a constitutionally based privilege flowing "from the supremacy of each branch within its own assigned area of constitutional duties" and from "the nature of the enumerated powers." However, the Court rejected the President's claim (at least in cases not involving military, diplomatic or sensitive national security matters) that invoking the privilege was vested absolutely in the Executive free of judicial review. Chief Justice Burger, speaking for the Court, instead invoked *Marbury v. Madison* (1803) for the proposition that "it is emphatically the province and duty of the judicial department to say what the law is"—a duty which the courts could not share with the Executive Branch. To accept a claim of absolute privilege, stated the Chief Justice, "would upset the constitutional balance of 'a workable government' and gravely impair the role of the courts under Art. III." While the claim of executive privilege was presumptively valid, the courts must determine, through *in camera* inspection, whether the claimed privilege should yield to some overriding interest in disclosure.

Applying these principles, the Court concluded: "[W]hen the ground for asserting privilege as to subpoenaed materials sought for use in a criminal trial is based only on the generalized interest in confidentiality, it cannot prevail over the fundamental demands of due process of law in the fair administration of criminal justice. The generalized assertion of privilege must yield to the demonstrated, specific need for evidence in a pending criminal trial." The order of the district court requiring that the subpoenaed materials be turned over to it was affirmed. However, the Court stressed that in determining what materials should be released or published, the district court was not to treat the President as "an ordinary individual" but was "to afford presidential confidentiality the greatest protection consistent with the fair administration of justice."

Executive privilege arose in *Nixon v. Administrator of Gen. Servs.* (1977), upholding the constitutionality of a federal statute governing public access to confidential papers, tape recordings, and other materials produced during the Nixon administration. Justice Brennan, writing for the Court, rejected President Nixon's challenge to the law, characterizing it as reflecting an "archaic view of the separation of powers as requiring three air tight departments of the government." The proper inquiry, said Justice Brennan, required a determination whether the challenged Act would prevent the Executive Branch from accomplishing its constitutionally assigned functions. In this instance, President Ford had signed the Act into law and President Carter had urged its validity, indicating that the Executive Branch was a partner in the Act's disposition of the presidential material. Further, the Executive Branch, through the GSA, remained in full control of the materials. Nor was the Act a violation of the executive privilege recognized in *United States v. Nixon* (1974) since it involved "a very limited intrusion by personnel in the Executive Branch sensitive to executive concerns." As in *United States v. Nixon*, the claim for confidentiality yielded to an overriding interest—the important congressional interest in preserving access to confidential materials for lawful government and historical use.

The difference between executive privilege claims in a civil proceeding as compared with such claims in a criminal context like that involved in *United States v. Nixon* was highlighted in a law suit brought by Sierra Club and Judicial Watch against Vice–President Cheney. They complained that a presidentially-appointed energy policy group included a number of private business executives and, therefore, was subject to federal open meeting and disclosure laws. The two groups sought discovery concerning the group's meetings and related documents. The Supreme Court, per Justice Kennedy, ruled that the Court of Appeals was mistaken in its assumption that a precondition to the government's separation of powers objections to the discovery requests was the assertion of executive privilege. Such a rule would exacerbate constitutional confrontations between the executive and legislative branches and should be avoided where possible. *United States v. Nixon* involved the Executive's interest in shielding the confidentiality of its communications as against the need for for relevant evidence in a criminal proceeding. That case specifically distinguished civil proceedings. *Nixon* did not oblige the Executive to undertake the burden of "critiquing the unacceptable discovery requests line by line" in civil proceedings such as this. *Cheney v. District Court for District of Columbia (2004).*

2.   EXECUTIVE IMMUNITY

United States v. Nixon (1974) and *Marbury v. Madison* (1803) establish that, at least in some instances, executive officers, including the President, are amenable to judicial process. But the extent of this judicial oversight is less clear. For example, could the courts have issued a coercive order if President Nixon had chosen to disobey the judicial order to turn over the Watergate tapes? Was President Nixon amenable to criminal processes while still in office or after he left office for acts done while President? The disposition of such issues under the separation of powers doctrine remains unanswered.

The Court has had occasion to address the question whether the President and his aides could be held civilly liable for their actions. *Nixon v. Fitzgerald* (1982), involved a suit by Fitzgerald, an Air Force management analyst, against former President Nixon and various executive officials, claiming that he had been illegally fired in retaliation for his testimony before a congressional committee. The Court, per Justice Powell, held 5–4 that the former President enjoyed absolute immunity from damages liability for acts within the "outer perimeter" of his official responsibility while in office. Presidential immunity was defined as "a functionally mandated incident of the President's unique office, rooted in the constitutional tradition of the separation of powers and supported by our history." Justice Powell found support for the principle in the absolute immunity accorded judges and prosecutors. Given the adversarial character of the presidential duties and the resulting probability of civil law suits, a qualified immunity would not provide an adequate guarantee to assure the effective performance of the President's duties. The interests of the civil litigant were outweighed by the separation of powers dangers of judicial intrusion "on the authority and functions of the Executive Branch." Alternative checks, such as impeachment, press and congressional scrutiny, Presidential concerns with maintaining influence and with reelection, reasoned Justice Powell, provided adequate assurance that the President would not be "above the law." The dismissal of an employee as part of a reorganization was found to be well within the outer perimeter of the President's official responsibility.

In a companion case, *Harlow v. Fitzgerald* (1982), the Court held that White House aides enjoy only a qualified immunity. "Government officials performing discretionary functions are shielded from liability for civil damages insofar as their conduct does not violate clearly established statutory or constitutional rights of which a reasonable person would have known." See *Mitchell v. Forsyth* (1985) [Attorney General entitled only to qualified immunity].

Should the Presidential immunity doctrine of *Nixon v. Fitzgerald* extend to private civil litigation arising out of actions unconnected with the President's official duties? Paula Jones alleged that President Clinton had made improper sexual advances to her while he was Governor of Arkansas and sued him for civil damages in federal court. President Clinton urged that the litigation be deferred until his term of office ended and that, at the very least, respect for the Presidential office required a stay of the proceedings. The Supreme Court unanimously disagreed. The Court held that the rationale of *Nixon v. Fitzgerald* did not apply. *Fitzgerald* was based on the rationale that the President should not be " 'unduly cautious in the discharge of his official duties.' " But this rationale did not hold for Presidential *unofficial* conduct. What is critical for immunity is not the identity of the actor but the nature of the function performed. Presidential immunity does not extend beyond official action. Separation of powers doctrine does not *require* that private actions against the President be deferred until he is out of office. *Clinton v. Jones* (1997). Nor was the argument that responding to litigation while in office would distract from the effective discharge of his duties any more persuasive. The trial court has discretion to manage such actions—"including deferral of trial"—so as to assure that interference with Presidential duties is avoided. Finally, the Court was careful to say that there were some issues related to Presidential immunity which it was not deciding. Since this case was not brought in state court, it was not necessary to decide whether the need to protect federal officials from local prejudice would present "a more compelling case for immunity." Nor was there need to decide "whether a court may compel the attendance of the President at any specific time or place." The Court assumed discovery could take place at the White House. Even if a trial was held "there would be no necessity for the President to attend in person."

PART TWO

INDIVIDUAL RIGHTS AND LIBERTIES

Limited government in the United States is achieved not only through the constitutional allocation of powers but also through the recognition of rights and liberties. The original Constitution contained few such specific guarantees. Art. I, Secs. 9 & 10, prohibit Congress and the states respectively from enacting bills of attainder, *i.e.,* legislative punishment without the benefit of judicial trial. The same sections proscribe federal and state enactment of retroactive legislation, *i.e., ex post facto* laws. The *Ex Post Facto* Clause, interestingly enough, has been interpreted to apply only to criminal legislation (even though the text is not so limited) and only if the effect of the law is to significantly burden the offender. *Weaver v. Graham* (1981) [state statute retroactively reducing a prisoner's gain time for good conduct held unconstitutional]. Art. I, Sec. 10 also provides that states shall not pass laws impairing the obligations of contract. This limitation operates on the federal government through the Due Process Clause of the Fifth Amendment.

None of these guarantees, however, have been interpreted so broadly as to extend meaningful protection to the fundamental interests of individuals. Indeed, many of the Framers felt that no specification of basic rights was needed since the national government could exercise only the limited powers delegated in the Constitution. For example, since Congress had no power to regulate the press, there was no need to guarantee freedom of the press. For the Framers, the limited powers of the federal government was the assurance of freedom. But the Antifederalists were fearful. As the price of ratification, they demanded the addition of what we now call the Bill of Rights.

In *Barron v. Mayor and City Council of Baltimore* (1833), the argument was made that the Bill of Rights was a limitation on the state governments as well as the federal government. John Marshall disagreed and ruled that, both as a matter of text and history, the states were not limited by the Bill of Rights. But a significant limitation on the state power was introduced into American constitutional law with the enactment of the Fourteenth Amendment which was to become the vehicle through which much of the contents of the Bill of Rights were made binding on the states.

The Fourteenth Amendment guarantee that no state shall deny the privileges or immunities of citizens of the United States might have served as a vehicle for applying the guarantees of the Bill of Rights to the states. At least it might have done so were it not for the Court's decision in the *Slaugh-*

ter–House Cases (1872). Justice Miller, for the
Court, began with the premise that the first sentence of the Fourteenth Amendment creates two
types of citizenship, federal and state. He then read
the second sentence of the Amendment as extending federal constitutional protection only to the
privileges and immunities of national citizenship.
But what are the privileges and immunities attach-
ing to federal and state citizenship? Justice Miller's
answer was that the fundamental rights of the
individual were derived from state law. The federal
guarantee was limited to those rights peculiar to
the citizen's relationship to the federal government,
e.g., to petition Congress, to use the navigable waters of the United States, the right to interstate
travel, etc. An alternative interpretation, *e.g.,* that
the privileges and immunities clause was meant to
extend all the fundamental rights traditionally associated with state citizenship to the national citizen
as a guarantee of federal law would, in Miller's
view, upset the historic relation of the federal government to the states. Congress and the Court
would become the perpetual censors of state legislation.

But arguably the precise intent of the Fourteenth
Amendment, as Justice Field stated in dissent, was
to upset the historic relationship of the states to the
federal government, particularly in relation to protection of the rights and liberties of the citizen.
After all, the Fourteenth Amendment in all its
sections was designed to bring legal freedom and
equality to the recently emancipated slaves. The

Privileges and Immunities Clause, in this view, was a means by which this objective was to be accomplished. Justice Miller's interpretation, however, gave the Clause no significance. Essentially all the rights that he was willing to find within it already had been recognized as federally guaranteed. On the other hand, Justice Field, dissenting in the *Slaughter–House Cases,* perceived the Fourteenth Amendment Privileges and Immunities Clause as guaranteeing those rights which belong to citizens of all free governments. "The fundamental rights, privileges and immunities which belong to him as a free man and as a free citizen, now belong to him as a citizen of the United States, and are not dependent upon his citizenship in any state." The practical effect of the *Slaughter–House Cases* was to read out the Privileges and Immunities Clause as a meaningful constitutional guarantee.

More than a century after the *Slaughter-House Cases*, the Supreme Court in a surprise move resurrected the Privileges and Immunities Clause of the Fourteenth Amendment. *Saenz v. Roe* (1999). A California law limiting families moving into the state during their first year of residence to the welfare benefits they would have received if they had remained in their former state was struck down under the Privileges and Immunities Clause. That Clause embraces the right to travel including that component of the right to travel which guarantees to United States citizens seeking to become permanent residents of another state the right to be treated like other citizens of that state. United

States citizens whatever their economic status have the right to choose to be citizens of the state where they reside. Justice Stevens declared for the Court: "The States, however, do not have any right to select their citizens." Legislation like the California law has to be justified by a stricter standard of review than the rationality or intermediate standard of review. The California law might serve a state's fiscal needs by reducing its welfare obligations somewhat but this did not justify discriminating between newly arrived citizens and longer residing citizens. The Citizenship Clause of the Fourteenth Amendment "expressly equates citizenship with residence." The Citizenship Clause does not allow for a system of degrees of citizenship based on length of residence. Possibly, the states may evaluate the *bona fides* of permanent residence before making state benefits available. Whether after *Saenz* the Privileges and Immunities Clause will become, like the Due Process and Equal Protection Clauses of the Fourteenth Amendment, a source of rights is at yet unclear. Justice Thomas, who like Justice Rehnquist dissented in *Saenz*, expressed the hope that the Privileges and Immunities Clause would not "become yet another convenient tool for inventing new rights."

CHAPTER V

DUE PROCESS OF LAW

A. THE PROCESS OF INCORPORATION

The Fourteenth Amendment Privileges and Immunities Clause failed as a vehicle for expanded federal constitutional limitations on the states. Instead, the Fourteenth Amendment Due Process Clause became the tool whereby various fundamental guarantees of the Bill of Rights were "incorporated" and made applicable to the states. The history of this development is characterized by controversy about what rights are included and the nature of the incorporation process.

In *Adamson v. California* (1947), two major due process methodologies were joined in combat. One theory—that defended by Justice Frankfurter in his concurring opinion in *Adamson*—argued that the Due Process Clause has an "independent potency" of its own, not defined by the Bill of Rights. The commands of due process were to be determined on a case-by-case basis by asking whether the particular procedures used by government "offend those canons of decency and fairness which express the notions of justice of English-speaking peoples." This theory, in Frankfurter's view, did not simply imple-

ment the idiosyncratic standards of the particular
judge but rather involved a quest to identify "accepted notions of justice."

For Justice Black, the *ad hoc* approach of Frankfurter would only lead to the revival of discredited
notions of natural law. The Fourteenth Amendment, taken as a whole, he argued, required the
application of the entire Bill of Rights to the states,
nothing more and nothing less. This "total incorporation" approach provided the guarantee of judicial
objectivity. If it were argued that, unlike the Frankfurter *ad hoc* theory, the Black theory had no
dynamic quality, Justice Black would respond: Precisely. For him, total incorporation assured certainty, objectivity, and conformance to the historical
intent of the Framers of the Fourteenth Amendment.

As often happens in the history of ideas, neither
the Frankfurter nor the Black theory in its pure
form prevailed. While the *ad hoc* approach enjoyed
a temporary ascendancy during the late fifties, its
demise quietly began in *Mapp v. Ohio* (1961). Later,
the new theory fashioned in *Mapp* was more boldly
proclaimed under the name "selective incorporation," meaning that some of the Bill of Rights
were binding on the states in accord with the teachings of Justice Black but the mode of their selection
was more in keeping with the flexible due process
theories of Justice Frankfurter.

In implementing this selective incorporation approach, the Court, at times, has asked whether the

particular guarantee of the Bill of Rights is "implicit in the concept of ordered liberty." More recently, the Court has asked, instead, whether the guarantee in question is "fundamental to the American scheme of justice," even though a "fair and enlightened system of justice" would be possible without the guarantee. *Duncan v. Louisiana* (1968) [Sixth Amendment right to jury trial incorporated as a part of due process liberty under the Fourteenth Amendment]. Through this process of selective inclusion, the states have been subjected to most of the principal guarantees of the Bill of Rights. The only provisions thus far not incorporated are the Second, Third, and Seventh Amendments, the right to grand jury indictment in the Fifth Amendment, and the Eighth Amendment's guarantee of freedom from excessive bail.

Duncan v. Louisiana (1968) set forth another basic principle of the incorporation approach. The Court held that an "incorporated" Bill of Rights guarantee applies against the states to the same extent and in the same manner that it binds the federal government. This approach, however, presents a problem. The Sixth Amendment guarantee of trial by jury, for example, had been thought to imply the use of a twelve-person jury and a unanimous verdict. But were the states to be fettered by these requirements? In a somewhat confusing line of cases, the Court has answered, "No." In *Williams v. Florida* (1970), the Court held that a twelve-person jury is not required under either the Sixth or the Fourteenth Amendment. In subsequent

cases, it was held that a jury of five persons would
violate due process [*Ballew v. Georgia* (1978)] as
would a state conviction by a non-unanimous six-
person jury [*Burch v. Louisiana* (1979)]. In *Apodaca
v. Oregon* (1972), the Court held that the requirement of unanimity was not a demand of Fourteenth
Amendment due process. But a split among the
justices left it uncertain whether the federal government itself was still bound by a Sixth Amendment
requirement of unanimity in a federal criminal
prosecution. Many commentators examining these
cases conclude that the Court has simply watered
down the guarantees of the Bill of Rights to accommodate the values of federalism. So, perhaps, in the
Court's post-*Duncan* due process cases, Frankfurter's flexible due process theory had a final inning.

B. SUBSTANTIVE DUE PROCESS

1. TRADITIONAL SUBSTANTIVE
DUE PROCESS

The due process liberty clause incorporates not
only the procedural guarantees of the Bill of Rights
but the substantive limitations of the Bill of Rights
as well. Thus, a state law burdening freedom of
speech can be attacked as an infringement of the
First and Fourteenth Amendment guarantee of
freedom of expression. But is the substantive limitation of due process liberty limited to the express, or
even the implied, guarantees of the Bill of Rights?

a. The Early Rise and Demise of Economic Due Process

Historically, business interests have sought a basis in the Constitution to protect property against the state economic regulation and intervention. A favored constitutional locus for this protection has been the Due Process Clause of the Fourteenth Amendment. Illustrative is the famous case of *Lochner v. New York* (1905), invalidating 5–4 a New York law prohibiting employers from employing workers in bakeries more than ten hours per day and sixty hours per week.

Justice Peckham, for the Court, found the law to be a significant interference with the liberty of contract protected by the Due Process Clause since "[t]he right to purchase or to sell labor is part of the liberty protected by this amendment." How did one know that the right to contract for one's labor was part of the content of the word "liberty" in the Due Process Clause? The Court had said so and this made it so. [See, *e.g., Allgeyer v. Louisiana* (1897)]. But even if the New York law was an interference with the guarantee of liberty, so construed, that did not necessarily mean that the law was unconstitutional since the state still might have latitude to legislate under its police powers. As Justice Peckham said: "Both property and liberty are held on such reasonable conditions as may be imposed by the governing power of the state." The due process issue, then, was whether the New York law was "an unreasonable, unnecessary, and arbitrary interference with the right of the individual to his personal liberty."

Applying this standard, the Court initially considered whether the law furthered the police power interest of the state. While the law under review in *Lochner* purported to be for the health of the workers, Justice Peckham questioned whether this was its real object and purpose. For him, the real legislative objective was the regulation of private labor contracts which was not within the realm of the state's police power. The ordering of private economic relationships was simply not a matter of the general welfare which the state was empowered to protect. This unjudicial probing for the true legislative purpose and narrow view of the police power have been cited by many commentators as constituting one of the principal defects of the *Lochner* approach.

But Justice Peckham declared further that even if the law were considered as a health measure, the law was unconstitutional. The Court found no reasonable foundation for holding that the law was necessary or appropriate for safeguarding the health of the public or the employees. An act "must have a more direct relation as a means to an end." But why was there no direct relationship here? Was the problem in *Lochner* only one of a deficiency of evidence? Perhaps counsel had simply failed to provide sufficient facts to establish that the maximum hours law furthered the permissible health interests of the state. After all, in other cases from the same period, the Court upheld maximum hour laws applied to the mining industry [*Holden v. Hardy* (1898)] and to maximum hours for women in the workplace [*Muller v. Oregon* (1908)]. In these cases, the health dangers arguably were either more apparent or were supported by a "Brandeis brief" detailing the factual basis for the reasonableness of the law in promoting the public health.

We would suggest, however, that the problem presented in *Lochner* transcended proof of reasonableness. *Lochner* closely scrutinized the *appropriateness* of the legislative means for promoting health interests of the workers. Justice Peckham examined alternatives that the legislature might have selected but chose not to. Simply, there was no deference to the legislative judgment during the reign of *Lochner*-style substantive due process but rather an intrusion of the judicial economic value choices in preference to those selected by the legislature.

It was this close judicial scrutiny of the legislative judgment that drew the impassioned dissents written by Justice Holmes and the first Justice Harlan. For Justice Harlan, there was adequate evidence whereby the legislature could reasonably conclude that long hours working in a bakery might endanger the health of the workmen. Only if economic enactments were "plainly, palpably, beyond all question" inconsistent with due process liberty should the Court, in Harlan's view, invalidate a legislative enactment.

Justice Holmes characterized the majority's decision as being based "upon an economic theory
which a large part of the country does not entertain" and chastised the majority for importing into
the Fourteenth Amendment "Mr. Herbert Spencer's Social Statics." For Holmes, the majority will,
as expressed by the legislature, prevails "unless it
can be said that a rational and fair man necessarily
would admit that the statute proposed would infringe fundamental principles as they have been
understood by the traditions of our people and our
law." There was no question in the present case
that a reasonable man could conclude that the New
York maximum hour law for bakers served a legitimate and permissible health interest of the state.

The judicial approach to economic due process in
Lochner provided the dominant motif for the early
part of the twentieth century. *Adair v. United
States* (1908); *Coppage v. Kansas* (1915); *Adkins v.
Children's Hospital* (1923). But it was the judicial
deference to the legislative judgment in economic
cases preached by Justices Holmes and Harlan in
their dissents which ultimately prevailed.

Constitutional doctrines usually do not die all at
once but slowly show signs of mortality. So it was
with *Lochner*-style substantive due process. A significant instance of the decline of Lochnerism is
found in *Nebbia v. New York* (1934), upholding a
New York minimum price law for milk. Gone was
the active probing of the legislative objective. Price
regulation, even though it involved the private economic relationship of a buyer and a seller, was held

to be still within the state's police power concern. Further, "a state is free to adopt whatever economic policy may reasonably be deemed to promote public welfare." If the means selected "have a reasonable relation to a proper legislative purpose, and are neither arbitrary nor discriminatory, the requirements of due process are satisfied, and judicial determination to that effect renders a court *functus officio*." *New Deal: More deference*

While this may sound like the reasonableness test employed in *Lochner,* the minimal judicial scrutiny of the legislative work product left little doubt that the Court was exercising a degree of deference to the legislature in marked contrast to the judicial activism of *Lochner.* Courts were not to judge the wisdom of the policy or the adequacy or practicability of the law for achieving that policy since they were "both incompetent and unauthorized" to do so. Only if the means were "demonstrably irrelevant" to the permissible state policy would the law violate due process. In this instance, the Court found that there was extensive legislative fact finding on the dangers of price instability in the milk industry that demonstrated the reasonableness of the milk price control law.

Nebbia began a process that was to result not merely in the demise of Lochnerism (judicial activism in socioeconomic cases under the guise of interpreting the Due Process Clause of the Fourteenth Amendment) but with a complete judicial role reversal. Where once there had been judicial activism, there was now candid judicial abdication.

b. Economic Regulation: Substantive Due Process Today

The judicial deference begun in *Nebbia* was soon transformed into a total withdrawal from review in economic regulation cases. The modern approach proceeds from principles such as those set forth in *Ferguson v. Skrupa* (1963), holding constitutional against a substantive due process attack a state law limiting the business of debt adjusting to lawyers exclusively. Justice Black, for the Court, stated: "We have returned to the original constitutional proposition that courts do not substitute their social and economic beliefs for the judgment of legislative bodies, who are elected to pass laws. Whether the legislature takes for its textbook, Adam Smith, Herbert Spencer, Lord Keynes, or some other, is no concern of ours. [R]elief if any be needed lies not with us but with the body constituted to pass laws."

This principle finds expression today in the rational basis approach which at least nominally is the test used for reviewing socioeconomic legislation. A law is presumed constitutional and the burden is on the challenging party to prove that the law is not rationally related to a permissible governmental interest. Further, "the existence of facts supporting the legislative judgment is to be presumed." *United States v. Carolene Products Co.* (1938). In practice, the review afforded is essentially no review at all. Illustrative is *North Dakota State Board of Pharmacy v. Snyder's Drug Stores, Inc.* (1973), where the Court upheld a state law requiring that applicants for pharmacy permits be limited either to those who were pharmacists or were corporations the majority of whose stock was owned by pharmacists. *Louis K. Liggett Co. v. Baldridge* (1928), had struck down very similar legislation. *Liggett* was overruled in *Snyder's Drug Stores*. The North Dakota legislature could rationally conclude that there was some relation between the legislative means and the end that pharmacies not be owned by those who knew nothing about them. This was so even though the means and the end were hardly a perfect fit.

It is important for the student to note that this deferential standard of due process review, or more precisely, judicial abdication, is used primarily for socioeconomic laws. It is not applicable when legislation burdens the exercise of fundamental rights. In the absence of a meaningful burden on a fundamental personal right, the student should use the deferential rational basis standard of review in analyzing the constitutionality of laws challenged on due process grounds. And, this means that the law is invariably upheld.

In discrete areas involving non-fundamental rights, however, a form of review slightly more exacting than the rational basis test may be used. Such a development appears to be in the making in the punitive damages area. A challenge to punitive damages awards based on both procedural and substantive due process involved a jury award of $10 million in punitive damages when the actual damages in the case awarded were only $19,000. Although the punitive damages award was sustained, the plurality opinion declined to adopt a rational basis approach that would sustain any punitive damages award no matter how large as long as it served some legitimate state interest in deterring or punishing wrongful conduct. The Due Process Clause of the Fourteenth Amendment imposes a substantive standard of reasonableness which acts as a limitation on punitive damages awards. *TXO Production v. Alliance Resources Corp.* (1993). Moreover, punitive damages cannot be left to the unreviewable discretion of a jury. A state law which prohibited judicial review of a punitive damages award was deemed to violate the Due Process Clause. *Honda Motor Co. v. Oberg* (1994). Building on these cases, the Court reversed an award by the Alabama courts of $2,000,000 in punitive damages and compensatory damages of $4000 in a case where a car manufacturer did not disclose that a car sold as new had actually been damaged prior to delivery. The punitive damages award constituted grossly excessive punishment prohibited by the Due Process Clause. Three guideposts were used to reach this result: (1) the degree of reprehensibility of the conduct, (2) the ratio between the punitive damages and the compensatory damages—here a ratio of 500 to 1, and (3) the difference between the punitive damages award and civil penalties in comparable cases. *BMW of North America, Inc. v. Gore* (1996).

Re-affirming the standards set forth in *BMW*, the Court held, 6–3, that a punitive damages award of $145 million when compensatory damages were just $1 million were excessive and violated due process.

The Court gave *BMW* further particularity by suggesting that few awards which exceeded a "single-digit ratio between punitive and compensatory damages" would satisfy due process. The Due Process Clause forbids "the imposition of grossly excessive or arbitrary punishments on a tortfeasor." Justice Kennedy, for the Court, ruled that "exacting judicial review" was appropriate to make sure a punitive damages award is not an "arbitrary deprivation of property." Evidence in the case indicated the punitive damages award was imposed in order to punish State Farm for allegedly fraudulent nation-wide conduct and lacked a "nexus to the specific harm suffered by the plaintiff." Justice Ginsburg, dissenting, objected to the Court's "foray into punitive damages;" such damages were within the domain of the states. Justice Scalia, dissenting, said *BMW* was incorrectly decided because the Due Process Clause provides no substantive protection against "excessive" or "unreasonable" punitive damages. *State Farm Mut. Auto. Ins. Co. v. Campbell* (2003).

c.   The Takings Alternative

Deprivations of property caused by governmental action obviously invoke consideration of the applicability of the Due Process Clause. Such situations could also invoke analysis of the "takings" alternative. Both the federal and state governments have the power of eminent domain, *i.e.* authority to take private property for public use. The Fifth Amendment specifically deals with takings by the federal government and provides that private property shall not be taken for public use without just compensation. The states are bound to provide compensation for takings of private property pursuant to the Just Compensation Clause of the Fifth Amendment as made applicable to the States through the Due Process Clause of the Fourteenth Amendment. *First English Evangelical Lutheran Church v. Los Angeles County* (1987).

The law on what constitutes a "taking" is fairly complex. A reasonable exercise of government power which may result in the reduction of property values does not in itself create a compensable "taking." "[W]hile property may be regulated to a certain extent, if regulation goes too far it will be recognized as a taking." *Pennsylvania Coal Co. v. Mahon* (1922). Factors which are relevant in determining whether a law is a "reasonable" regulation or a compensable taking include (1) the economic impact of the regulation on the party protesting it, (2) the extent to which the regulation interferes with distinct investment expectations, and (3) the nature of the governmental action, e.g. a physical occupation of the property. For example, a municipal zoning ordinance, enacted after the plaintiff has purchased the land in question, which limited the use of the land did not constitute a "taking." *Agins v. Tiburon* (1980). Residential uses for the land in question were still possible. The fact that the economically optimal use was foreclosed still did not extinguish beneficial use of the land. The significant

point was that the fundamental attributes of ownership remained intact.

A state law imposing a cap on the rent an oil
company can challenge the lessee-operator of a service station owned by that company cannot be
deemed an uncompensated taking just because the
law does not substantially advance the state's asserted interest in controlling retail gas prices:
"[T]he 'substantially advances' formula is not a
valid takings test." There must be an analysis of
the burden the law imposes on the claimant. Requiring courts to assay the effectiveness of a law
would involve examination of vast numbers of state
and federal regulations and would impose on courts
a task for which they are not suited. Such a doctrine would unwisely authorize courts to substitute
their predictions about the effectiveness of a law for
that of legislatures and administrative agencies.
Lingle v. Chevron (2005).

Just because a property owner has purchased his
property after notice of the enactment of state
wetlands regulations with respect to the property
did not preclude the property owner from challenging the regulations as a taking requiring compensation. A broad rule that a post-enactment purchaser
is deemed to have notice of an earlier state regulation and is, therefore, barred from claiming that the
regulation is a taking is repudiated. "The State may
not put so potent a Hobbesian stick into the Locke-
an bundle." Otherwise a post-enactment transfer of
title would free the state from any obligation to
revisit a land use restriction no matter how unrea-

sonable. If such were the rule, a state would be allowed "to put an expiration date on the Takings Clause." *Palazzolo v. Rhode Island* (2001).

Even a "temporary" loss of use of private property will constitute a taking requiring compensation for the period during which use of the property was denied. *First English Evangelical Lutheran Church* But one crucial determination is whether the regulation can be classified as a taking at all. Some of the more recent Supreme Court case law evidences a greater concern for property rights than in the past. It is possible that economic substantive due process may have taken new root in the Takings Clause.

A landowner who bought property on a South Carolina barrier island intending to develop it was prevented from doing so by state regulation banning construction in order to preserve the state's beaches. Despite the public interest served by the ban, there is a categorical rule in takings cases that total regulatory takings—depriving a property owner of all beneficial use of the property—must be compensated. An exception to this doctrine would exist if the state could show that regulation at issue is inherent in the landowner's title under state property or nuisance law. *Lucas v. South Carolina Coastal Council* (1992). *Lucas* dealt with a total taking. However, a temporary moratorium of 32 months on the development of property while a comprehensive land-use plan was being developed is not a *per se* categorical taking of the property. Whether a temporary moratorium effects a taking depends on the circumstances of the case. A contrary rule would impose a prohibitively expensive burden on the planning process and rush it as well in an effort to reduce the costs of compensating landowners. Indeed, such a rule might lead to the abandonment of a moratorium as a planning tool altogether. At the same time, the Court said it was not saying that a temporary moratorium could never constitute a taking. *Tahoe-Sierra Preservation Council, Inc. v. Tahoe Regional Planning Agency* (2002).

The Takings Clause also may limit the conditions government may impose on land use. When a California couple applied for a permit to tear down the house on their ocean-front property and build a new one, the state Coastal Commission said that a permit would be issued only on condition that the couple grant a public easement across the beach to allow people to move back and forth to other public beaches. The state might have denied the permit if it had determined that the proposed development would impair legitimate state concerns. But conditioning the permit would be valid only if the condition served the same governmental purpose as the ban. "[L]ack of nexus between the condition and the original purpose of the building restriction converts that purpose to something other than what it was." The Court invalidated the public easement condition imposed by the state as an uncompensated taking. *Nollan v. California Coastal Commission* (1987).

Although *Nollan* may have set the stage, a doctrine of unconstitutional conditions under the Takings Clause was clearly established in *Dolan v. City of Tigard* (1994). A hardware store owner in a small Oregon city sought a building permit to expand her store and pave a parking lot on her property. The city said it would grant the permit if the landowner would dedicate part of her property for flood control and traffic improvements. This involved dedication of land for a public greenway along a creek and a pedestrian bicycle pathway. Could the landowner be forced to choose between the building permit and her constitutional right to just compensation? The Court, per Chief Justice Rehnquist, struck down the condition 5–4.

Dolan established a two-part framework for analyzing whether a condition is a reasonable regulation or a taking requiring just compensation. The first part—based on *Nollan*—asks whether there is an essential nexus between a legitimate state interest and the condition at issue. The second inquiry requires "rough proportionality." The government must make an "individualized determination that the required dedication" is roughly proportionate to the impact of the proposed development. There was an essential nexus between legitimate government interests and the conditions imposed. No precise mathematical formula was required but the city had to make some effort to quantify its traffic findings. In summary, *Dolan's* two-part test for conditions sets forth a more demanding standard of review than rational basis. Justice Stevens complained in dissent in *Dolan* that the "regulatory takings" doctrine resurrected *Lochner*.

The possibility that economic substantive due process would commence a revival in the Court's Takings Clause jurisprudence was revived when the Court struck down a provision of the federal Coal Industry Retiree Health Benefits Act. The Court, 5–4, held that the part of that law which required companies formerly involved in coal mining retroactively to pay millions of dollars in lifetime health benefits to retired miners was invalid. *Eastern Enterprises v. Apfel* (1998).

Justice O'Connor for a plurality, consisting of herself, Chief Justice Rehnquist and Justices Thomas and Scalia, declared that the law at issue constituted a violation of the Takings Clause. The plaintiff here ceased its coal mining operations in 1965. The Coal Act substantially interferes with Eastern's reasonable investment backed expectations. Reaching back so far into the past to impose liability of great magnitude raises substantial questions of fairness.

Justice Kennedy concurred in the judgment but contended that the retroactive liability imposed in this case is one of those "rare instances" where a statute offends the limits imposed by substantive due process.

The Court's concern for property rights even when the economic value to the owner of those rights is quite minimal was shown in a case involving interest income generated by funds held in a state's Interest on Lawyers Trust Account (IOLTA) program. These funds were paid to a foundation which financed legal services for the poor in that state. The Court ruled, 5–4, per Chief Justice Rehnquist, that such funds were the private property of the owner of the principal and constituted property within the meaning of the Takings Clause. The Court left for another day whether a state's public use of these funds constituted a violation of the Takings Clause requiring "just compensation." *Phillips v. Washington Legal Foundation* (1998).

An IOLTA case following *Phillips* involved Washington state law requiring lawyers to place funds incapable of earning interest into IOLTA accounts. The Washington IOLTA program mandated that the interest on these IOLTA accounts be transferred to the Legal Foundation of Washington to be used for law-related charitable and educational purposes. The Court ruled, 5–4, per Justice Stevens that these requirements constituted a *per se* taking. Under *Phillips*, interest earned on IOLTA trust accounts is the private property of the owner of the principal. Nonetheless, no just compensation was owed to the owners. Just compensation is measured by the loss to the owner not by any gain running to the government. If there were no IOLTA program, the owners would not have earned any interest. Their funds would never have been placed in interest bearing accounts due to the high transactions costs. Therefore, the amount of just compensation owed to the owners was zero. *Brown v. Legal Foundation of Washington* (2003).

As the foregoing indicates, there is substantial
Supreme Court case law concerning what constitutes a taking. The meaning of the "public use"
requirement has received less attention. But the
Court provided a virtual road map for local governments on to how steer clear of violating the "public
use" requirement when the city of New London,
Connecticut formulated a carefully integrated development plan designed to stimulate employment,
increase the tax base and generally aid in the revi-
talization of an economically distressed area of the
city. To effectuate its plan, the city relied on a state
statute that authorized the use of the eminent
domain power in order to foster economic development. The city through its agent was able to buy
most of the real estate in the development plan
area. But several residents of the area refused to
sell. The properties owned by these residents were
not blighted nor in run-down condition but they
were sited within the development area. Condemnation proceedings were instituted against these recalcitrant owners. The owners' request that "a new
bright-line" rule be adopted that economic development could not qualify as a public use was rejected.
Economic development was a long-established and
legitimate public purpose. The argument of the
objecting owners that without "a new bright line,"
A's property could be transferred to B just because
B would "put the property to a more productive use
and thus pay more taxes" was deemed not descriptive of the case at hand. The key here was that the
property at issue here was part of a larger develop-

ment plan. The challenge brought by the individual owners had to be evaluated on the basis of the entire plan and "not on a piecemeal basis." The Court held, 5–4, per Justice Stevens, that the New London development plan was valid because it was comprehensive in character and formulated with appropriate deliberation. Given the "limited scope" of judicial review in such cases, the plan was entitled to judicial deference. The states, of course, were free to limit the exercise of the takings power if they chose. *Kelo v. City of New London* (2005).

Although joining in the Court's opinion in *Kelo*, Justice Kennedy observed that if a taking was designed "to favor a particular party with only incidental or pretextual public benefits," then a court using rational basis review should rule that such a taking would violate the "public use" requirement. Justice O'Connor, joined by Chief Justice Rehnquist and Justices Scalia and Thomas, dissenting, protested that as a result of the majority's decision in *Kelo* all real property in the country was under risk of condemnation. The beneficiaries of the decision would be those citizens with great influence and power resulting in the transferral of "property from those with fewer resources to those with more." Justice Thomas, in a separate dissent, urged a return to the original meaning of "public use" which he contended meant that government could only take property "if it actually uses or gives the public a legal right to use the property."

2. SUBSTANTIVE DUE PROCESS REVISITED: FUNDAMENTAL PERSONAL RIGHTS

a. In General

When federal or state legislation burdens the exercise of fundamental personal rights, the courts forsake the rational basis test in favor of more searching standards of review. When, for example, First Amendment rights are burdened by a law, the courts will not uphold the legislation even if it is rationally related to a permissible governmental objective. Rather, the courts will demand that government establish that the law is narrowly tailored to a compelling or substantial governmental interest.

Such heightened standards of review are most unlike the toothless rationality standard of review used presently in economic due process. In the fundamental rights area, the standard of review is truly searching. Nevertheless, even here, the standard employed is not always uniform. In many fundamental rights cases, the courts demand that the state establish that the law is necessary to a compelling state interest, *i.e.,* strict scrutiny. But, in other instances, the standard of review appears more tempered. Generally, it may be said that the degree of justification required of government tends to increase as the severity of the burden on the protected right increases. For example, a law totally prohibiting the exercise of the right is likely to be tested by a far more exacting standard than a law that only regulates the manner in which the right is exercised. See Chap. VII, *infra,* on freedom of expression.

But what are the "fundamental personal rights" that will trigger this exacting judicial scrutiny? The concept clearly includes express constitutional rights. For example, when First Amendment rights are burdened by state action, the courts will not apply simple rationality review, but will employ a more demanding standard of judicial review. It is also clear today that "fundamental personal rights" includes some non-enumerated rights. But it is very unclear how these rights are to be determined.

The modern debate is generally framed in terms of interpretivism versus noninterpretivism. Interpretivists argue that all constitutional rights must be found through interpretation of the Constitution itself. For example, freedom of association and belief can be implied from the express guarantees of the First Amendment. *N.A.A.C.P. v. Alabama* (1958). Interpretivists debate among themselves concerning the extent to which it is appropriate to go beyond the text of the Constitution to consider history and the constitutional structure and relationships established by the Framers (*e.g.,* the need to assure open political processes). They also debate over the closeness of the relationship demanded before new rights are implied from express rights. But, interpretivists all do agree that the only legitimate source for values and principles of decision is the Constitution itself. See J.H. Ely, *Democracy and Distrust* (1980).

Noninterpretivism, on the other hand, accepts that constitutional principles and norms can be found outside of the constitutional document. Noninterpretivists cite favorably early Court decisions such as *Meyer v. Nebraska* (1923) [state law barring the teaching of foreign languages to young children held to violate due process liberty of teachers and students] and *Pierce v. Society of the Sisters* (1925) [state law requiring all students to attend public schools held an unconstitutional interference with the liberty of parents to control their children's education]. See also *Skinner v. Oklahoma* (1942) [holding a law requiring sterilization of certain criminals violative of equal protection, but emphasizing the importance of marriage and procreation]. But noninterpretivists differ on what extra-constitutional sources are legitimate in discovering and fashioning these extra-constitutional rights. The two approaches which have received the most judicial acceptance are, first, reliance on values drawn from tradition and custom, and, second, a potentially dynamic approach identifying those values which are implicit in the concept of ordered liberty. Some commentators have urged the use of principles of morality, logic, and reason. See *e.g.,* M. Perry, *The Constitution, the Courts and Human Rights* (1982). Others simply argue that some interests are of such importance to the individual or society that they demand constitutional protection.

The basis for the departure from the rationality standard of review when fundamental personal rights are burdened is difficult to ascertain. If a law burdens an express constitutional right, perhaps more active review is understandable even though the right applies to state action only through its incorporation as part of Fourteenth Amendment liberty. But if the right is only judicially implied from the express rights, or is cut whole cloth through judicial use of extra-constitutional sources, what considerations justify judicial activism? In short, if *Lochner* was wrong, what makes close judicial scrutiny proper when the Court determines that the conduct being regulated involves an unenumerated fundamental personal right? After all, the *Lochner* Court invoked a right of contract implied from the liberty and property guarantees of the Fourteenth Amendment. For many critics of the fundamental rights approach, the invocation of a stricter standard of review at least where used to protect non-express interests such as privacy, travel, marriage or family life, is nothing more than substantive due process in new clothes. And, these critics continue, this use of the judicial power is nothing but natural law jurisprudence in a new form.

Some commentators have sought to justify active judicial scrutiny where fundamental personal rights are concerned by arguing that personal rights such as speech, association and belief, travel or privacy are more deserving of special judicial solicitude than purely economic property rights. They suggest a hierarchy or, at least, a tiering of constitutional rights. But see, *Lynch v. Household Finance Corp.* (1972), criticizing such a double standard. Sometimes this argument is bolstered by the claim that ordinary political processes may be inadequate to protect such personal rights. See *United States v. Carolene Products Co.* (1938) [Justice Stone's footnote 4]. A closely related justification is to focus on the judicial capabilities vis-a-vis the legislature. Legislatures have a higher degree of competence than courts in socioeconomic matters. But, the insularity and sensitivity of courts to minority beliefs and practices, it is argued, require that courts exercise special solicitude when personal rights are burdened.

A number of fundamental personal rights will be considered in the chapters on Equal Protection and First Amendment Rights. In the present chapter, the focus is on a range of interests involving marriage, family, sex, procreation, treatment, dying, and care and protection. Sometimes these interests are treated together under the single rubric of a Right of Privacy. In any case, it is in the context of these intimate interests that the problems generated by the "fundamental personal rights" approach to due process review become most apparent.

b. Contraception, Abortion and Sodomy

There is no right of privacy specifically guaranteed by the Constitution. Indeed, the Constitution does not mention marriage, family, or procreation. Nevertheless, in *Griswold v. Connecticut* (1965), the Court held, 7–2, that a criminal law prohibiting the use or the aiding or abetting of the use of contraceptives violated a constitutional right of privacy.

Justice Douglas, for the Court, was at pains to distinguish *Lochner* where the Court had sat as superlegislature. Unlike *Lochner*, which had involved only economic conditions, the Connecticut law "operates directly on an intimate relation between husband and wife and their physician's role in one aspect of that relation." The substantive due process of the *Lochner* era was to be distinguished, according to Justice Douglas, because, unlike the freedom of contract values cherished by Justice Peckham in *Lochner,* the privacy value had a textual constitutional source.

What was the textual source for a constitutional right of privacy? Justice Douglas found the right of privacy in the penumbras and emanations of the First, Third, Fourth, Fifth, and Ninth Amendments. In fact, Justice Douglas relied on two key concepts derived from the express rights. First, he emphasized a right of association flowing from the First Amendment which he concluded encompassed a protected status for the marital relationship. Second, enforcement of the criminal proscriptions against the use of contraceptives could involve police intrusion into the marital bedroom, which would implicate the privacy guarantees of the Third, Fourth, and Fifth Amendments. Since the state law employed means having a severe destructive impact on the privacy of the marital relationship, the Connecticut law was unconstitutionally overbroad.

Justice Douglas provided little explanation as to why the First Amendment's implied rights of political association extends to the marital relationship other than the fundamental importance to society of protecting the marital relationship. Further, since the defendants in the *Griswold* case were a physician and an official of the Planned Parenthood organization, there was no question in this case of the invasion of the marital bedroom. Why, then, did Justice Douglas feel the need to bring the right of privacy within the confines of the guarantees of the Bill of Rights? The answer is that Justice Douglas accepted Justice Black's premise that Fourteenth Amendment liberty incorporated all of the guarantees of the Bill of Rights but nothing else. In short, Justice Douglas tried to do homage to what today would be called an interpretivist approach. On the other hand, Justice Black, in dissent, remained faithful to the vaunted literalism of his *Adamson* dissent. The Bill of Rights was binding on the states by virtue of the enactment of the Fourteenth Amendment. But it was a more literal Bill of Rights that was binding on them. Justice Black said he liked his privacy as well as the next one, but this predilection did not mean that he could read privacy into the Bill of Rights when it was not there.

Concurring opinions in *Griswold* by Justices Goldberg and Harlan adopted a non-interpretivist approach in fashioning a right of privacy. The liberty guarantee, said Justice Goldberg, "is not restricted to rights specifically mentioned in the first eight amendments" but includes fundamental personal rights that have their source directly in the "liberty" clause of the Fourteenth Amendment. Justice

Goldberg cited the Ninth Amendment as a specific recognition that not all rights protected by the Constitution are specifically enumerated in the Constitution. How are fundamental rights to be identified? Justice Goldberg said the Court must look to the "traditions and (collective) conscience of our people" to determine fundamental principles, as well as experience regarding the requirements of a free society. For Justice Goldberg, "the entire fabric of the Constitution and the purposes that clearly underlie its specific guarantees demonstrate that the rights to marital privacy and to marry and raise a family are of a similar order and magnitude as the fundamental rights specifically protected."

Similarly, Justice Harlan contended that the Connecticut law violated basic values "implicit in the concept of ordered liberty." Fourteenth Amendment liberty, independent of any reliance on the Bill of Rights, embodied the traditional values of our society. Marital privacy was one of those values. In an earlier contraceptives decision, *Poe v. Ullman* (1961), Justice Harlan had stressed that tradition is a "living thing" and urged that certain liberty interests "require particularly careful scrutiny of the state needs asserted to justify their abridgment."

For the majority of the *Griswold* Court, a law that so intruded on protected marital privacy could not be justified on the basis of its rationality. As Justice White stated in a concurring opinion, when a law regulates "sensitive areas of liberty," the courts apply a strict scrutiny standard of review to the fundamental right protected by the liberty clause of the Fourteenth Amendment. The law must serve a subordinating state interest which is compelling and no less drastic means must be available to the state, if the law under review is to be upheld. In the *Griswold* situation, the state interest in discouraging extra-marital relations could not justify the intolerable burden placed on the marital relationship especially in light of the adultery and fornication laws available to protect the state interests.

Griswold v. Connecticut is firmly grounded in the traditional values associated with the marital relationship. Privacy, as fashioned in *Griswold,* is essentially an associational right born of the relation recognized by the state between marital partners. As such, it does not provide a basis for extending a right of privacy to non-marital relationships or personal sexual privacy generally. A key step toward the judicial recognition of an expanded right of sexual privacy came in *Eisenstadt v. Baird* (1972), holding unconstitutional a Massachusetts statute prohibiting the distribution of contraceptives to unmarried persons. While the case was decided on equal protection grounds, Justice Brennan, for the Court, provided a basis for breaking the privacy right loose from its marital moorings: "[T]he marital couple is not an independent entity with a mind and heart of its own, but an association of two individuals each with a separate intellectual and emotional make-up. If the right of privacy means anything, it is the right of the individual, married or single, to be free from unwarranted governmental intrusion into matters so fundamentally affecting a person as the decision whether to bear or beget a child."

It was this expanded concept of personal privacy that was to find expression in *Roe v. Wade* (1973), invalidating, 7–2, a Texas law prohibiting abortion except to save the life of the mother. Adopting a noninterpretivist position, Justice Blackmun for the Court concluded: "This right of privacy, whether it is founded in the Fourteenth Amendment's concept of personal liberty and restrictions upon state action, as we feel it is, or, as the District Court determined, in the Ninth Amendment's reservation of rights to the people is broad enough to encompass a woman's decision whether or not to terminate her pregnancy." What was the basis for this conclusion? Justice Blackmun cited all the detrimental consequences to a single woman such as Jane Roe which might result from being denied the ability to terminate an unwanted pregnancy. This suggested to many commentators that Justice Blackmun was asserting that the importance of an interest to a person was sufficient in itself to give the value a constitutional dimension—at least when enjoyment of the interest involved was being prohibited or burdened by state action.

The right of personal privacy, Justice Blackmun noted, is not absolute but must be considered in light of the state's interest in regulation. Given the fundamental character of the right involved, and the severity of a criminal penalty on the right, state limitations could be justified only by a "compelling state interest," and the state enactment "must be narrowly drawn to express only the legitimate state interests at stake." While the Court might have held simply that the Texas abortion law proscribing all abortions except those necessary to save the life of the mother was unconstitutionally overbroad, Justice Blackmun instead fashioned a trimester test. This approach attracted scathing criticism. The trimester approach was seen as a statute in the guise of a judicial opinion and therefore, in effect, a judicial usurpation of the role and power of the legislature.

In applying the strict scrutiny standard, Justice Blackmun initially dismissed the claim that the rights of the fetus to life should be included in the balance. The term "person" in the Fourteenth Amendment Due Process Clause, he reasoned, was not intended by its Framers to include the unborn. Turning instead to the state interests supporting abortion laws, Justice Blackmun concluded that the state has a compelling interest in maternal health, permitting reasonable regulation of abortions, only after the first trimester. Prior to that time, abortion produces less mortality than normal childbirth. During this initial trimester, "the attending physician in consultation with his patient is free to determine without regulation by the state, that, in his medical judgment, the patient's pregnancy should be terminated." Critics of *Roe,* however, ask why the state may not regulate abortion procedures during the first trimester in order to promote the health of the mother. Why are only the mortality tables relevant?

Justice Blackmun then went on to hold that the government has a compelling interest in the potentiality of life from the point of viability, *i.e.,* when the fetus can live apart from its mother: "If the State is interested in protecting fetal life after viability, it may go so far as to proscribe abortion during that period except when it is necessary to preserve the life or health of the mother." Again, it may be asked, why does the state interest in potential life become "compelling" only at viability? Certainly, a legislature could reasonably conclude that potential life begins at conception. In any case, under the *Roe* trimester standards, the Texas statute clearly swept too broadly.

For Justice Rehnquist, this decisional emperor clearly had no clothes. While accepting the premise that the Fourteenth Amendment guarantee of liberty includes more than the rights set forth in the Bill of Rights, that liberty is protected only against deprivation without due process. Social and economic legislation is to be judged solely by whether the law "has a rational relation to a valid state objective."

In the years following *Roe,* its opponents continued to insist that abortion was a non-constitutional issue. The Court was repeatedly asked to reconsider its decision and return the fashioning of abortion law to the state legislatures. The Court regularly rejected the invitation, reaffirming its holding in

Roe. See, *e.g.*, *City of Akron v. Akron Center for Reproductive Health, Inc.* (1983). The Court was required to apply *Roe* and its trimester scheme to a variety of state regulations which limited access to abortions. Some were upheld, but most were rejected under the stringent standards of *Roe*.

In 1989, the Court upheld a Missouri state abortion law which presented a major challenge to *Roe v. Wade*. In *Webster v. Reproductive Health Services* (1989), a three-Justice plurality, consisting of Justices Kennedy, Rehnquist and White, would have overruled the trimester framework. Justice Scalia, although also an advocate of scrapping the trimester framework, would have overruled *Roe* entirely. Much to the chagrin of Justice Scalia, Justice O'Connor, one of the new conservative appointees to the Court, saved the fragile shell that *Roe* had now become.

In 1992, the Court in *Planned Parenthood of Southeastern Pennsylvania v. Casey* considered yet another challenge to *Roe*. Retirements on the Court gave new hope to its opponents that *Roe*, clearly weakened by *Webster*, would at long last collapse altogether. Two stalwart adherents of *Roe*—Justices Marshall and Brennan—had left the Court. They were replaced respectively by Justices Thomas and Souter. Only Justice O'Connor's vote had saved *Roe* in *Webster*. Would the two new Justices provide the majority for overruling it altogether?

In the end result, a joint opinion for the Court, authored by Justices O'Connor, Kennedy and Souter, declared their adherence to the core—but not the whole—of *Roe.* The joint opinion reduced the protection afforded the woman's abortion decision. Why didn't the joint opinion reverse it altogether? The Court's answer to this was based in part on a fidelity to *stare decisis* and in part on a desire to protect the institutional image of the Court by not retreating under fire. Changing societal circumstances may require new constitutional responses and warrant departures from a rigid adherence to *stare decisis.* That was not the case here for several reasons. A whole generation had relied on *Roe* and structured its conduct accordingly. Moreover, the factual background underpinnings of *Roe* remained constant as had society's understanding of it.

Abortion was a unique act involving the "most intimate and personal choices a person may make in a lifetime." This dimension of personal liberty was what *Roe* sought to protect. The joint opinion in *Casey* based the constitutional protection for abortion in the liberty protected by the Fourteenth Amendment. The student will note that, despite the formal allegiance to *Roe,* the abortion decision in *Casey* does not use the terminology of "fundamental rights" in general or "right to privacy" in particular.

The joint opinion combined with support provided by the separate opinions of Justices Blackmun and Stevens forged a fragile majority of five to save *Roe's* "essential holding" which was described as having three parts: First, a woman has a right to choose to have an abortion prior to viability of the fetus and that choice can be exercised without undue interference by the state. Second, the state has a right to restrict abortions after fetal viability so long as the state regulation provides an exception to those pregnancies which endanger a woman's life or health. Third, from the very beginning of the pregnancy, the state has an interest in protecting the health of the woman *and* the life of the fetus that may become a person.

The joint opinion in *Casey* rejected the trimester scheme. Opinions by Justices Rehnquist and Scalia also rejected it, establishing a majority for repudiating the trimester scheme. This prompted Justice Scalia, who concurred in part and dissented in part, to characterize the Court's version of *stare decisis* as "keep-what-you-want-and-throw-away the rest." Nor was the trimester scheme the only part of *Roe* scuttled by the joint opinion. The strict scrutiny standard was also abandoned. In its place, the plurality said it would use an undue burden test. What is an undue burden? The joint opinion described it: "An undue burden exists, and therefore a provision of law is invalid, if its purpose or effect is to place a substantial obstacle in the path of a woman seeking an abortion before the fetus attains viability."

How does the undue burden test work in practice? The Pennsylvania Abortion Control Act which was under review in *Casey* contained five provisions which were challenged as violative of *Roe*. Four of the five provisions were held not to constitute an undue burden:

—A provision that a woman seeking an abortion must give her informed consent with an exception for medical emergencies prior to the abortion procedure was not an undue burden. Prior decisions had validated such a regulation so long as it was not designed to coerce the woman's choice. Indeed, informed consent was standard medical procedure.

—A provision that a woman be provided with certain information prescribed by the state 24 hours before the abortion proceeding was performed was not an undue burden. The state was permitted to insist that reflection precede the abortion decision. Insofar as *City of Akron v. Akron Center for Reproductive Health* (1983) had invalidated a 24 hour waiting period, it was repudiated. The Court did concede that some applications of this provision might yield a different result, *i.e.*, a poor woman who would not be able to have an abortion because she could not afford the expense of a waiting period. But this did not render the provision facially unconstitutional.

—A provision requiring the consent of at least one parent or, failing that, permission by a court in the case of a minor seeking an abortion was held not to be an undue burden. Such provisions had been upheld in the past. See, *infra*, *Hodgson v. Minnesota* (1990); *Ohio v. Akron Center for Reproductive Health* (1990).

—A provision that physicians give certain specified information about the nature of the abortion procedure, its health risks and the gestational age of the fetus was not an undue burden. The information in question was truthful and not misleading. The key to the conclusion that mandating such information does not constitute an undue burden is that the woman is still permitted to make the ultimate choice—to have an abortion. Even if the state seeks to promote childbirth, all the state is doing is to make sure that she is aware of a competing choice. To the extent that *City of Akron* and *Thornburgh v. American College of Obstetricians and Gynecologists* (1986) held otherwise, they were repudiated.

—The only regulation struck down as an undue burden in *Casey* dealt with spousal notification. Requiring a woman to secure a statement that she has notified her husband of her decision to have an abortion is an undue burden. Such a requirement places a substantial obstacle in the path of a woman since fear of spousal abuse might inhibit the abortion decision altogether.

The Court's holding on what was and what was not an undue burden put in sharp relief the difference between the undue burden standard of *Casey* and the strict scrutiny standard of *Roe*. State mandates requiring a 24 hour waiting period and that specified information be provided the woman by the physician had been struck down in *Thornburgh* and *City of Akron*. In those cases, the strict scrutiny standard had been employed. Clearly—at least as used in *Casey*—the undue burden standard was far more generous to state regulation of abortion than *Roe's* strict scrutiny standard.

Four Justices—Rehnquist, Thomas, Scalia and White—would have reversed *Roe* in its entirety. Justice Blackmun would have adhered to *Roe* in its entirety. Although an adherent of *Roe*, Justice Stevens said he would invalidate the very regulations upheld by the joint opinion and he would do so using the undue burden standard. This is because in applying the undue burden test, Stevens would weigh the woman's constitutional interest in deciding whether to go to full term more heavily than the state's non-constitutional interest in life. This approach may prove to have significance in the future. Justice Scalia castigated the "inherently standardless" quality of the undue burden inquiry. But paradoxically, the imprecision of the undue burden test may enable it to endure as the measure of regulation in the abortion area.

In *Stenberg v. Carhart* (2000) the Court, per Justice Breyer, 5–4, invalidated a Nebraska statute prohibiting "partial birth" abortions at any stage of pregnancy using the "undue burden" test. For the first time, the undue burden test supplanted the strict scrutiny standard of review in a Supreme Court case striking down an abortion regulation. The statute prohibited "partial birth abortions" which were described as the partial delivery of a "living unborn child before killing the unborn child and completing the delivery" except to save the life of the mother. The statute was fatally flawed. The statute lacked a requisite health exception for the mother since it forbade the use of certain procedures even when medically safer. The state was really forcing "many women into more risky situations" and was thereby impermissibly imposing significant health risks on women. The law also "unduly burdened" the abortion decision since the statute used language that could be interpreted to ban even the most frequently used method for performing pre-viability second trimester abortions. The consequence of this was to chill the use of this procedure by abortion providers. The dissenters vigorously contended that there was a moral difference between the abortion proscribed by the Nebraska law and other abortion procedures which a state could properly consider. Justice Scalia, dissenting, contended that the result of the Court's decision would be to give "live-birth abortion free rein."

A significant body of abortion case law has addressed the constitutional issues raised by the privacy rights of minors. While the Court has consistently recognized that "[m]inors as well as adults are protected by the Constitution and possess constitutional rights," it has also established that "the power of the state to control the conduct of children reaches beyond the scope of its authority over adults." *Carey v. Population Services International* (1977). Thus, the Court has employed a less demanding standard than strict scrutiny in reviewing state legislation limiting the access of minors to contraceptives and abortions. Nevertheless, in *Carey,* the Court struck down a total prohibition against non-prescription sales of contraceptives to minors since the law served no significant state

interest not present in the case of an adult. Similarly, a blanket requirement in state law that a parent
has an "absolute veto" over the abortion decision of
a minor child is unconstitutional. *Planned Parenthood of Central Missouri v. Danforth* (1976). On the
other hand, some parental or judicial consent sub-
stitutes for immature minors are constitutional.

A Minnesota parental notification statute which
required that a physician notify both parents of a
female minor seeking an abortion but which did
not provide for a judicial bypass was unconstitutional. Requiring notification of both parents serves
no legitimate state interest and could have harmful
effects on the pregnant minor—particularly in the
case of divorced or separated parents or of an abusive or dysfunctional family. However, the Minnesota statute also provided that a judicial bypass
procedure would go into effect if the dual parent
notification requirement was struck down. This bypass provision saved the statute. The judicial bypass procedure enables the minor to show a court
that she possesses sufficient maturity to make an
informed choice or it may allow her to show that
parental notification was not in her best interests.
Consequently, the bypass procedure corrects the
infirmities which would have otherwise rendered
the statute unconstitutional. *Hodgson v. Minnesota*
(1990). A Montana parental notification statute
which provides for a judicial bypass only on a showing by the minor that such notification is not in her
best interests is constitutional; the statute was not
unconstitutional because it did not provide for a

bypass when an *abortion* would be in the minor's best interests. *Lambert v. Wicklund* (1997).

Funding

A significant limitation on the privacy rights forged in *Roe* is indicated in the abortion funding cases. It is one thing to hold that the constitutional right of privacy inhibits the state's power to limit the abortion decision of a woman. However, it is another and different step to say that the right is not only protected but the state is obligated to make the right effective if the woman is indigent. Thus, in *Maher v. Roe* (1977), the Court held, per Powell, J., that the state is under no constitutional obligation to provide public funding for abortions of state welfare recipients. And this is true even though the state provides funding for normal childbirth: "The Connecticut regulation places no obstacles—absolute or otherwise—in the pregnant woman's path to an abortion. An indigent woman who desires an abortion suffers no disadvantage as a consequence of Connecticut's decision to fund childbirth. While the state may have made childbirth a more attractive alternative than abortion, it has imposed no restriction on the woman's decision to terminate her pregnancy that was not already present." But Justice Brennan declared in dissent: "What is critical is that the State has inhibited [the indigent woman's] fundamental right to make that choice free from state interference." In the view of the dissenters, the financial pressure exerted on the woman to bear the child constitutes a restraint making the exercise of the right more difficult and

thus infringes the fundamental right established by
Roe.

The principle of *Maher v. Roe* was pushed even
further in *Harris v. McRae* (1980). The Hyde
Amendment prohibits the use of federal funds even
for medically necessary abortions. Justice Stewart
invoked the principle of *Maher* and concluded for
the Court that the Hyde Amendment "places no
governmental obstacle in the path of a woman who
chooses to terminate her pregnancy, but rather, by
means of unequal subsidization of abortion and
other medical services, encourages alternative activity deemed in the public interest." In short, the *Roe*
right does not include "a constitutional entitlement
to the financial resources to avail herself of the full
range of protected choices." In dissent, Justice
Brennan protested that both "by design and in
effect" government was coercing indigent pregnant
women to bear children that they did not want.
Justice Stevens, dissenting, objected that the government was not employing neutral criteria in dis-
tributing its medical benefits: "If a woman has a
constitutional right the exercise of that right cannot
provide the basis for the denial of a [medical] benefit to which she would otherwise be entitled." Having decided to provide medically necessary benefits
to indigent women, the government could not constitutionally exclude benefits for the exercise of
what was, after all, a protected right. The majority
in *Harris v. McRae* did not agree.

Webster v. Reproductive Health Services (1989)
made clear just how little in the way of obligation is

imposed on the state to make the abortion decision effective—a Missouri state law prohibiting public employees and public facilities from being used for facilitating abortions not necessary to save the life of the mother was upheld. States are not obliged to commit any resources to facilitate abortions.

The Court has thus far rejected efforts to extend the privacy right protecting contraceptive and abortion choices to sexual privacy or matters of personal autonomy generally. *Bowers v. Hardwick* (1986) upheld, 5–4, a Georgia statute criminalizing sodomy against a constitutional attack by a homosexual engaged in homosexual activity in the privacy of his home. There was no fundamental due process right conferred on homosexuals to engage in sodomy. At the time the *Bowers* case came before the Court, 24 states and the District of Columbia had statutes punishing sodomy. It was insupportable, therefore, to contend that homosexual conduct was " 'deeply rooted in this Nation's history and tradition' or 'implicit in the concept of ordered liberty'." There should be "great resistance to expanding the substantive reach" of due process. Having disposed of the fundamental rights issue, the Georgia sodomy law was upheld as a rationally based moral choice by its citizens. In *Roe v. Wade,* the Court expressed doubt that the right of privacy could be extended to include the unlimited right to do with one's body as one pleases. The Court's treatment of private homosexual relations in *Bowers* confirms these doubts.

In *Bowers*, Justice Blackmun wrote a strong dissent, joined by three other Justices. The issue was not a fundamental right to engage in homosexual sodomy but a far more inclusive right to be let alone. Justice Powell, concurring, had suggested that the prohibition against cruel and unusual punishment might have been violated if there had been a criminal prosecution given the severe sentence which the state statute imposed. Justice Stevens, dissenting, criticized Georgia's prosecution of homosexual but not heterosexual sodomy. Liberty should be the same for all the state's citizens. Georgia had failed to demonstrate any valid or legitimate basis for targeting homosexuals alone. The dissent was a portent of what was to come.

Justice White's careful effort in *Bowers to* deny Fourteenth Amendment due process protection to individual choice in matters of sexual relations was reversed, per Justice Kennedy, 6–3, in *Lawrence v. Texas* (2003). The *Lawrence* Court struck down a Texas law which made it a crime for two persons of the same sex to engage in sodomy. The Texas law differed from the Georgia law in that the Texas law by its terms prohibited sodomy only when the participants were of the same sex. Relying on the Supreme Court's elaborations on the meaning of the word liberty in the Due Process Clause since *Griswold v. Connecticut*, the Court ruled that the Texas statute was invalid because it interfered with the due process right of individuals to control intimate choices with respect to adult sexual relations. Emphasizing that liberty involved the autonomy of the person, the Court repeated and re-affirmed the language in *Casey* that "the heart of liberty is the right to define one's own concept of existence, of meaning, of the universe, and of the mystery of human life." *Lawrence v. Texas* was remarkable not only substantively but doctrinally. No reference was made to the ruling in *Bowers* that there was no fundamental right to engage in homosexual sodomy. Nor was reference made to a fundamental right to privacy. Similarly, no reference was made to the strict scrutiny standard of review. Indeed, none of the established standards of review are referred to in the majority opinion in *Lawrence*.

The Court in *Lawrence* did, however, explain that *Bowers* had been undermined by time and contradicted by history. Sodomy in general rather then homosexual sodomy had been the target of state legislation in the nineteenth century. Homosexual conduct had been accorded new protection by societies similar to our own. Reference in that regard was made to a decision by the European Court of Human Rights. Recent tradition and new legal developments in law in this country demonstrated an "emerging awareness" that liberty extended significant protection to adults with respect to the manner in which they conduct their sexual relationships. Furthermore, *Romer v. Evans*, although decided on equal protection grounds, also made the holding in *Bowers* highly questionable. Significantly, Justice Kennedy quoted *Romer*: "Equality of treatment and the right to demand respect for conduct protected by the substantive guarantee of liberty are linked in important respects." The essence of the *Lawrence* opinion was that the Texas law criminalizing homosexual sodomy served to further no legitimate interest on the part of the state which could justify the intrusion the law presented to the lives and choices of the individuals affected, regardless of their sexual orientation.

Justice O'Connor, while concurring in the judgment, wrote a separate opinion indicating that she reached the same result as the majority opinion by relying on the Equal Protection Clause. She would not, therefore, overrule *Bowers*. Since the Texas legislation targeted homosexual conduct and not identical conduct engaged in by heterosexuals, the Texas law represented a state effort to harm a politically unpopular group. Such a state interest was illegitimate and required the use of a "more searching form of rational basis review" under which the law was invalid.

Justice Scalia, joined by Chief Justice Rehnquist and Justice Thomas, dissenting, criticized the Court for ignoring *stare decisis* and for a disingenuous use of rational basis review. Basically, Scalia accused the majority of achieving the result that would obtain from a holding that the right involved here was a fundamental one warranting the strict scrutiny standard of review while actually using what he assumed was a rational basis standard of review. In fact, the majority had been silent on what standard of review it in fact had used. In addition, Scalia reasoned that the "emerging awareness" of a right by adults to engage in consensual sexual relationships without state interference was by definition not "deeply rooted in the nation's history and tradition." Finally, Scalia attacked the majority's reliance on foreign law as irrelevant. In contrast, *Bowers* had not relied on values shared with any nation but our own. The state interest served by the Texas law at issue was a legitimate one. The Texas law rationally furthered the state interest in advancing the belief of its citizens that the sexual behavior that the law proscribed was immoral and should be subject to criminal sanction.

Both Justice Kennedy for the majority and Justice O'Connor in her concurrence disclaimed any intention to rule on the constitutional merits of state bans on same sex marriage. Nevertheless, Justice Scalia in dissent prophesied that *Lawrence* had opened the door for extending constitutional protection to same sex couples seeking to marry. In fact, *Lawrence* bore fruit rather quickly but in the context, at least formally, of state rather than federal constitutional law. In *Goodridge v. Department of Public Health* (Mass. 2003), the Supreme Judicial Court of Massachusetts held on the basis of the state constitution that Massachusetts could not deny the benefits of civil marriage to same sex couples. Although acknowledging that *Lawrence v. Texas* had not ruled on the constitutionality of state same sex marriage bans, the *Goodridge* opinion pointed to the declaration in *Lawrence* that the Fourteenth Amendment prohibited government interference into consensual adult expressions of intimacy or choice of intimate partner. Whether *Lawrence* will yield a federal constitutional law counterpart to *Goodridge* is a question that is now open.

In short, *Lawrence* has not resolved all of the constitutional law questions which laws disadvantaging gay people present. For example, the question of the standard of review which should be applied to such legislation is still unsettled. However, there is no question that *Lawrence* has greatly strengthened the ability of gay people to obtain constitutional protection against governmental actions which discriminate against them. *Lawrence* is a Due Process Clause counterpart to *Romer v. Evans*, *infra*, an earlier important development in this area under Equal Protection Clause.

c. Marital and Familial Rights

A right to marry has been judicially accepted as a guarantee of due process. Thus, in *Loving v. Virginia* (1967), a state statute prohibiting interracial marriage was struck down on both equal protection and due process grounds. Chief Justice Warren declared: "The freedom to marry has long been recognized as one of the vital personal rights essential to the orderly pursuit of happiness by free men. Marriage is one of the 'basic civil rights of man,' fundamental to our very existence and survival." So vital a right could not be abridged by statutes designed to accomplish invidious racial discrimination. Similar issues are often disposed of by the Court under the rubric of equal protection rather than due process. See *Zablocki v. Redhail* (1978), where Justice Stewart, concurring, referred to the Court's use of equal protection doctrine as "no more than substantive due process by another name." The calculus for determining which clause will be used is not readily apparent.

The Court has stated: "This Court has long recognized that freedom of personal choice in matters of marriage and family life is one of the liberties protected by the Due Process Clause of the Fourteenth Amendment." *Cleveland Board of Education v. LaFleur* (1974). When a law significantly burdens the exercise of critical choices in marriage and family life, the rationality standard of review is inappropriate and a stricter standard of review should be used.

Thus, in *Moore v. East Cleveland* (1977), a pluralityt stated: "[W]hen the government intrudes on choices concerning family living relationships, this Court must examine carefully the importance of the governmental interest advanced and the extent to which they are served by the challenged regulation." This standard, which sounds more like the intermediate standard of review than the strict scrutiny standard, was invoked by the plurality to strike down an ordinance limiting housing occupancy to members of a single family. Family was defined in such a way as to exclude the grandchild of a grandmother living in the house. In *Moore,* Justice Powell in a plurality opinion, did not invoke the right of privacy but instead adopted a substantive due process approach to protect "family rights."

The *Moore* facts, reasoned Powell, J., unlike *Lochner,* involved the basic values of our society. "Our decisions establish that the Constitution protects the sanctity of the family precisely because the institution of the family is deeply rooted in this Nation's history and tradition. It is through the family that we inculcate and pass down many of our most cherished values, moral and cultural." Nor was this constitutional protection limited to the nuclear family. The tradition of the extended family "has roots equally venerable and equally deserving of constitutional recognition."

In *Moore,* the city tried to defend its occupancy limitation ordinance as a reasonable means of preventing overcrowding with its ensuing burden on the community. While these were legitimate goals, the ordinance only marginally served them. Powell noted, for example, that the ordinance would permit a husband, wife and unmarried children to live together even "if the family contains a half-dozen licensed drivers each with his or her own car."

The four dissenters in *Moore* challenged both the judicial activism of the substantive due process methodology employed by Powell as well as the conclusions derived therefrom. In dissent, Justice White argued that the "judge-made constitutional law, employed by the plurality would intrude excessively into the ability of Congress and the state legislatures to respond to a changing social order." He warned: "What the deeply rooted traditions of the country are is arguable; which of them deserves the protection of the Due Process Clause is even more debatable." Justice Stewart, dissenting, questioned whether the interest of a person in sharing living quarters with a relative was of constitutional dimension. "To equate this interest with the fundamental decisions to marry and to bear and raise children is to extend the limited substantive contours of the Due Process Clause beyond recognition."

In *Michael H. & Victoria D. v. Gerald D.* (1989), a California statute which established a presumption that a child born to a married woman living with her husband is a child of the marriage if the husband is not impotent or sterile was upheld against a substantive due process claim. The statute was upheld despite the fact that blood tests performed on the putative natural father indicated a 98.07% probability of paternity, that the natural father had established a parental relationship with the child, and that the natural father had brought a filiation action to establish paternity and a right to visitation. In a plurality opinion, Justice Scalia, rejected the substantive due process claims of the natural father. Justice Scalia said that what was decisive was that the states did not in fact confer substantive parental rights on the "natural father of a child conceived within and born into an extant marital union that wishes to embrace the child." Michael H. had failed to prove a liberty interest. Persons in the situation of *Michael H.* and his married lover had never been "treated as a protected family unit under the historic practices of our society."

Justice Scalia would have gone further in *Michael H.* and fashioned a new and restrictive test for substantive due process. He argued in a footnote, in which he was joined only by Chief Justice Rehnquist, that the inquiry to determine whether a right was fundamental for substantive due process purposes should "refer to the most specific level at which a relevant tradition protecting, or denying protection to, the asserted right can be identified." In his view, there was such a specific tradition and it "unqualifiedly" denied protection to a parent in the situation of Michael H.

In *Reno v. Flores* (1993), Justice Scalia's analysis for the Court looked very much like his "most specific level" approach even though its use was not acknowledged. At issue in *Flores* was an Immigration and Naturalization Service (INS) regulation stating that alien juveniles in custody and facing deportation could be released to parents, guardians and adult relatives not in INS detention. In certain unusual and compelling circumstances, the juvenile could be released to another adult. Otherwise the INS could place the child in a government custodial facility which met federal standards. The alien juveniles launched a facial challenge to the regulation on the ground that it violated their right to "freedom from physical restraint." The Court upheld the regulation.

Justice Scalia asserted that the right of alien juveniles in *Flores* was not a fundamental right to freedom from physical restraint but a far narrower and hitherto unrecognized right. "[T]he right at

Scalias narrow
defining of the
purported right

issue is the alleged right of a child who has no
available parent, close relative, or legal guardian,
and for whom the government is responsible, to be
placed in the custody of a willing-and-able private
custodian rather than of a government-operated or
government-selected child-care institution." The
novelty of the claim was itself evidence that substantive due process did not require it. This alleged
right was certainly not " 'so rooted in the traditions
and conscience of our people as to be ranked as
fundamental.' " This would be so even if the right
at issue were characterized as the alien juvenile's
fundamental right to an individualized hearing to
ascertain whether private placement would be in
the juvenile's *best interest*. No such fundamental
right exists as long as the government was providing adequate care for the alien juvenile. Substantive
due process does not require the government to
substitute private placement for institutional custody where possible.

In *Michael H.*, Justice Scalia's narrow "most specific level" approach to substantive due process had
only attracted the support of Chief Justice Rehnquist. *Reno v. Flores* suggests at first blush that it
may have more of a future than was originally
thought. But it should be noted that Justice O'Connor, joined by Justice Souter, concurring in *Flores*,
recognized that there *was* a core liberty interest in
freedom from institutional confinement. Nevertheless, they felt that the INS regulation survived the
heightened scrutiny that substantive due process
imposed. Moreover, in dissent, Justices Blackmun

and Stevens asserted that the only novelty in *Flores* was Scalia's analysis. They objected to the Court's "narrow reading of the right at issue." The right at issue was nothing less than the right not to be detained at all. In short, the effort begun by Justice Scalia in *Michael H.*, and continued in *Flores*, to make substantive due process a less fertile source for the recognition of new constitutional rights and interests can still be expected to meet substantial resistance on the Court.

In *Troxel v. Granville* (2000), the Court re-affirmed the fundamental right of a parent to rear her children. A Washington state statute permitted any person to petition the court for visitation rights at any time if it was in the best interests of the child. Grandparents successfully relied on the law in the lower state court to gain greater visitation rights to the grandchildren than their mother wished. A plurality opinion per Justice O'Connor, joined by Rehnquist, Ginsburg and Breyer, concluded that the statute, as applied, unconstitutionally trespassed on a parent's fundamental right to make decisions about the "care, custody and control" of her children. The plurality noted that the mother had not sought to cut off visitation rights on the part of the grandparents. In addition, the state lower court had failed to give sufficient consideration to the presumption that a parent will act in the best interests of her child. The plurality stated that the "breathtakingly broad" law exceeded the limits set by the Due Process Clause of the Fourteenth Amendment and should be subjected to heightened scrutiny. Justice Thomas, concurring, contended that the plurality should have made it clear that the strict scrutiny standard of review applied since a fundamental right was involved— the right of parents to rear their children.

d. Right to Care and Protection

As the abortion funding cases indicate, the Court has generally insisted that there is no affirmative constitutional duty on the part of government to effectuate rights. Yet a right to care and protection by the government has occasionally been recognized. In the limited context where the State has custody of an individual, the Due Process Clause has been found to impose a duty on government to assume a measure of responsibility for that person's care and well-being. *Youngberg v. Romeo* (1982) held that a profoundly retarded individual who had been involuntarily committed to a state institution for the mentally retarded had some substantive due process rights. When the state institutionalizes such a wholly dependent person, the state then has a duty to provide certain services and care. The person in the state's custody has a liberty interest which would have to be balanced against the relevant state interests. In the context of *Youngberg,* the liberty interest would require the state to provide "minimally adequate or reasonable training to ensure safety and freedom from undue restraint." The judgment of medical professionals in such circumstances would be presumptively valid. That judgment could be validly superseded only when there was a showing of a "substantial departure from accepted professional judgment."

The Rehnquist Court has been unwilling to extend the *Youngberg v. Romeo* analysis very far. Thus, the state has been held not to deprive a child of his "liberty" when it failed to protect him from the physical abuse of his father. Complaints about physical abuse of the child had been made known to the county department of social services. Yet when the child was so badly beaten by his father that he suffered permanent brain damage, the state was held not to be sufficiently implicated to violate the due process guarantee. Chief Justice Rehnquist said that, unlike *Youngberg*, the harms suffered by the child did not occur while he was in the state's custody but while he was in the custody of his natural father. Even though the county department of social services had investigated the case, and might have removed the child, there was no affirmative right to government aid. The father was not a state actor: "While the State may have been aware of the dangers that Joshua faced in the free world, it played no part in their creation, nor did it do anything to render him more vulnerable to them." In dissent, Justice Brennan protested the Court's failure to understand "that inaction can be every bit as abusive of power as action, that oppression can result when a State undertakes a vital duty and then ignores it." *DeShaney v. Winnebago County Dept. of Social Services* (1989).

A city sanitary worker died of asphyxia while working in a manhole. The city had not trained its employees about the dangers of working in sewers nor had it provided safety equipment or even warnings. The city employee did not have a right under the Due Process Clause to be free from unreasonable risk of harm and to protection from the city's deliberate indifference. Only the most egregious executive action can be viewed as arbitrary from a constitutional perspective. The appropriate level of resources to be allocated to the training of sewer maintenance employees is a matter for local government and not for the federal judiciary. "[T]he Due Process Clause does not impose an independent federal obligation upon municipalities to provide certain minimal levels of safety and security in the workplace." *Collins v. City of Harker Heights* (1992).

A person's substantive due process right to life and personal security is not violated when death results from a deliberate or reckless indifference to life by a police high-speed auto chase to apprehend a suspect. Two criteria must be met to demonstrate a substantive due process claim. First, there must be no applicable provision of the Constitution more specific than substantive due process. Here there is no such specific provision. The Fourth Amendment does not apply because no "search or seizure" occurred here. Second, there must be, as required in *Collins v. Harker Heights,* an executive abuse of power so egregious as to be arbitrary. The appropriate standard for evaluating the latter is not deliberate or reckless indifference to life but conduct that "shocks the conscience" of the Court. Police high

speed chases conducted "with no intent to harm
suspects physically or to worsen their legal plight"
do not "shock the conscience" and thus do not
constitute a substantive due process violation. *Sac-*
ramento County v. Lewis (1998).

e. The Right to Refuse Treatment

An individual has a significant due process liberty
interest in refusing unwanted medical treatment.
However, the state's regulatory interest may sometimes outweigh the burden on the protected liberty
interest. For example, a state does not violate substantive due process if it authorizes the involuntary
treatment with drugs of a prisoner who suffers from
a mental disorder, is gravely disabled, and presents
a likelihood of serious harm to others or their
property. There was a valid rational relationship
between the prison regulation and the government
interest asserted to support it. The absence of a
ready alternative to involuntary medication fur-
nished additional evidence of the state policy's reasonableness: "[T]he Due Process Clause permits the
State to treat a prison inmate who has serious
mental illness with antipsychotic drugs against his
will, if the inmate is dangerous to himself or others
and the treatment is in the inmate's medical interests." *Washington v. Harper* (1990).

Nor is a state law necessarily punitive or violative
of substantive due process because it fails to offer
any legitimate "treatment." A Kansas statute provided that a person convicted for a sexually violent
crime can be involuntarily subjected to civil com-

mitment upon release from prison if he "suffers
from a mental disorder which makes [him] likely to
engage in predatory acts of sexual violence." The
state law was applied to an individual with a history
of molesting children. Involuntary civil commitment
does not offend ordered liberty if it follows appropriate procedures and evidentiary standards and is
applied to those unable to control their behavior
and who pose a danger to the public. There need
not be a finding of "mental illness." Treatment
need not be the state's overriding concern particularly where treatment is not possible for the affected class and the possibility remains that an ancillary purpose of the law was to provide treatment.
Kansas v. Hendricks (1997).

Does a person have a "right to die" or at least to
refuse life preserving treatment? This difficult issue
was presented when the parents of a young woman,
a victim of an automobile accident, unsuccessfully
sought an order from a Missouri court directing the
withdrawal of their daughter's artificial feeding and
hydration equipment because it was clear that "she
had virtually no chance of recovering her cognitive
faculties." The Supreme Court held, per Chief Justice Rehnquist, that a state may constitutionally
require clear and convincing evidence that the patient herself desires that life-sustaining treatment
be withdrawn. A patient has a significant liberty
interest in refusing unwanted medical treatment.
But the state has an interest in the preservation of
human life and in protecting the personal element
in the choice of life or death. These state interests

were sufficient to justify the imposition of heightened evidentiary standards. Such standards protect against abuse, promote more accurate fact finding and reflect the importance of the decision to withdraw medical life supports. *Cruzan v. Director, Missouri Dept. of Health* (1990).

Cruzan teaches that the state is not constitutionally required to confer decisional power in such matters on anyone but the patient. The state is not constitutionally obliged to accept the substituted judgement of even close family members. But, the Court was not called upon to resolve the question whether a state would be required to defer to the decision of a surrogate if evidence clearly established that the patient wanted the surrogate to make the decision to withdraw life supports for her.

f. No Right to Assisted Suicide

limit on decisional autonomy

A Washington state law made it a felony to knowingly cause or aid another to attempt suicide. The law was unsuccessfully challenged by terminally ill patients and physicians as an infringement of a liberty interest protected by the Due Process Clause. They asserted this liberty interest extended to physician assisted suicide. Chief Justice Rehnquist for the Court said there were two elements to the Court's substantive due process analysis. First, the Due Process Clause protects only those interests which are deeply rooted in the nation's history and traditions and which are implicit in the concept of ordered liberty. For 700 years the common law tradition has criminalized or sanctioned both suicide and assisted suicide. Second, the substantive due process cases demand a precise description of the asserted "fundamental liberty interest." These requirements served to limit the subjectivity inherent in due process adjudication. The Court is reluctant to expand substantive due process rights. Guideposts for decisionmaking are scarce and recognition of a right or liberty interest places it largely beyond public debate or legislative resolution. Furthermore, there is a threshold requirement that a challenged state action implicate a fundamental right. There is no "right" to commit suicide or to assisted suicide. A "right" to assisted suicide is not a fundamental liberty interest protected by the Due Process Clause. *Washington v. Glucksberg* (1997).

Although *Cruzan* recognized a significant liberty interest in refusing unwanted medical treatment or life support, this interest flowed not from some abstract protected concept of personal autonomy but from the common law tradition that forced medical treatment was a battery. Nor did the protection that *Casey* gave to personal choice concerning the attributes of personhood mean that all rights and liberties relating to personal autonomy were protected. The treatment of assisted suicide in the United States reflects the rejection of all efforts at recognition. The only standard the Washington law banning assisted suicide must meet is that it be rationally related to legitimate governmental interests. This standard is met since the state ban rationally promotes interests such as the preservation

of human life, protection of the integrity of the
medical profession, protection of vulnerable groups
such as the poor, the elderly and disabled and,
finally, the state concern that recognition of assisted suicide might lead to voluntary and even involuntary euthanasia.

The concern expressed in the *Glucksberg* concur-
rences for palliative care for the terminally ill suggest that the rigor of the Court's holding might be
mitigated in different circumstances. Using an approach espoused in Justice Harlan's influential dissent in *Poe v. Ullman* (1961), Justice Souter called
for balancing "the relative weights or dignities of
contending interests." Thus, the interest in assisted
suicide in terms of personal autonomy, human dignity and the avoidance of pain demanded careful
scrutiny of the state's contrary claim. Justice Souter did not "for all time" decide that the interests of
terminally ill patients were unworthy of protection.
Justice O'Connor pointed out that in Washington
state dying patients can obtain "palliative care even
when doing so would hasten their deaths." Justice
Stevens agreed that there is no constitutional entitlement to autonomy to the point of recognizing an
open-ended constitutional right to commit suicide.
Yet there were situations when an interest in has-
tening death is entitled to constitutional protection.
Justice Breyer said this was not the occasion to
decide whether a "right to die with dignity" was
fundamental. The avoidance of severe physical pain
would be essential to the success of such a claim.

g. Other Fundamental Rights

The constitutional protection afforded personal decisions involving abortion, contraception, marriage and family life indicates the general principle that laws significantly burdening fundamental personal rights are subjected to stricter judicial scrutiny. This principle will be reflected again in subsequent sections of this Nutshell dealing with First Amendment freedoms made applicable to the states through the Due Process Clause of the Fourteenth Amendment. This fundamental rights principle is also used to protect both rights that may be fairly implied from the constitutional text as well as rights that are judicially created, *e.g.,* the right of interstate travel. *Shapiro v. Thompson* (1969). Finally, the fundamental rights principle has provided the foundation for stricter review of governmental action under the Equal Protection Clause.

C. PROCEDURAL DUE PROCESS

Substantive due process is addressed to what government can do. Procedural due process inquires into the way government acts and the enforcement mechanisms it uses. When government deprives a person of an already acquired life, liberty or property interest, the Due Process Clauses of the Fifth and Fourteenth Amendments require procedural fairness. In testing the adequacy of government procedures, two questions are asked: First, is there a life, liberty or property interest at stake? Second, what procedures must be afforded to assure fair treatment?

1. LIFE, LIBERTY AND PROPERTY INTERESTS

At one time, the due process mandate of procedural fairness did not apply when governmental benefits or privileges rather than constitutional rights were denied. *McAuliffe v. Mayor of New Bedford* (Mass.1892) [dismissal of a policeman for political activities held to be solely a matter of government discretion]. But with an increasing appreciation of the adverse impact of government action on the individual, this right-privilege dichotomy eroded. Today, whether an interest is a right or a privilege, when it is intentionally denied, procedural due process must be afforded. *Goldberg v. Kelly* (1970) ["The Constitutional arguments cannot be answered by an argument that public assistance benefits are 'a privilege and not a right' "]. Further, government cannot condition receipt of public benefits on surrender of constitutional rights (*i.e.*, the Unconstitutional Conditions Doctrine).

But this does not mean that due process applies whenever government action intentionally denies an interest of value. In fact, the terms "life, liberty or property" have received an increasingly narrow interpretation in recent years. Indeed, many commentators would argue that the Court has restored the right-privilege dichotomy by giving highly restrictive meaning to the terms "liberty" and "property."

a. Property Interests

"Property" includes a wide range of significant, legally-recognized proprietary interests. The key concept in defining property today is "entitlement." When the government recognizes that an individual is legally entitled to a benefit, it thereby creates an expectancy that the benefit will not be arbitrarily terminated. A property interest is created. But note that entitlement applies only to "presently enjoyed" rights or interests; due process does not protect the person applying for benefits. *Board of Regents v. Roth* (1972).

The vital role played by entitlement can be appreciated by comparing *Roth* with *Perry v. Sindermann* (1972). In *Roth*, the Court held that a state untenured teacher, hired under a fixed one-year term, could be dismissed without reasons or a hearing. In concluding that the teacher had no property interest, Justice Stewart, for the Court, stressed that it is "the nature of the interest at stake," not the weight, that is critical. Property interests, he explained, "are created and their dimensions are defined by existing rules or understandings that stem from an independent source such as state law-rules or understandings that secure certain benefits and that support claims of entitlements to those benefits." In this case, there was no contractual provision for renewal of Roth's employment; no state statute or University policy "secured his interest in re-employment" or "created any legitimate claim" to re-employment. Simply, the state had not created any entitlement qualifying as a property interest.

In a companion case, *Perry v. Sindermann* (1972), the Court discovered such an entitlement in a school official Faculty Guide which could reasonably be interpreted to create a de facto tenure system. Property interests, said Justice Stewart, can arise from "mutually explicit understandings" that support a claim of entitlement. Thus, a teacher who had been employed for 12 years under a series of one year contracts could attempt to prove that the college, while lacking a formal tenure system, had in practice created an "unwritten common law" which was the equivalent of tenure.

In other cases, "property interests" have been found when government has aided in the collection of debts [*Sniadach v. Family Finance Corp. of Bay View* (1969) (wage garnishment)]; or in pre-judgment seizures [*North Georgia Fin., Inc. v. Di–Chem, Inc.* (1975) (the use and enjoyment of goods)]; or has terminated statutorily created welfare benefits [*Goldberg v. Kelly* (1970)]; or has imposed a ten-day suspension from a state guaranteed education [*Goss v. Lopez* (1975)]; or has terminated public employment [*Perry v. Sindermann* (1972)]; or has suspended a driver's license [*Bell v. Burson* (1971)]; or has terminated a state-created cause of action [*Logan v. Zimmerman Brush Co.* (1982)].

A troublesome area in defining "property" arises when the state creates an interest but prescribes various procedures for terminating it or otherwise conditions the interest. While a state is free to stipulate restrictions on a claim, it is the judicial function to determine whether the conditioned claim constitutes a "property" interest. For example, when the state conditions public employment to an extent that it is terminable at will, rather than "for cause," it has been held that the employment does not constitute a property interest. *Bishop v. Wood* (1976). But in *Cleveland Board of Education v. Loudermill* (1985), a statute entitling classified civil servants to retain their positions absent "misfeasance, malfeasance, or nonfeasance in office" was held to create a property interest in continued employment even though the state provided procedures for termination. Justice White, for the Court, stressed that the question of the substantive right of liberty or property is distinct from the procedural question: " 'Property' cannot be defined by the procedures provided for its deprivation any more than can life or liberty." The question of what procedures are due is a constitutional issue, not to be determined by the state statute.

b. Liberty Interests

The concept of "liberty" is far more amorphous than that of property, embodying principles of freedom that lie at the roots of our legal system. The Court has said that liberty "denotes not merely freedom from bodily restraint but also the right of the individual to contract, to engage in any of the common occupations of life, to acquire useful knowledge, to marry, establish a home and bring up children, to worship God according to the dictates of his own conscience and generally to enjoy those privileges long recognized as essential to the orderly pursuit of happiness by free men." *Meyer v. Nebraska* (1923). Using this statement as a guide, liberty interests generally fall under one of the following headings: (1) freedom from bodily restraint or "physical liberty"; (2) substantive constitutional rights; (3) other fundamental freedoms.

Liberty interests are burdened when physical freedom is curtailed by commitment, imprisonment, or when bodily integrity is impaired [*Ingraham v. Wright* (1977), corporal punishment of students by teachers]. Thus, the Constitution mandates extensive procedural protection for the accused in the criminal justice system and juvenile justice system. When the state seeks to revoke parole [*Morrissey v. Brewer* (1972)], or probation [*Gagnon v. Scarpelli* (1973)], due process must be afforded. A prisoner ordered back to prison after release under a preparole conditional supervision program is in a situation similar to revocation of parole and is entitled to the same due process protections. *Young v. Harper* (1997). Involuntary civil commitment to a mental institution demands due process. *Addington v. Texas* (1979) ["clear and convincing" evidence of dangerousness required for commitment]; *Parham v. J.R.* (1979) [parental commitment of child involves protectable liberty interest, requiring neutral fact finder's determination that admission requirements are satisfied]. Transfer of an incarcerated prisoner to a mental hospital involving stigma and subjection to mandatory treatment procedures requires written notice and a hearing with extensive procedural protections. *Vitek v. Jones* (1980).

However, the Court has indicated that not every "grievous loss" inflicted on a prisoner implicates a liberty interest. Once criminal due process is satisfied and a person is imprisoned, liberty has already been significantly curtailed and subsequent adverse action does not necessarily constitute a significant privation of liberty. Thus, transfer of a prisoner to a different institution [*Meachum v. Fano* (1976); *Olim v. Wakinekona* (1983)]; or rescission of discretionary parole prior to release [*Jago v. Van Curen* (1981)]; or, administrative segregation of prisoners [*Hewitt v. Helms* (1983)], have been held not to involve liberty requiring due process procedures.

Similarly, in *Kentucky Department of Corrections v. Thompson* (1989), the Court held that Kentucky prison regulations governing visitation did not create a liberty interest when visiting privileges for certain visitors were suspended. No entitlement had been created by the prison regulations. The regulations did not create by mandatory language the "substantive predicate" that would lead prisoners to reasonably expect that a visit would be allowed. Denial of access to particular visitors was well within the terms of confinement associated with imprisonment.

On the other hand, state law can create a specific entitlement to designated procedures for prisoners before adverse actions are taken by prison authorities. *Greenholtz v. Inmates of Nebraska Penal & Correctional Complex* (1979) [statute requiring parole for eligible inmate absent finding of designated grounds for denial of parole creates an entitlement].

Liberty also includes all of the incorporated rights (*e.g.,* freedom of expression and religion), as well as those substantive rights which have been implied from, or have been read into the Constitution (*e.g.,* association and belief, privacy). If a public employee is discharged because of her exercise of speech rights, liberty is burdened and procedural fairness is required. *Perry v. Sindermann* (1972) [But see, *Mt. Healthy City School Dist. Bd. of Educ. v. Doyle* (1977), indicating due process is not required if the employee would have been discharged for permissible reasons]. When parental rights in the care, custody and management of their children are terminated, due process is required. *Santosky v. Kramer* (1982) ["clear and convincing" evidence of unfitness required before terminating parental rights]. In short, when constitutional rights are severely burdened by government action, due process must be provided.

Finally, due process "liberty" encompasses a variety of fundamental interests relating to personal autonomy and choice. It is in this context that liberty is most ill-defined and tends to produce most conceptual confusion with "property" interests. Discharge from a particular job may not involve a property entitlement but government action which denies access to the common occupations of the community may well implicate due process liberty. See *Board of Regents v. Roth* (1972). Termination of one's ability to practice a profession can involve not only property but liberty interests as well.

The confusion in this murky area of liberty and property is best illustrated by the Court's treatment of reputational interests. Early cases had indicated that when government action "stigmatizes" a person, impairing her good name, reputation, honor, or integrity, the liberty clause requires that due process be afforded. See, *e.g.*, *Wisconsin v. Constantineau* (1971) [public posting of names of persons causing problems because of excessive drinking]. But in *Paul v. Davis* (1976), the Court indicated that injury to reputation, without more, does not require due process.

Paul v. Davis involved reputational injury resulting from police distribution of a flyer identifying Davis as an "active shoplifter." In fact, while Davis had been arrested, he was subsequently acquitted. Rather than suing for defamation in state court, Davis sued in federal court claiming a violation of his due process rights since he had not been afforded any hearing on the charges prior to circulation of the flyer. The Court, 5–4, rejected the claim "that reputation alone, apart from some more tangible interests such as employment, is either 'liberty' or 'property' by itself sufficient to invoke the procedural protection of the Due Process Clause." Justice Rehnquist, for the Court, instead indicated that interests attain the constitutional status of liberty or property "by virtue of the fact that they have been initially recognized and protected by state law." The public posting in *Constantineau*, explained Justice Rehnquist, had altered the plaintiff's legal right to purchase liquor. In the present case, the action of the police did not produce "a deprivation of any 'liberty' or 'property' recognized by state or federal law nor has it worked any change of respondent's status as theretofore recognized under the state's laws."

Taken literally, *Paul v. Davis* would limit "liberty" to constitutional rights and physical liberty. Beyond these interests only state created entitlements (*i.e.,* "property") would invoke the due process guarantee. Perhaps, *Paul* may simply reflect the Court's federalism concern with preserving state created causes of action—Rehnquist warned against making "the Fourteenth Amendment a font of tort law to be superimposed upon whatever systems may already be administered by the states."

2. THE PROCESS THAT IS DUE

Having determined that a liberty or property interest is significantly burdened, the Court must next assess what procedures are required in order to provide fundamental fairness. The answer to this inquiry depends heavily on the particular fact context involved, *e.g.,* welfare, prisons, schools. The important item for the constitutional law student is to understand the methodology employed by the courts in providing the answer. Remember that the inquiry into what process is due is a federal constitutional question to be answered by the courts in interpreting the meaning of "due process." The fact that the state has defined procedures for terminating an interest is not determinative of the demands of the federal Constitution. *Vitek v. Jones* (1980); *Logan v. Zimmerman Brush Co.* (1982); *Cleveland Board of Education v. Loudermill* (1985). Compare *Arnett v. Kennedy* (1974) (plurality opinion).

An example of the way in which the due process clause can override state definitions is the conclusive presumption doctrine. A statute creates such a presumption when it conclusively presumes that certain facts exist which permit categorizing individuals into a class and subjecting them to burdens not visited on others. The conclusive presumption doctrine holds that since the presumption may not be valid for each member of the class, denial of an opportunity to challenge the presumption violates due process. When critical due process interests of the individual are at stake, an opportunity for an individualized hearing to challenge the presumption must be provided. For example, school board rules requiring every pregnant school teacher to take a maternity leave without pay for a specified number of months before the expected birth of her child violated due process. Individualized determinations are necessary for due process to be satisfied. *Cleveland Board of Education v. La Fleur* (1974). A plurality of the Court contends that the conclusive presumption doctrine does not have its source in the requirements of procedural due process. The doctrine instead, it is argued, is based on the lack of fit between the classification established by the law and the policy underlying the classification, *i.e.* equal protection or a challenge to the policy itself, e.g. substantive due process. *Michael H. & Victoria D. v. Gerald D.* (1989).

While the Court has not provided systematic guidance on the values and objectives underlying the due process inquiry, primary emphasis has been given to assuring accuracy and avoiding arbitrariness in government decision-making. *Codd v. Velger* (1977) [employee claiming due process right to a hearing because of stigma resulting from discharge must allege that the charges are false]. Commentators have argued that this approach excessively narrows the judicial inquiry; the due process inquiry should also focus on process values such as individual dignity, participation, and equality of treatment. Once it is determined that due process interests have been adversely affected, the individual has at least the right, absent an emergency, to reasonable notice and some form of hearing on his claim.

But due process rights did not attach when Connecticut passed a "Megan's law" requiring that convicted sex offenders upon release had to provide a registry set up by the state Department of Public Safety with updated addresses and photographs for a period of ten years after release. Violent sex offenders were required to provide this information for life. In addition, sex offenders, upon release also has to provide DNA samples. The Department of Public Safety then publicized the registry via an Internet site. Members of the public could enter a zip code at the site and determine whether sex offenders lived in the area. The registry cautioned, however, (1) that the names were listed without reference to whether the sex offender listed was presently a danger and (2) that it was a crime to use the information in the registry to harass people on the list. John Doe, who was required to register under the law, challenged the law as a violation of procedural due process. Although the disclosures deprived him of liberty interests in his reputation and his status under state law, he had not been afforded a hearing on whether or not he was still a danger to the community. The Supreme Court rejected the procedural due process challenge. The Connecticut law required the publication of the names and whereabouts of *all prior* convicted sex offenders without reference to the offender's current dangerousness. Even if Doe could prove that he was not likely to be dangerous now, a hearing on on current dangerousness would be "a bootless exercise." *Connecticut Department of Public Safety v. Doe* (2003).

The scope of the procedural protection afforded beyond this minimum is determined by balancing the interests favoring summary determination against the interests of the individual in additional procedural protection. *Goss v. Lopez* (1975). Courts making this balancing determination employ a three-part test fashioned in *Mathews v. Eldridge* (1976), focusing on the following factors:

First, the private interest that will be affected by the official action; second, the risk of an erroneous deprivation of such interest through the procedures used, and the probable value, if any, of additional or substitute procedural safeguards; and finally, the government's interest, including the function involved and the fiscal and administrative burden that the additional or substitute procedural requirements would entail.

Applying these standards in *Mathews v. Eldridge,* in the context of termination of disability benefits, the Court found significant differences from *Goldberg v. Kelly* (1970), where the Court had required extensive procedural protection and a hearing prior to termination of welfare benefits under the Aid to Families with Dependent Children (AFDC) program. First, whereas AFDC benefits are based upon need, disability benefits are grounded upon findings unrelated to the worker's financial needs; there is likely to be less hardship on the disability claimant. Second, termination of AFDC benefits turns upon decisions by social workers that involve a high risk of error. Continued eligibility for disability, on the other hand, involves medical decisions having a higher degree of accuracy. Finally, a full administrative hearing in disability cases would involve high costs taken from scarce resources which might well decrease benefits.

The cost benefit calculus involved in using this balancing formulation is also illustrated by the Court's treatment of student discipline. In *Goss v. Lopez* (1975), involving a ten-day suspension from school for students engaged in misconduct, the Court balanced the need of the schools for discipline and order through immediate, effective action in combating misconduct against the stigma and loss of schooling suffered by students subjected to even a short 10–day suspension. At least minimal pre-suspension procedural protection, *i.e.*, an explanation of the charges and an informal opportunity to reply, was required.

Due process rights are not violated by a 27–day delay in holding an administrative hearing for the recovery of a towing fee. The fee was imposed on an individual whose car was towed from a place where parking was not allowed despite the fact that the no-parking sign was hidden behind trees. Using the factors set forth in *Matthews v. Eldridge, supra*, the Court ruled (1) that the harm to the petitioner was minimal because it could easily be recompensed by an interest payment, (2) the 27–day delay in presenting evidence was unlikely to cause factual errors; (3) the government interest was strong in terms of administrative necessity given the number of claims against the city and the city's limited resources. *Los Angeles v. David* (2003).

The Court displayed reluctance to excessively intrude on school administration and to constitutionalize school procedures in *Board of Curators v. Horowitz* (1978). Charlotte Horowitz had failed to graduate from medical school because of poor performance in clinical courses and concern for her personal hygiene. Although the Court acknowledged the severity of Ms. Horowitz's plight, it denied her claim to personally appear before the school's administrative board to defend her interests. The Court was unanimous in determining that due process had been satisfied by affording her a hearing and an appeal at which she could make her case in writing. But the Court was not unanimous on whether the procedures which had been provided were constitutionally required. Justice Rehnquist, for the Court, emphasized the differences between academic evaluation and the fact-finding and adversariness characteristic of adjudication, concluding "that the school went beyond [constitutionally required] due process." Justice Marshall, concurring, rejected this "dicta suggesting that respondent was entitled to even less procedural protection than she received." Instead, he compared the present case with *Goss,* stressing the greater severity of the personal harm, the risk of error in academic evaluation and the absence, compared to *Goss,* of any government interest in discipline and order.

When a medicated and disoriented patient was admitted to a state mental hospital as a "voluntary" admission where, as alleged, the state employees should have known otherwise, the failure of the state employees to follow a state statutory procedure for the involuntary admission of mentally ill patients was sufficient to state a claim under the Due Process Clause. In such circumstances, postdeprivation remedies were inadequate and due process mandated a proper predeprivation hearing. *Zinermon v. Burch* (1990).

But a state policy which established a nonjudicial procedure, staffed by medical professionals, for deciding the involuntary treatment with antipsychotic drugs of mentally ill felons did not violate procedural due process. Although the prisoner enjoyed a significant liberty interest in avoiding the unwanted administration of antipsychotic drugs, the state procedure, given the inmate's threat to the security of the prison environment, satisfied due process. The procedure afforded the inmate notice, the right to cross-examine witnesses, and the opportunity to attend the hearing. Since medical personnel would be making the treatment decision, a clear and convincing standard was not required and would not be helpful. *Washington v. Harper* (1990).

A new development in the law of institutional due process is that a state may not punish by involuntary commitment to a mental institution a person who has not been convicted and who is not now mentally ill. A state statute which permitted an individual acquitted on grounds of insanity to be committed to a mental institution until he was able to demonstrate that he was not dangerous to himself or others even though he was not mentally ill was invalid. The state has no punitive interest to justify involuntary commitment in these circumstances. But a state may confine a mentally ill person if it shows by clear and convincing evidence that the individual is presently mentally ill and dangerous. *Foucha v. Louisiana* (1992).

A state statute permitted guardians and members of the immediate family of a mentally retarded person who is the subject of an involuntary commitment to participate in the proceeding as if they were full parties. Applying *Mathews v. Eldridge*, the Court held that such participation by third parties did not violate due process. Their participation did not increase "the risk of an erroneous deprivation" of the mentally retarded person's liberty interest. Close relatives and guardians might be able to offer valuable insights concerning the mentally retarded person which would increase the accuracy of the commitment decision. The presence of additional parties in the commitment proceeding might, it is true, increase the likelihood of commitment if those parties favor commitment. But the due process clause does not require that a state adopt an alternative procedure just because the alternative might produce a result more favorable to the party challenging the existing procedure. *Heller v. Doe* (1993).

Finally, *Mathews v. Eldridge* should not be viewed as establishing an all-embracing test for procedural due process claims. *Dusenbery v. United States* (2002). Notice of seizure of the property of a federal prisoner convicted on drug charges by means of notice in a newspaper and by certified mail should not have been evaluated under the balancing test of *Mathews v. Eldridge*. *Mullane v. Central Hanover Bank & Trust Co.*(1950) which requires that the method of notice used must be reasonably designed to inform the affected parties of the government's action is the appropriate test for evaluating methods of notice under procedural due process. Under the reasonableness standard of *Mullane* proof of actual notice is not required.

The procedural standards set forth in *Mathews v. Eldridge* got a surprising revival in the enemy combatant context in a decision confronting the following issue: Can the Executive detain American citizens designated as "enemy combatants?" Furthermore, if the Due Process Clause applies, what process is due such detainees? Yaser Hamdi was a U.S. citizen apprehended by U.S. forces in Afghanistan. Justice O'Connor in a plurality opinion, joined in by Chief Justice Rehnquist and Justices Kennedy and Breyer, declared that Congress had in fact authorized his detention by virtue of the Authorization for Use of Military Forces (AUMF) enacted one week after the terrorist attacks on the World Trade Center and the Pentagon. The AUMF authorized the President to use "all necessary and appropriate force" against those associated with that attack. Since the plurality viewed the AUMF as authorizing Hamdi's detention, it was unnecessary to decide whether, as the government argued, the President's Article II powers were all that was required to authorize Hamdi's detention. In addition, the Court rejected the Executive's position that individual determinations concerning a citizen's enemy combatant status were beyond the competence of judiciary. Citizen enemy combatants were owed a process more rigorous than—as had been the case—the simple presentation to a court of a declaration by a defense department official that the individual in question was an enemy combatant. A citizen challenging his citizen combatant status should be evaluated under the test set forth in *Mathews v. Eldridge*. Applying that test, the plurality declared that a citizen-detainee had to receive notice "of the factual basis for his classification, and a fair opportunity to rebut the government's factual assertions

before a neutral decision-maker." Also, Hamdi
should have the right to counsel in the proceedings
on remand. Justices Souter and Ginsburg, concurring in part and dissenting in part, agreed that
these procedures were essential.

In addition, Justice O'Connor declared for the
plurality that there should be a presumption in
favor of the government's evidence and a shifting of
the evidentiary burden to the citizen-detainee. Finally, the plurality suggested that an opportunity to
litigate before a military tribunal might make resort to a judicial habeas hearing unnecessary. Justice Souter, joined by Justice Ginsburg, did not
agree that a military proceeding would suffice nor
did they agree with an evidentiary presumption in
favor of the government or a shifting of the burden
of proof. Justice Scalia, joined by Justice Stevens,
dissenting, contended that detention of American
citizens was constitutional only when the writ of
habeas corpus has been suspended or where the individual concerned has been committed to trial for
criminal prosecution. Since neither situation obtained here, Hamdi's detention in the view of the
two dissenters was unconstitutional. *Hamdi v.
Rumsfeld* (2004).

While the *Mathews v. Eldridge* balancing test
suggests an objective measure of the demands of
due process, the above cases indicate the subjective
value choices that are actually involved. Further,
many commentators find in the Court's calculus a
utilitarian bias that denigrates the intrinsic worth
of constitutional rights. Use of the calculus argu-

ably ignores the effects of governmental action on particular individuals and focuses on claimants generally. In assessing the Court's efforts to objectively measure the costs and benefits of administrative actions, a serious question is raised over the capacity of courts to weigh the competing interests at stake.

CHAPTER VI

EQUAL PROTECTION

The Fourteenth Amendment guarantees that "[n]o State shall make or enforce any law which shall deny to any person within its jurisdiction the equal protection of the laws." While there is no corresponding provision applicable to the federal government, the Fifth Amendment Due Process Clause applies the same limitation to the federal government. *Bolling v. Sharpe* (1954). While it has been argued that the Equal Protection Clause was intended only to require equal enforcement of the laws, it is established today that the Clause is a guarantee of equal laws, *i.e.,* that the law itself may be challenged as violating equal protection.

But what is the nature of this equal protection right? The Clause cannot be a proscription against legal classification since different treatment of persons and things that are not similarly situated is essential to lawmaking. Men and women, adults and children, aliens and citizens need not always be treated alike under the law. But it is also clear that these classes cannot be treated differently on an arbitrary basis. The Court's answer has been that a legal classification must be reasonable in relation to the objectives of the law.

In developing this general demand for reasonableness in government classifications, the Court has employed three different standards of review. During the Warren Court era, the Court developed a two-tiered system of equal protection review. In most socioeconomic cases, the Court employs a traditional rationality standard. If the classification is rationally related to a permissible government objective, equal protection is satisfied. But when a law intentionally employs a "suspect classification" or when a classification significantly burdens the exercise of a "fundamental right," strict scrutiny is applied. The burden is on the government to establish that the classification is necessary to a compelling governmental interest; there must be no less onerous alternative available. During the Burger Court years, a third approach emerged. Used mostly in gender and illegitimacy cases (quasi-suspect classifications), the "intermediate" standard of review requires that a classification be substantially related to an important government interest.

In fact, the Rehnquist Court may be moving towards an abandonment of a rigid three-tiered approach to equal protection review. In the main, the law of equal protection has consisted largely in working out the standards for judicial scrutiny of legal classifications. For a time, it appeared that a more indeterminate "reasonableness" standard might emerge in which the degree of judicial scrutiny would vary depending on the identity of the classes (or nature of the classifying trait, *e.g.*, race, sex, age), the severity of the burden imposed by the classification, and the nature of the government interests supporting the classification (*e.g.,* national security and foreign affairs will produce increased judicial deference. *Rostker v. Goldberg* (1981) [male only draft registration upheld]). From time to time various Justices—Marshall, Stevens, Rehnquist—have suggested that there is really only one standard of review and that the degree of judicial scrutiny should vary with the nature of the discrimination and the significance of the burden on fundamental interests. Whether these later variations or departures from the three-tiered theme will capture a majority of the Court is uncertain. At the present, the three-tiered approach remains dominant.

A. TRADITIONAL EQUAL PROTECTION

The traditional approach to equal protection review has been marked by extreme judicial self-restraint and a marked concern for limiting the judicial role vis–a–vis the legislature. While the Court occasionally frames the traditional equal protection standard in terms of whether a classification is based upon some difference having a "fair and substantial relation" to the legislative objective [*F.S. Royster Guano Co. v. Commonwealth of Virginia* (1920)], the standard most frequently used imposes on the challenging party the burden of proving that the classification is not "rationally related to furthering a legitimate government interest."

Massachusetts Board of Retirement v. Murgia (1976) [state law requiring retirement of police officers at age 50 held constitutional under rational basis test]. The judicial deference embodied in this test has almost invariably resulted in socioeconomic laws being upheld against equal protection challenges.

Government must have a *legitimate interest* in imposing a classification; the objective of the law cannot itself violate the Constitution. But what if the real objective of the law is impermissible or if the classification is not rationally related to the law's true purpose. The courts have shown extreme deference requiring only that the law serve some conceivable legislative purpose. As long as the classification rationally serves a legitimate objective that the legislature *might* have had, it will be upheld. *United States Railroad Retirement Bd. v. Fritz* (1980) [since there was a "plausible reason" for the congressional enactment, it was "constitutionally irrelevant whether this reasoning in fact underlay the legislative decision"]. This deference reflects concern over the propriety of judicial probing of the legislative purpose, the problem of identifying and proving the actual purpose of a collegial lawmaking body and concern that the legislature would simply re-enact the law while masking its impermissible objectives.

The classification must be *rationally related* to the law's objective. In challenging a law, the litigant might argue that the classification is under-or over-inclusive or a combination of the two. Under-inclusion arises when a law does not burden or benefit all those who are similarly situated. Over-inclusive classifications extend the benefit or burden of the law not only to those who are similarly situated with respect to the objective of the law but to others as well (*e.g.,* dragnet searches, internment of Japanese–Americans during World War II because of the danger of sabotage).

However, neither of these conditions is likely to make a classification unreasonable if the rationality standard is applied; only if the law is totally arbitrary will it fail. Perfectly drawn classifications in lawmaking are essentially impossible. The Court has stated: "A classification having some reasonable basis does not offend [equal protection] merely because it is not made with mathematical nicety or because in practice it results in some inequality." *Lindsley v. Natural Carbonic Gas Co.* (1911). Further, the *Lindsley* Court noted that "if any state of facts reasonably can be conceived that would sustain the classification, the existence of that state of facts at the time the law was enacted must be assumed." More recently, the Court has captured this principle by holding that a challenging party cannot prevail where an issue remains debatable. *Minnesota v. Clover Leaf Creamery Co.* (1981). The state need not choose the best means to accomplish its purpose but only select a rational means.

The judicial deference in rationality review is suggested by the Court's decision in *Railway Express Agency v. New York* (1949). A city ordinance banning advertising on trucks but exempting those advertising their own wares on their trucks was held not to violate equal protection. The law was designed to promote the permissible objective of public safety, stated Justice Douglas for the Court, and the local authorities "may well have concluded" that those advertising their own products would not present the same traffic problem in light of the nature and extent of their advertising. The Court deferred to the legislative capacity to assess "practical considerations based on experience." Nor was the fact that the city had not banned even more vivid displays relevant. "It is no requirement of equal protection that all evils of the same genus be eradicated or none at all." Government must be able to experiment and may deal with a problem one step at a time.

Justice Jackson, concurring, rejected the Court's rationale since there was not even a pretense that traffic hazards posed by the two classes of truck advertising differed. Instead, he urged that the legislature may also have had the objective of curbing the nuisance posed by truck advertising and that legitimate objective would make the classification rational. "[T]here is a real difference between doing in self-interest and doing for hire, so that it is one thing to tolerate action from those who act on their own and it is another thing to permit the same action to be promoted for a price."

This same deference exhibited in *REA* was employed by the Burger Court in rejecting a challenge to a state ban on nonreturnable milk containers while permitting use of other nonreturnable containers, *e.g.*, paperboard cartons. The legislature might have concluded that even a limited ban would foster greater use of environmentally desirable alternative containers. *Minnesota v. Clover Leaf Creamery Co.* (1981). A grandfather clause exempting two vendors from a general ban on pushcart dealers in the New Orleans French Quarter was sustained against an equal protection challenge. The city could rationally conclude that the exempted vendors had become part of the distinctive charm of the Quarter. *New Orleans v. Dukes* (1976).

A federal statute denying food stamps to strikers was sustained on traditional equal protection analysis. The federal statute denied eligibility for food stamps to households while a member was on strike; the statute also precluded an increase in the allotment of food stamps even though the striker's income had decreased. Conceding that the statute was harder against strikers than "voluntary quitters," the Court nonetheless upheld the statute since it bore a rational relationship to the legitimate government objective of avoiding favoritism in labor disputes. *Lyng v. International Union, UAW* (1988).

While invocation of the traditional rationality test in modern economic regulation cases has regularly resulted in rejection of the equal protection challenge, the Court is capable of putting some teeth into rationality review. This was presaged in a concurring opinion by Justice Blackmun in *Logan v. Zimmerman Brush Co.* (1982): "The State's rationale must be something more than the exercise of a strained imagination; while the connection between means and ends need not be precise, it, at the least, must have some objective basis." In *Metropolitan Life Insurance Co. v. Ward* (1985), the state interest in promoting domestic business was deemed not to be a legitimate purpose under the Equal Protection Clause when achieved through the imposition of a discriminatory domestic preference tax statute. And, in *City of Cleburne v. Cleburne Living Center* (1985), the Court held that requiring a special use permit for a proposed group home for the mentally retarded was not rationally related to any permissible government purpose and therefore violated equal protection.

Also illustrative of this less deferential approach is a state tax case where a West Virginia county assessed real property on the basis of its recent purchase price. The county made only minor modifications to assessments of properties not recently sold. This valuation scheme was held to violate equal protection since it resulted in a gross disparity in the assessed value of comparable properties over a long period of time. Equal protection tolerates some margin for mistake in the valuation of property for tax purposes and does not require constant reevaluation of all assessed properties on the basis of the latest market developments. But seasonal attainment of a rough equality among similarly situated taxpayers is required by equal protection. *Allegheny Pittsburgh Coal Co. v. County Commission* (1989). The Court, thus, has demonstrated that it will sometimes use in socio-economic cases a non-deferential "reasonableness" test which involves a real evaluation of the state interests supporting a classification and a true balancing of the competing interests.

An equal protection violation can occur even with respect to a "class of one." A property owner asserted that the city had tried to impose a 33–foot easement on her when seeking a hookup to the municipal water supply yet only a 15–foot easement had been required of other property owners. The property owner contended that the city was out to "get" her. The Court held that regardless of motive, an allegation of irrational and entirely arbitrary state action sets forth a claim under traditional equal protection analysis regardless of the number of individuals in the affected class. *Village of Willowbrook v. Olech* (2000).

A Kentucky law requiring a more demanding procedure for the involuntary commitment of the mentally ill than the mentally retarded was upheld, 5–4, against an equal protection challenge. The Kentucky law made two distinctions between the two classes. First, the burden of proof for the involuntary commitment of the mentally retarded was clear and convincing evidence but the burden of proof required for the mentally ill was beyond a reasonable doubt. Second, guardians and immediate relatives of mentally retarded persons were permitted to participate in the involuntary commitment proceedings of a mentally retarded person but not in such proceedings for a mentally ill person. Citing *Cleburne*, rational basis review was applied to the classification. Less demanding procedures for the mentally retarded than the mentally ill were rational because mental retardation was a static condition and was easier to diagnose. In addition, treatment of the mentally retarded tends to be less invasive than the treatment accorded to the mentally ill. Classifications which do not involve fundamental rights or "proceed along suspect lines" are accorded a "strong presumption of validity." *Heller v. Doe* (1993).

The traditional deferential rationality test is still the norm in economic regulation. An Ohio statute requiring its state universities to develop instructional workload standards for faculty and exempting those standards from collective bargaining did not violate Equal Protection. *Central State University v. American Association of University Professors* (1999). The Ohio Supreme Court had held that the state had failed to show any rational basis for singling out state university faculty among public employees generally from bargaining over their workload. The Supreme Court reversed and ruled that the Equal Protection Clause is not violated if disparity of treatment is rationally related to a legitimate government objective. Here the legislature, concerned that research was short–changing teaching, mandated uniform instructional workloads for public university faculty. The legislature could rationally conclude that collective bargaining over instructional workloads would undercut this legitimate governmental purpose.

The deferential standard for economic regulation was employed once again when Iowa imposed a tax rate on slot machines at racetracks that was higher than the tax rate set for slot machines on river boats. A racetrack association contended that since the purpose of granting race tracks authority to operate slot machines was to help them to recover from economic difficulties, the higher tax on race track slots was irrational and constituted a violation of equal protection. The Supreme Court, per Justice Breyer, held that the tax differential did not violate the Equal Protection Clause. The Iowa law permitting racetracks to have slot machines does in fact advance the racetrack's economic interest even though the simultaneous imposition of a higher tax on race track slot machines provides less economic help than might otherwise be the case: "[N]ot every provision in a law must share a single objective." While the differential between the tax on slot machines at racetracks compared to the lower rate on slot machines on river boats might disadvantage racetracks, it was beneficial to river boats who also were having economic difficulties. Applying the rational basis test, Justice Breyer stated that a law might "predominantly serve one general objective" and, at the same time, include "subsidiary provisions" that sought to accomplish other useful, even contrary, objectives. The result might be a law that balances objectives but "still serves the general objectives when seen as a whole." Such was the case here. The task of judicial review ends once a plausible basis on which the legislature may have relied for its enactment is identified. *Fitzgerald v. Racing Association of Central Iowa* (2003).

B. THE NEW EQUAL PROTECTION

1. CLASSIFYING TRAITS

While the traditional rationality test is generally used for equal protection review, the courts will employ a stricter scrutiny when government employs a suspect or quasi-suspect classification. For example, when the government intentionally acts on the basis of race or national origin (and sometimes alienage), strict scrutiny will be used. And when intentional gender or illegitimacy classifications are employed, the law will be tested using intermediate review. The judicial deference normally accorded governmental action is no longer appropriate when the government intentionally confers benefits or imposes burdens on the basis of such classifying traits.

But why isn't deference appropriate? What justification is there for judicial activism when such classifications are involved? Perhaps the suspect treatment of racial classifications could be explained simply as a matter of history: "[T]he clear and central purpose of the [Equal Protection Clause] was to eliminate all official state sources of invidious racial discrimination in the States." *Loving v. Virginia* (1967) [miscegenation laws held violative of equal protection and due process]. But this explanation would probably justify only judicial activism in race cases. A broader rationale can be found in the concept of "stigma" or "caste." When a particular group is regularly treated as inferior, ["implying inferiority in civil society," *Strauder v. West Virgi-*

nia (1880)], special judicial solicitude is appropriate. This concern is enhanced when the discrimination visited on the class is pervasive in the society. It is argued that government must treat persons on the basis of merit and not on the basis of immutable traits or stereotypes. See *Regents of the Univ. of California v. Bakke* (1978).

Another approach to the rationale making certain classifications suspect is grounded on Justice Stone's famous footnote four in *United States v. Carolene Products Co.* (1938): "[P]rejudice against discrete and insular minorities may be a special condition, which tends seriously to curtail the operation of those political processes ordinarily to be relied upon to protect minorities, and may call for a more searching judicial scrutiny." These specially disadvantaged groups, these insular minorities, have a special claim to judicial protection since the ordinary political processes for redressing injury are closed to them because of prejudice.

The discrimination that entails heightened judicial scrutiny may be contained in legislation. In *Loving v. Virginia* (1967), the Court held that a statute prohibiting marriages between the races violates equal protection. Chief Justice Warren, for the Court, noted that "the fact of equal application does not immunize a statute from the very heavy burden of justification which the Fourteenth Amendment has traditionally required of state statutes drawn according to race." The Court found "no legitimate overriding purpose independent of invidious racial discrimination that might justify

Purpose + Effect

the racial classification." See *Strauder v. West Virginia* (1880) [murder conviction of a Black by a jury from which Blacks were excluded by state law violates equal protection].

Alternatively, discrimination may be found in the administration of a racially-neutral law. *Yick Wo v. Hopkins* (1886) dealt with a law requiring a permit to operate a laundry unless the laundry was located in a brick or stone building. Yick Wo, a Chinese alien, was convicted for operating a laundry without a permit. His conviction was reversed. Whatever the merits of the statute itself, the law had been administered in a discriminatory manner. Statistics demonstrated that permits were denied to Chinese applicants while being granted to others. "Though the law itself be fair on the face yet, if it is applied and administered by public authorities with an evil eye and unequal hand, the denial of equal justice is still within the prohibition of the Constitution." The Court found no reason for the discrimination other than hostility to the race and nationality of the Chinese applicants. The administration of the law, therefore, violated equal protection.

Whether it is a law or its enforcement that is the subject of the litigation, the challenger must establish that the classification is intentional [de jure] before a stricter standard of judicial review will be used. While the discriminatory effect or impact of a law or administrative action may be evidence of discriminatory intent, "[a] purpose to discriminate must be present. Standing alone, [disproportionate impact] does not trigger the rule that racial classifi-

cations are to be subjected to the strictest scrutiny
and are justifiable only by the weightiest of considerations." *Washington v. Davis* (1976) [fact that
police qualifying test produces racially discriminatory results held insufficient to establish equal protection violation]. Discrimination need not be the sole
or even the primary basis for the law, but it must
be one of the objectives. *Village of Arlington
Heights v. Metropolitan Housing Dev. Corp.* (1977).
While discriminatory effects may suffice for some
congressional civil rights statutes [*Griggs v. Duke
Power Co.* (1971)], the key for constitutional litigation is whether the discrimination is intentional.
Hunter v. Underwood (1985) [state constitutional
provision disenfranchising persons convicted of a
crime of moral turpitude held violative of equal
protection because, while racially neutral on its
face, the original enactment was motivated by a
desire to discriminate against Blacks].

Must be intentional

The fact that the government adopts a policy
knowing discrimination will result does not satisfy
this requirement of intent. In *Personnel Adm. of
Massachusetts v. Feeney* (1979), a state law granting
a preference for veterans in state employment was
challenged as discriminating against women since
veterans are overwhelmingly males. In rejecting the
equal protection challenge, the Court stated: " 'Discriminatory purpose' implies more than intent as
volition or intent as awareness of consequences. It
implies that the decision-maker selected or reaffirmed a particular course of action at least in part
'because of,' not merely 'in spite of,' its adverse

effects upon an identifiable group." While the state legislature could foresee that use of the preference policy would disadvantage women, its objective was to benefit veterans, male or female—it acted "in spite of" the negative effect on women.

Discrimination may be overt or covert. A statute or a formal administrative rule or regulation may be discriminatory on its face. In *Palmore v. Sidoti* (1984), the Court, per Chief Justice Burger, held that a state court's overt consideration of community racial bias in determining child custody (the white mother was cohabiting with a black male) violated equal protection. Chief Justice Burger noted that the state court "was entirely candid and made no effort to place its holding on any ground other than race." While the objective of granting custody based on the best interests of the child represented a substantial interest, "[t]he effects of racial prejudice, however real, cannot justify racial classification."

Similarly, in a case involving a black accused, it was held that a prosecutor could not, consistent with equal protection, use peremptory challenges to exclude black jurors solely on their race. A showing of purposeful discrimination in selection of a jury makes out a prima facie case for the defendant. The state then has the burden of coming forward with a neutral explanation for its use of peremptory challenges against black jurors. *Batson v. Kentucky* (1986). [But cf. *Holland v. Illinois* (1990), where the equal protection issue was not raised by the defendant. Instead the defendant unsuccessfully contend-

ed that the use of peremptory challenges to exclude
all black jurors from the petit jury of a white
defendant violated his Sixth Amendment right to
trial by an impartial jury: "The Sixth Amendment
requirement of a cross-section on the venire is a
means of asserting, not a representative jury (which
the constitution does not demand), but an impartial
one (which it does)"]. *Batson* has been extended to
race-based peremptory challenges by the defense on
the theory that enforcement of such challenges by
the judicial process constitutes state action. *Georgia
v. McCollum* (1992). A Texas criminal court allowed
10 of the prosecution's 14 peremptory strikes
against African–American jurors for allegedly race-
neutral reasons that would have applied equally
well to white jurors who were not challenged and
who were permitted to sit on the jury. Peremptory
challenges had been used to exclude 91% of available African–American jurors but only 13% of non-
African–American jurors had been excluded on the
basis of peremptory challenges. "Happenstance is
unlikely to produce this disparity." The burden of
proof required by *Batson* had been met by the
defendant. In these circumstances, evidence existed
to support a prima facie case that an equal protection violation had occurred. *Miller-El v. Cockrell*
(2003). Subsequently, the Court held, 6–3, that
there was discrimination by the prosecution in sys-
tematically excluding blacks as jurors through the
use of peremptory challenges. *Miller-El v. Dretke*
(2005) Finally, the rule of *Batson* prohibiting race-
based peremptory challenges also applies to civil

litigation. *Edmonson v. Leesville Concrete Co.* (1991).

If the discriminatory intent is not overt, the challenger seeking to secure stricter review must prove that the facially neutral government action is, in fact, covert discrimination. Statistical impact may provide useful evidence of discriminatory intent, but absent a stark pattern of impact, unexplainable on other grounds, "impact alone is not determinative and the Court must look to other evidence." *Village of Arlington Heights.* Similarly, foreseeability or knowledge of discriminatory impact can provide evidence of covert prejudice. *Personnel Adm. of Massachusetts v. Feeney* (1979). Proof of discriminatory purpose can sometimes be found in the historical context in which government actions are taken, in departures from the usual substantive or procedural policies employed, or from contemporaneous statements by government decision-makers. *Village of Arlington Heights.*

In voting discrimination cases challenging use of at-large electoral systems, the courts have looked to the "totality of the circumstances" to determine if there is discriminatory intent. In *Rogers v. Lodge* (1982), the Court upheld a lower court finding of discriminatory intent by county officials based on evidence of the failure of any Black candidate to be elected, the impact of past discrimination on Black political participation, the failure of elected officials to consider the needs of the Black community, past racial discrimination in contexts other than voting, the socioeconomic conditions of the county's Blacks

and electoral requirements minimizing the voting
strength of racial minorities in the county.

An important point in this area is that the racial
animus complained of must derive from government
and not from private individuals. For example, after
a city council by ordinance had approved construction of a low income housing development, a citizen
group petitioned asking that the ordinance be submitted for a referendum vote as provided in the
town charter. The city's voters repealed the ordinance thereby preventing construction of the development. The state supreme court, however, found
that the referendum violated the state constitution.
Meanwhile, those supporting construction had filed
suit in federal court contending that the referendum was racially motivated. Furthermore, they alleged that city officials "by allowing the referendum
petition to stay the implementation of the site plan,
gave effect to the racial bias reflected in the public's
opposition to the project." They pointed to racially
discriminatory statements expressed by voters in
connection with the referendum. The Supreme
Court, per Justice O'Connor, held that the evidence
that racial bias motivated the city's decision to
delay the project until the referendum was insufficient to support a claim of denial of equal protection. By submitting the ordinance to referendum,
the city was simply following the facially neutral
provisions of the city charter. The actions of the city
officials were not motivated by any racial animus
nor had they acted *because of* racially discriminatory intent. Racist expression by private individuals in

connection with the referendum petition drive did not constitute state action; nor could they be attributed to government officials. *City of Cuyahoga Falls v. Buckeye Community Hope Foundation* (2003).

If the challenger proves discrimination was *a* factor motivating the government's action, the burden shifts to the government. The state may seek "to rebut the presumption of unconstitutional action" by showing that discriminatory purpose was not the basis for the discriminatory impact. *Washington v. Davis* (1976). It may also be possible for the state to avoid strict scrutiny by proving that it *would* (not could) have reached the same result even if discrimination had not been involved. *Village of Arlington Heights.* Essentially, the state argues that its racially-motivated action did not cause the harm. Alternatively, the state must overcome the strict standard of equal protection review.

a. Race and Ethnic Origins

Race is the paradigm suspect classification. As Chief Justice Burger explained in *Palmore v. Sidoti* (1984): "A core purpose of the Fourteenth Amendment was to do away with all governmentally-imposed discrimination based on race. Classifying persons according to their race is more likely to reflect racial prejudice than legitimate public concerns; the race, not the person, dictates the category." Simply, race should generally be a neutral factor in allocating public benefits and burdens. When race is used, the law is suspect and "subject to the most exacting scrutiny." *Palmore.* The government has the bur-

den of proving that the classification is necessary to
a compelling interest. Application of this standard
of review generally results in a holding that the law
violates equal protection. But see *Korematsu v.
United States* (1944) [exclusion of Japanese–Americans from areas of West Coast during World War II
upheld on grounds of extreme military danger from
sabotage]. The same strict scrutiny treatment has
been given to discrimination based on national origin. *Hernandez v. Texas* (1954) [discrimination
against Mexican Americans in selection for jury
service, reflecting "community prejudice," held un-
constitutional].

(1) *Segregation in Education.* Through most of
the 20th century, even officially-sanctioned racial
segregation in matters of "social, as distinguished
from political equality," was held not to violate the
Equal Protection Clause. *Plessy v. Ferguson* (1896)
[law requiring "equal but separate" railway accommodations for whites and blacks upheld]. But in
Brown v. Board of Educ. (1954), the Court held that
"[s]eparate educational facilities are inherently unequal and that laws requiring or permitting racial
segregation of schools violate equal protection."
While the Court in *Brown I* emphasized the harm to
children from educational segregation, the rejection
of state sanctioned racial segregation was summari-
ly extended to other public facilities.

Would racial segregation in the schools that was
not attributable to government action violate equal
protection? Today *Brown I* is treated by the courts
as a condemnation *only* of intentional or de jure

state segregation. *Keyes v. School Dist. No. 1* (1973). Racial segregation in the schools which is not proven to be the product of intentional government action (*i.e.*, de facto segregation) does not violate equal protection even if it is proven that children suffer from the educational racial segregation. The state has no constitutional duty to remedy racial segregation in schools which it has not caused. Thus, even a formerly de jure segregated school system which has desegregated is not constitutionally required to remedy segregation produced by changing social conditions. *Pasadena City Bd. of Educ. v. Spangler* (1976).

Determining when a school has "desegregated" has produced an uncertain standard. The Court has held that a public school district which has been under a judicial order to desegregate may still implement a new busing plan which would result in one race schools. But the school district must have complied in good faith with the initial judicial order and the vestigial remnants of past de jure discrimination must have been eradicated as far as practicable. Regulatory control of a federal court over a public school system should not continue beyond the time necessary to remedy consequences of "past intentional discrimination." *Board of Education of Oklahoma City v. Dowell* (1991). Moreover, the federal district court may relinquish supervision and control over a school district in incremental stages. The court's objective must be to remedy the violation and to restore to the local authorities a school system which is operating in compliance with the constitution. "A transition phase in which control is relinquished in a gradual way is an appropriate means to this end." *Freeman v. Pitts* (1992).

If a school district is found to have engaged in de jure racial segregation, what remedy is appropriate? The remedy in the *Brown* litigation might have been simply to order the immediate admission of members of the plaintiff class to the schools on a nonracial basis. But in *Brown v. Board of Educ.* (1955) (*Brown II*), the Court, perhaps anticipating strong public reaction, ordered only desegregation "with all deliberate speed." However, federal courts were instructed to retain jurisdiction, apply equitable principles (no specific standards were provided) and to assure that school boards engaged in good faith compliance to desegregate "as soon as practicable." *Brown II* is generally credited (or blamed) for having launched modern public law litigation where courts engage in large scale institutional reform to remedy a generalized injury to a large class.

The aftermath of *Brown II* was a slow process of resistance and desegregation. Eventually, the Court held that "[c]ontinued operation of segregated schools under a standard of allowing 'all deliberate speed' for desegregation is no longer constitutionally permissible. Under explicit holdings of this Court, the obligation of every school district is to terminate dual systems at once and to operate now and hereafter only unitary schools." *Alexander v. Holmes County Bd. of Educ.* (1969).

Today, if the courts find that a school system has engaged in de jure, intentional racial segregation, the school system has an affirmative duty to desegregate—"to take whatever steps might be necessary to convert to a unitary system in which racial discrimination would be eliminated root and branch." *Green v. County School Bd. of New Kent County* (1968). Any actions by a school board under this affirmative duty which have even the *effect* of impeding desegregation violate equal protection. *Wright v. Council of Emporia* (1972). Again, note that school systems that are only de facto segregated have no affirmative duty to desegregate and can act even if their actions have disparate racial impact. This same principle governs segregation between city and suburbs (*i.e.*, interdistrict litigation). A challenger must show "that racially discriminatory acts of the state or local school districts, or of a single school district have been a substantial cause of interdistrict segregation." *Milliken v. Bradley* (1974). De jure, intentional segregation establishes the constitutional wrong creating the affirmative duty to desegregate.

Even though a state has established race neutral policies to govern its system of state supported colleges, the state has not necessarily met its affirmative obligation to dismantle a de jure system of segregated higher education. Thus, admission requirements for Mississippi's public universities required higher standardized test scores for its historically white institutions than for its historically black institutions. Similarly, the historically white institutions offered more comprehensive programs and graduate degrees. These policies and practices, attributable to a heritage of de jure segregated higher education, have segregative effects, including the continuing racial identifiability of colleges within the state system and thus constitute impermissible state action. *United States v. Fordice* (1992).

When segregation is a product of a law requiring a dual school system as in *Brown II,* de jure segregation is clearly present. But as the courts began to confront northern style segregation involving covert racial discrimination, finding intentional or purposeful discrimination has been more problematical. Generally, the courts engage in a fact-based inquiry into purpose, focusing on policies and actions of the school board. In addition, certain judicially-crafted presumptions have proven valuable. If it is established that a substantial part of a school system is de jure segregated, there is a presumption that other segregation in the district is de jure. To rebut this presumption, the school board must prove that the de jure segregation was an isolated event, not affecting other parts of the system. *Keyes v. School Dist. No. 1* (1973). The existence of past de jure segregation in a district creates a presumption that present segregation is attributable to the past conduct. Further, "actions having a foreseeable and anticipated disparate impact are relevant evidence to prove the ultimate fact, forbidden purpose." *Columbus Bd. of Educ. v. Penick* (1979); *Dayton Bd. of Educ. v. Brinkman* (1979) (*Dayton II*).

When de jure segregation is established, the federal courts have broad equity powers to remedy the constitutional wrong. In *Swann v. Charlotte–Mecklenburg Bd. of Educ.* (1971), the Court provided guidance to lower courts for "balancing of the individual and collective interests." While lower courts may not require racial balance in the schools, the Chief Justice concluded that numerical ratios based on the racial composition of the students in the system (which were used by the lower court) provide "a useful starting point" in fashioning an effective remedy. A reasonable amount of busing where needed to remedy past discrimination was also approved. But the Chief Justice warned against use of busing where the time and distance involved threatens the health or education of the children.

Judicial approval of busing has provided a rash of federal and state efforts to curb use of this remedy. Congressional measures which simply curb use of federal funds for busing or limit the executive in seeking busing orders may be constitutional. But there is greater doubt whether Congress can prevent a federal court from ordering busing where it is the only effective way of remedying de jure segregation. In such cases, denial of the remedy can be viewed as effectively denying the constitutional right or might intrude on the judicial function in violation of the separation of powers.

State laws prohibiting the use of busing, at least when de jure segregation is present, are unconstitutional. *North Carolina State Bd. of Educ. v. Swann* (1971). State legislative efforts to curb *voluntary* busing programs aimed at de facto segregation have failed to generate any general principle. When the legislation alters the usual process for making school policy decisions by denying a school board the power to order busing, the law is based on the racial characteristic of the policy and violates equal protection. *Washington v. Seattle School Dist. No. 1* (1982). But a state constitutional amendment which would prevent state courts from ordering busing to remedy de facto segregation was upheld. The law was racially neutral on its face and was not enacted for a discriminatory purpose. School boards could still order busing. Equal protection does not prevent repeal of a particular judicial remedy which goes beyond the federal constitutional mandate. *Crawford v. Board of Educ. of Los Angeles* (1982).

The scope and the limits on a federal district court's power to remedy de jure racial segregation were delineated by Justice White for the Court in *Missouri v. Jenkins* (1990). A federal district court's order increasing local taxes to satisfy a school de-segregation decree violates the principles of federal/state comity. Although the federal district court may not itself raise taxes, it may order local governments to do so if it is necessary to implement its school desegregation decree even though the increase will exceed the limit on taxes imposed by state statute. The latter holding was objected to by four dissenters who complained, per Justice Kennedy, against the Court's "casual embrace of taxation imposed by the unelected, life-tenured federal" judiciary because of its disregard of "fundamental precepts for the democratic control of public institutions."

A federal court cannot order salary increases and remedial education programs just because student achievement levels were still at or below national norms. This aspect of the federal court's remedial decree was too far removed from the task of eliminating the racial identifiability of Kansas City schools and therefore was beyond the "admittedly broad discretion of the federal court." The nature and scope of the remedy are determined by the violation. The federal court decree must be directly responsive to the constitutional violation. *Missouri v. Jenkins* (1995).

Spallone v. United States (1990) outlined some further do's and don'ts for federal courts in the context of judicially imposed desegregation orders. A federal district court order which imposed monetary sanctions upon individual Yonkers city council members for failure to vote to implement a housing desegregation order was invalidated as an abuse of discretion. Judicial imposition of such sanctions on legislators constituted a perversion of the normal functioning of the legislative process because it caused legislators "to vote, not with a view to the interest of their constituents or of the city, but with a view solely to their own personal interest." On the other hand, imposition of a daily fine on the city for the duration of the contempt had a reasonable likelihood of success and was valid. In the event the sanction against the city failed to bring compliance with the judicial order, imposition of contempt citations against individual legislators until they voted to implement the judicial order would presumably be valid.

(2) *Affirmative Action*. Courts regularly use race as a basis for remedying past de jure segregation. *Swann v. Charlotte–Mecklenburg Bd. of Educ.* (1971). But a government agency may also voluntarily adopt race-conscious policies in awarding benefits in order to benefit racial minorities. Further, government frequently requires private parties who have not been found to have personally engaged in racial discrimination to take action that would benefit racial minorities. Is strict scrutiny appropriate for these intentional racial classifications? In short, what is the status of affirmative action programs under the equal protection guarantee?

In *Regents of the Univ. of California v. Bakke* (1978), the Court considered the validity of a special minority admissions program at University of California–Davis medical school. Under the plan, a separate committee considered applicants from four designated minority groups for 16 out of 100 available places. Alan Bakke, a white, was denied admission even though he had higher numerical scores than some special program applicants who were admitted. The Court held 5–4 that the Davis plan violated Title VI of the 1964 Civil Rights Act. More significantly, five Justices accepted the principle that a public university can use a race-conscious admissions program; that the use of racial considerations will not *per se* violate equal protection. But there was not agreement among these five justices

on when a race conscious admissions program
would pass constitutional muster.

Justice Powell, providing the critical swing vote, argued for the use of strict scrutiny in reviewing discrimination even if whites as a class are disadvantaged. Arguing for a principle of individualized justice, Powell stressed that equal protection is a personal right of an individual to be judged on the basis of individual worth and merit and not on the basis of class membership. Applying strict scrutiny, Powell concluded that, while remedying societal discrimination may be a compelling interest for some governmental institutions, a state medical school was not in a position to fashion an appropriate remedial program. Decisions based on race must be made by government policy makers in a position to narrowly tailor the race-conscious program to further the compelling interest with the least burden to the disadvantaged race (*i.e.*, structural due process). Promoting diversity in the student body, on the other hand, is a compelling interest for a university. However, the Davis quota system, in which consideration for 16 places was based solely on race, was not a "necessary" means for promoting diversity. Race could simply be considered a plus factor in admissions decisions. The Davis program, Powell concluded, violated both Equal Protection and Title VI and he joined with four other Justices who decided only that the Civil Rights Act was violated.

Four other Justices (led by Justice Brennan) argued for intermediate equal protection review. Whites as a class do not have any of the traditional

Strict
Scrut.

factors of suspectness. They are not the special
beneficiaries of the Fourteenth Amendment nor
have they historically experienced pervasive discrimination. They are not politically insular. And,
most important, the racial classification imposes no
stigma on them; whites are not viewed as a caste,
as morally inferior. While strict scrutiny was therefore inappropriate, rationality review was also inadequate. Benign classification often masks race
prejudice. Preferential treatment tends to foster
race consciousness in government and racial stereotypes that run counter to the ideal of success
based on individual merit and achievement. Brennan concluded that benign racial classification
"must serve important governmental objective and
must be substantially related to achievement of
those objectives." Since "minority underrepresen-
tation is substantial and chronic, and the handicap
of past discrimination is impeding access of minorities to medical school," the Davis program was
substantially related to government's interest in
remedying the discriminatory effects of societal discrimination.

In *Fullilove v. Klutznick* (1980), seven Justices
again accepted the principle that race conscious
programs to remedy discrimination may be constitutional. The Court 6–3 upheld, against a Fifth
Amendment challenge, a congressional statute requiring that 10% of federal public work project
funds be used by a grantee to purchase services or
supplies from businesses controlled by designated
minorities. Chief Justice Burger, in a plurality opin-

ion joined by Justices White and Powell, applied a "most searching examination," concluding that the program would satisfy either the strict scrutiny or intermediate review tests. Stressing the broad remedial powers of Congress, the Chief Justice noted that the program was limited in extent and duration and was narrowly-tailored to the end of remedying discriminatory treatment of minorities on public works projects.

Justice Powell, concurring, reaffirmed his support for a strict scrutiny standard which he found satisfied. Justices Marshall, Brennan and Blackmun, using their *Bakke* intermediate test, concurred. Justice Stevens dissented based on his conclusion that the Act was not narrowly tailored to achieve any remedial objective. Only Justices Stewart and Rehnquist, dissenting, adopted the view that "the government may never act to the detriment of a person solely because of that person's race. The color of a person's skin and the country of his origin are immutable facts that bear no relation to ability, disadvantage, moral culpability or any other characteristics of constitutionally permissible interest to government. In short, racial discrimination is by definition invidious discrimination." Even a race-conscious judicial decree is permitted only to remedy "the actual effects of illegal race discrimination."

In *City of Richmond v. J. A. Croson Co.* (1989), a city ordinance requiring prime contractors awarded city construction contracts to subcontract at least 30% of the dollar amount of each contract to "Minority Business Enterprises" was held, per Justice

O'Connor, to violate equal protection. A key development in *Croson* was its holding that the "standard of review under the Equal Protection Clause is not dependent on the race of those burdened or benefitted by a particular classification." Strict scrutiny should therefore be applied to all racial classifications: "Absent searching judicial inquiry into the justification for such race-based measures, there is simply no way of determining what classifications are 'benign' or 'remedial' and what classifications are in fact motivated by illegitimate notions of racial inferiority or simple racial politics." Justices Marshall, joined by Justices Blackmun and Brennan, dissented. They still adhered to use of an intermediate standard of review for remedial racial classifications.

Could a municipal minority set aside program ever meet a strict scrutiny standard? Justice O'Connor responded to this question in *Croson* by saying that elimination of government's passive support for private racial discrimination would be a compelling interest. However, Richmond's ordinance was not based on a record that showed specific statistical findings that the city was actually remedying specific past acts of illegal racial discrimination by the city. In addition, the city's plan was not narrowly drawn. Racial quotas should not be used where other means such as case-by-case consideration was possible. Rather than race-conscious remedies, racially neutral alternatives should be used. The city is required to consider the effects of its remedial program on third parties. It is also bound to limit the program's scope and duration.

Croson's larger meaning for the future of affirmative action has stimulated considerable controversy. The minority set aside upheld on the federal level in *Fullilove* was distinguished on two grounds. First, Congress has unique legislative enforcement powers under Sec. 5 of the Fourteenth Amendment. Second, Congress included a waiver procedure in its set aside program showing that Congress clearly recognized that the scope of the discrimination problem would vary from market to market. A question *Croson* was silent on, however, was whether its view that strict scrutiny applied to all racial classifications undermined the race conscious program upheld in the context of public university education in *Bakke*. However, *Bakke* is arguably distinguishable on the ground that, even under the *Croson* framework, the value of diversity in education represented by the use of race as a factor in admissions is a compelling governmental interest.

Croson had held that the strict scrutiny standard should be used for state mandated local racial classifications. *Fullilove* had stressed that race-conscious programs mandated by Congress warrant more deferential treatment. This deference to Congress was underscored when two FCC minority preference policies aimed at encouraging diversity of viewpoint in broadcast programming were held, 5–4, not to violate equal protection. One FCC policy at issue gave an "enhancement" to a license applicant which could show minority participation and management in its ownership. The other minority preference policy at issue was the "distress sale" policy which allowed a licensee facing revocation or non-renewal to transfer the license to a qualified minority-controlled firm without having to undergo an FCC hearing. The policies served First Amendment values and implemented the important government interest in promoting diversity of information and views in broadcast programming. Both the FCC and Congress had found that there was a substantial nexus between the minority preference programs and increasing minority ownership and participation in broadcasting. Moreover, the programs did not involve quotas and nonminorities were still able to compete for licenses. *Metro Broadcasting, Inc. v. FCC* (1990).

In short, the teaching of *Metro Broadcasting, Inc. v. FCC* (1990), per Justice Brennan, was that in light of the deference that should be accorded Congressionally mandated benign race-conscious programs, such programs, if substantially related to the achievement of an important governmental interest did not violate equal protection so long as they do not impose "undue burdens on nonminorities." The challenged FCC minority preference programs did not have to satisfy the strict scrutiny standard of review. Instead, in such circumstances, an intermediate standard of review should be applied.

Metro Broadcasting's holding applying the less rigorous intermediate standard of review to federal affirmative action programs proved to be short-lived. The vehicle for its demise involved a federal practice which gave general contractors on federal government projects a financial incentive to hire "socially and economically disadvantaged individuals." The Small Business Act provided that such individuals should be presumed to be members of specified minority groups. A prime contractor solicited bids from subcontractors. Adarand Construction Co., a nonminority subcontractor, submitted the low bid. Gonzales Construction Co., although not the low bidder, had been certified as a small business controlled by "socially and economically disadvantaged individuals" and was awarded the subcontract.

Adarand brought suit on the basis that the presumption in the Small Business Act discriminated on the basis of race in violation of the equal protection component of the Fifth Amendment. The Court held, 5–4, per Justice O'Connor, that all racial classifications whether enacted by federal, state or local governments must be evaluated under the strict scrutiny standard., *i.e.* must serve a compelling governmental interest and must be narrowly tailored to serve that interest. To the extent that *Fullilove* and *Metro Broadcasting* were inconsistent with that holding, those cases were overruled. *Adarand Constructors, Inc. v. Pena* (1995). Justice O'Connor noted that the Court below had not passed on whether subcontractor compensation clauses could be characterized as "compelling," or whether consideration had been given to the use of race neutral means to increase minority participation in government contracting, or whether the federal program here was structured to last longer than the discriminatory effects it was designed to eradicate. The Court, therefore, did not invalidate the challenged federal program but remanded the matter for consideration in the light of the principles announced.

Croson had established three principles—skepticism, consistency and congruence. Skepticism meant that any preference based on racial or ethnic criteria had to evaluated under a most searching examination. Consistency demanded that the standard of review under the equal protection clause could not be dependent on the race of the person burdened or benefitted by the particular classification. Congruence required that equal protection analysis be the same for government racial classifications whether state or federal. *Metro Broadcasting's* adoption of the intermediate scrutiny standard of review for Congressionally mandated "benign" racial classifications was contrary to prior precedent. First, it ran counter to the idea in *Croson* that strict scrutiny should be applied to all racial classifications. Second, *Metro Broadcasting* was a rejection of the congruence idea in *Croson* because *Metro Broadcasting* permitted benign racial classifications enacted by the federal government to be treated less skeptically than those of state and local governments. The three ideas that *Croson* established flow from the principle that both the Fifth Amendment and the Fourteenth Amendment protect persons and not groups. Finally, Justice O'Connor observed in *Adarand* that strict scrutiny was *not* " 'strict in theory but fatal in fact.' "Government is not disqualified from dealing with the practice and effects of racial discrimination by race-based action which satisfies the compelling interest and narrowly tailored test. Justice Souter, dissenting, thought that the *Adarand* view of strict scrutiny as applied to a remedial racial preference would in fact not function differently than "*Fullilove's* unlabeled standard."

Justice Ginsburg in dissent took a similar tack: "Today's decision thus usefully reiterates that the purpose of strict scrutiny 'is precisely to distinguish legitimate from illegitimate uses of race in government decisionmaking' "and to distinguish between permissible and impermissible uses of race in governmental racial classifications. In short, Justice Ginsburg argues that "benign" racial classifications may be able to survive the strict scrutiny standard set forth in *Adarand*. At least two on the Court—Thomas and Scalia—do not agree.

Justice Scalia, who otherwise joined the Court's opinion, contended that remedial "benign" discrimination could never meet the strict scrutiny standard of review: "[U]nder our Constitution there can be no such thing as either a creditor or a debtor race." Similarly, Justice Thomas insisted that government sponsored racial discrimination based on benign prejudice is just as noxious as discrimination inspired by malicious prejudice. In summary, it seems at the very least that the requirement in *Adarand* that all racial classifications be evaluated under a strict scrutiny standard—even in the light of the ameliorative language in Justice O'Connor's opinion—means that those seeking to validate such classifications, particularly on the federal level, will find it far more difficult to satisfy than in the past.

Croson and *Adarand* raised questions about whether affirmative action programs in the public educational arena could meet the strict standard of review. In *Bakke*, only Justice Powell had applied that standard. Acknowledging that the use of race as a factor in admissions in the public education context had not been considered since *Bakke*, the Court in *Grutter v. Bollinger* (2003) ruled, per Justice O'Connor, 5–4, that the affirmative action admissions program of the University of Michigan Law School did not violate equal protection. Justice O'Connor used the constitutional analysis, including the strict scrutiny standard, set forth by Justice Powell in his opinion in *Bakke*. This ended the debate about whether the Powell opinion, joined in its entirety only by him, was binding precedent. The compelling governmental interest component of the strict scrutiny standard was met. The law school had a compelling interest in securing a diverse student body. The law school sought a "critical mass" of students from otherwise under represented minorities because that was necessary to "further its compelling interest in securing the educational benefits of a diverse student body." Moreover, deference should be extended to the law school's judgment about the importance of diversity in the selection of its students because of the First Amendment interest in educational autonomy.

Diversity in the student body was also critical because of the importance of diversity in the military, business and supplying society's leadership. In using this broad view, the Court went beyond Justice Powell's approach in *Bakke* which focused on educational benefits. Furthermore, the law school program satisfied the narrow tailoring element of the strict scrutiny standard as well. The law school did not use quotas. Neither did it place racial groups on separate admissions tracks nor did it award a set number of points to applicants based on their minority racial status. This latter point served to distinguish the law school situation from the admissions program in the liberal arts college at the University of Michigan which in fact did award a set number of points to members of specified minority groups. Race or ethnicity could be a plus factor in admissions decisions but the key to satisfying the narrow tailoring requirement was "individualized consideration of each and every applicant." Although narrow tailoring did not demand exhaustion of every conceivable race neutral alternative, the Court declared that its expectation was that "25 years from now, the use of racial preferences will no longer be necessary to further the interest approved today."

Chief Justice Rehnquist, joined by Justices Scalia, Kennedy and Thomas, dissenting, complained that the majority's approach to the strict scrutiny standard was unprecedented in its deference. The law school's actual admissions practices was aimed not at achieving a "critical mass" but rather to make admissions offers to minority group applicants in direct proportion to their statistical portion of the

pool of applicants. Similarly, the dissent scoffed at
the 25 year limitation on the law school program.
The majority's expectation was much too vague.
Strict scrutiny required a time limit on a race
conscious program that was precise.

In *Gratz v. Bollinger* (2003), a companion case to
Grutter, Chief Justice Rehnquist for the Court, 6–3,
ruled that the admissions program at the liberal
arts college of the University of Michigan violated
equal protection. The program failed the narrow
 tailoring component of the strict scrutiny standard.
Members of specified racial minorities were awarded 20 points just based on their membership in the
specified minority groups. These 20 points constituted one-fifth of the total needed to assure admission. Although other factors were considered by the
college such as GPAs, SAT scores and high school
activities, the 20 point advantage that applicants
who belonged to the specified racial groups enjoyed
accorded resulted in the race factor being decisive in
assuring the admission "to virtually all minimally
qualified minority group applicants within the specific groups." In short, the individualized consideration which had served to validate the law school
program was lacking here. Indeed, Justice O'Connor who had written the majority opinion in *Grutter*
concurred in *Gratz* just on that basis. Furthermore,
the large number of applicants with which the
university had to deal did not excuse the failure of
the college to give each applicant the individualized
and holistic consideration which the strict scrutiny
standard and its narrow tailoring aspect required.

Justice Ginsburg, joined by Justices Souter and
Breyer, saw no unconstitutional infirmity in the

liberal arts college program. In implementing the equality requirement of the Equal Protection Clause it was important to distinguish between government policies whose objective was inclusion from those whose purpose was exclusion. The college program might be more candid about how it operated than the was the case with the law school program but that was "surely preferable to achieving similar numbers through winks, nods and disguises."

The increasing difficulty which government mandated race-conscious programs confront is particularly evident in the context of voter redistricting. The lead case was a ruling throwing doubt on the validity of North Carolina redistricting legislation which had created a district so irregular in shape that it resembled a " 'bug splattered on a windshield.' "White constituents alleged that the district was formed without regard to " 'compactness, contiguousness, geographical boundaries or political subdivisions.' "

The Court concluded that where state redistricting legislation is inexplicable on any other grounds than race, *i.e.*, the creation of a black Congressional district, such legislation should be accorded the same strict scrutiny that would be extended to other state legislation which classified citizens on the basis of their race, notwithstanding the fact that the district was created as a remedial response to the federal Voting Rights Act. On remand, if the charge of racial gerrymandering remained uncontradicted, the district court was ordered to consider whether the North Carolina plan was narrowly tailored to further a compelling governmental interest. *Shaw v. Reno* (1993).

Was the aversion in *Shaw* to a majority-minority district so irregular in shape as to defy any other explanation for its creation except race unique or did it presage a broader principle? When the Court struck down a Georgia redistricting plan established in response to the Federal Voting Rights Act which created three congressional districts with a black majority, the Court announced there was indeed a governing principle which transcended a district's geometry. The key to the equal protection violation is when race for its own sake and not other traditional race-neutral districting criteria—such as compactness, contiguity, respect for political subdivisions or communities characterized by real shared interests—is the critical factor in establishing the district. In that event, the districting must be subjected to strict scrutiny to ascertain whether it violates equal protection. There is a compelling governmental interest in remedying past racial discrimination but the plan here was designed simply to meet the preclearance requirements of the Justice Department. The bizarre shape of a district may show that race was the predominant factor in the district's creation but parties are not limited to that mode of proof. Evidence of legislative intent may also show that race for its own sake was the predominant factor. The Federal Voting Rights Act does not require the maximum possible number of majority-minority districts. The Federal Voting Rights Act is improperly invoked if it is read to require "the very racial stereotyping which the Fourteenth Amendment forbids." *Miller v. Johnson* (1995).

On appeal of the remand of *Shaw v. Reno*, the Court, per Chief Justice Rehnquist, held that the bizarrely shaped North Carolina Congressional district did in fact violate equal protection. Although other factors may have been present, race was the predominant factor in creating the district. The serpentine shaped district, the least geographically compact in the United States, was deliberately and admittedly formed to create a majority-minority district. Strict scrutiny was not satisfied. Since the majority-minority district in *Shaw* was not established in response to past discrimination, it could not serve as a compelling state interest. Even assuming that compliance with the federal Voting Rights Act itself can be a compelling state interest, the plan still failed because it was not narrowly tailored. The plan far exceeded the demands of the federal Voting Rights Act. *Shaw v. Hunt* (1996).

In an effort to comply with the Voting Rights Act of 1965 and with population changes disclosed by the 1990 census, the Texas legislature established a redistricting plan creating three majority-minority districts. Six Texas voters challenged the plan as an invalid racial gerrymander. The Court, per Justice O'Connor, struck down the plan. True, the plan disclosed mixed motives, *i.e.*, incumbency protection played a part in the shaping of the districts. But the bizarre shape of these districts and their lack of compactness showed that race was the predominant factor in formation of these districts. Two criteria must be satisfied for a state's interest in remedying past discrimination to be compelling: (1) the discrimination being remedied must be specific, identified discrimination and (2) there must be strong evidence that remedial action is necessary *prior* to the establishment of an affirmative action program. The only problem asserted to require remediation here was alleged vote dilution resulting from racial bloc voting. Such problems do not merit race-based districting unless, as *Shaw* indicated, race-neutral districting principles are employed and the "affected racial group's residential patterns" make it possible to create districts in which they will be in the majority. Even assuming that compliance with the Voting Rights Act itself can be a compelling state interest, the plan goes far beyond the requirements of that Act and is, therefore, not narrowly tailored. Accordingly, the plan fails the strict scrutiny standard. *Bush v. Vera* (1996).

In the aftermath of *Miller v. Johnson*, the Georgia legislature found itself unable to establish a redistricting plan. The federal district court entered into the breach and promulgated its own plan. Unlike the three majority-minority districts created by the original plan, the district court's plan created only one such district. This more modest plan was upheld because it applied traditional districting principles such as Georgia's historical preference for not splitting counties outside the Atlanta area and for not splitting precincts. The district court plan satisfied the Voting Rights Act and the Constitution. Even though the district court created only one majority-minority district instead of the previous plan's three such districts, the plan was still valid. *Abrams v. Johnson* (1997).

In response to *Shaw II,* the North Carolina legislature formulated a new districting plan. The federal district court granted the plaintiff's motion for summary judgment because it believed the facts showed that racial rather than political considerations motivated the districting plan. The disputed fact of motivation should not be decided at the summary judgment stage but should be resolved at trial given the sensitive nature of the redistricting process and the presumption of good faith that should be attributed to the legislative judgment. *Hunt v. Cromartie* (1999) (*Cromartie I.*) Two years later, the federal district court held that the districting plan was unconstitutional because it found that race was the dominant factor in drawing the district's boundaries. The Supreme Court, 5–4, per Justice Breyer, reversed and ruled that the district court's factual finding was clearly erroneous. The undisputed evidence showed that in North Carolina there was a close parallel between race and political behavior. The basic issue was whether the district boundaries were drawn because of race rather than political behavior and other traditional nonracial considerations. The demanding burden of proof that must be met by one seeking to set aside a districting plan had not been satisfied. *Easley v. Cromartie* (2001) (*Cromartie II*).

There is no rosetta stone which clearly deciphers all the complexities of the *Shaw* line of cases. This much, however, can be gleaned from the cases. A redistricting plan will be reviewed under strict scrutiny if race was the predominant factor in its creation. This can be shown either through the irregularity of the district's shape or other evidence of intent. Where traditional race neutral districting principles are found to have been subordinated to the allocation of voters by race in the creation of voting districts, such districts will be held to violate equal protection. But *Cromartie II* suggests that setting aside a voting district on the basis of race may be somewhat more difficult than in the past.

b. Alienage: The "Sometimes Suspect" Classification

The status of alienage classifications is confused. Generally, it can be said that when a state awards public benefits to citizens, but denies them to aliens, such classification is "inherently suspect and subject to close judicial scrutiny." Aliens are "a prime example, of a single 'discrete and insular' minority for whom such heightened judicial solicitude is appropriate." *Graham v. Richardson* (1971) [15 year durational residency requirement for alien eligibility for welfare benefits violates equal protection]. Critics of the use of strict scrutiny argue that alienage is not an immutable characteristic and that citizenship requirements are frequently used in the Constitution.

Application of the strict scrutiny standard has resulted in the invalidation of statutes barring aliens from competitive civil service positions [*Sugarman v. Dougall* (1973)] and from eligibility for membership in the state bar [*In re Griffiths* (1973)]. In *Nyquist v. Mauclet* (1977), a statute barring resident aliens from state financial assistance for education unless they indicated an intent to apply for citizenship was invalidated. See also *Plyler v. Doe* (1982) [discrimination against illegal aliens in providing free education held to violate equal protection].

Nevertheless, the Court has fashioned an important "political function" exception to this strict scrutiny principle. When aliens are excluded from voting or from positions "that are intimately related to the process of democratic self-government" [*Bernal v. Fainter* (1984), state law barring aliens from eligibility to become notaries public held unconstitutional], only rationality is required. When the government job relates to "political" rather than "economic" functions and involves broad discretion in the formulation and implementation of the state's self-definition, the state can choose to exclude those who are not part of the political community. Thus, a state may require that police be citizens since police officers "are clothed with authority to exercise an almost infinite variety of discretionary powers" involving the public. *Foley v. Connelie* (1978). The critical role played by teachers in shaping pupils for their roles as citizens and in preserving basic values was stressed by the Court in upholding the exclusion of aliens from public school teaching. *Ambach v. Norwick* (1979). Probation officers, like police and school teachers, were held to exercise official discretion over individuals, thus qualifying for the "political function" exception in *Cabell v. Chavez–Salido* (1982).

But the fact that a state designates a public official as occupying a critical political function will not be decisive. *Bernal v. Fainter* (1984) held 8–1 that the position of notary public does not qualify for the political function exception. Justice Marshall, for the Court, applied a two part test. First, Justice Marshall examined the specificity of the classification to determine if it was substantially over or under-inclusive which "tends to undercut the governmental claim that the classification serves legitimate political ends." While the exclusion applied to only one particular post and thus was not over-inclusive, there was greater concern over whether the law was under-inclusive since citizenship was not required for many state jobs involving similar functions. But the Court found a second inquiry dispositive—a notary public does not "perform functions that go to the heart of representative government." Justice Marshall characterized the functions of a notary as clerical and ministerial. Such officials are not, he said, "invested with policy-making responsibility or broad discretion in the execution of public policy" involving authority over individuals. The state failed to show that the law "furthers a compelling state interest by the least restrictive means practically available."

Strict scrutiny is thus a "sometimes" test when state alienage classifications are challenged. Also, strict scrutiny does not apply to federal laws based on alienage. The federal power over immigration and naturalization produces greater judicial deference. When federal classifications are challenged as violative of the Fifth Amendment, the courts ask only whether the classification is reasonable. *Mathews v. Diaz* (1976) [alien eligibility for federal medical assistance benefits conditioned on 5–year residency and application for permanent residence upheld]. This federal prerogative in matters involving immigration and naturalization has also been used as a basis for finding federal preemption of state laws burdening aliens. *Toll v. Moreno* (1982) [state university policy denying tuition benefits to certain aliens conflicts with federal immigration policy].

c. Gender Classification: Intermediate Review

It is doubtful that the framers of the Fourteenth Amendment ever contemplated that the Equal Protection guarantee would become a vehicle for challenging legal disabilities imposed on women. Prior to the 1970's, gender classifications were generally upheld against equal protection challenge using the highly-deferential rationality standard of review. The discriminatory laws being challenged generally reflected a paternalistic attitude regarding the need to protect "the weaker sex" and assumptions about a woman's proper place in society. *Goesaert v.*

Cleary (1948) [state law excluding women from being licensed as bartenders, but exempting wives and daughters of male bar owners, upheld]. But in 1971 a major shift occurred. In *Reed v. Reed* (1971), the Court unanimously struck down a state law giving men a preference over women as administrators of estates. The state claimed that the law rationally served the public interests in avoiding disputes and in limiting the workload of the probate courts. Chief Justice Burger, however, castigated the preference as "the very kind of arbitrary legislative choice forbidden by the Equal Protection Clause." While the opinion used the language of rationality, the review was more searching and demanding. But if not rationality, what standard should govern gender classification?

Justice Brennan, for a plurality in *Frontiero v. Richardson* (1973) [federal law allowing male servicemen to claim their spouse as dependent but requiring servicewomen to prove the spouse's dependency held unconstitutional], argued for strict judicial scrutiny. He cited the historic discrimination against women, the numerous "gross, stereotypical distinctions between the sexes" in the laws, the "pervasive, although at times more subtle, discrimination" against women today, and the immutability of the sex characteristic which "frequently bears no relation to ability to perform or contribute to society," as rendering sex classifications "inherently suspect." But critics of strict scrutiny for gender classifications have challenged Justice Brennan's efforts to analogize discrimination against women with the suspectness accorded race and ethnicity classifications. Justice Powell in *Bakke* asserts that "the perception of racial classifications as inherently odious stems from a lengthy and tragic history that gender-based classifications do not share." While gender-based laws do often reflect stereotypical thinking about women, critics argue that there is no stigma imposed nor does the classification reflect any assumption that women as a class are morally inferior. And, critics add, women are not a "discrete and insular minority"—they have been guaranteed the vote since 1920 and constitute a numerical majority.

The challenge to a stricter review standard for gender classifications is more compelling when the discrimination is visited upon males as a class. Certainly men have not been politically insular, have not suffered from pervasive historical discrimination and bear no stigma or sense of inferiority from separate treatment. On the other hand, any allocation of government benefits or burdens based on gender, rather than merit, challenges the ideal of individualized justice. Use of the immutable characteristic of sex, whether the discrimination is directed against women or men, often perpetuates gender stereotypes.

Today, gender classifications are subject to an intermediate standard of review: "Classifications by gender must serve important governmental objectives and must be substantially related to achievement of those objectives." *Craig v. Boren* (1976). *Craig* held unconstitutional a law prohibiting the sale of 3.2% beer to males under the age of 21 and to females under 18. While the state had an important interest in traffic safety, statistics offered by the state on the incidence of drunk driving among males and females did not establish that the gender discrimination was closely related to that objective. Justice Rehnquist in dissent challenged the Court's use of a new standard of equal protection review. Both the phrases "important objective," and "substantial relation," he argued, "are so diaphanous and elastic as to invite subjective judicial preferences or prejudices."

In *J.E.B. v. Alabama* (1994), the Court extended *Batson v. Kentucky* (1986) and its ban on race-based peremptory challenges to gender-based peremptories: "[G]ender, like race, is an unconstitutional proxy for juror competence and impartiality." Gender-based peremptories by state actors perpetuated "invidious, archaic and overbroad" stereotypes about the relative abilities of men and women. Aren't *all* peremptory challenges based on social stereotypes? Peremptory challenges not based on group characteristics such as race or gender do not reinforce historical patterns of state and socially imposed race and gender discrimination.

The student should not assume that the stricter review used in gender cases mirrors strict scrutiny and will necessarily result in a determination of invalidity. At times, the Court not only hedged on the appropriate degree of scrutiny in middle tier equal protection but has engaged in an analysis markedly similar to rationality review. In *Michael*

M. v. Superior Court of Sonoma County (1981), the Court held 5–4 that California's statutory rape law, making only men liable for the criminal conduct, does not violate equal protection. Justice Rehnquist's plurality opinion, while reciting the *Craig* intermediate review test, described this standard as simply giving "sharper focus" to the traditional rationality standard. Noting that men as a class are not "in need of the special solicitude of the courts," Justice Rehnquist stressed that a gender classification which "realistically reflects the fact that the sexes are not similarly situated in certain circumstances," will be upheld.

While *Craig* and *Hogan* appeared to probe for the actual or true legislative purpose in enacting the law, *Michael M.* tends to stress the reality of mixed legislative objectives and avoids judicial probing of the claimed state objective. The Court, however, did not suggest that any conceivable purpose would support the gender classification. The state's proffered objective, *i.e.,* preventing illegitimate teenage pregnancies, was to be accepted since it was "at least one of the 'purposes' of the statute." That the law may also have been enacted for "an alleged illicit legislative motive" of protecting the virtue and chastity of young women could not be used to strike down the otherwise constitutional law. Turning to the relation of the gender classification to the state's "strong" social welfare objective, Justice Rehnquist stressed that men and women are not similarly situated with respect to the law since only women could become pregnant. It followed that the state could direct deterrence to males who do not suffer from the consequences of their illicit conduct. This was not a law that "rests on the baggage of sexual stereotypes" but a law that "reasonably reflects the fact that the consequences of sexual intercourse and pregnancy fall more heavily on the female than on the male."

All-female or all-male state sponsored educational institutions have been a source both of litigation and of difficulty for the Court. Illustrative is *Mississippi University for Women v. Hogan* (1982), where the Court struck down (5–4) a women-only admissions policy at a state nursing school. While the plaintiff Hogan could audit courses at the women's school, in order to obtain credits he would have to travel a considerable distance to a state-supported coeducational nursing school: "A similarly situated female would not have been required to choose between foregoing credit and bearing that inconvenience." While the state claimed that the admissions policy served compensatory objectives (*i.e.*, affirmative action), Justice O'Connor for the Court concluded that the state had failed to establish that this was its actual objective given the lack of any disadvantage suffered by women in entering nursing. Instead, the policy tended to perpetuate stereotypic notions and that, she asserted, is illegitimate. Even if the policy were intended as compensatory, Justice O'Connor added, the state had not proven that the policy was "substantially and directly related to its proposed compensatory objective." Allowing males to audit classes undermined any claim that women would be adversely affected by the presence of males. Since the state did not provide a males-only nursing school, the Court did not address the validity of such a "separate but equal" policy. For the dissent, the fact that the state policy added to the educational choices available to women with only a minimal personal inconvenience to the plaintiff meant that only rationality review was appropriate. There simply was no stereotyping involved and no sex class discrimination involved. Even using heightened review, the dissent argued that the state policy was substantially related to promoting diversity in educational choices.

The next case of this kind to come before the Court was Virginia Military Institute (VMI) and its all-male admissions policy. The U.S. sued VMI alleging that its male only admissions policy violated equal protection. The lower federal courts held Virginia had not advanced any state policy which could justify offering VMI's unique educational program to men but not to women. Virginia was given three options: (1) admit women to VMI, (2) establish a parallel institution or program, (3) remove state support thus freeing VMI to operate as a private institution. Virginia chose the second option and developed a parallel program for women, the Virginia Women's Institute for Leadership (VWIL), at Mary Baldwin College. There were significant disparities between Mary Baldwin and VMI. SAT scores, endowment, faculty salaries and number of Ph.D's on the faculty were all lower at Mary Baldwin. The federal district court nonetheless upheld

the VWIL program against an equal protection challenge. The two programs did not have to be mirror
images of each other: "VMI marches to the drum;
Mary Baldwin marches to the melody of a fife. Both
will arrive at the same destination." The Fourth
Circuit, applying a substantial comparability test,
held that women in the VWIL program at Mary
Baldwin would receive a substantially comparable
education to that offered by VMI.

Justice Ginsburg for the Court acknowledged that
some state policies were served by making the
training offered at VMI available only to men. Single-sex education provided some important educational benefits. VMI's famous "adversative"
method, the so-called "rat line," would have to be
altered if women were to be admitted. A state may
want to provide diversity in the educational opportunities it offers its citizens. But instead of a preference for diversity, the history of higher education in
Virginia discloses barriers to women in higher education. The argument that the admission of women
would destroy VMI's adversative system is more in
the nature of a self-fulfilling prophecy than a prov-
en fact. Sex is not a proscribed classification. The
physical differences between men and women are
enduring. Sex classification may be used to compensate women for economic disabilities or to advance
employment opportunities for women. But such
classifications cannot be used to perpetuate an inferior status for women. In *Mississippi University for
Women*, the state justified the exclusion of men
form its nursing school on the ground that it was

engaged in educational affirmative action and its all female admission policy was compensated for discrimination against women. Using a searching review, the Court there found no close relationship between the asserted objective and the actual purpose underlying the discriminatory classification. Using this standard of review the Court concluded Virginia had failed to demonstrate an "exceedingly persuasive justification" for excluding women from the citizen soldier education offered by VMI. The remedy offered by Virginia—the VWIL program at Mary Baldwin is not proportionate to the constitutional violation. *United States v. Virginia* (1996).

The substantial comparability standard used by the Fourth Circuit was too deferential and did not comply with the intermediate standard of review and the "exceeding persuasive justification" necessary to meet that standard. The VWIL program was a "pale shadow" of VMI in curriculum, quality of the faculty "funding, prestige, alumni support and influence." A remedial decree must fit the constitutional violation and seek to eradicate both past and future discrimination. VMI's male only policy was left unaffected by the remedy approved by the lower courts. Virginia must show that its remedial proposal directly addresses and relates to the violation. A remedy must be crafted which will end the exclusion of women from state sponsored educational opportunities for which they are fit. Some alterations by VMI would, of course, be necessary to afford members of each sex privacy and some adjustments in aspects of VMI's physical training program, would also be necessary.

Justice Scalia, dissenting, said that although the Court had rejected the use of strict scrutiny in sex classification cases, the Court in essence now adopted it by substituting the "exceedingly persuasive justification" standard for the intermediate standard of review. The Court finds that VMI's single-sex policy is unconstitutional because several women may be willing or able to undertake VMI's training program: "Intermediate scrutiny has never required a least-restrictive means analysis." The intermediate standard does not require a perfect fit between ends and means. But yet this what the Court's "exceedingly persuasive justification standard" demands.

VWIL at Mary Baldwin College was carefully designed by professional educators to provide an all-female program that would provide similar outcomes to those provided by VMI's all-male program. The VWIL program could have been designed to more closely mirror that offered by VMI complete with rat line and barracks-like quarters. But such an approach would have offered no prospect of success. Expert testimony as found by the courts below showed that there was a legitimate pedagogical basis for the different means employed by VMI and VWIL to achieve substantially similar results.

In summary, for Justice Scalia, the appropriate analysis would have inquired whether the exclusion of women by VMI was "substantially related to an important governmental interest." Virginia has one private all-male and four all-female private colleges. Virginia's decision to fund one public all-male institution on the adversative model is substantially related to an important state policy—diversity in education. The Court's opinion to the contrary, Justice Scalia insisted, marked the death knell of government sponsored single-sex education in the United States.

The above cases suggest that in applying middle tiered review, the Court will generally not invalidate laws for want of an important legislative objective. Instead, whether the classification substantially serves the important objective is the focal point of dispute. The more a law is perceived as resting on archaic stereotypes rather than on identifiable differences between the sexes, the more it is likely to be held violative of equal protection. As a consequence of *United States v. Virginia*, the intermediate standard of review may be applied more rigorously than in the past in light of the "exceedingly persuasive justification" now demanded of it.

(1) *Affirmative Action.* Gender classification, like race classification, can be employed for the benign objective of compensating women for past discrimination. However, the problem of identifying if an allegedly benign law is actually a product of romantic paternalism and reflects sexual stereotypes has proven difficult. As *Mississippi Univ. for Women v. Hogan* indicates, the Court will not simply accept a state claim of affirmative action but will probe to determine if the law is truly compensatory. See

Califano v. Goldfarb (1977) [presumption that widows but not widowers are dependent used in determining Social Security death benefits is based on an "archaic and overbroad generalization." Discrimination against female workers who receive less insurance protection for their spouses than male workers, violates equal protection].

Even if a law is treated as a benign classification favoring women, the Court will probably employ an intermediate standard of review in determining if the discrimination against males is justified—the classification must be shown to be substantially related to the compensatory objective. Remedying past discrimination against women is invariably held to be an important interest. But once again, the problem is whether the gender classification is sufficiently related to the compensatory end. In *Orr v. Orr* (1979), the Court struck down a state law authorizing alimony awards to wives but not husbands. While the objective of helping needy spouses and compensating women for past discrimination during marriage were deemed sufficiently important, the Court determined that sex, in this instance, was not "a reliable proxy for need." Since individualized determinations of financial need were already part of the divorce proceedings, there was no reason to presume that women generally were needy. "Where as here, the State's compensatory and ameliorative purposes are as well served by a gender neutral classification as one that gender-classifies and therefore carries with it the baggage of sexual stereotypes, the State cannot be permitted to classify on the basis of sex." See *Wengler v. Druggists Mut. Ins. Co.* (1980) [law presuming wives' dependency for determining workers' compensation health benefits held unconstitutional. While providing for needy spouses is an important objective, the administrative convenience achieved by presuming dependence is an inadequate justification].

While the above cases establish that the state's invocation of a benign objective will not invariably survive equal protection scrutiny, a truly benign classification has a fairly good chance of surviving stricter scrutiny. Compensation for past discrimination is accepted as an important government interest. And if the law is tailored to remedying specific past discrimination against women, it will be upheld. See, *e.g., Kahn v. Shevin* (1974) [state property tax exemption for female widows, but not male widowers, upheld]; *Schlesinger v. Ballard* (1975) [law providing for later mandatory discharge for female military officers, because of lesser opportunities for women officers to be promoted, upheld]; *Califano v. Webster* (1977) [social security formula permitting women to exclude more low wage earning years than men, based on past discrimination against women, upheld]. But, once again, if the law is simply stereotyping, or if it is merely administratively convenient to use gender, the law will probably fail the stricter scrutiny standard.

(2) *Mothers and Fathers.* Laws built on stereotypes concerning the roles of mothers and fathers in relation to their children are likely to be held viola-

tive of equal protection under intermediate review. For example, a law permitting the mother, but not the father, of an illegitimate child, to veto the child's adoption, regardless of the child's development or the relation of the father to the child, violates equal protection. *Caban v. Mohammed* (1979). However, when a law is perceived by the Court, not as a gender classification, but as discrimination within a particular class, a rationality test has been used. Thus in *Parham v. Hughes* (1979), the Court held that a law barring a father who has not legitimated a child from suing for wrongful death as a means of promoting legitimization does not violate equal protection. Only the father, not the mother, could legitimate the child. Men and women therefore were not similarly situated and need not be treated alike. The law discriminates only against those fathers who have failed to legitimate their child.

A federal statute required that children born out-of-wedlock and outside the U.S. to U.S. citizen fathers must obtain proof of paternity by the age of 18 in order to obtain U.S. citizenship. No such formal proof was required of children born in such circumstances to U.S. citizen mothers. The Court held that the statute did not offend the equal protection component of the Fifth Amendment. *Miller v. Albright* (1998). No opinion attracted a majority of the justices. Justice Stevens, joined by the Chief Justice, rejected the claim that a heavier burden was placed on unmarried male citizens to transfer citizenship to their children to that placed on unmarried female citizens. The different situation of males and females in this regard necessitated different requirements. This distinction did not reflect stereotypical thinking about males and females. The statute's objective was to assure that a person born out-of-wedlock and outside the U.S. who claimed U.S. citizenship have a blood relationship with an American citizen. Congress assumed that mothers will be present at the birth of the child and the event will be listed in a hospital record and a birth certificate. The additional requirements imposed on children of U.S. fathers was based on gender based differences, *i.e.*, fathers are less likely than mothers to have the opportunity to develop relationships. In short, just because a statute makes gender-based distinction does not necessarily mean that it reflects a gender stereotype. In *Nguyen v. INS* (2001), the Court, 5–4, per Justice Kennedy, ruled that the statute at issue in *Miller* did not violate equal protection. That issue had not been resolved by a majority of the Court in *Miller*. The *Nguyen* Court ruled that the statute's distinction between unwed U.S. citizen mothers and unwed U.S. citizen fathers was in substantial furtherance of an important government objective. The statutory distinction was based "on the significant difference between their respective relationships to the potential citizen at the time of birth."

d. Illegitimacy Classification: Intermediate Review

Illegitimacy classifications, while not subject to strict scrutiny, have been reviewed under a middle tier standard since the 1960's. *Levy v. Louisiana* (1968) [law barring unacknowledged illegitimates from recovering for wrongful death of mother held to violate equal protection]; *Weber v. Aetna Casualty & Surety Co.* (1972) [law barring illegitimates from collecting death benefits violates equal protection]. However, the Court has been highly ambivalent over the precise standard to be applied [see *Labine v. Vincent* (1971), upholding an intestate succession law subordinating illegitimate children to other relatives, using a deferential form of judicial review] and even more uncertain as to how heightened review is to be applied in particular fact contexts. While the rationale for a heightened judicial scrutiny has sometimes been found in the "fundamental personal rights" attached to the familial relationship, the Court has more often emphasized the questionable character of illegitimacy as a classifying trait: "the legal status of illegitimacy is, like race and national origin, a characteristic determined by causes not within the control of the illegitimate individual and bears no relation to the individual's ability to participate in and contribute to society."

The ambiguity in application of heightened review in illegitimacy cases is indicated by comparing *Trimble v. Gordon* (1977) and *Lalli v. Lalli* (1978). In *Trimble,* the Court 5–4 struck down an Illinois law barring illegitimate children from inheriting intestate from their fathers unless they were acknowledged and the parents married; the law was not substantially related to a permissible state interest. While the state interest in protecting legitimate family relationships was proper, this end could not be pursued by means of sanctions against illegitimate children. The state had "substantial" interests in dealing with the difficulty of proving paternity and the danger of spurious claims but the law was not "carefully tuned to alternative considerations." The law broadly disqualified illegitimate children even where paternity could be established.

But in *Lalli,* the state interest in a just and orderly disposition of property on death and the problems of proving paternity were sufficient to uphold a state law providing that illegitimate children could inherit intestate from the father only if a court had determined paternity during the father's lifetime. The law was upheld even though it admittedly barred inheritance by some illegitimates where paternity could clearly be established. In a plurality opinion, Justice Powell stated that unlike the law in *Trimble,* the means were not "so tenuous that [the law] lacks the rationality contemplated by the Fourteenth Amendment; it did not disqualify an unnecessarily large number of [illegitimate] children."

In spite of *Lalli,* the Court has continued to apply intermediate review. In *Mills v. Habluetzel* (1982), a Texas law requiring that a paternity suit to establish child support had to be brought before the illegitimate child is one year old was unanimously held "not substantially related to a legitimate state interest." And, in *Pickett v. Brown* (1983), a unanimous Court held a two year statute was not "substantially related" to the state interest in avoiding stale or fraudulent claims. In *Clark v. Jeter* (1988), Pennsylvania's state statute requiring suits to establish paternity to be brought within six years of an illegitimate child's birth was invalidated on equal protection grounds. Even a six year period of limitation did not necessarily provide a reasonable opportunity to assert a claim on behalf of an illegitimate child. *Jeter* applied the intermediate standard of review. The six year period was not substantially related to the state's interest in preventing litigation of stale or fraudulent claims. Other Pennsylvania statutes permitted paternity to be litigated much longer than six years after the illegitimate child's birth.

While it is difficult to draw any principles from the Court's application of heightened equal protection review in illegitimacy cases, it does appear that laws based on stereotypes or prejudice against illegitimates or that impose insurmountable or extremely burdensome obstacles to illegitimates securing equal treatment with legitimate children will be held unconstitutional. While the state may be able to cite important interests which support the laws, the Court will determine that the means used are not "substantially related" to the achievement of the state objective.

e. Discrimination on the Basis of Sexual Preference

The Supreme Court in *Bowers v. Hardwick* (1986) ruled that homosexuals did not have a fundamental due process right to engage in homosexual activity. The Court did not pass, however, on whether legislation discriminating against homosexuals would offend the equal protection clause. A Colorado case raised the equal protection issue. A number of Colorado cities and towns enacted ordinances which barred discrimination based on sexual orientation. A statewide referendum, initiated by opponents of these measures, resulted in the adoption of "Amendment 2" to the Colorado state constitution. Amendment 2 was read to prohibit all legislative, executive or judicial action designed to protect homosexual persons from discrimination. Aggrieved municipalities and homosexual persons brought suit in the state courts to challenge the constitutional validity of Amendment 2. The upshot of this litigation was that Amendment 2 was held to infringe on the fundamental right of homosexuals to engage in the political process. The Amendment failed to meet the strict scrutiny standard and its enforcement was enjoined.

Colorado argued Amendment 2 simply denied gays and lesbians special rights and instead treated them like everyone else. Justice Kennedy for the Court called this contention implausible. In fact, the Amendment changed the legal status of homosexuals and placed them in a "solitary class" of persons who were precluded, as was no other group, from securing specific legal protection against discrimination in both the private and public sectors. Enumeration of the group discriminated against is the way the law renders the "duty not to discriminate concrete."

Amendment 2 imposed a "special disability" only on homosexuals and denied them safeguards others already have or do not need. Equal protection law recognizes, of course, that any classification disadvantages some and advantages others. Unless some fundamental right is burdened or some suspect class targeted, the classification will be upheld if it has a rational relationship to some legitimate objective. But Amendment 2 violated even the conventional—and usually deferential—rational relationship standard. Amendment 2 imposed a broad and "undifferentiated disability on a single named group."

The state asserted that Amendment 2 was based on respect for freedom of association and the liberties of landlords or employers and that it was a way of conserving state resources to better fight discrimination against other groups. But the very breadth of Amendment 2 went far beyond these special justifications. No rationale could explain Amendment 2 except animus toward the group against whom it was directed.

Central to equal protection law—indeed to the rule of law itself—is the idea that government remains "open on an impartial basis to all who seek its assistance." To disqualify an entire class from obtaining specific protection from the law is without precedent. Amendment 2 is invalid since it bears no rational relationship to any legitimate state objective. A state cannot "deem a class of persons a stranger to its laws." *Romer v. Evans* (1996).

Justice Scalia, joined by Chief Justice Rehnquist and Justice Thomas, dissented and contended that the Court's ruling that homosexuals as a class could not be disfavored by the law contradicted *Bowers*. If it was rational for the state to criminalize homosexual conduct, why was it irrational simply to deny favor or protection to those with a tendency to engage in such conduct? Law, contrary to what the Court says, is not impartial. Sexual practices such as polygamy have been, and still are, criminalized. The Constitution says nothing about the practice or status of homosexuality. Society's treatment of that practice and status should be decided by normal democratic means, not by the elite class from which the members of the Supreme Court are selected.

Romer marks the advent of some constitutional protection for homosexuals as a class. Although it uses the rational relationship test—the least protective standard of review—to secure that protection, *Romer*'s holding that animus against an entire class by the state is inherently irrational breaks new ground and may extend beyond gay and lesbian rights. *Romer* is also important for what it did not decide. *Bowers* was not reversed. Homosexual activity is still not viewed as a fundamental right nor are homosexuals treated as a suspect class. The Court's opinion in *Romer* did not even cite *Bowers*. But clearly, the *Bowers* precedent is shaky.

f. Other Bases of Classification

Romer demonstrates that the present Court remains unlikely to add new classifying traits to the lists of suspect and quasi-suspect classifications. Homosexuality is still not treated as either a quasi-suspect or suspect classification. Nor are age classifications [*Massachusetts Board of Retirement v. Murgia* (1976)] and wealth classifications [*James v. Valtierra* (1971) public housing referendum, *Harris v. McRae* (1980), abortion funding for indigents], for example, are not suspect and are subject only to rationality review.

In rejecting mental retardation as a suspect classification in *City of Cleburne v. Cleburne Living Center* (1985), Justice White, for the Court, stated: "[W]here individuals in the group affected by a law have distinguishing characteristics relevant to interests the state has authority to implement, the Courts have been very reluctant, as they should be in our federal system and with our respect for separation of powers, to closely scrutinize legislative choices as to whether, how and to what extent those interests should be pursued. In such cases, the Equal Protection Clause requires only a rational means to serve a legitimate end." Since mental retardation is a characteristic that government can legitimately employ in many decisions, *e.g.*, benign laws to aid the retarded, the Court would not treat legislative action embodying differential treatment as suspect. Using a non-deferential rational basis standard, the Court held that the application of the zoning law to exclude a group home for the mentally retarded was not rationally related to a legitimate government purpose. While *Cleburne* might have provided the rationale for *Romer*, the Court did not use it and instead moved the rational relationship test in a new direction.

2. FUNDAMENTAL RIGHTS

Suspect classifications analysis focuses on the basis on which classifications are drawn. But stricter equal protection review can also be triggered by what is lost as a result of a classification. If a classification significantly burdens the exercise of a fundamental right, strict judicial scrutiny will be applied, *i.e.,* the classification must be necessary to a compelling government interest. Again the student should note the Court's increasing discontent with a rigid tiered approach to equal protection law. There are indications that the Justices are moving towards a sliding scale approach similar to substantive due process review.

The clearest example of fundamental rights equal protection law arises when a law discriminates in the right to engage in protected constitutional activity. For example, when a classification significantly burdens the exercise of express First Amendment rights, traditional rationality review is inappropriate. If a law bars all picketing of schools [*Police Dept. of Chicago v. Mosley* (1972)] or residences [*Carey v. Brown* (1980)], except for labor picketing, such content-based discrimination is more closely scrutinized. "When government regulation discrimi-

nates among speech related activities in a public
forum the Equal Protection Clause mandates that
the legislation be finely tailored to serve substantial
state interests, and the justifications offered for any
distinctions it draws must be carefully scrutinized."
Ibid. See *Larson v. Valente* (1982) [charitable solicitation law operating to discriminate against non-
traditional religion such as Moonies held violative of
the Establishment Clause].

Similarly, if a law discriminates in the exercise of
implied rights a stricter mode of judicial review will
be applied. As indicated below, laws significantly
burdening the right of interstate travel [*Shapiro v.
Thompson* (1969)] or the right to marry [*Zablocki v.
Redhail* (1978)], have been subjected to a more
probing judicial scrutiny.

The most challenging aspect of fundamental
rights equal protection involves stricter review of
classifications burdening the exercise of rights derived from the Equal Protection Clause itself. When
government classification significantly burdens
equality of access to the exercise of the franchise or
equality of access to criminal or civil justice, strict
scrutiny will be used even though there is no independent right. The Equal Protection Clause itself
protects against discrimination in regard to these
fundamental interests. While the Court has not
repudiated the Warren Court legacy in this area of
fundamental rights and interests, the Court has
shown little inclination to use the Equal Protection
Clause as a font for equalizing social inequalities.
See *Dandridge v. Williams* (1970) [welfare]; *San*

Antonio Ind. School Dist. v. Rodriguez (1973) [education].

a. Interstate Travel

There is no express right to travel in the Constitution. Nevertheless, in holding that a one-year durational residency requirement for welfare assistance violates equal protection, the Court stated: "Since the classification here touches on the fundamental right of interstate movement, its constitutionality must be judged by the stricter standard of whether it promotes a *compelling* state interest." *Shapiro v. Thompson* (1969). The source of this fundamental right to travel interstate has never been clearly established by the Court although it is generally treated as an implication of our federalist system embodied in the very structure of the Constitution. In any case, when a state requires that newcomers live in the state for a fixed period of time as a condition of eligibility for benefits otherwise available on an equal basis to residents, the Court has generally invoked fundamental rights equal protection and closely scrutinized the laws. *Memorial Hospital v. Maricopa County* (1974) [one year durational residency requirement for indigents receiving public medical care held violative of equal protection]; *Dunn v. Blumstein* (1972) [one year durational residency requirement for voting held violative of equal protection]; *Shapiro.*

But not every burden on interstate migration is subjected to strict scrutiny review. *Bona fide* residency requirements are generally upheld using rationality review. *McCarthy v. Philadelphia Civil Service Com'n* (1976) [law requiring city employees to be city residents upheld]; *Martinez v. Bynum* (1983) [residence requirement for free public education upheld]. Such laws do not discriminate on the basis of travel but upon whether or not the claimant has acquired residence. Upon achieving such residence, the person participates fully in the program.

In *Sosna v. Iowa* (1975), the Court applied rationality review in upholding a one-year durational residency requirement for divorce. In distinguishing previous durational residency requirements held invalid, Justice Rehnquist explained that the recent traveler was not "irretrievably foreclosed from obtaining some part of what she sought; her access to the courts was merely delayed." The distinction appears to turn on the significance of the burden on the right of interstate migration. When the state law deters or imposes a significant "penalty" on the exercise of the right, strict scrutiny is used. *Shapiro* involved loss of basic necessities of life. Justice Marshall in *Maricopa County* stated: "Whatever the ultimate parameters of the Shapiro penalty analysis, it is at least clear that medical care is as much a 'basic necessity of life' to an indigent as welfare assistance. And, government privileges or benefits necessary to basic sustenance have often been viewed as being of greater constitutional significance than less essential forms of governmental entitlements." Apparently, delay in securing a divorce is not a sufficient "penalty" on travel as to merit strict scrutiny. See *Starns v. Malkerson* (D.Minn.1970) [one year durational residency requirement for lower tuition rates at state universities upheld]; *Jones v. Helms* (1981) [distinctions in the sanction for a parent who abandons a child which depends on whether the defendant left or remained in the state upheld since defendant's own conduct qualified his right to travel].

In some travel cases, the Court has verbally employed the rationality test but struck down the state law. For example, the Court in *Zobel v. Williams* (1982), held that a statutory scheme, whereby Alaska distributed income derived from its natural resources to adult citizens based on the length of each citizen's residence violated equal protection. Unlike the durational residency cases, no Alaska resident was totally denied benefits for failure to satisfy a threshold waiting period. Instead, "fixed permanent distinctions between an ever increasing number of perpetual classes of *bona fide* residents, based on how long they have been in the State" determined the amount of benefits. In this case, the state interests in creating an incentive for establishing residence in Alaska and encouraging prudent management of the funds and resources were not rationally served by distinctions drawn between those already resident in the state. The asserted state interest in recognizing past contributions of citizens was "not a legitimate state purpose" since it would "open the door to state apportionment of other rights, benefits and services according to length of residence." Since the discriminatory treatment could not pass even the rationality test, the Court found it unnecessary to determine if "enhanced scrutiny" would be appropriate. Thus the Court did not determine whether discrimination in access to funds not earmarked for any particular purpose such as welfare or medical services would constitute a "penalty" on the fundamental right triggering strict scrutiny. See *Attorney Gen. v. Soto–Lopez* (1986) [state employment preference limited to veterans residing in the state at the time of entering military service held unconstitutional. Plurality used strict scrutiny, citing right to travel and equal protection. Concurring justices used a rationality test].

A new approach to state legislation infringing the right to travel was evidenced by *Saenz v. Roe* (1999), where a state law limiting the welfare benefits of newly arrived citizens during their first year of residence was invalidated. Instead of using the fundamental rights/equal protection rationale of *Shapiro v. Thompson, supra*, the Court instead revitalized the Privileges and Immunities Clause of the Fourteenth Amendment and the right to travel embraced by that Clause. See Part Two, Individual Rights and Liberties. Newly arrived *bona fide* citizens are entitled to the same public benefits enjoyed by other citizens of the state and the Privileges and Immunities Clause of the Fourteenth Amendment forbids discrimination against them based on their exercise of the right to travel to another state to establish permanent residence. *Saenz* is significant because its Privileges and Immunities rationale may indicate an implicit break on the part of the Court with the fundamental rights branch of equal protection law. The rationality review approach employed in *Zobel* may also illustrate the present Court's disinclination to use *Shapiro*-type analysis.

b. Marriage and Family Life

Zablocki v. Redhail (1978), involved a Wisconsin criminal statute requiring court approval for marriage of any parent having child support obligations. Approval would not be given if support obligations were not being met or if the individual could not prove that the out of custody children would not become public charges. In invalidating the law, Justice Marshall, for the Court, stated: "[Since] the right to marry is of fundamental importance, and since the classification at issue here significantly interferes with the exercise of that right, we believe that 'critical examination' of the state interests advanced in support of the classification is required." As a result of the Wisconsin classification, persons (especially the poor) could be coerced into foregoing their right to marry or be absolutely prevented from getting married. This impact was a significant burden on the right. While the state interests in counseling parents regarding support obligations and assuring the welfare of out of custody children were "sufficiently important state interests," the means were not "closely tailored to effectuate only those interests."

But as *Zablocki* suggests, if the challenged classification does not significantly interfere with the decision to marry, only rationality review is appropriate. *Califano v. Jobst* (1977) [exception to rule terminating disability benefits upon marriage, providing continued benefits for persons who marry another disabled entitled to benefits, upheld using rationality review]. Consider also the abortion funding cases, involving funds for maternity care but not for abortion. In *Harris v. McRae* (1980), the Court held that since there was no violation of the constitutionally protected substantive right, (*i.e.,* no significant burden) the rational basis test was applicable. The Hyde Amendment was rationally related to the legitimate government objective of protecting potential life.

c. Voting

The Fifteenth Amendment, § 1, prohibits abridgment of the franchise by the federal or state government on the basis of race, color or previous condition of servitude. *Gomillion v. Lightfoot* (1960) [racially discriminatory gerrymander held violative of Fifteenth Amendment]. But the Court has never held that there is a general constitutionally protected right to vote. States possess broad power to define residence, age and citizenship qualifications and may choose to fill offices by appointment rather than election. However, if the state does grant the franchise, then the Equal Protection Clause requires equality of access to the franchise. The Court's allegiance to this principle was demonstrated in *Rice v. Cayetano* (2000) which invalidated a Hawaii statute limiting the vote for the board of trustees which managed public trust lands to descendants of the native people of Hawaii. When Hawaii was granted statehood in 1959, the federal government set aside a large bloc of public lands to be managed as a public trust for, among other purposes, the "betterment of the conditions of native Hawaiians." The State unsuccessfully argued that the law, *inter alia,* was similar to the special treatment of Indian tribes. But the Court held that the Fifteenth Amendment demands that voters be treated not "as members of a distinct race but as members of the whole citizenry." The idea that citizens of a designated race are more qualified to vote on an issue than others contradicts the "central meaning of the Fifteenth Amendment."

Is the equal protection mandate satisfied if the government acts rationally? The Court has held that the right to vote is a fundamental interest in democratic society because it is "preservative of other civil and political rights," *Reynolds v. Sims* (1964). When government classification significantly burdens its exercise a more searching review is usually required. This principle applies whether the electoral scheme denies or merely dilutes the franchise.

(1) *Voting Qualifications.* In *Harper v. Virginia State Bd. of Elections* (1966), the Court held state poll taxes violative of equal protection. While Justice Douglas, for the Court, relied in part on wealth discrimination as suspect, it was his treatment of voting discrimination that has endured. While noting the close relation of voting to express First Amendment rights, Justice Douglas did not deem it

necessary to fashion a right to vote: "For it is enough to say that once the franchise is granted to the electorate, lines may not be drawn which are inconsistent with the Equal Protection Clause." The states could not fix voter qualifications that "invidiously discriminate." Nor was rationality review appropriate. Since voting was fundamental, "classifications which might restrain [it] must be closely scrutinized and carefully confined." Since wealth or fee paying had no relation to one's ability to participate intelligently in the electoral process, the poll tax requirement violated equal protection.

Limiting the franchise for school district elections to parents of school children and property owners and lessees was held violative of equal protection in *Kramer v. Union Free School Dist. No. 15* (1969). Chief Justice Warren, stressing the importance of non-discriminatory participation in the electoral process to representative government, employed strict scrutiny review. The ordinary presumption of constitutionality, he argued, was based on the assumption that the state law-making institutions are structured fairly. When this assumption is challenged in the lawsuit, "exacting judicial scrutiny" is required. Applying this standard, the disenfranchisement failed. Assuming that the state might limit the vote to those primarily interested in the electoral outcome, the classification was not tailored to achieve that goal. The classification included many with only a limited interest in the election while excluding many citizens having a distinct interest in school district decisions. See *Cipriano v.*

Houma (1969) [limitation of franchise to property taxpayers for approving issuance of revenue bonds held unconstitutional]; *Phoenix v. Kolodziejski* (1970) [restriction of voting for general obligation bonds to property taxpayers held unconstitutional]. The basic principle is that when state classifications restrict the franchise on grounds other than residence, age, and citizenship, the law cannot stand unless the state can demonstrate that the limitation serves a compelling state interest. *Hill v. Stone* (1975) [requiring majority of property tax-payers to approve sale of bonds for city library held unconstitutional].

But there is an exception to this basic principle for "special interest" elections. In *Salyer Land Co. v. Tulare Lake Basin Water Storage Dist.* (1973), the Court applied the rational basis test in upholding an electoral scheme which limited the franchise to landowners and allocated votes by the assessed value of the land. Strict scrutiny was deemed inappropriate for reviewing the water district's election system because of "its special limited purpose and of the disproportionate effect of its activities on landowners as a group." Essentially the water district was not an entity exercising general governmental powers and a limitation of the franchise to those with a "special interest" in its activities was reasonably related to achieving the statutory objectives. See *Ball v. James* (1981) [limitation of franchise to landowners and weighted voting scheme for electing directors of a large water reclamation district upheld under the rationality test]. But *Ball* should be compared with *Quinn v. Millsap* (1989) where a Missouri constitutional provision requiring ownership of real property as a condition for membership on a board of freeholders was held to violate equal protection on the basis of a rationality standard of review. That the board did not exercise general governmental powers was deemed irrelevant. The right to be considered for public service is guaranteed by equal protection even if the board only recommends proposals and does not enact laws directly. Appreciation for community issues and concern for the community does not rationally depend on property ownership. State objectives could have been achieved by more narrowly tailored means. *Ball* was distinguished in *Millsap* on the ground that the water reclamation district at issue in the former had a peculiarly narrow function and a special relationship to the class of landowners.

Durational residency requirements provides another context in which fundamental rights equal protection has been used to overturn restrictions on the franchise. While *bona fide* residency requirements for voting do not violate equal protection, durational residency requirements which significantly burden both the fundamental interest in voting and the right to travel are frequently held invalid using strict scrutiny. *Dunn v. Blumstein* (1972) [one year state residency requirement held to violate equal protection]. But some limited term durational residency requirements shown to be necessary to serve the state interest in preventing election fraud have survived searching review. *Mar-*

ston v. Lewis (1973) [50 day durational residence requirement upheld].

(2) *Diluting the Franchise.* Equal protection also safeguards against electoral schemes which significantly burden the *effectiveness* of the votes of particular classes of voters. For example, state apportionment schemes which undervalue the votes of particular voters deny "the opportunity for equal participation by all voters." *Reynolds v. Sims* (1964). In *Reynolds,* the Court held that the Equal Protection Clause requires that the seats in both houses of a bicameral state legislature must be apportioned on a population basis. This "one-person, one-vote" principle was applied to congressional districting in *Wesberry v. Sanders* (1964) pursuant to Art. I, Sec. 2, which requires that members of Congress be chosen "by the people of the several states." While the principle applies to all local government units [*Hadley v. Junior College Dist.* (1970)], the unit may be so specialized in purpose and limited in powers as not to qualify as governmental. See *Salyer Land Co.*

But the *Reynolds* Court also indicated that "mathematical exactness or precision is hardly a workable constitutional requirement. Somewhat more flexibility may be constitutionally permissible with respect to state legislative apportionment than in congressional districting." In fact, the courts have required that states "come as nearly as practicable to population equality" in congressional districting. In rejecting a .7% maximum percentage deviation between districts in *Karcher v. Daggett*

(1983), the Court noted that the state must show "with some specificity that a particular objective required the specific deviation in its plan." In state districting, however, the Court has permitted minor deviations without any state justification [*White v. Regester* (1973), upholding average deviation of 2% and maximum deviation of 9.9%] and substantial deviation when justified by the state's interest in preserving its traditional political boundaries. *Mahan v. Howell* (1973) [16.4% deviation upheld]; *Brown v. Thomson* (1983) [16% average deviation and maximum deviation of 89% upheld where grant of a single seat to a county entitled to it numerically was not a significant cause of the population deviations].

Multimember districting, while it may impede particular groups from achieving political power proportionate to their numbers, does not, without more, violate equal protection. *City of Mobile v. Bolden* (1980). But when an examination of the "totality of the circumstances" establishes that the electoral scheme was borne of an intent to racially discriminate (*i.e.,* a suspect classification), the Fourteenth Amendment is violated. *Rogers v. Lodge* (1982). Similarly, giving a minority disproportionate political power by requiring an extraordinary majority [*Gordon v. Lance* (1971), 60% referenda approval for incurring bond indebtedness upheld] or concurrent majorities [*Town of Lockport v. Citizens for Community Action* (1977), separate majority of urban and rural voters required for new county charters upheld], does not necessarily violate equal protection.

Another method by which the value of the franchise can be diluted is through limitations on access of candidates and parties to the ballot. Restrictions prevent voters from expressing their preferences through their vote. In fact, such restrictions on access place "burdens on two different, although overlapping, kinds of rights—the right of individuals to associate for the advancement of political beliefs and the right of qualified voters, regardless of their political persuasion, to cast their votes effectively." *Williams v. Rhodes* (1968) [variety of state requirements limiting the access of new political parties to ballot held violative of equal protection because it gave Democrats and Republicans "a complete monopoly"]. On the other hand, restrictions on access are said to serve important state interests "in protecting the integrity of their political process from frivolous or fraudulent candidacies, in ensuring that their election processes are efficient, in avoiding voter confusion caused by an overcrowded ballot, and in avoiding the expense and burden of run-off elections." *Clements v. Fashing* (1982) [state laws limiting an office holder from running for a different office held not violative of equal protection using a rational basis test].

In most cases, the Court has applied strict scrutiny to such access restrictions, requiring the state to demonstrate that the differential treatment is "necessary to further compelling state interests." But a plurality of the Court in *Clements v. Fashing* stated: "Not all ballot access restrictions require 'heightened' equal protection scrutiny." The plurality argued that it is necessary to examine each law to determine the extent of the burden it imposes— "The inquiry is whether the challenged restriction unfairly or unnecessarily burdens 'the availability of political opportunity.' *Lubin v. Panish.*"

The imposition of filing fees on indigent candidates as a necessary condition of access (*i.e.,* no alternative means of access is provided) is likely to be held unconstitutional. *Bullock v. Carter* (1972); *Lubin v. Panish* (1974). But the fate of laws requiring that candidates or parties demonstrate a certain level of community support in order to secure access is far less certain. If the law "affords minority political parties a real and substantially equal opportunity for ballot qualification," it can be upheld even under a strict scrutiny standard. *American Party of Texas v. White* (1974) [ballot access requirement that parties which had not demonstrated significant voter support in previous elections provide petitions signed by 1% of voters and limiting pool of signatories to those who had not participated in another party's primary or nominating process upheld]; *Storer v. Brown* (1974) [one year disaffiliation provision upheld as furthering state's compelling interest in the stability of its political system]. On the other hand, if the provisions are virtually exclusionary of independents and minority parties, the requirements will be held invalid. *Anderson v. Celebrezze* (1983) [early filing deadlines for petitions of independent candidates seeking ballot access but not for candidates of major parties held to violate freedom of political association but relying heavily on equal protection cases]; *Williams v. Rhodes*. The Court's approach in the *Anderson* case suggests that the First Amendment analysis might receive increased attention from courts as an alternative to fundamental rights equal protection.

In *Bush v. Gore* (2000), the Court declared, *per curiam,* that the right to vote protects more than the "initial allocation of the franchise." Equal protection also extends to the manner in which the right to vote is exercised. If a state legislature vests the right to vote in Presidential elections in its citizens, such a right is fundamental. The reason such a right is fundamental "lies in the equal weight accorded to each vote and the equal dignity owed to each voter." Relying on *Harper v. Virginia Board of Elections* (1966), *supra*, the *per curiam* opinion declared that once the vote was granted on equal terms, the state could not subsequently "by later and disparate treatment, value one person's vote over that of another." The Court ruled that the recount ordered by the Florida Supreme Court could not be conducted in a manner that would be consistent with equal protection standards. Uniform rules to determine voter intent with respect to the meaning of disputed ballots were lacking. When a state court orders a state wide recount, some assurance must be provided of equal treatment and fundamental fairness as votes are counted from county to county.

Justice Stevens, in dissent, conceded that the use of differing substantive standards to ascertain voter intent in different counties raised difficult problems. But the key point was that a "single, impartial magistrate" will ultimately resolve any such difficulties arising from the recount procedure. What must underlie "this federal assault on the Florida election procedure" is a lack of confidence in the impartiality of the state judges who would otherwise make the ultimate decisions. Florida had left it to each county to determine what balloting system to use. If the approach to equal protection was too literal, the decisions of the "vast majority of state legislatures" to leave to local authorities decisions about what voting system and what ballot design to use will all be subject to equal protection challenge. The Court's response to this contention was to stress the uniqueness of this case.

d. Access to Justice

A highly confused area of equal protection law involves the treatment of economic obstacles such as fee requirements limiting access to criminal and civil justice. The primary source of confusion is the proper role of equal protection and procedural due process analysis. In *Griffin v. Illinois* (1956), the Court held that the state must provide free transcripts to indigent criminal defendants where a transcript was required to obtain "adequate and effective" appellate review. Justice Black, in a plurality opinion, invoked both due process and equal protection principles. On the latter issue, he acknowledged that the state was under no constitutional duty to provide appellate review. But while there was no constitutional right to appeal, "that is not to say that a state that does grant appellate review can do so in a way that discriminates against some convicted defendants on account of their poverty. There can be no equal justice where the kind of trial a man gets depends on the amount of money he has." Justice Harlan, dissenting, argued that the plurality, even while acknowledging the absence of any constitutional right to an appeal, was drawing from the Equal Protection Clause itself "an affirmative duty to lift the handicaps flowing from difference in economic circumstances." Equal protection, he argued, demands equal treatment, but does not require a state to "give to some what it requires others to pay for."

The equal protection approach to the problem of access to criminal justice was even more clearly accepted by the Court in *Douglas v. California* (1963). In upholding the right of indigent criminal defendants to appointed counsel on their first state appeal as of right, the Court, per Justice Douglas, branded the state's refusal to provide counsel as "discrimination against the indigent." Justice Douglas acknowledged that "absolute equality" in access to justice was not constitutionally required, but contended that counsel was of critical importance in the "*one and only appeal* an indigent has as of right." The state had drawn "an unconstitutional line between rich and poor." *Compare Ross v. Moffitt* (1974) [no right to appointed counsel for indigent on discretionary appeal].

And once again Justice Harlan challenged the Court's reliance on equal protection analysis. He accepted that the Clause prohibited discrimination, "between 'rich' and 'poor' *as such.*" But he argued that this was very different from saying that equal protection "prevents the State from adopting a law of general applicability that may affect the poor more harshly than it does the rich, or, from making some effort to redress economic imbalances while not eliminating them entirely." While the states may have a moral obligation to alleviate the effects of poverty, "[t]o construe the Equal Protection Clause as imposing an affirmative duty to cure economic disparities," he argued, "would be to read into the Constitution a philosophy of leveling that would be foreign to many of our basic concepts of the proper relations between government and society." Indeed, he questioned whether the state could ever satisfy an affirmative duty to equalize access to the justice system.

Griffin–Douglas focused on an ill-defined vital interest in equal access to criminal justice coupled with an obvious concern for discrimination against indigents. Yet there was no independent constitutional right at stake in the cases and wealth was not identified as a suspect classifying trait. It is the combination of the important interest and the indigency classification that demanded closer judicial scrutiny under the Equal Protection Clause and which provided the unique theme of *Griffin–Douglas. Williams v. Illinois* (1970) [provisions for "working off" a fine, resulting in confinement beyond the statutory maximum held to violate indigent's equal protection rights]; *Tate v. Short* (1971) [imprisonment alternative to fine held violative of equal protection]. *Compare Ross v. Moffitt; Fuller v. Oregon* (1974) [state recoupment of funds expended to provide counsel to an indigent if a convicted indigent is able to repay upheld].

The exact relationship of equal protection and due process in cases involving access to criminal justice remains problematical. Recently, the Court reiterated that both clauses are implicated. Due process applies because of its demand for a fair opportunity to obtain an adjudication on the merits; equal protection applies because of the differential treatment of two classes of defendants. *Evitts v. Lucey* (1985) [due process right to *effective* assistance of counsel on first appeal as of right was violated]. In *Ake v. Oklahoma* (1985), the Court used the Due Process Clause as the basis for requiring states to provide free psychiatric assistance to indigent defendants in some criminal cases. The Court employed the *Mathews v. Eldridge* procedural due process test, balancing the defendant's interest in psychiatric assistance, the government interest that would be affected by affording the safeguard and the risk of erroneous deprivation if psychiatric assistance was not provided.

The problem of indigent access to justice has also arisen in the civil context. In *Boddie v. Connecticut* (1971), the Court struck down a state imposition of fees on welfare recipients seeking a divorce. Justice Harlan, for the Court, employing the Due Process

Clause, emphasized two key factors: (1) the importance of the marriage relationship in our society's hierarchy of values; and, (2) the state monopolization of the means for ending that relationship. But what if these conditions were not present in other fee cases? In *United States v. Kras* (1973), the Court upheld a $50 fee for bankruptcy proceedings. The interest of the debtor in discharge of the debt burden was not deemed as "fundamental" as the marriage interest in *Boddie* and there were alternative means of debt settlement available to the debtor. Due process was not violated. See *Ortwein v. Schwab* (1973) [filing fee for appeal from adverse welfare board decisions upheld]. The importance of the two part *Boddie* inquiry was most recently indicated in *Little v. Streater* (1981), where the Court held that Connecticut's failure to pay for blood grouping tests for indigent defendants in paternity actions violated due process: "Because appellant has no choice of an alternative forum and his interest, as well as those of the child, are constitutionally significant, this case is comparable to *Boddie* rather than to *Kras* and *Ortwein*."

A state cannot deny a mother's right to appeal from the termination of her parental rights because of her inability to pay record preparation fees in advance. *M.L.B. v. S.L.J* (1996). The *Griffin* principle that once a state affords appellate review, the door to equal justice may not be bolted has not been confined entirely to the criminal context. In *Boddie* and elsewhere, the Court has recognized a "narrow category of civil cases" where the state must provide access to its courts without regard to the ability of a party to pay court fees. Included in this category are cases involving state intrusions into family relationships involving basic associational rights about marriage, family life and the rearing of children such as termination of parental rights. Both equal protection and due process concerns are implicated here. The equal protection concern relates to the validity of shutting out would-be appellants simply because they cannot pay court fees. The due process concern relates to the "essential fairness of the state-ordered proceeding anterior to adverse state action." In the *Griffin*-line of cases, due process and equal protection concepts converge.

In *Christopher v. Harbury* (2002), a "backward-looking" right of access to the courts claim was unanimously rejected by the Supreme Court. There was a constitutional right of access to the courts but the constitutional basis of that right remained unsettled. Past precedents had grounded the right in the Privileges and Immunities Clause of Article IV, the Petition Clause of the First Amendment, the Fifth Amendment's Due Process Clause and the Fourteenth Amendment's Equal Protection and Due Process Clauses. The claim arose from the complaint of Jennifer Harbury, widow of a Guatemalan rebel, captured, tortured and executed by the Guatemalan army. She claimed that the CIA knew of her husband's capture and shared this information with the National Security Council and the State Department but not with her. Indeed, these agencies told Harbury they had no knowledge of her husband's whereabouts. They said were investigating the case. Her basic contention was that if the United States government had shared the information they possessed concerning her husband, or if they had at least not misled her into believing they were trying to assist her, she might been able to take appropriate legal action which would have saved her husband's life. The Court held that a right of access to the courts claim, "whether anticipated or lost," which looks backward, has to describe with precision the underlying cause of action. This Harbury had failed to do. Judicial inquiry into such foreign affairs matters raised separation of powers issues and could impinge on matters committed to the non-judicial branches of government.

e. The Limits of Fundamental Rights

The fundamental rights strand of equal protection law fashioned by the Warren Court appeared to offer an alternative to substantive due process and its taint of "Lochnerism." Indeed, it was sometimes called "Substantive Equal Protection." Further, the developing case law suggested that the states might be under an affirmative constitutional duty to equalize access to important government benefits and services such as welfare, education, housing and medical care. Perhaps the Equal Protection Clause could be a vehicle for attacking economic inequalities in the society.

But the Burger Court sharply curtailed these expansive interpretations of equal protection. In *San Antonio Ind. School Dist. v. Rodriguez* (1973), the Court considered whether Texas violated equal protection by funding education through property taxes, producing marked interdistrict disparities in per pupil expenditures, because of the disparate property values in the districts. The Court, per Justice Powell, employed rational basis analysis and held 5–4 that equal protection was satisfied. In rejecting strict scrutiny, Justice Powell first determined that the law did not operate to the disadvantage of a suspect class. There was no showing that the poor as an identifiable class live in property poor districts. Nor had it been shown that they suffered "an absolute deprivation of the desired benefit;" Justice Powell noted that equal protection "does not require absolute equality or precisely equal advantages." Finally, discrimination based on school district wealth was not suspect. District wealth possessed "none of the traditional indicia of suspectness." Justice Powell concluded that the Texas funding scheme "does not operate to peculiar disadvantage of any suspect class." See *Maher v. Roe* (1977) and *Harris v. McRae* (1980), the abortion funding cases, rejecting wealth as suspect. The Court similarly rejected strict scrutiny based on fundamental rights analysis. While acknowledging that education may be the most important function of state government, Justice Powell asserted that "the importance of a service performed by the state does not determine whether it must be regarded as fundamental for purposes of examination under the Equal Protection Clause." The critical conclusion was that there is no "right to education explicitly or implicitly guaranteed by the Constitution." Efforts to link education to First Amendment rights and voting failed since the Constitution does not guarantee "the most *effective* speech or the most *informed* electoral choice."

Justice Powell did note that even if it were assumed that there is a constitutional right to "some identifiable quantum of education," there was no evidence that this basic minimum was not provided. Indeed, whereas prior cases had involved deprivations or interferences with free exercise of a right, Texas was affirmatively seeking to extend education. Since Texas has made a rational choice on allocating its scarce tax resources in a way to protect local autonomy over education, it was not the function of the courts to override its choices. See *Dandridge v. Williams* (1970) [state maximum grant law setting a ceiling on AFDC welfare benefits upheld using rational basis test].

Nevertheless, it was Justice Powell who provided the crucial fifth vote in *Plyler v. Doe* (1982), holding that Texas' failure to provide undocumented school age children the free public education that it provides to citizens and legally admitted aliens violates equal protection. Justice Brennan, a dissenter in *San Antonio,* now wrote for the Court. While he acknowledged that "public education is not a 'right' granted to individuals by the constitution," he observed that "education has a fundamental role in maintaining the fabric of our society." Justice Brennan similarly accepted that illegal aliens are not a suspect class. But the children of illegal entrants are special members of an "underclass," part of a "permanent caste" denied the benefits provided to citizens and lawful residents. In language reminiscent of that used in illegitimacy cases, Justice Brennan noted that the Texas law "imposes a lifetime of hardship on a discrete class of children not accountable for their disabling status." In light of the costs of lost education that the discrimination visited on "innocent" undocumented children, the law could "hardly be considered rational unless it furthers some substantial goal of the state." Applying this intermediate standard of review, the Court found the Texas law unconstitutional. Justice Powell, concurring in *Plyler,* distinguished *Rodriguez* on grounds that, in *Rodriguez,* "no group of children was singled out by the state and then penalized because of their parent's status." Further, in *Rodriguez* there was not "any group of children totally deprived of all education as in this case."

Plyler is a noteworthy departure from rationality review absent any suspect classification or fundamental right. *Plyler* could be seen as providing an alternative to the strict tiered equal protection review used by the Warren Court—the degree of scrutiny varies with the nature of the classifying trait and the importance of the interest burdened as well as the severity of the burden (*e.g.,* is the law a "penalty" on a fundamental interest). But *Plyler* more likely should be seen, as the dissent contended, as simply a result-oriented case, providing minimal doctrinal development in equal protection law. See *Martinez v. Bynum* (1983) [state *bona fide* residency requirement denying free tuition benefits to children living in the district for the primary purpose of attending free public schools upheld using rationality review].

In *Kadrmas v. Dickinson Pub. Schools* (1988), the Court, 5–4, per Justice O'Connor, upheld, as against an equal protection challenge, a North Dakota statute authorizing school districts which chose not to "reorganize" into larger districts to charge a fee for school bus service. Unlike the situation in *Plyler*, the school child in *Kadrmas* was not being disadvantaged by the state because of the illegal conduct of her parents. The child was denied access to the school bus "only because her parents would not pay the same user fee charged to all other families". Furthermore, the statute was rationally related to the state's legitimate interest in fulfilling the expectation of residents of reorganized districts that a consequence of reorganization would be free busing arrangements. *Kadrmas* refused to apply either the strict scrutiny standard or the less exacting "heightened scrutiny" standard which had been applied in *Plyler*. Indeed, *Plyler* was pointedly described as not having been extended beyond its "unique circumstances."

In summary, the future of fundamental rights equal protection analysis appears to be a limited one. Strict scrutiny analysis is unlikely to be extended to reach new interests not already protected. The Rehnquist Court appears, if anything, even less disposed than the Burger Court to expand further the domain of the fundamental rights branch of the new equal protection.

CHAPTER VII

FREEDOM OF EXPRESSION

A. THE BASIC DOCTRINE

1. THE RATIONALE OF SPEECH PROTECTION

The First Amendment provides that "Congress shall make no law abridging the freedom of speech." The text of the First Amendment clearly has Congress, *i.e.,* the federal government, as its addressee. It probably was not intended to reach the states. But in 1925 the Supreme Court declared that the Due Process Clause of the Fourteenth Amendment protected freedom of expression against state infringement. *Gitlow v. New York* (1925).

What is the nature of the guarantee of freedom of expression? It cannot reasonably be claimed that the Constitution extends its protection to all verbal and non-verbal communication. As Holmes said: "The most stringent protection of free speech would not protect a man in falsely shouting fire in a theatre and causing a panic." *Schenck v. United States* (1919). But why not? There are no qualifications to the guarantee of freedom of speech in the text of the First Amendment. The key is that the Constitution prohibits laws "abridging the freedom

373

f speech" and not all laws restricting communication.

What does "the freedom of speech" embrace? The historical intent of the Framers is disputed and does not provide much guidance. But some guidance can be obtained after the fact, as it were, by considering the functions the First Amendment serves. For some, freedom of expression is a vital ingredient of the pursuit of truth, especially political truth. Thus, Justice Holmes believed that "the best test of truth is the power of the thought to get itself accepted in the competition of the market." *Abrams v. United States* (1919). This marketplace of ideas rationale for free expression had its origins in English constitutional history. Thus, in the seventeenth century, John Milton, in a famous essay, *The Areopagitica,* protested government licensing and censorship of the press: "[W]ho ever knew truth put to the worse, in a free and open encounter?" Modern refinement of this doctrine contends that the state must allow dialogue to continue no matter how noxious that dialogue. Only when the social order is drastically threatened is government permitted to punish a speaker. As Justice Brandeis put it in *Whitney v. California* (1927): "Only an emergency justifies repression."

But is the marketplace of ideas model of the First Amendment realistic? Critics question the notion of absolute truth as the objective of political dialogue. The marketplace theory rests on a presumption of rationality—a citizenry of intelligent decisionmakers seeking and empowered to govern a free society.

er, such laws are to be subjected to the regimen of stricter judicial scrutiny. From this modern principle of searching scrutiny of governmental action infringing free expression we derive the basic doctrines and tests of First Amendment law.

2. A DOCTRINAL OVERVIEW

a. Content Control v. Indirect Burdens

The Supreme Court has stated that "above all else the First Amendment means that government has no power to restrict expression because of its message, its ideas, its subject matter, or its content." *Police Department of Chicago v. Mosley* (1972). Nevertheless, the Court has frequently upheld laws imposing content-based restrictions on speech. Two approaches are used to reconcile such holdings. First, some speech has been thought of as categorically excluded from First Amendment protection or at least is given a lesser degree of protection under the First Amendment. In *Chaplinsky v. New Hampshire* (1942), the Court stated: "There are certain well-defined and narrowly limited classes of speech, the prevention and punishment of which have never been thought to raise constitutional problems." Thus, as a general rule, one does not ask whether particular obscene publications are protected by the First Amendment. Obscenity has been considered the kind of expression with which "the freedom of speech" is not concerned. Laws restricting its availability were therefore not restricted by the First Amendment.

But is this how twentieth century society really functions? Free societies threatened by totalitarian adversaries may not dare to wait. Critics of the marketplace argue that in an age of concentration of control of the mass media there are too few stalls in the market for the marketplace theory still to be viable.

Alexander Meiklejohn posited an influential rationale for free expression. He said that the Framers were interested in political freedom and in making democracy work. The citizen-critic of government must be given the information to enable him to do his political duty. Otherwise he cannot control his governors. As Meiklejohn put it, "public speech," speech involving the political arena, is absolutely protected. Speech involving private life—business communications, for example—is not absolutely protected but is to be accorded only the general protection provided by the Due Process Clause. Critics ask: Is the Meiklejohn theory meant to be descriptive of reality or is it only a utopian ideal?

An alternative to these social utilitarian models is the view that freedom of speech is valuable in itself in promoting individual self-realization and self-determination. The rational individual requires information and an opportunity to express her own ideas if she is to grow. This theory may be called the individual liberty or self-realization model.

From these theories flows the principle that laws limiting freedom of expression are not to be reviewed under the deferential rationality test. Rath-

The categorical approach to free expression problems received a significant qualification in *R.A.V. v. City of St. Paul* (1992) where an ordinance sanctioning fighting words in the context of race, religion or gender was struck down. Justice Scalia, for the Court, held that no category of expression was "entirely invisible" to the First Amendment. Obscenity may be regulated, it is true, but only with regard to its "distinctly proscribable content." Thus, a city council ordinance prohibiting "only those legally obscene words that contain criticism of the city government" would violate the First Amendment. Three justices, concurring, deplored this revisionism in the traditional understanding of the First Amendment status of unprotected categories of expression. They insisted that since such categories involved speech that was worthless in First Amendment terms, government could regulate as it chose. But the *R.A.V.* majority held that content discrimination within a particular category of even otherwise unprotected expression merited First Amendment protection and was subject to strict scrutiny review.

A second approach is to employ a weighted form of "balancing" test to determine whether the government content control constitutes an impermissible "abridgement" of "the freedom of speech." The balancing or justification approach may be cast as a formula such as the clear and present danger doctrine. Or it may come in the form, as is often the case today, of a court extending strict scrutiny to content-based legislation, *i.e.,* government must demonstrate that the law under review is narrowly tailored to meet some overriding or compelling governmental interest. Finally, the judicial inquiry may amount to little more than *ad hoc* balancing of the speech and governmental interest in conflict even when the law is content-based. Alternatively, government regulation may be content-neutral and impose only an indirect burden on freedom of speech. In such cases, a less demanding form of judicial review is used. *Konigsberg v. State Bar of California* (1961) [refusal to answer lawful inquiries concerning bar applicants' qualifications is a permissible basis for denying admission].

The courts engage in a balancing of the competing interests to determine if a content neutral regulation is reasonable. For example, a broad municipal ordinance governing sound trucks, vesting extensive discretion in police officials, was held unconstitutional. *Saia v. New York* (1948). A more narrowly-drawn sound truck ordinance, prohibiting "loud and raucous noises" on the streets, was constitutional. *Kovacs v. Cooper* (1949). Similarly, a New York City ordinance which regulated the volume of amplified music at a bandshell in Central Park by requiring use of sound-amplification equipment and a sound technician provided by the city was constitutional. Here again the regulation was deemed narrowly tailored because the substantial governmental interest in controlling the sound volume was served in a direct and effective way by requiring use of the city's sound technician but allowing the sponsor autonomy concerning the sound mix. *Ward v. Rock Against Racism* (1989).

A total ban on residential canvassing, handbilling, and solicitation [*Martin v. Struthers* (1943)] or a law vesting excessive discretion in officials over the content of such solicitation [*Hynes v. Mayor and Council of Oradell* (1976)], is unreasonable—it approximates content control. On the other hand, a limited reasonable regulation designed to protect the privacy of homeowners will be upheld. *Breard v. Alexandria* (1951) [ban on residential magazine sales without homeowners consent upheld]; *Rowan v. United States Post Office Dept.* (1970) [statute permitting homeowners to stop offensive home mailings is constitutional]. Narrowly drawn, reasonable content-neutral regulations of the time, place and manner of public protest, designed to promote valid local interests such as traffic flow and public safety, will be upheld. *Grayned v. City of Rockford* (1972).

The student should be aware that the degree of judicial scrutiny in this balancing of interests can vary markedly from case to case. Perhaps the most frequently used standard for measuring the reasonableness of such indirect regulation is that fashioned in *United States v. O'Brien* (1968): "A government regulation is sufficiently justified if it furthers an important or substantial government interest; if the governmental interest is unrelated to the suppression of free expression; and if the incidental restriction of alleged First Amendment freedoms is no greater than is essential to the furtherance of that interest."

Finally, a helpful guide to the rationale for subjecting content-neutral regulations to intermediate rather than strict scrutiny is provided by *Turner Broadcasting System, Inc. v. FCC* (1994). Unlike content-based regulations, content-neutral regulations present less risk that they will exclude particular ideas or points of view from public discourse. In *Turner*, "must carry" obligations imposed by federal legislation requiring cable systems to carry a designated number of local broadcast signals were reviewed under the *O'Brien* intermediate level of scrutiny "applicable to content-neutral restrictions that imposed an incidental burden on speech." Clearly, distinguishing content-neutral from content-based regulations is difficult. Indeed, the Court pointed out that content-neutral regulations that appeared to be neutral on their face could be deemed content-based if their "manifest purpose is to regulate speech because of the message it conveys." But the must carry regulations were not imposed to regulate on the basis of the subject-matter or viewpoint of a message but because Congress believed that the future of free broadcasting was placed in economic jeopardy because of the "physical characteristics of cable transmission."

The fact that a regulation is content-neutral and is subject to a less exacting standard of scrutiny than a content-based one does not necessarily mean that it will survive a First Amendment challenge. When a city ordinance prohibited homeowners from displaying all signs except residence identification signs, "for sale" signs and signs warning of safety hazards, the Court struck it down. The Court assumed that the ordinance was content-neutral Nonetheless, entirely too much protected expression was prohibited by the ordinance. Political, religious and personal messages were completely precluded from being communicated by means of residential signs and no adequate substitute existed. *City of Ladue v. Gilleo* (1994).

Finally, unlike the more deferential treatment given to content-neutral regulations, content-based regulations are scrutinized much more strictly. New York's "Son of Sam" law creating a mechanism applying the income from works of criminals who describe their crimes first to the criminal's victims and then to creditors was struck down. There was no doubt that the "Son of Sam" law was content-based. The state imposed a burden on income derived from expressive activity placed on no other income. Further, the burden was placed only on activity with a particular content, *i.e.*, works in which an author described his crimes. A content-based law is presumptively invalid under the First Amendment. Such a law could be upheld only if it met the strict scrutiny standard. Did the law serve a compelling state interest? Was it narrowly drawn to achieve those interests? Although the state interests in victim compensation and preventing criminals from profiting from their crimes were compelling, the law was not narrowly drawn. Indeed, it was impermissibly overinclusive. For example, the law applied even to works of authors describing crimes for which they had never been convicted. *Simon & Schuster, Inc. v. Members of the New York State Criminal Victims Board* (1991).

b. Vagueness and Overbreadth

In most First Amendment litigation, the constitutional challenge is directed at the validity of the law "as applied" to the particular litigant. Under this "as applied" approach, a judicial determination of unconstitutionality does not render the law itself invalid but only renders void the particular application of the law. The law must be unconstitutional as applied to the plaintiff. Pursuant to the third party standing rule, a litigant will not be permitted to challenge possible but unrelated unconstitutional applications to others of an otherwise valid law.

There is, however, another vitally important approach. In addition (or as an alternative) to challenging the validity of the application of the law to himself, the litigant may challenge the validity of the law itself by arguing that the law is facially unconstitutional in that it is vague and/or overbroad. A court decision in the plaintiff's favor in such circumstances results in the invalidation of the law. Further, the litigant is allowed to raise the rights of third parties not before the Court who could not be reached under a properly drawn law. This is so even though the litigant himself is not affected by the overbreadth and could be validly regulated by a statute that was neither overbroad nor vague. Because of concern about the chilling effect of vague and overbroad laws on protected constitutional expression, an exception is made to the third party standing rule.

The doctrines of vagueness and overbreadth are closely related but distinct. Vagueness is concerned with the clarity of the law. A law must be drawn with sufficient clarity so that it informs people of the conduct they must take to avoid the sanction of the particular law. Under procedural due process, a statute is not constitutionally fair if it fails to give such information. However, an unclear statute may have First Amendment as well as a procedural due process impact. A law regulating expression has to be especially clear because, if it is not specific, protected expression may be chilled or suppressed.

The doctrine of overbreadth is concerned with the precision of a law. A law may be facially clear but may sweep too broadly if it indiscriminately reaches both protected and unprotected expression. For example, a law that prohibits three or more persons from congregating on a street corner and engaging in activity that is "annoying" to passers-by is both vague and overbroad. *Coates v. Cincinnati* (1971). Protected expression can be chilled or suppressed by such a law. Administrators are permitted to roam free and curtail protected expression. Herein lies the vice of overbreadth. Even though the litigant might be engaged in unprotected expression, the statute could be applied to protected speech.

Closely related to the overbreadth doctrine is the less burdensome alternatives test, often used in

First Amendment litigation. Even if the government has a compelling objective, if that objective could be achieved by a law less burdensome on protected expression, the First Amendment demands that these less drastic means be used.

The overbreadth doctrine is under attack within the Court. It has been described as "strong medicine" to be "employed by the Court sparingly and only as a last resort." *Broadrick v. Oklahoma* (1973). The judicial critics challenge the propriety of a court's invalidation of a law based on possible, imagined applications of the statute that may in fact never arise. They point out that it is not an appropriate judicial function to anticipate constitutional issues which are not directly presented by parties actually affected.

Broadrick v. Oklahoma (1973), fashioned a significant exception to the overbreadth doctrine. "[W]here conduct and not merely speech is involved, we believe that the overbreadth of a statute must not only be real but substantial as well, judged in relation to the statute's plainly legitimate sweep." While this principle, as formulated, applied only to speech-related conduct and not pure speech, the potential scope of this demand for "substantial overbreadth" was left essentially uncharted. It has always been clear that not any possible unconstitutional application of a statute would render it facially invalid. *Broadrick,* however, suggests a sharp limitation on those occasions when the overbreadth doctrine will be invoked. In fact, there has been an increasing tendency to invoke the requirement of "substantial overbreadth" even when reviewing a law burdening pure speech.

The Court has not retreated from its policy of insisting on substantial overbreadth before it will apply the overbreadth doctrine. In *Virginia v. Hicks* (2003), a municipal public housing authority responding to problems created by nonresident criminals and drug dealers entering its public housing development adopted a trespass policy. The policy authorized police to notify those nonresidents unable to show a legitimate business or social reason for their presence that they must leave and not return on pain of being arrested for trespass. A defendant who subsequent to notification nevertheless returned and was arrested for trespass challenged the policy as unconstitutionally overbroad. The defendant contended that the policy was being used to exclude individuals engaged in protected speech. The Court, per Justice Scalia, ruled that the defendant had not shown that the policy was "substantially overbroad in relation to its legitimate sweep." The defendant had failed to show that the "no-return notice" had been given to anyone engaged in protected speech, In fact, the policy could be constitutionally applied to a substantial number of individuals such as loiterers and drug dealers who were not engaged in such speech. The defendant was arrested not because of any speech he intended to engage in but because he violated the "no-return notice" policy of the housing authority. If any applications of that policy did violate the First Amendment, those violations could be dealt with on as-applied basis rather than through the "strong medicine" of the overbreadth doctrine.

c. The Doctrine of Prior Restraint

Historically, freedom from prior restraint was what English lawyers meant when they spoke of freedom of the press. Indeed, the earliest understanding of the First Amendment was that it provided freedom from prior restraint. This freedom protected the printed word prior to publication and forbade prior administrative restraint. In other words, the doctrine of prior restraint forbade censorship in advance of publication. This should be distinguished from subsequent punishment through breach of the peace, disorderly conduct, or tort damages, all of which might be imposed *after* expression has taken place.

Freedom from prior restraint has been deemed in the past more important than freedom from subsequent punishment. Why is this? The bias against prior restraint is grounded in large part on the fact that the expression never enters the marketplace of ideas. In the case of subsequent punishment, on the other hand, at least the public has been given an opportunity to hear and judge the communication in controversy. The speaker in a system of subsequent punishment remains responsible for the consequences of his speech. Since concern for the marketplace is a primary motivating force underlying the bias against prior restraint, it is not surprising that the modern doctrine of prior restraint reaches a variety of forms of government restraint which operate prior to expression. Thus, even an injunction issued by a court which bears a special responsibility for protecting freedom of expression falls within its parameters. *Near v. Minnesota ex rel. Olson* (1931). Similarly, in more recent times, forms of expression other than printed materials have been accorded freedom from prior restraint. *Walker v. Birmingham* (1967) [street demonstration].

In its modern form, the doctrine provides that prior restraints are highly suspect both substantively and procedurally and are subject to a rebuttable presumption of unconstitutionality. In seeking to justify use of such a restraint the government bears a heavy burden of proof. Generally, the Court has professed to employ the clear and present danger doctrine in reviewing such prior restraint systems. *Nebraska Press Association v. Stuart* (1976). Such cases also involve controls on speech content which independently require use of strict judicial scrutiny. In *Nebraska Press*, the gag order designed to prevent prejudicial pretrial publicity was aimed at journalists. Where a gag order targeted lawyers, the Court did not use the clear and present danger doctrine. Instead, since lawyers were officers of the court, the gag order was evaluated under the less demanding "substantial likelihood of material prejudice" standard. *Gentile v. State Bar of Nevada* (1991). In a brief *per curiam* decision, the Court, 6–3, in *New York Times Co. v. United States (The Pentagon Papers Case)* (1971) invalidated a lower court restraint on the publication of a classified study dealing with the Vietnam war policy of the

United States. The Court's *per curiam* decision did little more than cite the failure of the government to meet the heavy burden of justification for the use of a prior restraint. This was followed by nine separate opinions detailing each Justice's views on the issue presented.

A difficulty with evaluating the role of the prior restraint doctrine in the case is that a number of the justices were deeply troubled by the issuance of a restraint against the press in the absence of a federal statute authorizing such a restraint. Some of the justices felt that the presence of a statute, coupled with a fact pattern involving an alleged threat to national security, might satisfy the heavy burden of justification necessary to authorize a prior restraint. In the absence of such a statute, the simple declaration by the Executive that publication would involve a "grave and irreparable threat to the public interest" was insufficient to override the heavy presumption against prior restraint.

Since the First Amendment grants "greater protection from prior restraints than from subsequent punishment," it has been deemed essential to define the characteristics of prior restraint with precision. *Alexander v. United States* (1993). For example, when the government seized $9,000,000 worth of books and videos belonging to the owner of businesses dealing with sexually oriented materials pursuant to the forfeiture provisions of RICO (the federal Racketeer Influenced and Corrupt Organizations Act), the owner contended that since his RICO conviction was based on prior convictions under

federal obscenity laws the RICO forfeiture constituted prior restraint. A prohibition of "future presumptively protected expression in retaliation for
prior unprotected speech" was, in this view, a prior
restraint. Indeed, most of the seized materials had
not been adjudicated to be obscene. Nonetheless,
the forfeiture was held not to be a prior restraint
but a valid criminal sanction which had been preceded by a full criminal trial. The punishment was
for past acts not future speech. The owner was still
free to engage in expressive activities in the future.
Alexander v. United States (1993).

The *Alexander* case was a refusal to extend prior
restraint doctrine. In *Madsen v. Women's Health
Center, Inc.* (1994), the Court, per Chief Justice
Rehnquist, eroded traditional prior restraint doctrine by refusing to characterize a state court injunction as an impermissible prior restraint. The
injunction prohibited antiabortion protesters from
demonstrating within a 36 foot buffer zone around
a health clinic that performed abortions as an impermissible prior restraint. Although some injunctions are prior restraints, "not all injunctions which
may incidentally affect expression" are prior restraints. The injunction was not content-based, as
in the *Pentagon Papers* case. The protesters were
not prevented from expressing their views but were
just prohibited from doing so in the buffer zone
around the clinic. *Madsen v. Women's Health Center, Inc.* (1994).

*Schenck v. Pro–Choice Network of Western New
York* (1997) upheld an injunction imposing a num-

ber of restrictions, similar to those upheld in *Madsen*, on anti-abortion protesters aimed at preventing them from blocking access to abortion clinics or engaging in other illegal conduct. But the Court invalidated the so-called "moving" or floating buffer zone prohibiting protests within fifteen feet of any person or vehicle entering or leaving an abortion clinic. The "moving" buffer zone, unlike a "fixed" buffer zone, prevents a person from communicating a message from a normal conversational distance or from handing leaflets to people entering or leaving the clinic. There is a lack of certainty inherent in such a restraint that causes it to pose a substantial risk that speech protected by the First Amendment will be curbed.

The demanding procedural protections for content-based permit systems such as those mandated for subject-matter censorship boards, see *Freedman v. Maryland, infra*, are not applicable to content-neutral permit systems. Conferring waivers on favored selected groups is not valid but affording limited discretion to the licensing entity with respect to a content-neutral permit system encourages rather than limits freedom of speech. *Thomas v. Chicago Park District* (2002).

3. THE CLEAR AND PRESENT DANGER DOCTRINE

Perhaps the most significant formulation of First Amendment doctrine has been the clear and present danger doctrine. As used by Justice Holmes in

Schenck v. United States (1919), the doctrine dealt with what evidence is admissible to establish violation of the Espionage Act. Holmes' answer was that a publication could be used to convict when "the words used are used in such circumstances and are of such a nature as to create a clear and present danger that they will bring about the substantive evils that Congress has a right to prevent. It is a question of proximity and degree." It is doubtful that Holmes was really reformulating First Amendment doctrine in *Schenck*. Indeed, he seemed to adopt the prevailing "bad tendency" test, then in its ascendancy, since he states: "If the act (speaking, or circulating a paper), its tendency and the intent with which it is done are the same, we perceive no ground for saying that success alone warrants making the act a crime."

But by the time of *Whitney v. California* (1927), Justice Brandeis, in a concurrence which became more influential than the opinion of the Court, provided a statement of the danger test which yielded a greater measure of protection to free expression than the *Schenck* formulation. Brandeis said that for government to suppress speech, "[t]here must be reasonable ground to believe the danger apprehended is imminent. There must be the probability of serious danger to the State." For Brandeis, speech could not be denied protection "where the advocacy falls short of incitement and there is nothing to indicate that the advocacy would be acted on." Further, the danger test was now used by Holmes and Brandeis not merely as an evidentiary standard but as a test for judging the validity of a law even where the legislature had determined the speech in question to be dangerous.

In *Gitlow v. New York* (1925), the Court, per Justice Sanford, upheld a New York statute punishing criminal anarchy. Justice Sanford began from the premise that when the legislature determines that speech is so inimical to the general welfare "every presumption is to be indulged in favor of the validity of the statute." It is only where the statute is an "arbitrary and unreasonable" use of state police power that it violates freedom of expression. Since the legislature could reasonably conclude that utterances inciting to the overthrow of government by unlawful means are to be suppressed, "[the legislature] may, in the exercise of its judgment, suppress the threatened danger in its incipiency." Justices Holmes and Brandeis objected to this reasoning and dissented. For them, the clear and present danger test was fully applicable to judicial review of the legislative judgment. As Justice Brandeis explained in *Whitney,* the legislative declaration regarding the need for legislating "creates merely a rebuttable presumption that these conditions have been satisfied."

The *Whitney* formulation of the danger test by Brandeis received both formal espousal and a near trashing in the famous case of *Dennis v. United States* (1951), where a plurality opinion by Chief Justice Vinson upheld the validity of the federal anti-subversive law, the Smith Act, against First Amendment attack. Chief Justice Vinson declared that the formulation of the danger test which the Court accepted was the test announced by Brandeis in *Whitney*. But, it is doubtful that Brandeis would have claimed the test for his own in light of the application it received. Vinson placed heavy emphasis on the need for government to respond to the Communist threat; the danger test could not mean that government "must wait until the *putsch* is about to be executed, the plans have been laid, and the signal awaited." Rather, government could move against the conspiracy or attempt at overthrow, even though the attempt was obviously doomed at the outset. Probability of success could not be the criterion and imminence could not be the measure of government power. The Court adopted a new formulation of the danger test fashioned by Chief Judge Learned Hand in the federal court of appeals below: "In each case [courts] must ask whether the gravity of the 'evil', discounted by its improbability, justifies such invasion of free speech as is necessary to avoid the danger."

Even this watered-down version of the danger test was unacceptable for Justice Frankfurter who concurred in the judgment. No formula could capture the delicate balance of interests. While this statement would appear to envision judicial balancing of the competing speech and national security interests, in fact Justice Frankfurter argued that the balancing was the function of the Congress. The judicial function was limited to assuring that there was a reasonable basis for the legislative judgment. Shades of Justice Sanford in *Gitlow!*

The emasculation of the danger test in *Dennis* was somewhat mitigated by *Yates v. United States* (1957), which also involved the Smith Act. Interestingly, *Yates* was not technically speaking a First Amendment case. The legal issue presented was a statutory question—the meaning of the prohibition against advocacy of violent overthrow of the government in the Smith Act. What kind of "advocacy" did the Smith Act prohibit? Justice Harlan for the Court in *Yates* repaired some of the damage to free expression done by *Dennis* by interpreting the statute to proscribe "advocacy of action" rather than "advocacy of abstract doctrine or ideas." Now this was an approach reminiscent not of Justice Sanford but of the Brandeis formulation of the danger test in *Whitney*. This liberalizing decision may have been due to the waning support for the rabid anti-Communism of McCarthyism. In any event, it was not a thorough resurrection of the Holmes–Brandeis test since Justice Harlan never purported to use the danger test in *Yates*. Similarly, there is no mention of imminence or probability of success. The true Brandeis–Holmes faith achieved a fuller but still somewhat altered restoration in the case of *Brandenburg v. Ohio* (1969).

In *Brandenburg,* the Court, *per curiam,* invalidated a state statute punishing criminal syndicalism, *i.e.,* the advocacy of violence in industrial disputes in the workplace. For the Court, *Dennis–Yates* had established the principle that freedom of expression does not permit a state "to forbid or proscribe advocacy of the use of force or of law violation except where such advocacy is directed to inciting or producing imminent lawless action and is likely to incite or produce such actions." The *Brandenburg* Court never mentioned the danger test and cited only cryptically to *Dennis* and *Yates*.

Some commentators interpret *Brandenburg* as adopting an "incitement" test which focuses on the nature of the speech in question. Freedom of speech is absolutely protected, they argue, but speech which incites to the violent overthrow of government is not First Amendment speech. Such expression is categorically excluded from protection. Other commentators read *Brandenburg* as a merger of the Holmes–Brandeis danger test, which focuses on the context in which the speech occurs, with an incitement test. In order to punish speech, the speaker must both use the language of action and the context must be sufficient to establish imminence and the probability of the occurrence of the serious substantive evil which the government is seeking to prevent.

The debate over the meaning of *Brandenburg* is indicative of the continuing controversy over the value of the danger test itself. For some critics the test provides inadequate protection for First Amendment interests offering little more protection to the speaker than ad hoc balancing provides. Other critics see the danger test as affording inadequate protection to vital governmental interests. Hidden within the language of the danger test, they argue, is found functionally a strict scrutiny standard. In this view, demanding judicial superintendence of the legislative judgment in areas such as national security is inappropriate because it curtails the democratic will. In any case, it may well be that where in the past the danger test was invoked, the courts today will use the strict scrutiny test.

4. SYMBOLIC CONDUCT

Conduct is frequently used as a means of communicating messages, *e.g.,* picketing, handbilling, advertising. This "speech plus conduct" is subject to reasonable regulation. But conduct can also constitute the message itself. Conduct can embody an idea: "Symbolism is a primitive but effective way of communicating ideas. The use of an emblem or flag to symbolize some system, idea, institution, or personality, is a short cut from mind to mind." *West Virginia State Bd. of Educ. v. Barnette* (1943) [compulsory flag salute law held unconstitutional]. But not all conduct is meant to be communicative and not all expressive conduct is protected by the First Amendment. The anarchist who shoots a public official to express opposition to government cannot wrap himself in the protective cloak of the Constitution. What standards determine when symbolic conduct will enjoy First Amendment protection?

The initial task is to define when conduct will be treated as speech for First Amendment purposes. In fact, when the Court does not wish to apply First Amendment protection to conduct, it will sometimes simply assume arguendo that even if the conduct is "speech," the law is a reasonable regula-

tion of the "speech." *United States v. O'Brien*
(1968) [draft card burning during Vietnam War
protests assumed to be symbolic speech]; *Clark v.
Community for Creative Non–Violence* (1984) [over-
night sleeping in public park as part of protest
assumed to be expressive conduct]. Even in cases
where First Amendment protection is extended to
conduct, the Court often fails to discuss why the
conduct constitutes speech. *Tinker v. Des Moines
Independent Community School Dist.* (1969), merely
stated that the wearing of black armbands by public
high school students to protest the Vietnam War is
"closely akin to 'pure speech.' "Unfortunately this
approach often ignores the importance of the conduct in question as a means of expressing the
speaker's message. *Spence v. Washington* (1974),
overturning a flag misuse statute applied to a protestor who had affixed a peace symbol on the flag
and flown it from his window, did confront the task
of defining symbolic speech. The Court examined
the factual context and environment in which the
conduct took place, and determined that (1) there
was an intent to communicate a particularized message of opposition to war and violence, and (2) the
message would be received and understood by others.

Assuming that the conduct at issue qualifies as
First Amendment speech under *Spence,* what degree of constitutional protection should such symbolic speech receive? Does expressive conduct enjoy
the same constitutional protection as oral speech?
In *Tinker,* the Court said that the conduct (black

armbands) enjoyed "comprehensive protection under the First Amendment." The ban, which appears to have been treated as a content-based regulation, was unconstitutional absent a showing that the exercise of the right would "materially and substantially interfere with the requirements of appropriate discipline in the operation of the school." This latter showing is the real test set forth in *Tinker*. While this test appears to require something less than the clear and present danger test requires, that was probably due to the school house context in which the expression occurred.

United States v. O'Brien (1968), most clearly defines the governing standards. In *O'Brien*, Chief Justice Warren, for the Court, began from the premise that when speech and nonspeech are combined in conduct, an incidental restriction of expression resulting from regulating the nonspeech element could be justified only if the following conditions are satisfied: (1) the regulation must further an important or substantial governmental interest; (2) the government interest must be unrelated to the suppression of free expression; and, (3) the incidental restriction on alleged freedom must be no greater than is essential to the furtherance of that interest. The *O'Brien* test is of major importance since it is one of the most frequently-used standards for reviewing content-neutral laws which incidentally burden speech.

In applying this balancing standard, the *O'Brien* Court refused to probe the congressional motive in proscribing draft-card burning which might have proven that the law was based on the content of the speech, requiring a more stringent standard of review. Instead, the law was said to serve the content-neutral, important objective of promoting the effective operation of the Selective Services System. Even assuming that this was the objective of law, the challengers argued that it was already adequately served by other laws—the incremental advantages gained by one more law was not worth the added burden on First Amendment rights. *O'Brien* adopted a less demanding approach to means-end analysis. Since no alternative law would as effectively serve the governmental interest, the law was valid. This watered-down approach to balancing has been severely criticized but it has emerged as the dominant judicial approach for reviewing content-neutral regulation.

The *O'Brien* approach to interest balancing is also reflected in *Clark v. Community for Creative Non–Violence* (1984). While the National Park Service permitted the erection of tent cities in Lafayette Park and on the Mall in Washington, D.C., as part of a demonstration on the problems of the homeless, the Service invoked regulations against camping in the parks in rejecting requests to allow the demonstrators to sleep in the tents. The Court, per Justice White, rejected the claim that this refusal violated the First Amendment. Justice White in *Clark* invoked *O'Brien's* rules for symbolic conduct as well as the standards for judging the reasonableness of regulation of the manner of expression in the public forum concluding that the two standards were essentially the same.

The dissenters in *Clark* leveled an objection frequently made against the Court's application of the *O'Brien* standards: "[T]he Court has dramatically lowered the scrutiny of government regulations once it has determined that such regulations are content-neutral." The challenge of the critics is not to the *O'Brien* standards themselves but to the Court's use of them, especially its assessment of the relation of the law to the admittedly important government interest. Critics assert that the Court does not give sufficient weight to First Amendment values in the balance and that the Court does not ask whether the added incremental effectiveness afforded by using the law in question is really worth the costs in freedom of expression. More generally, the critics question whether the Court is not diluting the standards of First Amendment review because the expression takes the form of conduct rather than pure oral speech.

But the student should not assume that symbolic expression is never accorded full protection. When the government regulates the content of symbolic expression, it constitutes a direct and significant burden on expression. In such circumstances the *O'Brien* rules do not apply because those rules apply only to incidental burdens. For example, when a demonstrator as a means of political protest burned an American flag at the Republican National Convention in Texas, his conviction under a Texas statute which prohibited desecration of a venerated object was set aside as inconsistent with the First Amendment. The expressive and overtly political nature of the flag burner's conduct at the convention was obvious. The state may not presume that provocative or offensive words will produce disorder. The flag burning did not constitute "fighting words." An interest in preventing breach of the peace was not served when no disturbance occurred or was threatened. The state's asserted interest in preserving the flag as a symbol of "nationhood and national unity" proved too much because such concerns come to the fore only when the "person's treatment of the flag communicates a message." The precept that government cannot "prohibit expression simply because it disagrees with its message" is not conditional on the mode chosen for expression of the idea. Government cannot limit the symbols which the people use to communicate their messages. The contention that the flag cannot be used for communicating has no limiting principle. Can the Presidential seal or the Constitution itself be similarly placed off limits? The Court, applying the strict scrutiny standard of review, held, 5–4, that the state interests asserted did not justify criminally punishing a person for communicating political protest by means of burning a flag. *Texas v. Johnson* (1989).

After the decision in *Texas v. Johnson*, the Congress passed the Flag Protection Act of 1989 which made criminal the conduct of anyone who "knowingly mutilates, defaces, physically defiles, burns, maintains on the floor or ground, or tramples upon" the United States flag. The United States prosecuted certain individuals for violating the Act by setting fire to the American flag. Was the new Flag Protection Act sufficiently different from the Texas law? The Texas law had "targeted expressive conduct on the basis of the content of its message." Nevertheless, it was clear that the interest of Congress in the Act was related to the suppression of free expression. The language of the statute revealed Congress's interest "in the communicative impact of flag destruction." Almost every term used in the statute was concerned with disrespectful treatment of the flag. The Flag Protection Act was cast in broader terms than the Texas law; yet it still suffered from the same fatal infirmity. It suppressed expression because of concern for its "likely communicative impact." Once again the Court held, 5–4, that the prosecutions for flag burning could not stand consistent with the First Amendment. *United States v. Eichman* (1990).

The controversy over flag burning resulted in a renewed emphasis on a fundamental principle: "If there is a bedrock principle underlying the First Amendment, it is that the Government may not prohibit the expression of an idea simply because society finds the idea offensive or disagreeable." *Texas v. Johnson*. When regulation of symbolic activity is content based, the most exacting level of scrutiny will be applied. *United States v. Eichman* (1990).

The First Amendment status of expressive activity may be in more flux, however, than the flag desecration cases indicate. A state law which prohibited non-obscene nude dancing was upheld 5–4 even though such dancing was conceded to be expressive activity protected by the First Amendment. This concession seemed to deprive the activity of protection at the same time it conceded it. Chief Justice Rehnquist in a plurality opinion described the prohibited non-obscene nude dancing as "expressive conduct within the outer perimeters of the First Amendment, though only marginally so." Perhaps because of its "outer perimeter" First Amendment status, the plurality concluded that the state law could be evaluated under the *O'Brien* test. The substantial state interest prong of *O'Brien* was satisfied since the law furthered the state interest in "order and morality." The critical prong of *O'Brien* requiring that the law be unrelated to the suppression of free expression was said to be satisfied since the law was deemed to be directed at public nudity not at any erotic message communicated by the dancing. The plurality indicates a willingness to accord a lower degree of protection to some forms of hitherto protected expressive activity such as indecent dancing. Justice Souter concurred on the ground that under the doctrine of *Renton v. Playtime Theatres, Inc.* (1986) the state law could be justified as directed at preventing the adverse secondary effects flowing from adult entertainment establishments. Justice Scalia concurred on the ground that the law banning non-obscene nude dancing did not present First Amendment issues at all since it was a general law not directed at expression. *Barnes v. Glen Theatre, Inc.* (1991).

5.   FREEDOM OF ASSOCIATION
AND BELIEF

a.   The Source of the Right

Freedom of association is not specifically mentioned in the Constitution. As early as the seventeenth century, John Locke wrote of the importance of private associations in checking concentrations of power and protecting liberty. In modern society, association is a vital means for competing in the marketplace of ideas and controlling government. Interest groups and political parties compete for public attention and support and, in that process, they further the values of democratic government. As the Supreme Court stated in *N.A.A.C.P. v. Alabama* (1958): "[I]t is beyond debate that freedom to engage in association for the advancement of beliefs and ideas is an inseparable aspect of the 'liberty' assured by the Due Process Clause of the Fourteenth Amendment, which embraces freedom of speech."

But when a city ordinance restricts admission to certain dance halls to persons between the ages of 14 and 18, the exclusion of adults from these dance halls does not violate any First Amendment right of association. There is no generalized right of "social association." It is expressive association to further First Amendment objectives which the First Amendment protects. Protecting the opportunity for minors and adults to dance together does not fall in that category. *City of Dallas v. Stanglin* (1989).

Similarly, freedom of belief is not an express constitutional guarantee. But, like association, it has developed into a right implied from the First Amendment guarantee and due process liberty. "If there is any fixed star in our constitutional horizon, it is that no official, high or petty, can proscribe what shall be orthodox in politics, nationalism, religion, or other matters of opinion." *West Virginia State Bd. of Educ. v. Barnette* (1943).

b. Membership and Associational Action

Suppose government were to make it a crime to be a member of the Ku Klux Klan? Such a law, if approached *in vacuo,* would violate freedom of association and belief. Associations often have multiple objectives, some might be legal and some might not be. To punish mere membership alone is essentially to create guilt by association. Thus, freedom of association precludes the consideration in a capital sentencing hearing of defendant's membership in a white racist organization which had neither committed nor endorsed unlawful or violent acts. The First Amendment prevents the use of defendant's abstract beliefs in a sentencing proceeding when those beliefs have no relevance to it. *Dawson v. Delaware* (1992).

In *Scales v. United States* (1961), the Court held that individual membership in an association could be criminally punished only if the government were required to show, (1) knowledge or scienter of the illegal objectives of the association; (2) specific intent to further those illegal objectives; and (3) "active" membership. It is probable that the reference to illegal objectives would be synchronized by a contemporary court to meet the requirements of the modern revised clear and present danger doctrine. *Brandenburg v. Ohio* (1969). The group must be shown to have a specific intent to incite, not merely to advocate illegal conduct. *Noto v. United States* (1961). The severity of these requirements have effectively terminated government prosecution of group membership. The student should note, however, that as stringent as these requirements are, they do not require that punishment be based on actual harmful conduct.

If constitutional protection of association is to be meaningful, it must extend to activities in furtherance of the group's objectives. Legislation burdening lawful activities must be judicially scrutinized. In *Aptheker v. Secretary of State* (1964), the Court struck down a federal law prohibiting members of so-called subversive action organizations from even applying for a passport. The law violated the freedom of travel found to be embodied in the freedom of association, an instance, it might be said, of a right twice derived. In *N.A.A.C.P. v. Claiborne Hardware Co.* (1982), the Court held that neither the NAACP nor its members could be held liable for damages arising from a civil rights boycott, absent a showing of illegal conduct causing the resultant harm. "The right to associate does not lose all constitutional protection merely because some members of the group may have participated in conduct or advocated doctrine that itself is not protected." Damages could not be imposed based on the results of non-violent protected activity. Unless the government established that the NAACP had authorized the illegal conduct causing the injury, imposing liability would "impermissibly burden the rights of political association." A protected political boycott like the one in *Claiborne* should be distinguished from an unprotected economic boycott. A boycott by an association of court-appointed lawyers representing indigents for the purpose of obtaining an increase in their compensation was a restraint of trade under the antitrust laws and was quite unlike the civil rights protestors in *Claiborne* who had sought no "special advantage for themselves." *FTC v. Superior Court Trial Lawyers Association* (1990).

The student should not assume that the principles set forth above require government to treat all groups equally. For example, the fact that government chooses to extend certain tax breaks to some groups but refuses to support the lobbying activities of others via tax advantages does not violate the First Amendment. "Congress has simply chosen not to pay for [the organization's] lobbying. We again reject the 'notion that First Amendment rights are somehow not fully realized unless they are subsidized by the State.' " *Regan v. Taxation With Representation of Washington* (1983).

The idea expressed in *Regan* that the "legislature's decision not to subsidize the exercise of a fundamental right does not infringe the right" was relied on again in *Lyng v. International Union, UAW* (1988). A federal statute provided (1) that no household would be eligible to participate in the food stamp program while any of its members was on strike, and (2) that no household would be permitted to receive an increase in its food stamp allotment because the income of a striking member of the household had decreased because of the strike. The statute was upheld against contentions that the statute infringed a striker's right to associate with her family as well as the freedom of association rights of strikers and their unions. The statute did not order individuals not to dine together nor did it directly and substantially interfere with family life. Similarly, the statute did not order union members "not to associate together for the purpose of conducting a strike." Concededly, strikers would be better off if food stamps were available during a strike but freedom of association did not "require the Government to furnish funds to maximize the exercise" of the "striker's right of association."

c. Group Registration and Disclosure

A vital aspect of freedom of association and belief is the right to maintain privacy regarding those beliefs and group ties. Anonymity is a vital means of avoiding the chilling effect of threats and harassment. Nevertheless, the Court has not forged a consistent doctrine indicating when the First Amendment will protect against compelled disclosure of group membership or other information concerning group activities. Cases from an earlier era dealing with subversive organizations tended to adopt an *ad hoc* balancing analysis giving extreme deference to legislative justifications based on national security. *Barenblatt v. United States* (1959) [contempt conviction for refusing to answer congressional committee's questions concerning witness' associational relationships upheld]; *Communist Party of the United States v. Subversive Activities Control Bd.* (1961) [compelled registration and disclosure of Communist Party membership list upheld].

However, other cases, typically dealing with groups perceived as "legitimate," have been reviewed under a strict scrutiny standard. *Gibson v. Florida Legislative Investigation Comm.* (1963) held that before a state legislature could compel the NAACP to disclose membership list information, it had to "convincingly show a substantial relation between the information sought and a subject of overriding and compelling state interest." In explaining the basis for heightened review, the Court noted that the state was not seeking to secure information about Communist activity. Rather, it was the NAACP, which was in no way alleged to be a subversive organization, that was the focal point of the state's inquiry. *Gibson; Brown v. Socialist Workers* (1982).

How are these two lines of cases to be reconciled? One interpretation would be that the *ad hoc* balancing test and its susceptibility to allowing disturbing exceptions to freedom of association has been overtaken by the strict scrutiny standard of the later cases. Another view is that each line of cases is still creditable; *Barenblatt* and its government-favored balancing approach has neither been reversed nor discredited by the Court. The more stringent standard of review is reserved by the Court to protect activities deemed "legitimate" under the First Amendment. This suggests the view that the right of association implied from and protected by the First Amendment is to join together to pursue objectives consistent with the goals of the First Amendment. It is not a general right of association.

d.   Public Benefits and Government Employment

Public benefits and government employment have traditionally been treated as privileges rather than rights. If government employment and public benefits are privileges, it is argued, it follows that government is free to impose such conditions on the receipt of such benefits as it deems appropriate. Today, this right-privilege dichotomy has been largely discarded and replaced by principles such as the unconstitutional conditions doctrine. Government cannot condition the receipt of public benefits or enjoyment of public employment upon the surrender of constitutional rights.

In the context of freedom of association and belief, unconstitutional conditions reasoning means that the government cannot freely condition an individual's access to benefits from the public sector

on the basis of what would constitute interference
with her political and associational freedom. Of
course, this does not mean that government must
open sensitive job positions to obvious national security risks. But it does require that governmental
rules and regulations concerning access to public
employment, for example, be narrowly drawn with
precision and clarity. Illustrative is *United States v.
Robel* (1967), which invalidated provisions of federal
law prohibiting members of communist-action organizations from engaging in "any employment in
any defense facility." The Court, per Chief Justice
Warren, struck down this statutory prohibition as a
vague and overbroad intrusion on First Amendment
rights: "[T]he statute sweeps indiscriminately
across all types of associations with communist-
action groups, without regard to the quality and
degree of membership." The government must, said
the Chief Justice, use "means which have a 'less
drastic' impact on the continued vitality of First
Amendment freedoms."

Unfortunately, the use of the overbreadth doctrine in *Robel* to invalidate the sweeping federal law
did little to illuminate how a properly drawn loyal-
ty-security program might be framed. Paradoxically,
if the Court had chosen to put a savings construction on the statute, the *Robel* decision might have
provided greater clarification on the line between
permissible and impermissible conditions. As a consequence of the Court's approach, the *Robel* decision is now usually dismissed as a form of interest

balancing even though the Court specifically refused to adopt a balancing test.

How should a loyalty security program be drafted to withstand First Amendment attack? It appears that a statute must satisfy the requirements outlined in *Scales v. United States* (1961). Although *Scales* arose in a criminal setting, even in the civil context of a *Robel*-type situation, the requirements of *Scales* apply, *i.e.*, there must be individual *scienter* of the organization's illegal objectives and specific intent to further those objectives, and active membership. If the statute meets these demanding criteria, it is likely to survive First Amendment scrutiny. Conversely, if the statute is not narrowly drawn in these terms, or if it is not drawn with clarity, it is likely to be held unconstitutionally vague and overbroad. The student should remember that even if a law survives such a facial inquiry, it still must be applied to particular individuals in a constitutional manner, *e.g.*, whether the law is limited to sensitive government employment.

In addition to the First Amendment problems raised by government efforts to force disclosure of group memberships and political beliefs, public inquiries may also raise issues of self-incrimination. May government force its employees to disclose incriminating information under threat of discharge? *Garrity v. New Jersey* (1967), held that confessions given under such coercion cannot be used as a basis for subsequent criminal prosecution. Further, the employee cannot be forced to surrender his privilege against self-incrimination as a condition of continued employment. *Gardner v. Broderick* (1968). But if the employee is granted full immunity from criminal prosecution, and the questions asked are relevant to the job, she cannot refuse to answer. Refusal to cooperate with a lawful inquiry here as in the bar cases can become an independent basis for either denial of a public benefit or discharge from public employment.

e. The Right Not to Associate—Compelled Speech

The corollary of freedom to speak, to believe, and to associate is the freedom not to speak, not to believe, and not to associate. In part, recognition of these corollary rights reflects concern with freedom of conscience. When government intrudes into the private realm, its activities must necessarily be more restricted than when it regulates public conduct or expression. *Stanley v. Georgia* (1969) [private possession of obscene matter cannot constitutionally be made a crime]. The corollary rights also reflect appreciation of the need to allow an individual to determine for herself what identity or personality she will present to the world. Government cannot force an individual to identify with a belief or idea with which she disagrees. "A system which secures the right to proselytize religious, political, and ideological causes must also guarantee the concomitant right to decline to foster such beliefs." *Wooley v. Maynard* (1977). But these corollary rights are not absolute. As the Court said in *Roberts v. United States Jaycees* (1984): "Infringements may be justified by regulations adopted to serve compelling state interests, unrelated to the suppression of ideas, that cannot be achieved through means significantly less restrictive of associational freedoms."

In *Abood v. Detroit Board of Education* (1977), the Court held that compulsory service fees charged under a closed shop agreement (permitted by state law) which were used for the ideological or political objectives of the union (which were not necessarily shared by those paying fees) were unconstitutional. "[A]t the heart of the First Amendment is the notion that the individual should be free to believe as he will, and that in a free society one's beliefs should be shaped by his mind and his conscience rather than coerced by the State."

Similarly, an "integrated state bar" (which conditions the right to practice on membership in and payment of dues to the state bar) cannot use the dues of its members to finance political and ideological activities with which its members disagree. The Court rejected an attempt to distinguish *Abood* by reliance on the "government speech" doctrine which provides that government necessarily must take positions if it is to govern effectively. Use by the state bar of mandatory dues for political and ideological purposes could not be so justified. Unlike a government agency, the funds of the state bar came from dues not legislative appropriations and its functions were essentially advisory. The "integrated bar" was held to be governed by *Abood*. The state bar could fund activities which were germane to its goals but it could not fund activities of an ideological nature. *Keller v. State Bar of California* (1990).

Students at the University of Wisconsin challenged a mandatory student activity fee which was used in part to fund student organizations engaged in political or ideological speech. The state university contended that its mandatory student activity fee was used to fund speech appropriate to the mission of the university. The Supreme Court, reversing the lower federal courts,validated the fee. The Court acknowledged that *Abood* and *Keller* had limited the mandated subsidy to speech germane to the purposes of the union or bar association involved in those cases. However, the Court concluded that a standard of germaneness was simply not feasible in a university setting. To ask the university to identify expression germane to its mission is opposed to the very idea of a university. Nor was it for the Court to say what was or was not germane. This ruling does not mean that objecting students are unprotected because a requirement of viewpoint neutrality still obtains with respect to state university funding of student activities. *Board of Regents of University of Wisconsin System v. Southworth* (2000).

And in *Wooley v. Maynard* (1977), the Court held unconstitutional the application of criminal sanctions to Jehovah's Witnesses who covered over the motto on their New Hampshire automobile license plate, "Live Free or Die." Their claim that they should not be compelled to proclaim agreement on their private property (*i.e.,* the license plate) with a state-composed message that offended their deepest religious and ideological convictions was upheld. The Court concluded that the state's interests in fostering appreciation of state history and state pride were insufficiently compelling to override the First Amendment rights at stake.

The principle that not every burden on the interests of a group to choose its members freely, or of an individual who declines to provide any support for an idea, will be protected, is reflected in *PruneYard Shopping Center v. Robins* (1980). *PruneYard* presented the question whether the California court's interpretation of the free expression provisions of its own Constitution could be used to force shopping center owners to permit pamphleteering within the shopping mall. The shopping center owner claimed a First Amendment right of non-association against being compelled to provide a forum on his property for the speech of others. The Supreme Court upheld the decision of the California court's ruling that the owner's First Amendment rights had not been infringed.

How is *PruneYard* to be distinguished from *Abood, Keller* and *Wooley?* First, *Wooley* involved ideas coming from the state itself. Second, the shopping center, by the choice of the Shopping Center owners, was open to the public. Third, there was little likelihood that the views expressed by the pamphleteers would be identified with those of the owners. Fourth, to the extent that such a danger was present, the owners could simply disavow the views being expressed. In short, the more a government regulation compelling some activity imposes a personal and direct burden on the rights of association and belief, the more it is likely to infringe the First Amendment right. See *Pacific Gas & Elec. Co. v. Public Util. Com'n* (1986) [state utility commission order requiring a private utility company to provide space in its billing envelopes four times a year to a private interest group critical of the utility held unconstitutional. The utility may be forced either to appear to agree with the group's message or to respond].

In some cases, the governmental interest in the regulation may be so overriding as to justify an admitted intrusion on the corollary rights. In the *Abood* case, for example, the Court upheld compulsory fees used for collective bargaining purposes even though some workers might be opposed to collective bargaining or strikes. *Abood* concluded that the legislative assessment of the important contribution of the union shop to industrial peace constitutionally justified the interference with associational rights.

Roberts v. United States Jaycees (1984), upheld an interpretation of the Minnesota Human Rights Act barring gender discrimination by public business entities to apply to the males-only membership rules of the United States Jaycees. The Jaycees attacked the Act as a vague and overbroad intrusion on First Amendment rights. Justice Brennan for the Court in *Roberts* distinguished two senses of freedom of association. First, the Jaycees' exclusion of women did not involve the constitutional protection afforded "intimate human relationships." Unlike marriage, family, or childbirth, "the local chapters of the Jaycees are neither small nor selective. Moreover, much of the activity central to the formation and maintenance of the association involved the participation of strangers to that relationship." Second, while the Act did burden the right to associate for expressive purposes protected by the First Amendment by interfering with the internal organization and affairs of the group, "Minnesota's compelling interest in eradicating discrimination against its female citizens justifies the impact that application of the statute to the Jaycees may have on the male members' associational freedoms."

Similarly, a New York City law prohibiting discrimination in clubs with over four hundred members which provided benefits to businesses and nonmembers was not unconstitutionally overbroad. The law on its face did not significantly diminish "the ability of individuals to form associations that will advocate public or private viewpoints." If there was any overbreadth in the New York law, cure would have to await case-by-case analysis of situations where such overbreadth was in fact present. *New York State Club Association v. City of New York* (1988).

When a group of gay, lesbian and bisexual persons of Irish descent sought to join the St. Patrick's Day parade in Boston, the private group organizing the parade refused to permit them to participate.

The Massachusetts courts held that the state's public accommodations law required the inclusion of the excluded groups and that such inclusion did not violate the organizing group's First Amendment rights. The Supreme Court, per Justice Souter, unanimously reversed. Every unit in a parade influences the message conveyed by its organizers. The state courts' application of the Massachusetts public accommodations law forced the parade organizers "to alter the expressive content of their parade." An important aspect of the idea of free speech is that one who chooses to speak also has a right to choose what not to say. *Hurley v. Irish–American Gay, Lesbian and Bisexual Group* (1995)

In *Boy Scouts of America v. Dale* (2000), the Court once again protected an organization's right of "expressive association" against state anti-discrimination laws. James Dale, the assistant coordinator of a Boy Scout troop, was dismissed from his position when he announced that he was gay. Dale's challenge to his dismissal under a New Jersey anti-discrimination law failed. Chief Justice Rehnquist for the Court, 5–4, ruled that the right of expressive association of the Boy Scouts trumped the New Jersey law. The state failed to show a compelling interest which warranted overriding that right. This case resembled *Hurley* rather than *Roberts*. No serious burden was imposed on the association by the public accommodations law in *Roberts*. But requiring Dale's continued presence in the Boy Scouts, given his public avowal of his sexual orientation, would incorrectly send a message that the Boy Scouts approved of homosexual conduct and, as in *Hurley*, would violate the right of expressive association of the organization. Justice Souter, for the dissenters, thought that the Court should have weighted the state interest in remedying discrimination more heavily than the organization's right to promote its moral views.

Marketing orders issued by the Secretary of Agriculture under the Agricultural Marketing Agreement Act of 1937 assessing fruit growers for the cost of generic advertising of their products were subjected to a First Amendment challenge by the growers. Should the orders be evaluated under the rational basis test used for economic regulation or under the heightened review used in the First Amendment context? The Court held, per Justice Stevens, that the presumptive validity standard used in economic regulation should be applied to the marketing orders. Although the fruit growers were compelled to fund generic advertising, this was part of a broader collective regulatory program which already curbed the freedom of the fruit growers to act as they chose. There were three reasons why First Amendment considerations were not implicated by these orders: (1) no restraint was imposed on any grower's freedom to communicate any message; (2) no person was compelled to engage in any actual or symbolic speech; and (3) the orders did not compel the growers to support or finance any political or ideological views. This was an economic regulation case not a First Amendment case. Therefore, neither the First Amendment test for commercial speech set forth in *Central Hudson Gas & Elec. Corp. v. Public Service Commission of New York, infra,* (1980) nor the Court's compelled speech cases applied. *Glickman v. Wileman Brothers & Elliott* (1997).

A federal law mandated that fresh mushroom handlers pay assessments which were chiefly used to pay for advertising to promote the sale of mushrooms. The Supreme Court upheld a mushroom producer's First Amendment challenge which asserted that the assessment constituted invalid compelled speech. The Court has permitted compelled speech or subsidies only in the context of an overriding associational purpose. In *Glickman,* unlike the case here, the subsidy was part of a general regulatory system. Here the only purpose the assessment serves is to promote the very advertising scheme which the challenger protests. He does not wish to advertise the sale of mushrooms; he wishes to advertise that his mushrooms are superior. Compelled subsidies for speech are not valid where the principle objective of the program is speech itself apart from a larger regulatory regime. *United States v. United Foods, Inc.* (2001). The Court, per Justice Scalia, upheld a federal assessment on beef producers to be used to promote the consumption and marketing of beef and related products. *United Foods* was distinguished on the ground that the advertising there concerned private rather than government speech. Here the speech involved is government speech. Compelled support of government programs, even government programs which one opposes, is "perfectly constitutional." *Johanns v. Livestock Marketing Association* (2005).

In summary, claims based on the right not to associate may be defeated by a finding that there is no significant intrusion on the right or by the determination that a burden is justified by a compelling governmental interest. *PruneYard* and *Glickman* indicate that not every form of compelled expression significantly intrudes on First Amendment rights. *Roberts* suggests that where a state policy of requiring freedom from gender discrimination collides with associational freedom, the state policy can override the liberty claim. Although the Court did not say so in *Roberts,* the case is certainly capable of being seen as an example of equal protection policy triumphing over liberty considerations. See also *Runyon v. McCrary* (1976) [discrimination in private schools on the basis of race held to violate civil rights laws even as against claims of privacy, educational freedom, and associational freedom]. At the same time, when the right of "expressive association" is severely intruded upon, that right will prevail over equality interests. *Hurley* and the *Boy Scouts* case make clear that a private organization's right of expressive association must be deferred to in the absence of an overriding compelling governmental interest.

B. THE DOCTRINE APPLIED

1. EXPRESSION IN THE LOCAL FORUM

In the "fifties" and "sixties," a civil rights social revolution occurred in the United States. Through sit-ins, demonstrations, parades, and picketing, civil rights demonstrators protested the continuing survival of Jim Crow legislation in the southern and border states. When the states and municipalities involved responded through legislation, the demonstrators usually found successful refuge in the First Amendment. *Edwards v. South Carolina* (1963); *Cox v. Louisiana* (1965); *Brown v. Louisiana* (1966). In 1977, the American Nazis announced plans to march through Skokie, Illinois, a predominantly Jewish suburb of Chicago. Skokie's population included many survivors of Nazi concentration camps. When the village of Skokie responded by seeking injunctions and announcing new ordinances to prevent such marches, the Nazis contended that these measures offended the First Amendment. These contentions prevailed. *Collin v. Smith* (7th Cir. 1978).

Whatever one's reaction to these events, they dramatically illustrate the dilemma of reconciling the rights of speech and assembly in the public forum with a community's right to maintain peace and order. Indeed, the context of the Skokie cases is particularly troubling. Who may properly claim freedom of speech? For what modes of expression? In order to answer these questions, it is necessary first to draw a distinction based on the nature of the regulation. It must be determined whether the local community is seeking to regulate the content of the speech, *i.e.,* the message being communicated, or is merely seeking to regulate the conditions under which the expression will occur in a content-neutral way, *e.g.,* regulating the time, place, and manner under which expression, regardless of its content, can occur.

a. Controlling Speech Content: Inciting, Provocative and Offensive Language

Whenever government undertakes to regulate speech and assembly because of the content of what is being communicated, it bears a heavy burden of justification. Frequently, the courts invoke the modern clear and present danger test in reviewing convictions under a breach of the peace or disorderly conduct law. For example, *Hess v. Indiana* (1973), reversed a disorderly conduct conviction of a demonstrator in an antiwar protest who had used words such as "we'll take the fucking street later." *Hess* declared that such language was nothing more than advocacy of illegal action at some future time. Since there was no incitement to imminent disorder, or indeed any evidence of an intent to produce such imminent disorder, the fact that the words might have a tendency to lead to violence was inadequate to meet the requirements of the modern clear and present danger test. *Brandenburg v. Ohio* (1969). See also *Cohen v. California* (1971), where the Court held that the defendant could not be convicted of disturbing the peace absent a showing of intent to incite to illegal conduct.

An alternative approach can be found in *Chaplinsky v. New Hampshire* (1942), where a Jehovah's Witness called the town constable "a goddamned racketeer and a damned fascist." A breach of the peace conviction was upheld because the state supreme court had given a curative gloss to the breach of the peace law limiting it to words with a "direct tendency to cause acts of violence by the persons to whom individually the remark is addressed." The U.S. Supreme Court explained in *Chaplinsky* that there are some categories of expression which are not protected freedom of speech, including fighting words, "those words which by their very utterance inflict injury or tend to incite an immediate breach of the peace." Such expression is "of such slight social value as a step to truth that any benefit that may be derived is clearly outweighed by the social interest in order and morality." In short, fighting words, like obscenity, do not fall within the protected scope of the freedom of speech.

The student should note the important features of the fighting words doctrine as it operates. First, as defined by *Chaplinsky,* the doctrine had two parts. It encompassed offensive or abusive language which by its very utterance inflicts injury. It also included language which by its very nature, judged by the probable reaction of a person of common intelligence, is likely to produce a violent reaction. Second, the doctrine, as framed, was limited to face-to-face verbal encounters which at the moment they are uttered invite physical reprisal or otherwise are likely to produce disorder. Third, the doctrine does not look to the actual danger of the particular situation but focuses on the abstract character of the words—are they of a kind likely to provoke retaliation by the average addressee?

The fighting words doctrine, however, has been severely limited since its announcement in *Chaplinsky*. The doctrine suggested that a speaker could be restricted because of the reactions of the audience. It thus seemed to endorse the concept of a heckler's veto. *Terminiello v. Chicago* (1949), rejected the principle that the hostile reaction of a crowd would provide justification, consistent with the First Amendment, for silencing a speaker. Justice Douglas said in fact that it was the purpose of the First Amendment to invite dispute.

But *Feiner v. New York* (1951), appeared to endorse a broader version of *Chaplinsky*. Irving Feiner spoke at the American Legion picnic in Syracuse, New York. Among other things, he called the Mayor "a champagne-sipping bum." The crowd moved toward the speaker. Who should be arrested, the speaker or the crowd? The police arrested the speaker. The Supreme Court, 5–4, upheld the conviction by drawing a distinction between Feiner's situation and a hostile audience scenario. While a speaker could not be silenced merely because of the reactions of a hostile audience, in this case the speaker was deemed to have been inciting a riot. *Feiner* had created a "clear and present danger of disorder." But is this only after-the-fact rationalization? Logistically, it is always easier to arrest the speaker than the crowd. Similarly, it is not difficult to portray a noisy and insulting speaker as inciting. The dissenters found no danger of imminent disorder on the *Feiner* facts; the majority did. *Feiner* shows that the clear and present danger test can be manipulated to silence offensive speakers.

Nevertheless, *Feiner* has increasingly been read narrowly. When a speaker intentionally provokes a hostile reaction and imminent disorder is probable, his speech is not protected, and the police may move against him. See *Cohen v. California* (1971). But if a speaker is engaged in protected expression, if he is not intentionally inciting the crowd to violence, he is to be protected. Police must then move against the hostile crowd. *Gregory v. Chicago* (1969). What happens if the police cannot control the crowd and violence is imminent remains unclear. In such an emergency, whether or not the speaker should be stopped, he usually will be.

There was a second part to the *Chaplinsky* "fighting words" doctrine. The Court had indicated that insulting or abusive language (*i.e.*, words which by their very utterance inflict an injury) also fell outside the First Amendment. But *Cohen v. California* severely undermined this concept. Cohen had been convicted of disturbing the peace by "offensive conduct" for wearing a jacket bearing the words "Fuck the Draft" in a Los Angeles courthouse. In reversing the conviction, Justice Harlan rejected the proposition that the Court could excise, as offensive conduct, particularly scurrilous expression from the public discourse. There was a great danger in government selecting certain expression and placing it off-limits: "[O]ne man's vulgarity is another's lyric." Further, Justice Harlan stressed that speech often serves an emotive, non-cognitive value. In prohibiting a certain manner of expression, there was great danger that the ideas themselves would be suppressed.

The fighting words doctrine, although it has been altered, has never been overturned. The prohibition against punishing offensive language, while a source of dispute on the present Court, remains unaltered. The line between fighting words and offensive language is ill-defined. Yet it is an important distinction. Fighting words—absent content discrimination among subsets of fighting words [*R.A.V. v. City of St. Paul* (1992) *infra*]—can be prohibited consistent with the First Amendment. Offensive speech cannot be. The reason that the nature of fighting words has not been clarified is, in part, that the Court has increasingly used the devices of vagueness and overbreadth to invalidate disorderly conduct and breach of the peace statutes on their face.

In *Gooding v. Wilson* (1972), a Georgia breach of the peace statute was held unconstitutionally overbroad in that the Georgia courts had not limited the statute to fighting words as defined in *Chaplinsky*. The Court concluded that the statute as interpreted made it "a 'breach of the peace' merely to speak words offensive to some who hear them, and so [swept] too broadly."

The *Gooding* technique of using vagueness and overbreadth to invalidate a statute, thereby avoiding the need to define fighting words with particularity, has been employed frequently in subsequent cases. See, *e.g., Lewis v. New Orleans* (1972) (*Lewis I*), *Lewis v. New Orleans* (1974) (*Lewis II*), *Rosenfeld v. New Jersey* (1972). Indeed, Justice Blackmun joined by Chief Justice Burger and Justice Rehnquist, dissenting in *Lewis II,* stated: "Overbreadth and vagueness in the field of speech have become result-oriented rubber stamps attuned to the easy and imagined self-assurance that 'one man's vulgarity is another's lyric.'" To pass muster under the prevailing judicial doctrine, then, a statute must be limited to fighting words used in personal face-to-face encounters, or incitement to imminent and probable illegal conduct. The laws must not cross the line to reach speech which is merely offensive or annoying. The student should remember that if a statute is narrowly drawn, it would then become necessary to determine whether the defendant's words in the particular case are constitutionally protected words (*i.e.,* is the law constitutional "as applied").

In addition to the many limitations which have been placed on the "fighting words" doctrine since its inception, a major limitation was added in *R.A.V. v. City of St. Paul* (1992). Justice Scalia declared for the Court 5–4 that there were "no categories of speech entirely invisible to the Constitution." A St. Paul ordinance which punished fighting words that insult or provoke violence "on the basis of race, color, creed, religion, or gender" was unconstitutional on its face. The ordinance had been applied to white youths who had burnt a cross in the yard of a black family. The city was unsuccessful in defending the ordinance on the ground that it punished fighting words. Categories of speech may be regulated consistent with the First Amendment "because of their constitutionally proscribable content." For example, libel can be made actionable because of the damage it inflicts on reputation but libel actions cannot be limited only to those actions where government officials have been criticized. All "fighting words" can be punished but a subset of fighting words which is punished because of the viewpoint they express cannot be. Such regulation of fighting words is impermissible content discrimination.

The St. Paul ordinance in *R.A.V.* could not be justified as a "secondary effect" [See *Renton v. Playtime Theaters, Inc.* (1986)] because of the city's interest in protecting vulnerable minority groups which had suffered discrimination. The consequences of the proscribed speech flowed from the listener's reaction to the speech—an impermissible ground for the regulation of speech. Although the ordinance served a compelling interest in promoting racial, religious and ethnic harmony, the ordinance was still invalid since there were content-neutral alternatives available, *i.e.*, the proscription of all fighting words.

Justice Scalia's opinion for the Court in *R.A.V.* drew fire from the concurring justices on two grounds. First, the holding undermined the entire categorical approach to free expression problems. Justice White, concurring, said the holding contradicted "repeated statements [in earlier cases] that certain categories of expression are 'not within the area of constitutionally protected speech.'" Justice White said the Court's new underbreadth doctrine served no useful function because it protects expressive activity that is "evil and worthless in First Amendment terms" simply because government had not regulated more rather than less speech. Second, *R.A.V.* undermined the purpose of strict scrutiny analysis in First Amendment cases since a narrowly drawn law which met the strict scrutiny standard was nevertheless invalid since it had not regulated *enough* speech. Such an approach to strict scrutiny analysis robbed it of all utility as a First Amendment tool. In sum, *R.A.V.* takes a radically new approach to the fighting words doctrine and to the categorical approach to First Amendment problems in general. *R.A.V.* suggests that hitherto unprotected categories of expression will merit First Amendment protection if regulation of them reflects impermissible content-based discrimination.

An exception mentioned in *R.A.V.*, however, may serve as a significant limit on its scope. Categories of speech can be regulated consistent with the First Amendment. Such a category is the true threat category. In *Virginia v. Black* (2003), true threats were defined to include statements "where the speaker means to communicate a serious expression of intent to commit an act of unlawful violence" to particular individuals or groups. A prohibition on true threats provides protection to individuals from "the fear of violence," the disruption such fear occasions and from the possibility that the threatened violence will actually occur. Cross-burning with an intent to intimidate is a form of true threat. A Virginia statute made it a felony to burn a cross from another person's property "with the intention of intimidating any person or group of persons." Defendants charged the law was invalid under *R.A.V.* The Court, per Justice O'Connor, conceded that the law discriminated on the basis of content but ruled that it was not invalid under *R.A.V.* Although it was true that cross-burning has a strong racist identification, the Virginia law did not "single-out for opprobrium" only cross-burning on that disfavored topic as had been the case with the St. Paul ordinance. Content discrimination is not impermissible when the basis for it consists "entirely of the very reason the entire class of speech as issue" was proscribable. Cross-burning undertaken with the intent to intimidate can be proscribed by the state "because burning a cross is a particularly virulent form of intimidation." Historically, cross-burning has long suggested imminent violence. Therefore, the state could choose to regulate this "subset of intimidating messages." The state may single out forms of intimidation "most likely to inspire fear of bodily harm."

A significant aspect of *Virginia v. Black* is the distinction it makes between cross-burnings which fall into the true threat category and are unprotected and cross-burnings as ideological statements which constitute protected speech. Another provision of the Virginia law illustrates the distinction. The provision made the burning of a cross prima facie evidence of an intent to intimidate an individual or group of individuals. The state courts interpreted this provision so that the burning of a cross alone constituted sufficient evidence from which one could infer the requisite intent. So construed, this provision was unconstitutional because it ignored that very context which would show whether a particular cross-burning was intended to intimidate or was instead a protected expression of a racist ideology. As interpreted, the provision chilled protected political speech by increasing the likelihood that those engaging in cross-burning by itself would be subject to prosecution and conviction.

Virginia v. Black raises new questions. What about other controversial symbols? Does the display of the swastika constitute a true threat? Perhaps, courts will answer this question by distinguishing between swastika displays with an intent to intimidate and displays that have no such intention. In dissent, in *Virginia v. Black*, Justice Thomas objected to this distinction. In light of the "horrific effect cross-burning has on its victims," Thomas thought it was reasonable to presume an intent to intimidate from the act of cross-burning alone.

R.A.V. affects the future of new candidates for unprotected First Amendment category status such as hate speech. Some legal scholars have argued that racial epithets, and hate speech in general, serves to perpetuate the subordinate status of minority groups. Hate speech does not invite discussion but instead produces a demeaning silence on the part of its victims. Some universities have developed hate speech codes and legislatures have considered enacting legislation punishing hate speech. At an earlier time, when hate speech was known as group defamation, an Illinois criminal libel statute punishing group defamation was upheld 5–4. *Beauharnais v. Illinois* (1952). Justice Frankfurter suggested for the Court that racial libel constituted unprotected expression because it robbed members of minority groups of human dignity and deprived them of economic and educational opportunities. However, *Beauharnais* proved to be a First Amendment dead end. The Illinois statute was repealed and *Beauharnais* has not met with favor in subsequent Supreme Court decisions.

Since *R.A.V.* held that a content-based proscription of a subset of "fighting words" such as hate speech is impermissible, the future of hate speech regulation just dealing with "fighting words" is not bright. Even if racist speech as a broad category were proscribed, such regulation would likely fall afoul of the doctrine of *Cohen v. California* that offensive speech may not be proscribed simply on the ground of its offensiveness.

For the proponents of hate speech regulation, a development which provides some encouragement is *Wisconsin v. Mitchell* (1993) which upheld a Wisconsin law enhancing criminal penalties when the victim of the crime has been selected because of race. Motive is an appropriate factor in sentencing and when the motivation for crime is the racial identity of the victim, such motivation can be considered. *R.A.V.* was distinguished on the ground that the law struck down there was aimed at expression while enhanced penalties for racial crimes were by definition directed at non-speech conduct. In *Apprendi v. New Jersey* (2000), the Court held that the fact that a hate crime sentence enhancing penalty was placed in the sentencing part of the state criminal code did not relieve the state from trying the issue of biased purpose—-an essential element of the offense—before a jury under the beyond a reasonable doubt standard. The question of whether hate crime sentence enhancement is valid under the First Amendment was not directly raised but the Court pointedly noted that it had specifically rejected such a challenge in *Wisconsin v. Mitchell.*

b. Access to Public Property—The Public Forum

While government regulation of protected First Amendment speech in the public forum because of its content is subject to strict scrutiny, content-neutral regulation which only indirectly burdens free speech is not seen as imposing as severe a burden on First Amendment values. *Greer v. Spock* (1976). Thus, time, place and manner regulation of the context in which speech occurs (*i.e.,* an indirect burden on free speech, *supra*) is subjected to a less searching balancing inquiry. *Perry Education Ass'n v. Perry Local Educators' Ass'n* (1983). The degree of judicial scrutiny of the government regulation frequently turns on the nature of the place being regulated. Public property may be characterized as a traditional public forum, a limited or designated public forum, or a nonpublic forum.

Streets, sidewalks, and parks are "quintessential public forums" which "have immemorially been held in trust for the use of the public, and, time out of mind, have been used for purposes of assembly, communicating thoughts between citizens, and discussing public questions." *Hague v. CIO* (1939). See *Edwards v. South Carolina* (1963) [state capitol grounds are a traditional place for public protest]. While these traditional public fora are open for speech, the right of access must be exercised "in subordination to the general comfort and convenience, and in consonance with peace and good order." *Hague.* In short, competing uses of the forum must be harmonized.

Because traditional public fora are "natural and proper places for the dissemination of information and opinion" [*Schneider v. State of New Jersey* (1939), ordinance forbidding all handbilling is not justified by concern over street littering], any restriction based on the *content* of the message must be narrowly tailored to serve a compelling state interest. *Carey v. Brown* (1980) [prohibition on residential picketing except for labor picketing held unconstitutional]. But even an indirect government regulation of the context of expression is subject to stringent standards. Government may "enforce reasonable time, place and manner regulations as long as the restrictions are content-neutral, are narrowly tailored to serve a significant government interest, and leave open alternative channels of communication." *United States v. Grace* (1983) [law barring all picketing and leafletting on the sidewalks surrounding the Supreme Court held unconstitutional].

In the context of the traditional public forum, the distinction between a content-based regulation and a content-neutral time, place or manner regulation is a crucial one. Exemplifying this distinction is *Boos v. Barry* (1988), which invalidated under the First Amendment a District of Columbia regulation prohibiting the display of signs within 500 feet of a foreign embassy if the signs tended to bring the embassy's government into disrepute. Although not viewpoint-based, the sign prohibition was a content-based regulation of core political expression. Even assuming the regulation's justification that shielding embassy personnel from critical speech protected their dignity was compelling, the regulation was not narrowly tailored since less restrictive alternatives were available to protect the dignity interest.

But a regulation permitting dispersal of demonstrators within 500 feet of an embassy was valid. The lower court had narrowly interpreted this congregation clause to permit dispersal of demonstrators only when the police reasonably believed that a threat to the security of the embassy was present. So interpreted, this content-neutral regulation was not facially overbroad; it was instead a reasonable place and manner regulation.

The Court has held that a right of minimum and equal access to the public forum for expression extends beyond the traditional public forum to government property designated as a "limited public forum." But what is the scope of this limited public forum? Not all public property is open to speech and protest by the public generally: "The State, no less than a private owner of property, has power to preserve the property under its control for the use to which it is lawfully dedicated. [People who want to propagandize do not] have a constitutional right to do so whenever and however and wherever they please." *Adderley v. Florida* (1966).

In an effort to more clearly define the scope of the "public forum," the Court at times has applied a generalized inquiry into the compatibility of the expressive activity with the normal use to which the property is put. *Brown v. Louisiana* (1966) [quiet sit-in protest in a public library held to be constitutionally protected]; *Grayned v. City of Rockford* (1972) [school property may be part of public forum subject to reasonable time, place and manner regulation].

A more narrow, but increasingly dominant approach, is to look to the government's intent. Under this designated forum approach, the compatibility of the expressive activity with the nature of the property is only one factor to be considered along with the relevant policies and practices of the government to ascertain whether the government intended to designate the place as a limited public forum. *See, e.g., Widmar v. Vincent* (1981) [university policy of opening meeting facilities to student groups created a limited public forum from which religious groups could not be constitutionally excluded].

An example of limited public forum analysis is provided by *Heffron v. International Society for Krishna Consciousness* (1981). A state fair rule limiting the sale or distribution of goods and materials to fixed locations was challenged by the Hare Krishnas, who sought more personal encounters. The rule was held to be a reasonable time, place and manner regulation. A state fair held on public property, reasoned the Court, involves a limited public forum designed to efficiently present the products and views of a great number of exhibitors to a large number of people in a limited area. The fixed location rule was applied even-handedly to all distributors; it was therefore content-neutral. It was narrowly-tailored to serve the significant government interest in maintaining orderly movement of the crowds. No alternative regulation would deal adequately with the problem. The Court rejected a selective access approach exempting the Krishnas from the fixed place rule—other religious and non-religious groups seeking support for their activities were equally entitled to access as the Krishnas. Finally, the rule did not prevent communication; it did not deny access to the forum nor prevent the Krishnas from pursuing their personal encounters outside the fairgrounds.

Recently, the Court has increasingly avoided this somewhat demanding form of judicial scrutiny by characterizing the public property subject to the regulations as not being part of the public forum. In *Cornelius v. NAACP Legal Def. & Educ. Fund* (1985), Justice O'Connor stated: "Control over access to a nonpublic forum can be based on subject matter and speaker identity so long as the distinctions drawn are reasonable in light of the purpose served by the forum and are viewpoint neutral." Thus, the city may limit access to the advertising space on city buses. *Lehman v. Shaker Heights* (1974). Military bases are not ordinarily a part of the public forum even when they are open to the public. *Greer v. Spock* (1976); *United States v. Albertini* (1985) [protestor who had been banned on security grounds from access to a base because of past protest activity could be excluded even during military open house]. Jail house grounds are not part of the public forum. *Adderley v. Florida* (1966). There is no right of public access to home mail boxes for unstamped mail. *United States Postal Service v. Council of Greenburgh Civic Ass'ns* (1981).

Nonpublic forum analysis is exemplified by *Perry Education Ass'n v. Perry Local Educators' Ass'n* (1983). A local school district had entered into an agreement with the exclusive bargaining agent for the teachers to deny access to the teachers' mailboxes to a rival union. The Court, 5–4, upheld the school district's action. Justice White, for the Court, began by rejecting the rival union's efforts to invoke the public forum doctrine. The district did not have a policy of unrestricted public access to the mailboxes. Selective access afforded certain civic groups engaged in activities of interest to students did not render the property open to the general public—at most the district had created a limited forum open to groups of a similar character.

Applying principles used for a nonpublic forum, Justice White concluded that the restriction on access turned "on the status of the respective union rather than their views," *i.e.,* it was viewpoint neutral; there was no ideological bias. The restriction was reasonable in serving the district's interest in preserving the property for its designated use—only the exclusive bargaining agent had responsibility to all of the teachers. The rival union retained "substantial alternative channels" for communication with the teachers. For the four dissenters, the case involved an "equal access claim" which should not turn on whether the mailboxes were designated a public forum.

The problem of determining whether a facility, even though public property, constitutes a public forum is itself an intensely difficult one. For example, a postal service regulation barred solicitation of contributions on postal premises. Did the application of the regulation to prohibit solicitation of contributions by a political advocacy group on the post office sidewalk violate the First Amendment? Justice White held for a plurality that it did not. The postal sidewalk was not a traditional public forum; it lacked the characteristics of a general public sidewalk. It was not a public thoroughfare but led only from the parking lot to the post office. Even though some individuals and groups had been

442 FREEDOM OF EXPRESSION Pt. 2

permitted to speak, leaflet, and picket on postal premises in the past, there was also a regulation extant prohibiting disruption. The sum of these factors did not dedicate postal property to expressive activity. Relying on *Perry*, the plurality declared that selective access did not transform public property into a public forum. *United States v. Kokinda* (1990).

Just as the postal sidewalk in *Kokinda* was not a public forum, so an airport terminal operated by a public authority was not a public forum either. Why were these facilities categorized as nonpublic fora? The distinction between public and nonpublic fora was governed by whether government was acting as a lawmaker or as a proprietor. The heightened review which applied when the government managed a public facility as a regulator or licensor would not be invoked when the government functioned as a proprietor managing the internal operations of a public facility. *International Society for Krishna Consciousness, Inc. v. Lee* (1992).

Airport terminals were not traditional public fora. Airport terminals, unlike the village green, had not been historically open to expressive activity. Airport terminals existed to facilitate air travel not expression. In such circumstances, the no-solicitation rule was a reasonable content-neutral regulation. For an airport terminal to be categorized as a limited or designated public fora, government must have an intention to open the facility to public discourse. Justice Kennedy, in a concurrence, rejected the idea that the public forum category should be confined to those facilities which had historically been so categorized. The purpose of the public forum doctrine was to protect expression from government interference. Closing off recognition of new public facilities as public fora ran counter to this objective. The First Amendment had responded to changing technologies in other contexts and it should do so here as well. Justice Kennedy contended instead that the use of the public facility should dictate whether it was a public forum. If physical characteristics and easy public access made a public facility appropriate and suitable for expressive activity, then it should be characterized as a public forum.

Kokinda held the challenged regulation's application to sidewalk solicitation valid using the reasonableness standard applied in the case of nonpublic fora. The regulation did not involve content or viewpoint discrimination. Solicitation was inherently disruptive of the business of the postal service and impeded normal traffic flows. Furthermore, a categorical ban on solicitation was reasonable since it would be too difficult to enforce more limited regulations for all the nation's post offices. Justice Kennedy concurred but reached that result after using the heightened review standard applied to content-neutral time, place and manner regulation, *i.e.,* is the regulation narrowly tailored to serve significant government interests? Does it leave open alternative channels of communication?

Similarly, in *International Society for Krishna Consciousness v. Lee* (1992), a government-operated airport terminal regulation which prohibited the solicitation and receipt of funds within the terminal did not violate the First Amendment. But a public authority-operated airport terminal regulation banning the distribution of written or printed materials violated the First Amendment. *Lee v. International Society for Krishna Consciousness* (1992). Using the foregoing public forum analysis, four Justices ruled that so extensive a prohibition was not narrowly drawn nor did it leave open ample alternative means of communication. Justice O'Connor using *nonpublic* forum analysis reached the same conclusion. The total ban on the distribution of leaflets or pamphlets was invalid because it was unreasonable. Unlike the disruption associated with solicitation such as pedestrian traffic delay and congestion, the peaceful distribution of leaflets or pamphlets was clearly not incompatible "with a large, multi-purpose forum" such as an airport terminal.

The student should note that while the above discussion focuses on regulations of the *place* for expression, government may also impose narrowly drawn, reasonable regulation of the *time* and *manner* of protest. In focusing on the manner of expression, the Court has suggested that "speech plus" conduct does not enjoy the same constitutional protection as "pure speech." Thus, Justice Goldberg in *Cox v. Louisiana* (1965) [obstructing public passage law held facially vague and overbroad] rejected any suggestion that the Constitution affords "the same kind of freedom to those who would communicate ideas by conduct such as patrolling, marching, and picketing [as] to those who communicate ideas by pure speech." While balancing is employed in such "speech plus" cases, the Court tends to weigh the scales in favor of regulation.

In balancing the competing interests in these public forum cases, the Court will frequently use the standard fashioned in *O'Brien:* "A government regulation is sufficiently justified if it furthers an important or substantial government interest; if the governmental interest is unrelated to the suppression of free expression; and if the incidental restriction of alleged First Amendment freedoms is no greater than is essential to the furtherance of that interest." The Court has characterized this test as involving essentially the same inquiry as is used in public forum analysis. See *Clark v. Community for Creative Non–Violence* (1984).

In *Members of City Council of Los Angeles v. Taxpayers for Vincent* (1984), the Court used *O'Brien* in upholding an ordinance prohibiting the posting of signs on public property including lamp posts. Justice Stevens, for the Court, characterized the law as a regulation of the *manner* of communication. The law was said to serve aesthetic interests, *i.e.,* barring a visual assault on citizens, which were "basically unrelated to the suppression of ideas." The ordinance was not substantially broader than necessary since it was aimed at the exact source of the evil. Visual clutter is a product of the medium itself; the substantive evil is not merely a byproduct of the conduct, *e.g.,* litter from handbilling. Borrowing from the public forum cases, the Court noted that adequate alternative channels of effective communication, at the public places where the signs would have been posted, were available, *e.g.,* handbilling. But Justice Stevens found no support for the challenger's invocation of the public forum doctrine. Rather, he suggested that lamp posts would not qualify as a traditional or limited public forum.

While the Court's balancing approach in the public forum cases or under *O'Brien* purports to be searching, the application of the test appears much less demanding. The "significance" of the government's interest often is little more than a requirement of a real, not imagined interest; the Court does not generally weigh the government's interest in a particular law against any increased intrusion on First Amendment values from its use; while a narrow tailoring of means to ends is verbally endorsed, the availability of alternative means of expression tends to diminish the demand for a close fit. With the development of the nonpublic fora concept, the protection available for open and equal access is even more restricted. Content neutrality is abandoned in favor of viewpoint or ideological neutrality; reasonableness of means often is little more than a minimal rationality standard; selectivity of access to the forum is accepted. A geographic fixation with the location of the speech replaces balanced assessment of the competing interests.

In summary, when government regulates expressive activity in the public forum, time, place and manner controls must be precise and must be able to be justified without reference to the content of the speech. A control, however, does not become content-neutral just because it incidentally burdens some speakers more than others. *Renton v. Playtime Theatres, Inc.* (1986). In addition, the Court has declared that although time, place and manner controls must be narrowly tailored to accomplish the substantial government interests they professedly serve, "narrowly tailored" does not mean the same thing as a "least restrictive alternative" test. The inquiry as to whether the control is narrowly tailored is less demanding than a less restrictive alternative test would be. All that is required is a showing that the government interest to be served would be accomplished less effectively in the absence of the control or regulation. *Ward v. Rock Against Racism* (1989).

c. Access to Private Property

State action is a key concept in imposing constitutional obligation. But is it possible that the First Amendment creates rights of access even in the context of private property? Can private property ever become part of the public forum? The possibility that the First Amendment can create a right of public access against an owner's consent was suggested by *Marsh v. Alabama* (1946). In reviewing a trespass conviction of a Jehovah's Witness for handbilling on the streets of a business district of a company town, the Court stated: "The more an owner, for his advantage, opens up his property for use by the public in general, the more do his rights become circumscribed by the statutory and constitutional rights of those who use it."

Marsh's suggestion that privately owned property could be dedicated to the public use generated a tortured series of cases involving access for speech purposes to privately owned shopping centers. In *Amalgamated Food Employees Union Local 590 v. Logan Valley Plaza, Inc.* (1968), an injunction barring informational picketing at the center was overturned. The shopping center was deemed a "functional equivalent" of the business district in *Marsh;* property rights of the store owners were closer to public property than to the private property rights of homeowners.

A caveat to the access rights recognized in *Logan Valley* came in *Lloyd Corp. v. Tanner* (1972). Only if there is a relationship between the object of the protest and the site of the protest, *i.e.,* the shopping center, do First Amendment rights attach—there was "no open-ended invitation to the public for any and all purposes." Then, in *Hudgens v. N.L.R.B.* (1976), *Logan Valley* was overruled. Conditioning access to the shopping center on the subject of the protest, reasoned the Court, constituted an invalid content-based restriction on expression.

Marsh apparently survives but in a highly limited form. Only when privately owned property has taken on essentially all of the attributes of a public property does it become subject to constitutional obligations. Absent some legally imposed duty, private property remains private, subject to the dominion of the owner to exclude those he chooses. But note that a right of access to private property can be created by state law. *PruneYard Shopping Center v. Robins* (1980) [state guarantee of public access for speech purposes to privately owned shopping center does not violate owner's right not to associate].

The fact that private property is not part of the public forum does not mean that government is free to bar access by the public to the homeowner. When a speaker seeks to communicate with homeowners through handbilling, solicitation, etc., First Amendment rights must be balanced with the state interest in protecting the interests of the homeowner, especially the interest in privacy and freedom from annoyance. A total government ban on door-to-door handbilling has been held invalid. *Martin v. Struthers* (1943). But in *Breard v. Alexandria* (1951), a more limited ban on commercial solicitation without the homeowner's consent was upheld. Soliciting the homeowner, then, is subject to reasonable regulation designed to protect citizens against crime and undue annoyance. But any such regulation must be drawn with "narrow specificity." *Hynes v. Mayor and Council of Oradell* (1976).

When a regulation, is found to impose a "direct and substantial limitation on protected activity," it can be justified only if the government demonstrates that it serves "a sufficiently strong, subordinating interest that [government] is entitled to protect." In *Village of Schaumburg v. Citizens for a Better Environment* (1980), the Court invalidated an

ordinance of the Village prohibiting charitable solicitations unless the charity used at least 75% of its
receipts for charitable purposes. The law only pe-
ripherally promoted the state's admittedly substantial interest in protecting the public from fraud,
crime, and annoyance. Less intrusive means than
banning solicitation were available.

But *Village of Schaumburg* was distinguished in
Madigan v. Telemarketing Associates (2003). Telemarketers told the public when soliciting for a
charity that a substantial portion of each dollar
contribution would go to benefit the charity. In fact,
only 15 cents out of every dollar raised was made
available to the charity. The Attorney General of
Illinois filed a complaint that such statements constituted fraud. The Illinois state courts dismissed
the suit as barred by the First Amendment relying
on *Schaumburg*. The Supreme Court reversed declaring that charitable solicitation is protected under the First Amendment but fraudulent charitable
solicitation is not. Under the First Amendment,
telemarketers cannot be charged with fraud just
because fund raising costs exceed an arbitrary statutory percentage limit but *Schaumburg* had left a
"corridor open for fraud actions" with regard to
false or misleading solicitations.

But a content-neutral ordinance banning targeted
picketing, i.e., picketing "before or about" any residence, is constitutional. As construed, the ordinance
only reached picketing focused on, or taking place
in front of, a particular residence. The regulation of
such focused picketing served the significant gov-

ernment interest in the protection of residential privacy: "The devastating effect of targeted picketing on the quiet enjoyment of the home is beyond doubt." As construed, the ordinance left open ample alternative means of communicating a message. The prohibition on targeted picketing was narrowly tailored since it eliminated no more than the precise evil it sought to correct—targeted picketing of "captive" residents presumptively unwilling to receive the message. *Frisby v. Schultz* (1988).

In *Watchtower Bible and Tract Society of New York, Inc. v. Village of Stratton* (2002), Jehovah's Witnesses challenged a village ordinance which provided that a canvasser must obtain a permit before engaging in door-to-door advocacy of any cause and, upon request, must display the permit which contains the canvasser's name. The Court reviewed the ordinance not only as it applied to religious proselytizing but also as it applied to anonymous political speech and the distribution of handbills. The Court conceded that, if the ordinance reached only commercial activity and solicitation of funds, it could be viewed as tailored to serve important interests such as protection of privacy and fraud and crime prevention. But since the ordinance was applied to non-commercial canvassers for religious and political causes, the ordinance is invalid, even though ministerial in nature, for three reasons. First, the requirement that the canvasser's name be identified in the permit application and be available for public inspection calls for the surrender of rights to anonymity protected by the First Amendment. Second, requiring a permit to exercise the right to speak burdens those whose religious or patriotic scruples preclude applying for such a permit. Third, the ordinance stifles spontaneous speech. It was not necessary to identify an appropriate standard of review. Given the breadth of the ordinance and the character of the regulation, First Amendment concerns outweigh the governmental interests of privacy and crime prevention. A resident is annoyed by a knock on the door whether the solicitor has a permit or not. Similarly, it is unlikely that a criminal is deterred from crime for lack of a permit.

d. Licensing, Permits and Injunctions

A narrowly drawn, content-neutral, reasonable time, place and manner control is constitutional even if it comes in the form of a prior restraint. *Cox v. New Hampshire* (1941) [city requirement for a fee and license for parades or processions held constitutional]. But, as is the case for prior restraints generally, when government employs licensing or permit systems, it bears a heavy burden of justification. *Organization for a Better Austin v. Keefe* (1971) [state court injunction against distribution of leaflets charging blockbusting overturned]. One aspect of the suspectness of such controls is the requirement that adequate standards be provided in the law to guide the administrator. Broad delegations of authority, even when cast as content-neutral, indirect controls, invite censorship of unpopular views.

A licensing system that provides no standards is overbroad and invalid on its face. *Kunz v. New York* (1951). If standards are provided, they must be clear and precise regardless of the way in which the law is applied. In *Shuttlesworth v. Birmingham* (1969), the city ordinance provided for issuance of a parade permit unless the administrator determined that "the public welfare, peace, safety, health, decency, good order, morals or convenience require that it be refused." The defendant, who had marched without a permit, successfully argued that the law was invalid on its face. As the Court concluded, it vested "virtually unbridled and absolute power" in the administrator. While the state courts had narrowly construed the law, the Supreme Court determined that it was impossible for protestors to anticipate this limited interpretation at the time of protest.

Similarly, a facial challenge to a Lakewood, Ohio ordinance which gave the Mayor unfettered discretion to deny a permit for the placement of coin-operated newspaper dispensing devices on city sidewalks was successful. Under the ordinance, the Mayor could deny such a permit whenever he deemed it in the public interest. No reasons were required to be stated. Unlimited authority to condition a permit on any terms the licensor deemed "necessary and reasonable" violated the First Amendment. Neutral licensing criteria are required: "Therefore, a facial challenge lies whenever a licensing law gives a government official or agency substantial power to discriminate based on the con-

tent or viewpoint of speech by suppressing disfavored speech or disliked speakers." *City of Lakewood v. Plain Dealer Publishing Co.* (1988).

A Forsyth County, Georgia ordinance requiring
applicants for a permit to conduct a parade or
assembly on public property to pay a permit fee of
up to $1000 to the county administrator was uncon-
stitutional. As in *City of Lakewood*, an overly broad
licensing discretion had been impermissibly lodged
in a government official. Ostensibly, the amount of
the license fee was based on the costs of providing
security for the parade. But this meant that the fee
could in fact depend on the administrator's estimate
of the degree of hostility the expressive activity, *i.e.*,
the parade, was likely to generate in the community. That there was a $1000 cap on the permit fee
did not make it content-neutral. Censorship was
still possible since the amount of the fee could
clearly be related to the content of the speech.
Forsyth County, Georgia v. Nationalist Movement
(1992).

Injunctions are also prior restraints subject to
close judicial scrutiny; precision of regulation is
required of the judicial order as well as the municipal ordinance. *Near v. Minnesota ex rel. Olson*
(1931). Nevertheless, courts have tended to be more
tolerant of this form of control. At least the decision
that the expression is subject to regulation is made
by a judicial decision-maker. One aspect of this
tolerance lies in the obligation to obey the facially
invalid injunction. In *Shuttlesworth,* Justice Stewart, for the Court, said that a person faced with a

facially invalid licensing law "may ignore it, and
engage with impunity in the exercise of the right of
free expression for which the law purports to require a license." But in *Walker v. Birmingham*
(1967), involving an injunction issued during the
same demonstration, Justice Stewart rejected the
right of the protestors "to ignore all the procedures
of the law and carry their battle to the streets." The
theory appears to be that the rule of law requires at
least an initial respect for the judicial injunction. If
there is a judicial process available allowing prompt
review of the injunction and the protestor fails to
use it, he is barred from collateral attack in the
contempt proceeding. But note that if the state fails
to provide strict procedural safeguards, including
"immediate appellate review," the injunction does
not bind. See *National Socialist Party of America v.
Village of Skokie* (1977). A similar principle governs
the right to disobey a facially valid law which is
being applied unconstitutionally. The protestor
must seek judicial review of the administrative action before taking to the streets. *Poulos v. New
Hampshire* (1953).

2. COMMERCIAL SPEECH

a. From *Valentine* to *Virginia Pharmacy*

In 1942, the Supreme Court read "purely commercial advertising" out of the First Amendment.
Valentine v. Chrestensen (1942) [municipal anti-lit-
ter ordinance could be constitutionally applied to
handbilling containing both political and commer-

cial messages]. However, the Court provided no rationale for this categorical exclusion of commercial speech from First Amendment protection nor did it define the meaning of commercial speech. What would be the status of a paid advertisement in a newspaper containing a political message but soliciting funds? See *New York Times v. Sullivan* (1964). Should any offer to buy or sell, *i.e.*, purely commercial speech, be excluded from "the freedom of speech" protected by the Constitution?

Some commentators have argued against extending First Amendment protection to commercial speech. They point to the minimal value of commercial advertising to the citizen-critic in the process of self-government and the limited role such communication has in self-development. The potential effect of extending full First Amendment protection to commercial speech given the plethora of government regulation of economic transactions also has been of concern. Nevertheless, in *Virginia State Bd. of Pharmacy v. Virginia Citizens Consumer Council, Inc.* (1976) [state statute prohibiting pharmacists from advertising the price of prescription drugs held unconstitutional], speech which does "no more than propose a commercial transaction" was brought within First Amendment protection. Justice Blackmun, for the Court, focused on the interests of the advertiser, consumers (especially poor and aged consumers), and the society, in drug price advertising. It is in the "public interest," he contended, to assure that private economic decisions regarding the allocation of resources in our free enterprise economy "in the aggregate, be intelligent and well informed. To this end, the free flow of commercial information is indispensable." The importance of this free information flow in fashioning intelligent opinion regarding how the economic system should be regulated was cited to indicate the value of commercial speech in self-governing. See generally *Linmark Assocs., Inc. v. Willingboro* (1977) [town's prohibition on posting of "For Sale" and "Sold" signs on real estate as a means of curbing white flight held unconstitutional].

To bring commercial speech within the freedom of speech guarantee, however, does not mean that such speech enjoys the same degree of First Amendment protection as "core" First Amendment expression, *e.g.,* political speech. *Virginia Pharmacy* characterized commercial speech as having greater hardiness and objectivity and as being easier to verify than other kinds of protected speech. Thus more extensive government regulation is acceptable than for more sensitive forms of expression. One consequence flowing from this conclusion is that false, misleading, and deceptive commercial speech enjoys no First Amendment protection. *Friedman v. Rogers* (1979) [state statute prohibiting practicing optometry under a trade name upheld]. Compare *New York Times v. Sullivan* (1964) [false defamatory speech protected under First Amendment, absent a showing of actual malice]. Similarly, commercial speech that proposes an illegal transaction is not protected speech. *Pittsburgh Press Co. v. Human*

Relations Com'n (1973) [ban on sex-designated help wanted ads upheld].

b. The Advent of the *Central Hudson* Test

But the unwillingness of the Court to equate commercial speech and political speech is not limited to erroneous expression. In commercial speech cases, the Court forgoes the ordinary strict scrutiny standard of review applied to content regulation in favor of a less stringent balancing analysis. *Central Hudson Gas & Electric Co. v. Public Service Com'n* (1980) [total state ban on promotional advertising by utilities held unconstitutional], established a four part test designed to indicate when commercial speech should be afforded First Amendment protection. *First,* the speech or message must not be false, misleading or involve illegal activity. *Second,* the governmental interest served by the regulation at issue must be substantial. *Third,* the regulation must directly advance that interest. *Fourth,* the regulation must not be more extensive than necessary to serve the governmental interest. *Virginia Pharmacy* had declared that blanket bans on truthful and non-misleading commercial speech were not permitted. The *Central Hudson* test was more malleable since such suppression is possible if four part test is not met. Clearly, the *Central Hudson* test does not employ a strict scrutiny approach to the regulation of commercial expression. On the other hand, it is not as deferential to government regulation as the rational basis test associated with

Valentine v. Chrestensen. The *Central Hudson* test is basically an intermediate standard of review.

The fourth prong of the *Central Hudson* test has been modified. A regulation, if narrowly tailored, can meet the "necessary" prong of the *Central Hudson* test even though the regulation is not the least restrictive means of furthering the substantial government interests. *Board of Trustees of State University of New York v. Fox* (1989). *Fox* did not signify that the means selected to achieve a governmental goal were entirely without significance in commercial speech cases. Thus, the Court struck down a municipal ban, which in the interest of safety and esthetics, banned commercial newsracks but not newspaper newsracks. The ban affected only 62 commercial newsracks but left 1500 to 2000 newsracks still on the streets. Clearly, the safety and aesthetic benefits to be derived from a ban with such minimal impact were marginal. The city had failed to calculate the costs and benefits flowing from the burden on speech which it had imposed. *Fox* required a "reasonable fit" between the government goal and the means selected to achieve it. *Cincinnati v. Discovery Network, Inc.* (1993).

Some First Amendment rules have less—or no— force in the context of commercial speech. Given the lesser danger of chilling hardy commercial speech, the overbreadth doctrine [*Bates v. State Bar of Arizona* (1977)], and the prior restraint doctrine [*Central Hudson Gas v. Public Service Commission* (1980)], do not apply to commercial speech. A challenge to a regulation of commercial speech on its face will not be invalidated on overbreadth grounds.

The *Central Hudson* test will permit the regulation of truthful advertising about lawful but potentially harmful activity. Thus regulation of advertising of legalized casino gambling which prohibited such advertising directed at Puerto Rico residents but permitted the same advertising directed to residents on the mainland was upheld. Deference to the legislature should be accorded to the legislature as to the appropriateness of the means used to accomplish the state's interest under *Central Hudson*. After all, Puerto Rico could have banned gambling altogether. If government has the authority to completely ban the activity, it necessarily has "the lesser power to ban advertising" of that activity. *Posadas de Puerto Rico Associates v. Tourism Company of Puerto Rico* (1986). But the future for *Posadas* was not bright. *44 Liquormart v. Rhode Island* (1996), *infra*, undermined *Posadas*. Four Justices, per Justice Stevens, repudiated *Posadas* and its idea that "attempts to regulate speech are more dangerous than attempts to regulate conduct."

Given that commercial speech is subject to a less demanding standard of review than other protected speech, it might be expected that the Court would have fashioned a fairly clear definition of what constitutes "commercial speech." But such is not the case. In *Bolger v. Youngs Drug Prods. Corp.* (1983), the Court considered the constitutionality of a federal law prohibiting the mailing of unsolicited advertisements for contraceptives as applied to certain promotional and informational material. Most of the mailings were held to fall "within the core notion of commercial speech—'speech which does no more than propose a commercial transaction.'" But much of the material did more than offer to deal, thus presenting "a closer question." Clearly the fact that the expression was embodied in an advertisement did not necessarily make it commercial speech. See *New York Times v. Sullivan* (1964). Neither the references to products nor the economic motivation for the mailings rendered the speech commercial. However, "[t]he combination of *all* these characteristics" provided a basis for invoking the *Central Hudson* test. The fact that the advertising sought to link the product to current public debate was deemed inadequate to elevate the expression to the fully protected category. Applying *Central Hudson,* neither the government interest in barring offensive material from unwilling recipients nor its interest in aiding parents of minor children justified the law's sweeping prohibition of the mailings at issue.

In retrospect, the resolution in the extent of First Amendment protection to be accorded to commercial speech signified by *Virginia Pharmacy* has proven to be less dramatic than originally anticipated. The refusal to apply many of the traditional protective doctrines of First Amendment law and the decision to categorically exclude false and misleading commercial speech from any constitutional protection certainly limits the constitutionalization of commercial speech. Further, the strict scrutiny regimen has not been applied in the commercial speech context.

Although certainly not as demanding as strict scrutiny, the *Central Hudson* test, as applied by the Court, is increasingly less deferential to regulation. A unanimous Court invalidated a federal statutory provision prohibiting beer labels from displaying alcohol content but not labels on hard liquor and wine. The regulation did not directly and materially advance the asserted governmental interest justifying the regulation as required by the third prong of the *Central Hudson* test. Federal law permitted the disclosure of the alcohol content in beer advertising except in the 18 states which prohibit disclosure. If the federal government's purpose was to bar "strength" wars about which beer had the highest alcohol content, it made no rational sense to exclude advertising from such a policy. The provision also failed the fourth prong of the *Central Hudson* test— it was more extensive than necessary. Congress had alternatives available to it which were less intrusive to the First Amendment protection accorded to commercial speech such as the direct limitation of the alcohol content of beer. *Rubin v. Coors Brewing Co.* (1995).

When a liquor retailer challenged a Rhode Island statutory ban against advertisement of retail liquor sales except at the place of sale, the Court held that (1) the Twenty-first Amendment giving the states authority to regulate alcoholic beverages within their borders did not qualify First Amendment protection; and (2) the ban on advertising liquor prices anywhere but at the point of sale violated the First Amendment. Although unanimous in result, the Court was badly split on the rationale. Justice Stevens, for a plurality of four, said when, as here, a state imposes a ban on "the dissemination of truthful, nonmisleading commercial messages for reasons unrelated to the preservation of a fair bargaining process," there was much less reason not to apply "the rigorous review that the First Amendment generally demands." Justice Stevens, citing *Central Hudson*, said the price advertising ban should be reviewed with "special care" since wholesale bans on truthful speech usually do not survive constitutional review. *44 Liquormart v. Rhode Island* (1995).

In *44 Liquormart*, Stevens said he would abandon *Posadas*: "[B]anning speech may sometimes prove far more intrusive than banning conduct." Conceding *Posadas* had been quite deferential in accepting the state's asserted interest, Justice O'Connor pointed out that post-*Posadas* cases has required a closer look at whether the commercial speech restriction directly advanced the state's interest and is narrowly tailored. The established *Central Hudson* test itself called for striking down the statutory ban since it was more extensive than necessary to serve the state's interest. There was no need to apply Justice Stevens' more stringent version with its insistence on review requiring "special care." Justice Thomas asked the Court to scuttle the *Central Hudson* test and return to the *Virginia Phar-*

macy principle "that all attempts to dissuade legal choice by citizens by keeping them in ignorance are impermissible." Justice Scalia shared Justice Thomas's "discomfort with *Central Hudson*." But since the Court was unclear about what should replace that test, he applied the existing *Central Hudson* test.

In *44 Liquormart*, four Justices, per Stevens, thought *Posadas* was wrong and Justice O'Connor declined either to follow it or overrule it. *Posadas* survived but just barely. The status of *Central Hudson* after *44 Liquormart*, although more secure than *Posadas* was, is unclear. The juxtaposition by Justice Stevens of "special care" review with the *Central Hudson* test was puzzling. Stevens applied *Central Hudson* in *44 Liquormart* but the gloss he gave it when applied to bans on truthful nonmisleading advertising, *i.e.*, review with "special care," seemed *sub silentio* to move *Central Hudson* from an intermediate standard of review closer to a strict scrutiny one.

A federal law banning truthful and non-misleading broadcast advertising of casino gambling in states where such gambling is legal violates the First Amendment. Applying the *Central Hudson* test, the Court declared that the federal law at issue was so studded with exemptions permitting gambling that it failed to meet the *Central Hudson* prong requiring that a regulation directly and materially advance the government interest involved, *i.e.*, discouraging casino gambling. The idea expressed in *Posadas* that because government has power to prohibit a product or activity altogether, therefore, it has authority to restrict speech about that product or activity was repudiated. The power to prohibit a product or activity does not in itself deprive truthful, non-deceptive commercial speech of its First Amendment protection. The appropriate alternative for government is to more directly regulate in a manner which is less intrusive of the "First Amendment rights of commercial speakers and the public." *Greater New Orleans Broadcasting Association, Inc. v. United States* (1999).

Provisions of a Massachusetts law prohibiting outdoor advertising of smokeless tobacco or cigars within 1000 feet of schools or playgrounds and indoor point-of-sale advertising of the same unless set more than 5 feet from the floor were struck down as violations of the First Amendment. Although the outdoor advertising restrictions met the third prong of the *Central Hudson* test requiring that a regulation directly advance the governmental interest, *i.e.*, preventing access to tobacco by those underage, it violated the fourth prong of *Central Hudson* that regulation be no more restrictive of speech than necessary. The indoor advertising restriction failed to meet either the third or the fourth prongs of the *Central Hudson* test: "Not all children are less than 5 feet tall, and those who are certainly have the ability to look up and take in their surroundings." The tobacco companies which challenged the regulations had asked the Court to abandon the *Central Hudson* test and apply the strict scrutiny standard of review but the Court responded that the *Central Hudson* test provided an adequate basis for decision. *Lorillard Tobacco Co. v. Reilly* (2001).

In *Thompson v. Western States Medical Center* (2002), the Supreme Court, per Justice O'Connor, struck down, 5–4, a federal law exempting drug compounding from FDA regulation. The process whereby a pharmacist or physician mixes or alters ingredients to create a medication suited to the needs of a particular patient is called drug compounding. The federal law afforded the exemption as long as the provider did not solicit the prescription or advertise or promote the compounded drug. The law was held to be an unconstitutional regulation of commercial speech under the *Central Hudson* test. Protecting both the new drug approval process and the drug compounding process itself serve important governmental interests. But even assuming that the federal law's ban on advertising compounding drugs satisfied the *Central Hudson* prong requiring that a regulation "directly advance" the governmental interests served by the regulation, the law still failed to satisfy that prong of *Central Hudson* requiring that a regulation of speech be no more extensive than necessary to serve those interests. Where government may achieve its objectives in a way that does not interfere with commercial speech, those alternatives should be used. For example, the use of commercial scale manufacturing or testing equipment in drug compounding could be banned as could offering compounded drugs at wholesale. The ban on advertising compounded drugs is not justified despite the fact that it may be motivated by a concern that it will cause patients to persuade their physicians to prescribe drugs for them they do not need. Such a concern is based on the premise, deemed impermissible in *Virginia Pharmacy* and *44 Liquormart*, that if people are given truthful information they will make bad decisions.

In *Thompson*, Justice Breyer, dissenting, thought that the Court applied the "commercial speech doctrine too strictly." The government's regulatory rationale was given insufficient weight and the availability of non-speech alternatives too easily assumed. Commercial speech rarely interferes "with the functioning of democratic political processes" and did not warrant the use of the Court's "strictest speech-protective tests." In summary, *Thompson* continues the trend in the Court's recent commercial speech cases whereby the Court professes to use the *Central Hudson* test but the type of review actually used is more consistent with the rigorous review associated with the strict scrutiny standard.

c. Lawyer Advertising

Lawyer advertising has proven an especially fruitful area for litigation probing the parameters of the constitutional protection afforded commercial speech. Shortly after *Virginia Pharmacy, Bates v. State Bar of Arizona* (1977) held that a blanket ban on lawyer price advertising in newspapers for routine legal services violates freedom of speech. But the Court acknowledged concern over deception of the consumer and stressed the narrow confines of its ruling. *Bates* was dealing with a total prohibition on price advertising and not a narrowly tailored regulation. Nor was it addressing the "peculiar problems" posed by advertisements relating to the quality of the legal services offered or broadcast advertising.

The concern with the danger of deception of consumers manifested in *Bates* found expression in the judicial imprimatur given state prophylactic regulation of in-person solicitation for pecuniary gain (*i.e.*, ambulance chasing). *Ohralik v. Ohio State Bar Ass'n* (1978). Compare *In re Primus* (1978) [ACLU lawyer may "further political and ideological goals of the association," *i.e.*, core political values, by informing potential clients of the possibility of litigation free from state sanction based on the *potential* danger of deception]. While prophylactic measures were approved in the context of face to face solicitation, state efforts to curtail potential deception have generally not fared well. *Zauderer v. Office of Disciplinary Counsel of Supreme Court of Ohio* (1985), struck down a state court reprimand of an attorney for newspaper ads soliciting business from those injured by using Dalkon Shields. There was no showing that the ads were false or misleading. Nor could the state sanction the use of illustrations of the shields in the ad since the representation was not inaccurate; the fear of potential public deception and the state interest in the dignity of the profession were deemed insufficient to justify a total ban on illustrations. A law designed to further the state's interest in preventing consumer confusion by curbing potentially misleading advertising must be "no broader than is reasonably necessary to prevent the deception." See *In re R.M.J.* (1982). For example, *Peel v. Attorney Registration and Disciplinary Commission of Illinois* (1990) held that a categorical state prohibition on advertising a lawyer's certification as a trial specialist failed to meet the heavy burden required where "dissemination of actual factual information to the public" was involved even though there was some potential for misleading consumers.

May an attorney who is also a CPA and a certified financial planner (CFP) use those designations after her name in advertising? A Florida state agency which had reprimanded an attorney for so doing was held to violate the First Amendment. The prong of the *Central Hudson* test which required that the regulation at issue must directly advance a substantial state interest was not served by the reprimand. The advertising was not misleading nor had there been any showing that any member of the public had been misled. There was a constitutional presumption which favored "disclosure over concealment." *Ibanez v. Florida Department of Business and Professional Regulation, Board of Accountancy* (1994).

In *Zauderer,* the Court did uphold state discipline of the attorney for failure to disclose in his ads that a client might be liable for litigation costs if the lawsuit failed: "Because the extension of First Amendment protection to commercial speech is justified principally by the value to consumers of the information such speech provides, [the lawyer's] constitutionally protected interest in *not* providing any particular factual information in his advertising is minimal." Rejecting the *Central Hudson* test for evaluating this minimal burden on speech from disclosure laws, the Court asked only if the requirements were reasonably related to the state interest in preventing deception of consumers.

In *Shapero v. Kentucky Bar Association* (1988), a state regulation prohibiting lawyers from sending truthful nondeceptive letters to potential clients facing particular types of legal problems was invalidated. The risk of overreaching and undue influence from mailed solicitation was deemed less than would be the case with in-person solicitation. A targeted letter invaded the recipient's privacy no more than at-large mailing of the same letter. Generally, lawyer advertising in the form of mailed solicitation has received more First Amendment protection than does in-person solicitation. But a Florida Bar Rule barring personal injury lawyers from sending targeted direct-mail solicitations to victims and their relatives for thirty days after an accident was upheld. *Shapero* was distinguished on the ground that it was not focused on the privacy rights of victims and that the ban there case did not have a limited time frame. Applying the *Central Hudson* test, the Court, 5–4, per Justice O'Connor, held that Florida had a substantial interest in protecting the privacy of victims and in preventing the erosion of confidence in the bar resulting from mail solicitation by lawyers intruding upon the grief and vulnerability of accident victims. *Florida Bar v. Went For It, Inc.* (1995).

A state ban on in-person solicitation by Certified Public Accountants was held to violate one of the prongs of the *Central Hudson* test. *Edenfield v. Fane* (1993). The Court distinguished *Ohralik* where a ban on in-person solicitation by lawyers was upheld. The state in *Edenfield* had not shown that its ban directly advanced a substantial state interest. Unlike lawyers, CPA's are not schooled in the art of persuasion. Therefore, CPA in-person solicitation was not inherently susceptible to over-reaching nor were innocent people likely to be misled.

3.   DEFAMATION AND PRIVACY

a.   Rise of the Public Law of Defamation

New York Times v. Sullivan (1964), declared that where an elected public official sues a "citizen critic" of government for defamation, the First Amendment should alter the normal operation of a state's private law of libel. Analogizing the rendition of heavy damages in a civil libel action in such circumstances to the old and discredited crime of seditious libel, the Court, per Justice Brennan, concluded in a famous passage that the "central meaning" of the First Amendment guaranteed the right of the "citizen critic" to criticize his government. The First

Amendment was said to reflect this nation's "profound commitment to the principle that debate on public issues should be uninhibited, robust, and wide-open, and that it may well include vehement, caustic, unpleasantly sharp attacks on government and public officials." Just as the government official enjoys immunity to freely perform his governmental duties, so also the "citizen critic" must enjoy a qualified immunity from civil damages in order to permit him to perform his duty in a democratic government.

A difficult task was presented to the Court in *Sullivan*. How to reconcile the reputational interest of the public official plaintiff with the interest in freedom of expression of the citizen critic, in this case the *New York Times*? Since the Court was not prepared, even in these circumstances, to obliterate the reputational interest, it created a qualified immunity for the citizen critic defamation defendant. This qualified privilege, as described by Justice Brennan, required proof of actual malice by the defamation plaintiff if he is to be successful: "The constitutional guarantees require a federal rule that prohibits a public official from recovering damages for a defamatory falsehood relating to his official conduct unless he proves that the statement was made with 'actual malice'—that is, with knowledge that it was false or with reckless disregard of whether it was false or not." Justice Brennan, by using the actual malice test, essentially reads out from First Amendment protection defamatory expression that meets the actual malice standard. In this sense, the "actual malice" test performs a similar function to the definition of obscenity in First Amendment law; the definition of actual malice separates what is protected speech from what is not.

The Supreme Court has held that a lower court finding of actual malice must be independently reviewed by appellate courts since the actual malice finding is a question of constitutional fact. *Bose Corp. v. Consumers Union* (1984). Although an appellate court must examine the statement at issue and the surrounding circumstances to decide whether it constitutes protected speech, a jury's credibility determinations are reviewed under the "clearly erroneous standard" and not a de novo review standard. *Harte–Hanks Communications, Inc. v. Connaughton* (1989). Furthermore, *Herbert v. Lando* (1979), declined to recognize an editorial privilege precluding pre-trial discovery into actual malice. Actual malice involves judgments about state of mind and the journalistic process which makes it necessary for a plaintiff to have access to such information in order to prove actual malice.

The doctrine set forth in *Sullivan* rapidly expanded. It was applied to non-elected public officials. *Rosenblatt v. Baer* (1966). It was then expanded to private sector public figures even though the analogy to seditious libel appeared to be stretched to the breaking point. *Curtis Publishing Co. v. Butts* (1967). These developments were not applauded by everyone on the Court. Justice Douglas asked cryptically in *Rosenblatt* whether the night watchman was a government official for purposes of *Sullivan.* What he suggested was that the content of the defamation was more important than the status of the plaintiff. This view found expression in a plurality opinion of the Court in *Rosenbloom v. Metromedia, Inc.* (1971). Three of the Justices—Brennan, Blackmun, and Burger—were willing to see the actual malice privilege extended to matters of public interest generally. In their view, the public interest in the communication in controversy should be the touchstone for the applicability of the actual malice privilege rather than the status of the plaintiff.

b. The Modern Public Law of Defamation

The *Rosenbloom* plurality's desire to make the content of the defamation the critical factor in the new public law of libel was rejected in *Gertz v. Robert Welch, Inc.* (1974). The Court held, 5–4, per Justice Powell: "[S]o long as they do not impose liability without fault, the States may define for themselves the appropriate standard of liability for a publisher or broadcaster of defamatory falsehood injurious to a private individual."

Justice Powell reasoned that the reputational interest of the private plaintiff enmeshed in the defamation controversy permitted a greater degree of state action. The private plaintiff lacked the means of self help available to the public plaintiff. Further, there was "a compelling normative consideration" for a different rule—the private figure had not voluntarily entered the vortex of public controversy or debate. On the other hand, concern for the dangers of self-censorship by the citizen-critic faced with a potential defamation action led to the extension of constitutional protection even to the private figure defamation plaintiff. States cannot impose strict liability. Further, at least in matters where there is a public interest, presumed and punitive damages would be precluded absent a showing of actual malice. Compensatory damages would still be available as long as the standard of liability was not a strict one. Although presumed damages were thus curtailed, compensatory damages were defined in such a way as to include some of the former domain of presumed damages. For example, the Court made it clear that damages for embarrassment, humiliation, and pain and suffering would be included under the rubric of compensatory damages.

Gertz, a milestone case, further extended the reach of the First Amendment into the private law of libel. Particularly significant was its rule that the First Amendment would not tolerate strict liability and that the minimum for liability would be negligent misstatement. The states, however, were free to create a rule more generous to the defamation defendant than negligent misstatement.

Gertz had not indicated whether its limitations on state defamation law were applicable in all private plaintiff defamation actions. Did the rules, for example, apply to non-media defendants? A case which seemed to pose this issue precisely was *Dun & Bradstreet, Inc. v. Greenmoss Builders, Inc.* (1985). A credit reporting agency had inaccurately reported that a construction company had filed for bankruptcy. Arguably, the credit reporting agency was not a media defendant. Were presumed and punitive damages therefore available in the absence of proof of actual malice? In a plurality opinion, the Court said such damages were available and the ordinary rules of Vermont libel law should apply. However, the plurality opinion said that the critical distinction was not whether the defendant was a media defendant. The critical issue was whether the public communication involved a matter of public concern. The *Gertz* rules apply only to matters of public concern that are "at the heart of the First Amendment's protection." Justice Powell reasons that "speech on matters of purely private concern is of less First Amendment concern." In the view of the *Dun & Bradstreet* plurality, the credit rating of a construction company which had been communicated only to a very small group of people was not a matter of public concern.

Philadelphia Newspapers, Inc. v. Hepps (1986), ruled 5–4 that plaintiffs suing newspapers for libel in matters of public concern must prove that the statements complained of are false. However, the Court did observe that when the defamatory matter is of exclusively private concern and the plaintiff is a private figure, constitutional requirements do not necessarily demand such special protection for the media. Subsequently, *Hepps* was used to reject a First Amendment privilege for matters of opinion in defamation cases. Liability for a statement of opinion which includes or implies false, defamatory statements of fact is not barred by the First Amendment. *Milkovich v. Lorain Journal Co.* (1990). First Amendment interests were sufficiently protected by the *Hepps* rule that the plaintiff prove falsity and by the requirement that the plaintiff must prove fault. *Milkovich* emphasized that a defamation action cannot prevail unless the statement at issue can reasonably be interpreted as stating actual facts about an individual. This may allow defense counsel to find shelter in a modified opinion privilege by contending that the opinion expressed should not have been interpreted to have asserted actual facts.

Another reaffirmation of the *New York Times–Gertz* rules is illustrated by the Court's refusal to allow the tort of infliction of emotional distress to do an end run around the *Times* doctrine. Hustler Magazine, a "skin" magazine, published a parody of right-wing evangelist Rev. Jerry Falwell portraying him having a sexual encounter with his mother in an outhouse. A judgment awarding damages to Falwell for emotional distress was unanimously reversed by the Supreme Court. Public plaintiffs— public officials and public figures—could not recover for intentional infliction of emotional distress in the absence of a showing that the publication complained of contained a false statement of fact which was published with actual malice. One of the elements of emotional distress is "outrageousness." But such a showing in a First Amendment context was too subjective because it would enable juries to impose liability based on the content of the publication or the identity of the parties. Moreover, the publication had been labeled "parody"; it could not reasonably have been interpreted as stating facts concerning Falwell. *Hustler Magazine v. Falwell* (1988). In summary, despite its many critics and its myriad technicalities, the *Times* doctrine still reigns.

c. Identifying the Public Figure Plaintiff

Since the focal point of the *Gertz–Sullivan* rules is still the status of the defamation plaintiff, it becomes critically important to understand the criteria for identifying who is a public figure. In *Gertz,* Justice Powell stated: "In some instances an individual may achieve such pervasive fame or notoriety that he becomes a public figure for all purposes and in all contexts. More commonly, an individual voluntarily injects himself or is drawn into a particular public controversy and thereby becomes a public figure for a limited range of issues. In either case, such persons assume special prominence in the resolution of public questions." Drawing on this dichotomy, subsequent cases have distinguished the all-purpose pervasive public figure from the limited-purpose public figure.

The pervasive public figure concept has been severely limited by the courts. Before an individual will be totally exposed to media attention, the courts require that his name almost be a household word, *e.g.,* Johnny Carson. Such a personality, it is thought, has access to the media to rebut defamatory attacks and has voluntarily thrust himself into the public spotlight.

The limited purpose public figure has proven more difficult to identify. *Time, Inc. v. Firestone* (1976), rejected efforts to apply the public figure label to Dorothy Firestone, Palm Beach socialite, who was involved in a racy divorce scandal. Justice Rehnquist, for the Court, applied a bifurcated test. First, in order for a person to be a public figure, the defamation must involve public controversy. Second, the plaintiff's involvement in that controversy must be voluntary. Applying these standards, Justice Rehnquist refused to equate matters of public controversy with matters of public interest. While the public might be keenly interested in Mrs. Firestone's marital travails, her divorce did not involve questions of overriding public concern. She had not voluntarily sought out public attention to make her divorce a matter of public debate. Her appearances in society pages did not in themselves make her a public figure. It would, of course, have been a different case if Mrs. Firestone had used the divorce litigation in which she was involved as the launchpad for airing her own views on divorce and marriage.

Hutchinson v. Proxmire (1979) refused to extend the public figure label to a scientist, a federal grant recipient, who sued Senator Proxmire for criticism concerning the value of his research. The scientist had neither sought public attention nor was he sufficiently well known to have access to the media. Similarly, in *Wolston v. Reader's Digest Association, Inc.* (1979), the plaintiff, who had pled guilty to a contempt citation for refusing to respond to a subpoena, sued Reader's Digest for falsely describing him, many years later, as a Soviet agent who had been found guilty of contempt. Wolston's activities may have made him newsworthy in that he attracted media attention. But this did not mean that he voluntarily thrust himself into a particular public controversy sufficient to make him a public figure. While Justice Powell in *Gertz* had suggested that a person might involuntarily become a public figure, these later cases failed to develop such a notion.

d. The Public Law of Privacy

There is a public law of defamation. Has the law of privacy also been constitutionalized? Does the First Amendment limit the state's ability to award civil damages for other tortious conduct involving expression such as invasion of privacy? *Time, Inc. v. Hill* (1967), considered this question in the context of the state award of civil damages for inaccurate portrayal of the plaintiff to the public in a way highly offensive to the reasonable person, *i.e.*, false light privacy. Life Magazine had done a picture story of the ordeals of the Hill family who had been held hostage by escaped convicts. While the story was newsworthy, parts had been fictionalized. Under New York law, Hill had a cause of action for privacy regardless of whether the publication was defamatory.

The Supreme Court, per Justice Brennan, set aside the damage award: "[T]he constitutional protection for speech and press preclude the application of the New York statute to redress false reports of matters of public interest in the absence of proof that the defendant published the report with knowledge of its falsity or in reckless disregard of the truth." A new public law of privacy was created. Its foundations reflected the principles of *New York Times v. Sullivan* (1964). Fear of damage awards, reasoned Justice Brennan, would yield self-censorship; negligence-based liability provided inadequate protection for the press. On the other side of the scales, the plaintiff's privacy interest was given short shrift since exposure of one's self is part of modern life—"The risk of this exposure is an essential incident of life in a society which places a primary value on freedom of speech and the press."

Time, Inc. deals with false light privacy which is closely related to defamation. But what of the "true" privacy action involving accurate publicity given to intimate facts concerning the private life of the plaintiff in a way offensive to a reasonable man? In *Cox Broadcasting Corp. v. Cohn* (1975), involving public disclosure of a rape victim's name in violation of state law, the Supreme Court reversed an award of damages. But the Court limited its holding to accurate disclosures of matters of public record; the victim's name had appeared in the indictment. In, *Florida Star v. B.J.F.* (1989) invalidated under the First Amendment a damages award against a newspaper for negligently publishing the name of a rape victim obtained from a public police report. The report had been released in violation of police department procedures and of a state statute banning the publication of the names of rape victims.

An award of civil damages was not a narrowly tailored means of protecting privacy. Other means less restrictive of protected speech were available to government. The Court strongly relied on a principle that had been set forth earlier in *Smith v. Daily Mail Publishing Co.* (1979): "If a newspaper lawfully obtains truthful information about a matter of public significance then state officials may not constitutionally punish publication of the information absent a need to further a state interest of the highest order."

If the contents of an illegally intercepted communication are disclosed, does the First Amendment provide any protection for such speech? This question arose in the context of a labor dispute. A union's chief negotiator and its president had a conversation over a cellular phone about a proposed teachers strike at a local high school and the possibility of violence in connection with collective bargaining negotiations in order to counter the obstinacy of the board of education. The conversation was intercepted, taped and given to the media. The individuals whose conversation had been taped without their consent sued the media for damages. The plaintiffs sued under federal and state wiretapping laws prohibiting the interception and taping of such conversations as well as the act of intentionally disclosing to others the contents of such conversations.

The Court, per Justice Stevens, ruled that the federal wiretapping law (and the state law as well) was a "content-neutral law of general applicability." The key to whether a law is content-neutral is whether the government regulation of the expressive activity is justified apart from the content of the speech. Here the legislation was designed to protect the privacy of electronic communications. The legislation was not justified by a reference to content nor did the legislation make any distinctions based on the content of the intercepted conversation.

But the prohibition against disclosure of intercepted communications was clearly a regulation of pure speech. The Court ruled that the legislation as applied to the conversation at issue violated the First Amendment. Three points, the Court observed, were critical. First, the media defendants did not play any role in the legal interception. Second, their access to the information on the tape was lawful even though the information was intercepted unlawfully. Third, the contents of the conversation was a matter of public concern. Justice Stevens rejected the government argument that prohibiting disclosure would deter illegal interception of communication because there was no empirical evidence to support it. The stronger government argument that anxiety about public disclosure of private communications would chill private speech was also rejected. On these facts, enforcement of the wiretapping laws ran counter to the core First Amendment objective of protecting publication of truthful information of *public* concern. The Court reserved for another time the question of whether the First Amendment permitted regulation of disclosure of trade secrets or of truthful publication of *private* matters which were not related to public affairs. When a prohibition against disclosure constitutes a regulation of pure speech involving matters of public concern, the principles of *Time, Inc. v. Hill* and *New York Times Co. v. Sullivan* come into play. The teaching of these cases is that some loss of privacy is a necessary consequence of protecting participation in the public arena. *Bartnicki v. Vopper* (2001).

Justice Breyer, joined by Justice O'Connor, concurring, *Bartnicki*, stressed the narrowness of the Court's holding. Justice Breyer wanted to make it clear that the Court was not holding that privacy would always take a subordinate position when balanced against other interests. Government was still free to fashion flexible remedies to cope with whatever dangers future technology might present to the personal privacy of individuals. Chief Justice Rehnquist, joined by Justice Scalia and Thomas, dissenting, contended that "public concern" was an "amorphous concept" and, worse yet, the Court did not define it. The Court's opinion contradicted rather than served First Amendment interests since it chilled the speech of those who communicate with each other by means of electronic technology. The statutory ban on disclosure made the ban on illegal interception of electronic communication more effective. Furthermore, the Court subordinated the interest in individual privacy which at a minimum should include "the right to be free from surreptitious eavesdropping on, and involuntary broadcast of, our cellular telephone conversations."

In sum, there has been no Supreme Court response to the fundamental question: can liability be imposed for truthful disclosure of private facts? Lower courts grappling with the problem have generally rejected any absolute constitutional privilege for truthful publication. Instead, they have tended to focus on the public interest in disclosure and the "outrageousness" of the disclosure. As for whether disclosure of illegally intercepted conversations can be prohibited, *Bartnicki* provides some assistance since it holds that the First Amendment protects such disclosure when it touches on a matter of public concern, although it fails to define public concern.

4. OBSCENITY AND INDECENCY

Roth v. United States (1957) determined that, as a matter of history and function, obscenity was "utterly without redeeming social importance." Obscenity was "not within the area of constitutionally protected speech or press." Since obscenity is categorically excluded from First Amendment protection, it enjoys only the protection afforded by the due process mandate of rationality in law-making. Obscenity control, apart from protecting juveniles and unconsenting adult passersby from exposure, serves the legitimate state interests in maintaining "the quality of life and the total community environment, the tone of commerce in the great city centers, and possibly, the public safety itself." *Paris Adult Theatre I v. Slaton* (1973).

Since *Roth,* the central constitutional task in obscenity cases has been identifying what expression qualifies as "obscenity." It is a question of definition. Today, each element of a three-part test must be satisfied. It must be determined: "(a) whether the average person, applying contemporary community standards, would find that the work, taken as a whole, appeals to the prurient interest, (b) whether the work depicts or describes, in a patently offensive way, sexual conduct specifically defined by the applicable state law, and (c) whether the work, taken as a whole, lacks serious literary, artistic, political, or scientific value." *Miller v. California* (1973). While the *Miller* formulation is designed to limit the Supreme Court's censorial role and promote local determination of obscenity, First Amendment values are to be protected "by the ultimate power of appellate courts to conduct an independent review of constitutional claims when necessary." See *Jenkins v. Georgia* (1974) [obscenity conviction for showing film "Carnal Knowledge" reversed since nude scenes did not constitute "hard core" sexual conduct].

The first part of the inquiry, the prurient interest test, was derived from *Roth*. Prurience is constitutionally defined as material appealing to a shameful or morbid interest in sex. It does not include a normal interest in sex. But see *Brockett v. Spokane Arcades, Inc.* (1985) [overbroad definition of prurient to include lust does not support holding that the entire statute is facially invalid]. *Roth* rejected the earlier *Regina v. Hicklin* (1868) standard that focused on the possible impact of the material, or even isolated parts of a work, on those persons most susceptible to its negative influences. In *Roth,* Justice Brennan, for the Court, determined that the *Hicklin* approach provided inadequate protection to material protected by the First Amendment. The Court instead required consideration of the effect of the work, taken as a whole, on the "average person, applying contemporary community standards." However, if the material is targeted to appeal to the peculiar susceptibilities of a particular group, courts will apply a variable obscenity standard measuring the impact on such a group. *Ginsberg v. New York* (1968) [minors]; *Pinkus v. United States* (1978) [sexually deviant groups]. See *Erznoznik v. Jacksonville* (1975) [state cannot proscribe exposure to all nudity, even for minors].

Obscenity is limited to "patently offensive" representations of sexual conduct (not violence) which is specifically defined by applicable law. Patently offensive refers to depiction of sexual conduct that "goes substantially beyond customary limits of candor and affronts contemporary community standards of decency." *Miller.* See *Manual Enterprises, Inc. v. Day* (1962). *Miller* undertook to provide examples: "(a) patently offensive representations or descriptions of ultimate sexual acts, normal or perverted, actual or simulated, (b) patently offensive representations or descriptions of masturbation, excretory functions, and lewd exhibitions of the genitals." While this listing is not exhaustive [*Jenkins v. Georgia* (1974)], obscenity controls must be written or judicially interpreted to be limited to such material or the law suffers from overbreadth. See *Ward v. Illinois* (1977) [state statute read to embody *Miller* standards and applied to materials describing sado-masochistic acts held constitutional]. Patent offensiveness, coupled with the pruriency test, is generally considered as restricting obscenity to hard-core pornography.

Both pruriency and patent offensiveness are determined by "contemporary community standards." But what is the relevant community? In *Miller,* the Court rejected the contention that only a national community standard, free of local biases, would provide adequate First Amendment protection and allowed lower courts to use local standards in defining what is obscene. Subsequent cases have made it clear that the state may choose to omit reference to any particular geographic community, state or local, although it may do so. If a geographic reference is omitted, each juror is free to ascertain the contemporary community standard. *Jenkins v. Georgia* (1974); *Hamling v. United States* (1974) [federal prosecutions]. The relevant community includes all adults, including sensitive persons, but excludes children. *Pinkus v. United States* (1978). Since the jury is applying community standards in determining pruriency and patent offensiveness, expert evidence is not required. *Paris Adult Theatre I v. Slaton* (1973).

Ashcroft v. American Civil Liberties Union (2002) raised the issue of whether the use in the Child Online Protection Act (COPA) of "community standards" to identify material harmful to minors is consistent with the First Amendment. The Court's "prior community standards jurisprudence," it was argued, should not be applicable to the Internet and the Web since the latter cannot control the "geographic scope of the recipients of their communications." The Court held that the use of "community standards" did not in itself make COPA facially unconstitutional nor did it render the law substantially overbroad. In evaluating the standards of pruriency and patent offensiveness, the application of a national community standard was not necessary. The jury could be charged to apply "contemporary community standards" without more. The unique characteristics of the Internet did not require departure from the principle that if the publisher permits its content to be transmitted to a particular community, it is the responsibility of that publisher to conform to the standards of that community.

One of the notable effects of *Miller* was its rejection of an earlier test requiring that material be "utterly without redeeming social value" in order to be labeled obscene. *Memoirs (A Book Named "John Cleland's Memoirs of A Woman of Pleasure") v. Attorney General of Comm. of Massachusetts* (1966). Chief Justice Burger, for the *Miller* Court, castigated this as "a burden virtually impossible to discharge under our criminal standards of proof" since it requires proof of a negative. In its place, *Miller* asks whether the work in question lacks "*serious* literary artistic, political or scientific value." Unlike

the other two tests which involve fact determinations for the jury, the redeeming serious value element appears to involve an increased judicial role
and not to be governed by the open-ended community standards. See *Smith v. United States* (1977).

There is one exception to the *Miller* tripartite
test. Even if material does not satisfy the standards,
the material may be rendered obscene by the way in
which it is published. A distributor can be convicted
of selling obscene material if he exploits the sexually provocative aspects of the material, *i.e.,* pandering. *Ginzburg v. United States* (1966) [mailings
from Intercourse and Blueball, PA and Middlesex,
N.J. evidenced the "leer of the sensualist" which
permeated the advertising].

Miller represents the first time since *Roth* that a
majority of the Court agreed on a test of obscenity.
Justice Brennan, the author of the opinion in *Roth*,
recanted in dissent in *Miller* accepting the bankruptcy of the search for a sufficiently specific and
clear definition of obscenity. He concluded that the
concept was inherently vague, producing a lack of
fair notice, a chill on protected speech and a constant institutional stress. For him the answer was
to limit obscenity control to the context of protecting juveniles and unconsenting adults. *Paris Adult
Theatre I v. Slaton* (1973) (Brennan, J., dissenting).
A majority of the Court, however, continues to
adhere to the path defined in *Roth–Miller*.

Although the Court has gone so far as to hold
that there is no constitutional bar to the inclusion

of substantive obscenity offenses under a state criminal RICO law, *Sappenfield v. Indiana* (1989), the state power to regulate obscenity recognized in *Roth–Miller* does not provide a *carte-blanche* to government. Obscenity control must be pursued consistent with other constitutional values. For example, the State may not invade the privacy of the home or a person's private thoughts by punishing a person for the mere possession of obscene materials in his home—"If the First Amendment means anything, it means that a State has no business telling a man, sitting alone in his own house, what books he may read or what films he may watch." *Stanley v. Georgia* (1969). *Stanley*, however, did not extend to a state law prohibiting the possession or viewing of child pornography; the state interest in the physical and psychological well-being of minors served to distinguish *Stanley*. The state had a compelling interest in protecting child pornography victims and in destroying the "market for the exploitative use of children." *Osborne v. Ohio* (1990). Furthermore, the right of privacy protected in *Stanley* appears to be limited to the home. The First Amendment provides no protection to consenting adults seeking to view obscene films in an adult movie theater. *Paris Adult Theatre I v. Slaton* (1973).

A corollary of the demand for specific limits on states in defining obscenity is that government cannot generally proscribe "indecent" publications consistent with the First Amendment. Whether cast as a criminal prosecution or a civil regulation, the *Miller* three-part test governs. *Paris Adult Theatre*

I v. Slaton (1973). For example, a law condemning drive-ins showing films containing nudity as a public nuisance when visible from the public streets was held to be an excessive intrusion on First Amendment values. *Erznoznik v. Jacksonville* (1975). A zoning ordinance which excludes all live entertainment including non-obscene nude dancing while permitting other commercial activity, has been held to be an overbroad intrusion on First Amendment rights. *Schad v. Mount Ephraim* (1981). Compare *New York State Liquor Auth. v. Bellanca* (1981) [state may ban nude dancing in establishments serving liquor pursuant to its police powers to prevent disturbances and the 21st Amendment].

But when the state undertakes to regulate the location of adult-only establishments pursuant to its zoning powers, the Court has treated such laws as time, place and manner controls rather than as content regulations requiring stricter scrutiny. Such laws imposing only an indirect burden on speech must serve a substantial government interest and must leave open reasonable alternative avenues of communication. *Young v. American Mini Theatres, Inc.* (1976), upheld 5–4 Detroit's "Anti–Skid Row" ordinance requiring dispersal of places of adult entertainment. The Court, per Justice Stevens, stressed that the law was a reasonable means of furthering the city's important interest in regulating land use for commercial purposes in order to preserve the quality of urban life. Unlike *Schad, supra,* there was evidence of harm from the regulated conduct. The Detroit law in *American Mini Theatres* was perceived as involving only a minimal indirect burden on First Amendment values since there was no claim that adult establishments were denied access to the market or that the law was ideologically biased. In a part of his opinion which did not win majority support, Justice Stevens contended that non-obscene erotic expression enjoys a lesser degree of First Amendment protection than political speech. Four justices in dissent expressly rejected Justice Stevens' bid for a two-tier approach to the value of speech.

Renton v. Playtime Theatres, Inc. (1986) rejected a First Amendment challenge to a Renton, Washington ordinance which regulated the location of adult theaters. Chief Justice Rehnquist for the Court set forth the "secondary effects" doctrine: the ordinance was aimed at the "secondary effects" of adult theaters rather than at the suppression of unpopular views. A city may rely on any evidence reasonably believed to be relevant and need not develop independent evidence of harm. The ordinance was aimed at responding to problems associated with adult theaters such as crime, the lowering of property values, the decline of commercial districts and lessening the quality of urban life. The ordinance was content-neutral, served the foregoing interests and, at the same time, provided for alternative opportunities for communication for the affected speech. The "secondary effects" doctrine provides an important defense to First Amendment challenges to land use regulation of sexually oriented movies, theaters and bookstores. The possibility that the "secondary effects" doctrine might cast a wider net and be exploited to shield content-based regulation from First Amendment attack was not addressed.

In *City of Los Angeles v. Alameda Books, Inc.* (2002), the Court further explained the showing required to satisfy *Renton*. Justice O'Connor for the Court relied on the *Renton* "secondary effects" doctrine to uphold a Los Angeles ordinance prohibiting the presence of more than one adult entertainment business in the same building. Although cities, in order to prevail, are required to demonstrate evidence that the ordinance serves an important governmental interest, they are not required to show that no other approach would support that interest. *Renton* does not set so high a hurdle for cities seeking merely to respond to the "secondary effects of protected speech." A city may rely on any evidence that shows a reasonable relationship "between speech and a substantial, independent government interest." If the ordinance challenger is able to cast doubt on the city's rationale, the burden is then on the city to supplement the record to support the asserted relationship. Justice Kennedy, concurring in the judgment, made the startling disclaimer that *Renton*-type ordinances were not content-neutral but instead were "content-based and we should call them so, even though he would still use the lesser standard of review." Justice Souter in dissent further complicated the waters by contending that a *Renton*-type regulation "though called content-neutral, occupies a kind of limbo between full-blown, content-based restrictions and regulations that apply without any reference to the substance of what is said."

Justice Stevens' two-tiered approach to indecent expression appeared again in *FCC v. Pacifica Foundation* (1978) but again won only plurality support. The Court endorsed FCC sanctions against a radio broadcaster for airing a program involving indecent, but not obscene, language. A majority of Justices were content with emphasizing the "uniquely pervasive presence" of broadcasting in our lives rendering us captive to unexpected programming and the unique accessibility of broadcasting to children. But Justice Stevens, for a three-judge plurality, again argued that the indecent content of the speech permitted greater government consideration of the expression's social value in the particular context. Two justices, concurring, and two justices, dissenting, rejected the assertion that the case should turn on the social value assigned by the Court to the speech. Two other justices did not reach the question.

Justice Stevens observed in *Pacifica* that "of all forms of communication, it is broadcasting that has received the most limited First Amendment protection." This lesser protection should not be applied indiscriminately, however, to all electronic media. For example, a total Congressional ban on dial-a-porn, *i.e.*, sexually-oriented indecent, but not obscene telephone messages, was held unconstitutional. The total ban was subjected to the more exacting form of review used for content control and was invalidated because it was not narrowly tailored to achieve a compelling government interest and because it failed to use the least restrictive means. *Pacifica* was distinguished. Dial-a-porn requires more of an affirmative act by the recipient than just turning on the television set. There was no captive audience. Unwilling listeners could avoid exposure to it. Furthermore, there were technological means available to protect children short of a total ban. *Sable Communications of California, Inc. v. FCC* (1989).

In *Denver Area Educational Telecommunications Consortium, Inc. v. FCC* (1996), three provisions of the Cable Television Consumer Protection and Competition Act of 1992 were subjected to First Amendment challenge. Sec. 10(a) authorizing cable operators to refuse to carry leased access programming depicting "sexual or excretory activities or organs in patently offensive ways as measured by contemporary community standards" was upheld. Justice Breyer, joined by Justices Stevens, O'Connor and Souter, ruled that Sec. 10(a) was valid. *Sable*, *Ginsberg* and *Ferber* had all found that there was a compelling governmental interest in protecting children from exposure to patently offensive sexually-related material. In addition, the problem Congress addressed in cable through Sec. 10(a) was similar to the *Pacifica* situation. Cable television broadcasting was just as accessible to children as over-the-air broadcasting and just as pervasive a presence. Further, Sec. 10(a)

authorized but did not *require* the cable operator to ban indecent material on leased access channels.

The Court, per Justice Breyer, struck down Sec. 10(b) which obligated the FCC to issue rules requiring cable operators transmitting indecent material to segregate such programming on a separate channel which is blocked unless the cable subscriber specifically requests that it be unblocked. The Court rejected the argument that these "segregate and block" requirements were the least restrictive means of achieving the compelling governmental interest in protecting children. Putting aside the question whether *Pacifica* required some lesser standard of review in the indecent speech context, Sec. 10(b) was held violative of both the strictest and less strict First Amendment standards. Sec. 10(b) was not "narrowly tailored" to meet its legitimate objective. Congress knows how to use less restrictive means when dealing with similar issues as is illustrated by the requirement in the 1996 Telecommunications Act that future television sets be manufactured with a V-chip—a device that identifies and blocks sexually explicit or violent programming. This latter approach is much less restrictive than Sec. 10(b) since it does not require the viewer to receive all "patently offensive" programming or none.

Sec. 10(c) which required the FCC to issue regulations authorizing cable operators to deny the use of public, educational and governmental channels [public access channels] for programming containing "obscene material, sexually explicit conduct, or

material soliciting or promoting unlawful conduct"
was struck down. Justice Breyer, joined by Justices
Stevens and Souter, said that the government had
failed to show that there was a sufficient problem
regarding the broadcast of "patently offensive" programming to children on public access channels to
justify the restrictions imposed by Sec. 10(c). Moreover, the provision increased the risk that certain
borderline types of offensive programming would
not be broadcast. Justice Kennedy, joined by Justice
Ginsburg, also thought that Sec. 10(c) was invalid
but they applied the strict scrutiny standard and
they rejected the idea that a lower *Pacifica*-type
standard of review was appropriate. In summary, in
Denver Area, some indecency regulations were upheld and some struck down. But the critical point is
that a majority of the Court did not evaluate cable
indecency regulation under a strict scrutiny standard of review.

However, in *United States v. Playboy Entertainment Group, Inc.* (2000), the Court, per Justice
Kennedy, that the "signal bleed" provision of the
Telecommunications Act of 1996 was an invalid
content-based regulation which failed to meet the
narrowly tailored requirement of the strict scrutiny
standard. "Signal bleed" occurs when, due to inadequate signal scrambling or blocking, an image appears on the television screen that is discernible.
"Signal bleed" in the case of sexually explicit cable
channels presents a problem if there are children in
the viewing audience. The 1996 Act mandated that
cable operators either scramble sexually explicit

channels or limit transmission of such programming to specified late hours when children were less likely to be in the audience. Local cable operators chose to transmit sexually explicit programming during the late evening "safe harbor" hours. This response created a nationwide daytime ban on this type of non-obscene but sexually explicit cable programming. The "signal bleed" provision of the 1996 Act was not narrowly tailored because it was not the least restrictive means that the government could have selected either in terms of effect on free expression or from the perspective of protecting children from involuntary exposure to sexually explicit content. The 1996 Act already contained a much less restrictive mechanism which permitted viewers to block such programming on an individual basis. The government, therefore, should have promoted this voluntary blocking alternative.

The Court has agreed to apply the strict scrutiny standard of review to content-based regulation of the Internet. Provisions of the Communications Decency Act of 1996 (CDA) prohibited transmission of indecent material on the Internet to persons under 18 or the sending of a patently offensive message on the Internet to persons under 18. Such content-based blanket restraints on speech could not be fairly characterized as time, place or manner regulations. Acknowledging that each medium of expression presented its own problems, the Court pointed out that in broadcasting, for example, special contexts required more deferential standards of review as exemplified in the *Red Lion, infra*, and *Pacifica, supra*, cases. The Internet, unlike broadcasting, does not suffer either from technological scarcity nor is it as "invasive" as radio or television. Sexually explicit sites are unlikely to be reached by accident. Accessing information on the Internet requires more deliberate and informed steps than simply turning on a dial: "[O]ur cases provide no basis for qualifying the level of First Amendment scrutiny that should be applied to this medium."

Applying this strict scrutiny standard of review, the Court invalidated the challenged provisions of the CDA; they lacked the precision required of content-based regulation. Sexual expression which is indecent although not obscene is protected expression. In order to prevent the access by minors to sexual expression deemed harmful, the CDA suppresses speech which adults have a right to receive and to speak to each other about. This burden on adult speech is not acceptable if less restrictive means can be employed to secure the governmental interest. The government had not proved otherwise nor did Congress make any findings to that effect. Furthermore, the district court found that software may be available allowing *parents* to deny their children access to material which they believe to be harmful. Thus, the CDA regulations are not narrowly tailored. In summary, the Court held that strict scrutiny is the appropriate standard of review for content-based regulation of the Internet and that the lesser broadcasting standards of review are not appropriate. *Reno v. ACLU* (1997).

There is one context in which the Court has accepted indecency as sufficient for government suppression. In *New York v. Ferber* (1982), the Court upheld a New York statute prohibiting knowing promotion of photographic or other visual reproductions of live performances of children engaged in non-obscene sexual conduct. The *Miller* standards were not applied; instead, the Court treated child pornography, as a "category of material outside the protection of the First Amendment." While the Court specifically indicated that the *Miller* pruriency and patent offensiveness tests did not apply to child pornography, the status of the "serious social value" test in the new category remains unclear. While the Court acknowledged the possibility that some educational, medical or artistic work might fall within the New York statute, it concluded that the problem could be handled on a case by case basis and that there was no "substantial overbreadth." Justice White, for the Court, in justifying categorical exclusion of child pornography, stressed the compelling state interest in protecting minors, the close relation of the distribution of the films and photographs to the sexual abuse of children and the motivation for the production of such materials resulting from sales and advertising revenues.

Another example of the Supreme Court's solicitude toward child pornography legislation involved an Ohio statute criminalizing the possession and viewing of child pornography. The statute might have succumbed to an overbreadth challenge since it punished "simple nudity, without more." However, the Ohio Supreme Court had given the statute a narrowing construction so that it only reached nudity "where such nudity constitutes a lewd exhibition or involves a graphic focus on the genitals." As narrowed, the statute was not impermissibly overbroad. *Osborne v. Ohio* (1990).

In *Ashcroft v. Free Speech Coalition* (2002), Justice Kennedy for the Court held that the Child Pornography Prevention Act (CPPA) dealing with virtual child pornography infringed freedom of speech. The CPPA extended the federal ban on child pornography to sexually explicit images that were produced to give the impression that they depicted minors or children but in fact did not do so. Like the law reviewed in *Ferber*, the CPPA restricts protected expression but, unlike the law considered in *Ferber*, the CPPA does not involve the state's interest in protecting children. The production of the work, not its content, was the focus of the New York law in *Ferber*. But the CPPA bans speech that "records no crime and creates no victims by its production." The government argued that the CPPA should be validated because people might use virtual child pornography in order to seduce children. But if adults otherwise have a right to hear speech, that speech may not be totally banned simply to shield children from it. Furthermore, the mere tendency of speech to lead to unlawful activity cannot justify banning such speech. The government argued that it was difficult to prosecute pornographers using real children because of the difficulty of distinguishing pictures using real chil-

dren from computer imaging. But protected speech
may not be suppressed in order to ban unprotected
speech. The overbreadth doctrine mandates that
unprotected speech may not be prohibited if a substantial amount of protected expression is thereby
chilled or banned. The CPPA also banned expression which is protected under *Miller* and which does
not fall under the *Ferber* exception permitting regulation of child pornography which uses real children. The CPPA banned the distribution or advertising of sexually explicit images created by adults
who look like children or which were produced to
give that impression that children were being used
through the use of computer imaging. This part of
the CPPA is not saved by invoking the pandering
rationale of *Ginzburg v. United States* (1966). The
CPPA punished possession even though those in
possession bore no responsibility for how such expression was marketed. The CPPA, unlike the law
in *Ginzburg,* does not require as a condition for
regulation a context of "commercial exploitation."
Far more precision is required under the First
Amendment. In sum, the CPPA was fatally overbroad.

While the discussion in this section focuses on the
substantive law of obscenity, the student should
note that procedural problems are especially preva-
lent in obscenity regulation. For example, while the
prior restraint doctrine is applicable to obscenity
regulation [*Bantam Books, Inc. v. Sullivan* (1963);
Vance v. Universal Amusement Co. (1980), heavy
burden on government to justify issuance of injunc-

tion on future filming based on past showing of obscene films], the courts have upheld film censorship. *Times Film Corp. v. Chicago* (1961). However, when administrative or judicial censorship is used, the Court requires that defined procedural norms be satisfied. These norms, set forth in *Freedman v. Maryland* (1965), require that three procedural requirements must be met: (1) the government authority or censor has the burden of demonstrating that the material is unprotected; (2) there must be a prompt judicial proceeding if a valid final restraint on publication is to be imposed; and (3) the government authority or censor must either issue a license for publication or exhibition or go to court to justify the refusal to do so. The *Freedman* standards reflect a clear preference for a judicial determination of the question of obscenity in order to protect First Amendment values.

If the regulatory or licensing scheme does not involve the exercise of administrative discretion with respect to the content of the publication or movie at issue, there is some disagreement about whether all the *Freedman* requirements must be met. A Dallas ordinance regulating zoning, licensing and inspections of "sexually oriented businesses" such as adult bookstores, video centers and theaters was invalidated as constituting a prior restraint which failed to meet the *Freedman* requirements. The Dallas ordinance was held invalid since it failed to place limits on the time within which the decision maker may issue the license and failed to provide for prompt judicial review as required by

Freedman. Three members of the Court believed, however, that since no censorship was involved in the Dallas licensing scheme, the *Freedman* requirement that the city must go to court to justify the restraint need not be met. Three justices would have applied all three *Freedman* standards. Three others believed that none of the *Freedman* standards were applicable where content censorship was not present. *FW/PBS, Inc. v. City of Dallas* (1990).

5. FREEDOM OF THE PRESS

The First Amendment protects against abridgment of the freedom of speech "or of the press." Does this clause provide special protection to the media as an institution? The Court has not accepted the idea that the Press Clause has a meaning independent of the Speech Clause. See *First Nat. Bank of Boston v. Bellotti* (1978) (Burger, C.J., concurring, criticizing the theory that the Press Clause has a separate meaning). Claims for special press privileges and immunities not available to ordinary citizens have been rejected. *Branzburg v. Hayes* (1972). But this does not mean that the press enjoys no special constitutional protection as the eyes and ears, the surrogate, of the public on matters of public interest. We have already seen the constitutional protection afforded the press against prior restraints (*i.e., Pentagon Papers; Nebraska Press*) and post hoc burdens on publication (*e.g., New York Times v. Sullivan,* involving defamation law). Further, laws which treat the press differently are subjected to stricter judicial scrutiny. See *Minne-apolis Star & Tribune Co. v. Minnesota Com'r of Rev.* (1983) [special state use tax imposed solely on the use of paper and ink in publishing invalid absent "a counterbalancing interest of compelling importance that it cannot achieve without differential taxation" even though press enjoyed favored tax treatment].

a. Newsgathering

Is the constitutional protection afforded the media limited only to publication or does the Constitution also provide protection to the process of gathering the news? In *Branzburg v. Hayes* (1972), this question arose in the context of a claim for a "journalist's privilege" to resist disclosure of information to a grand jury. The Court, per Justice White, accepted the premise that "newsgathering is not without its First Amendment protection" for "without some protection for seeking out the news, freedom of the press could be eviscerated." But this did not mean the press enjoyed some special immunity or "a constitutional right of access to information not available to the public generally." The First Amendment, said Justice White, did not require invalidating every "incidental burdening of the press."

The Court 5–4 rejected any absolute or qualified journalist privilege to refuse disclosure of the names of informants or other information beyond that enjoyed by any citizen. Justice White noted that reporters remain free to seek out the news by legal means; any inhibition from forced disclosure was deemed "widely divergent and to a great extent speculative." Against this "consequential, but uncertain burden" on information-gathering, the public interest in "fair and effective law enforcement"—the interest of the public to every person's evidence—was held to be sufficiently overriding. As long as the grand jury inquiry is conducted in good faith, the questions asked are relevant and there is no harassment, the journalist must cooperate. Further, *Branzburg* expressed concern that if such a privilege were recognized, the courts would face the administrative difficulty of defining what constitutes "the press." See also *Zurcher v. Stanford Daily* (1978) [issuance of ex parte search warrant authorizing search of student news offices for photographs of riot held constitutional].

A crucial, and subsequently highly influential, swing vote in *Branzburg* was cast by Justice Powell. In a separate concurrence, Justice Powell indicated that a claim of privilege might be available on a case-by-case basis as a result of balancing the competing interests in disclosure and confidentiality. Indeed, Powell asserted that the Court's opinion meant that "the courts will be available to newsmen under circumstances where legitimate First Amendment interests require protection." Many commentators suggest that as a result of Powell's position, a majority of the *Branzburg* Court actually endorsed a qualified privilege.

Justice Stewart, for three dissenters in *Branzburg,* urged recognition of a qualified journalist privilege requiring government seeking to force disclosure to prove: (1) that there is probable cause to believe that the journalist possesses clearly relevant evidence relating to law violation; (2) the absence of any means of acquiring the evidence less destructive of First Amendment rights; and (3) that there is "a compelling and overriding interest in the information." This approach has enjoyed marked success in lower courts especially in the civil context where law enforcement interests are not as pronounced.

A case where journalist's privilege was honored in the breach rather than in the observance was *Cohen v. Cowles Media Co.* (1991). A reporter had promised an informant to keep his identity secret. However, the editors reversed the reporter since disclosing the identity of the informant was deemed more newsworthy than the original information obtained from the informant. The informant sued for damages. Does the First Amendment prevent an informant from securing damages under state promissory estoppel law when a newspaper breaches its promise to him that in exchange for information from him the newspaper will keep his identity confidential? Justice White for the Court answered that it did not. The case fell under the principle that generally applicable laws do not violate the First Amendment just because their enforcement against the press has incidental effects on newsgathering.

The newsgathering rights of the press were similarly circumscribed in *Wilson v. Layne* (1999). Reporters were invited to join police officers on a "media ride along" in order that they might observe and photograph the execution of an arrest warrant. Although the fugitive was not at home, his parents were. They sued the police officers for violation of their Fourth Amendment rights. Although the press has an interest in informing the public about the criminal justice system, this cannot justify a media ride-along intrusion into a private home. It violates the Fourth Amendment for police officers to bring the media or third parties into a private home in the execution of an arrest warrant when their presence was not in "aid of the execution of the warrant."

Another context in which the constitutional protection afforded newsgathering arises is that of access to government institutions, documents and other information in possession of the government. Unlike most First Amendment issues, which involve the limits on government coercive powers, the issues in this area have a decided affirmative orientation. Is government under an affirmative constitutional duty to provide media access to information in its possession? Is there a constitutional right to know what government is doing?

Once again the Court has been unreceptive to special rights of access for the press. As long as there is no discrimination against the press, "newsmen have no constitutional right of access to prisons or their inmates beyond that afforded to the general public." *Pell v. Procunier* (1974) [state prison regulations prohibiting press interviews with specific inmates upheld as reasonable regulation, at least where alternative methods of communication

are available]. See *Saxbe v. Washington Post Co.*
(1974) [similar holding for federal prisons]. But
note that neither *Pell* nor *Saxbe* determined whether the public has a First Amendment right of access
which the media would share as "the necessary
representative of the public's interest in the context
and the instrumentality which affects the public's
right." (Powell, J., dissenting). In both *Pell* and
Saxbe, the public did enjoy visitation rights and
mail privileges with prisoners. [See *Procunier v.
Martinez* (1974), prison mail censorship must be no
greater than is necessary to further the substantial
government interests in security, order and inmate
rehabilitation].

Houchins v. KQED, Inc. (1978), revealed the
sharp divisions in the Court on the access question.
Chief Justice Burger, joined by Justices White and
Rehnquist, found the *Pell* requirements of equal
access to prisons satisfied and went on to suggest
that the public could be denied any prison access.
The Chief Justice stressed the absence of any constitutional guidelines for confining judges in fashioning and applying such a right of public access.
Justices Stevens, Brennan, and Powell, dissenting,
argued for a public right of access: "The preservation of a full and free flow of information to the
general public has long been recognized as a core
objective of the First Amendment to the Constitution." Justice Stewart, concurring, appeared to reject a constitutional duty on government to provide
public access to information but argued that, if
public access is provided, " 'effective access' may

require different rules for the media than for the general public," *e.g.,* cameras and recording equipment and more frequent interview schedules may be required. As this suggests, the subject of access to the prisons for public and press alike remains uncertain. Perhaps the best that can be said is that if the public is given access, the press may not be denied access and may be entitled to preferences in the name of "equal and effective access."

The claim of a constitutional right of access to government institutions has found substantial acceptance in the context of judicial proceedings. *Gannett Co., Inc. v. De Pasquale* (1979), held that the Sixth Amendment guarantee of the accused to a public trial gives neither the press nor the public an enforceable right of access to a pretrial suppression hearing. But after this initial setback, *Richmond Newspapers, Inc. v. Virginia* (1980), a landmark decision, recognized 7–1 that the First Amendment limits the power to close a criminal trial. *Richmond Newspapers, Inc.* held that "[a]bsent an overriding interest, articulated in findings, the trial of a criminal case must be open to the public." Since no findings had been made to justify closure, the trial court erred in closing the trial.

But the Court in *Richmond Newspapers* became fragmented in defining the nature of the emerging access right. Chief Justice Burger, for the Court, joined by Justices Stewart and White, emphasized the historic foundation of a "presumption of openness" in criminal trials as the basis for an implied right to attend criminal trials. The Court stressed the relationship of the open criminal trial to the effectuation of the guaranteed rights of speech, press and assembly. Justice Brennan, joined by Justice Marshall, concurring, was willing to recognize a First Amendment "public right of access" based on the "structural role [that the First Amendment plays] in securing and fostering our republican system of self-government." The present law which left the question of closing to the unfettered discretion of the trial judge was inadequate to satisfy the presumption of openness.

In subsequent cases, the Court has reaffirmed this qualified right of access to at least some criminal justice proceedings and employed a heightened scrutiny standard in reviewing trial court closures. In *Globe Newspaper Co. v. Superior Court* (1982), a state statute requiring that trials of designated sex offenses be closed during the testimony of minor witnesses was held unconstitutional. While accepting that the state interest in protecting the physical and psychological well-being of minors is compelling, Justice Brennan, for the Court, concluded that the law was not "a narrowly tailored means" of achieving the objective case-by-case determination of the need for closure.

Chief Justice Burger, for the Court in *Press–Enterprise Co. v. Superior Court* (1984) [*Press-Enterprise I*], held *Richmond Newspapers* applicable to voir dire examination of prospective jurors as a vital part of the criminal trial. The trial court's failure to consider alternatives to closure was considered critical in the case. The presumption of openness also attaches to at least some pretrial criminal proceedings. After considering the history of openness of preliminary hearings and the values of public access to such proceedings, the Court recognized a qualified First Amendment right of access. *Press-Enterprise Co. v. Superior Court* (1986) [*Press-Enterprise II*]. Only specific findings that there is a substantial probability of prejudice to the defendant's fair trial rights and the absence of reasonable alternatives would justify closure under the standards of *Press-Enterprise I*.

Similarly, a blanket Puerto Rico rule that the preliminary hearing should be private unless the defendant chooses otherwise violates the First Amendment. Despite the contention that the unique history and traditions of Puerto Rico show a special sensitivity for the honor and reputation of the citizenry, the "established and widespread tradition of open preliminary hearings among the states" controls. As in *Globe Newspaper Co.*, the concern that publicity will prejudice the rights of the defendant if the preliminary hearing is open must be dealt with on a case-by-case basis. *El Vocero de Puerto Rico v. Puerto Rico* (1993).

In summary, newsgathering may enjoy some constitutional protection but not too much. Unlike the broad First Amendment protection provided when government controls expression or publication, the courts have been hesitant in granting protection to the newsgathering process. In fact, it may be preferable to speak of information-gathering since the Press Clause adds little, if anything, to the Speech

Clause and journalists are largely fungible with other citizens. To the limited extent that the First Amendment creates a qualified privilege to resist forced disclosure of information to the government, it is a right of citizens generally. If there is an affirmative right of access to government institutions and information in government hands, which seems doubtful outside of the courtroom context, it is a right of the public.

b. Public Access to the Media

The most common scenario for government restraint on publication arises when government seeks to prevent or punish the media for publication. But what if the government seeks to compel the media to publish messages that would not otherwise be adequately presented in the marketplace? The First Amendment protects not only the rights of the speaker but also "the right of the public to receive suitable access to social, political, aesthetic, moral, and other ideas and experiences." *Red Lion Broadcasting Co. v. FCC* (1969) [FCC fairness doctrine, requiring discussion of public issues and fair coverage to competing positions, held constitutional]. In *Red Lion,* the Court added: "It is the right of the viewers and listeners, not the rights of the broadcasters, which is paramount." Can a legislature force the media to publish material in the national interest in order to further this First Amendment right of the public?

In the case of the print media, the Court has rejected a First Amendment right of public access.

In *Miami Herald Publishing Co. v. Tornillo* (1974), the Court unanimously held unconstitutional a state statute granting political candidates a right of reply to published criticism. Chief Justice Burger, after documenting the case of media concentration distorting the marketplace of ideas, nevertheless rejected use of government coercion to force the press to print what they would otherwise not print. While "a responsible press is an undoubtedly desirable goal, press responsibility is not mandated by the Constitution and like many other virtues it cannot be legislated." The Chief Justice reasoned that coerced publishing penalizes the press for past publication by adding to the costs of printing and by occupying valuable newspaper space. The fear of such sanctions, he warned, might lead editors to avoid controversial publications. Editorial control and judgment over the size and content must remain with the press, not with the government. See *Pacific Gas & Elec. Co. v. Public Utilities Com'n* (1986) [compelled access for private group to private utility's billing envelopes violates principles of *Tornillo*]. Whether a right of reply statute, as an affirmative remedy for defamation, would be valid under *Tornillo* has not been decided. See *Rosenbloom v. Metromedia, Inc.* (1971).

A First Amendment based right of public access to the broadcast media was rejected in *CBS v. Democratic Nat. Comm. (CBS v. DNC)* (1973), where the Court, per Chief Justice Burger, upheld an FCC ruling that a broadcaster who meets his statutory responsibilities for fair coverage is not required to accept editorial advertisements. The FCC was justified in concluding that such a right of access would not serve the public interest since it would be weighted in favor of the financially affluent with the means to purchase editorial time. While broadcasting is subject to government regulation, the Chief Justice stated that editing is what editors are for. Finally, Chief Justice Burger expressed concern that FCC monitoring of a constitutional right of access would intrude the government "into a continuing case-by-case determination of who should be heard and when." The Court concluded that the dangers of greater government surveillance of journalistic discretion outweighed any public access benefits to be gained.

While *CBS v. DNC* declared that the First Amendment of its own force did not mandate a right of access to the electronic media, the Court pointed out that it left open situations where the statute or the FCC by regulation might mandate some form of public access. Although *Tornillo* stressed journalistic freedom over newspaper content, broadcasting is subject to greater government regulation in the public interest. In upholding the fairness doctrine against First Amendment challenge in *Red Lion,* the Court noted the scarcity of radio frequencies as justifying government regulation aimed at preventing monopolization of the media marketplace by private broadcast licensees. In other cases, the Court has stressed the pervasiveness of broadcasting in our lives and its accessibility to children as justifying greater government control over content. See *FCC v. Pacifica Foundation* (1978).

CBS v. FCC (1981) recognized the legitimacy of specific as compared with general rights of access; the Court upheld the Federal Election Campaign Act establishing a statutory right of reasonable access for federal political candidates. *CBS v. FCC* stressed that the statute only "creates a *limited* right to 'reasonable' access that pertains only to legally qualified federal candidates and may be invoked by them only for the purpose of advancing their candidacies once a campaign has commenced." This was not a "general right of access to the media" significantly impairing journalistic discretion regarding what to air, but a limited law designed "to assure that an important resource—the airwaves—will be used in the public interest."

A state-owned public broadcast station sponsored a political candidate debate and excluded Ralph Forbes, a third party candidate. Forbes contended that the debate was a public forum to which he had a First Amendment right of access. Generally speaking, the Court declared, per Justice Kennedy, public broadcast stations are not public forums. Relying on *CBS v. DNC*, the Court observed such a characterization was antithetical to the journalistic and editorial role of broadcasters: "Claims of access under our public forum precedents could obstruct the legitimate purpose of television broadcasters." However, relying on *CBS v. FCC*, the Court conceded that public candidate debates are in a special category and should be viewed "as a forum of some type." In this regard, the Court stressed the voluntary action of the broadcaster in sponsoring the debate and the importance of electoral speech. But a designated public forum is created by purposeful action which opens public property to public access not when, as here, access is simply granted to selected speakers. The political candidate debate here restricted participation to candidates for a specific post and then only on the basis of the extent to which they had attracted public support. Forbes was excluded not because of his viewpoint but because he had not generated sufficient public support to warrant his inclusion. A debate of this type is a nonpublic forum from which Forbes could be excluded by the public broadcaster "in the reasonable viewpoint neutral exercise of its journalistic discretion." *Arkansas Educational Television Commission v. Forbes* (1998).

What is the appropriate First Amendment standard for new electronic technologies such as cable television? In *Turner Broadcasting System, Inc. v. FCC* (1994), the Court considered a First Amendment challenge to provisions of federal cable legislation which imposed so-called must-carry obligations on cable operators. These requirements obliged cable systems to transmit the signals of a certain number of local over-the-air broadcast stations. The cable operators contended that their First Amendment rights were violated since these provisions required them to transmit that which they would prefer not to transit. The Court declared that cable operators are engaged in speech and that the *Red*

Lion approach to broadcast regulation which allowed substantial government regulation was not appropriate for cable. The multi-channel capacity of cable contrasted sharply with the spectrum limitation problems which characterized over-the-air broadcasting.

Nevertheless, the *Turner* Court held that the must-carry legislation constituted content-neutral regulation which should be evaluated under the *O'Brien* test. Substantial governmental interests were served by the must-carry provisions such as ensuring that "broadcast television remains available as a source of video programming for those without cable." *Tornillo* did not govern since the must-carry provisions were content-neutral in application. Unlike the right of reply statute in *Tornillo*, must-carry obligations were not activated by any particular message transmitted by cable operators. Nor did the must-carry provisions impose any content-based penalty. But the must-carry rules may suppress more speech than was necessary. Therefore, the Court remanded the case to the district court in order to develop a more complete factual record on issues such as whether, without must-carry, local over-the-air free broadcasting would be placed in economic jeopardy.

In *Turner Broadcasting System, Inc. v. FCC* (1997), the Supreme Court affirmed, 5–4, per Justice Kennedy, the lower court determination on remand that substantial evidence warranted the Congressional judgment that the must-carry provisions furthered substantial governmental interests in preserving the survival of local over-the-air broadcast stations. Under the intermediate standard of review, the government may use any means it chooses so long as they promote a substantial governmental interest that would be achieved less effectively without the regulation and do not burden substantially more speech than necessary. The evidence shows that the majority of cable operators have not been hindered by must-carry. Any burdens imposed by must carry are likely to diminish as cable channel capacity increases. The burden imposed by must-carry was related to the benefits it afforded. The Court concluded that must carry was narrowly tailored to preserve over-the-air broadcasting for the 40% of American households which do not subscribe to cable. The manner in which the competing economic interests of broadcasting and cable are reconciled are for Congress and not the courts to decide as long as the regulations are content-neutral and supported by substantial evidence as is the case here.

In *Denver Area Educational Consortium, Inc. v. FCC* (1996), the Court considered First Amendment challenges to three provisions of the 1992 Cable Act regulating indecency on leased access and public access cable channels. See, *supra,* the indecency section of this chapter. Justice Breyer, joined by Justices Stevens, O'Connor and Souter, declined to identify or embrace a particular First Amendment standard. For example, he declined to accept or reject Justice Thomas' view "that the interests of the owners of communications media always subor-

dinate the interests of all other users of a medium."
Nor did he accept Justice Kennedy's view that a
leased access channel is a common carrier and that
content regulation of such a channel should be
evaluated under strict scrutiny. Justice Breyer refused to adopt a categorical First Amendment standard for cable regulation: "But no definitive choice
among competing analogies (broadcast, common
carrier, bookstore) allows us to declare a single rigid
standard, good for now and all future media." The
trouble with "categorical approaches" is that they
import into cable regulation law developed in quite
different contexts. Given the pace of change in
telecommunications, it was premature to select
"one analogy or one specific set of words now."
Instead, Justice Breyer used a kind of balancing test
which closely scrutinizes cable regulation "to assure
that it properly addresses an extremely important
problem without imposing, in light of the relevant
interests, an unnecessarily great restriction on
speech."

In summary, while the Court has recognized that
the First Amendment includes the right of the
public to hear, this has not been converted into a
constitutional right of access to the media. For print
and broadcast media alike, the Court has emphasized the importance of journalistic discretion over
content. While broadcasting is subject to a greater
degree of government regulation than the print
media, the Court has increasingly emphasized the
limited nature of the federal government's regulatory authority. The Court even seemed to introduce a

heightened standard of review with respect to government content controls on broadcasting. In *FCC v. League of Women Voters* (1984) [federal statute forbidding broadcasters receiving grants for public broadcasting from engaging in editorializing held unconstitutional], the Court stated that only when a restriction is narrowly tailored to further substantial governmental interests will such content regulation be upheld. Nevertheless, as *CBS v. FCC* indicates, a limited statutory right of reasonable access to the broadcast media can survive First Amendment scrutiny. Similarly, the Court's willingness in the *Turner* cases to view statutorily imposed must-carry obligations on cable systems as content-neutral, and thus valid, illustrates that some measure of regulation of new electronic media such as cable is permissible. Finally, the *Denver Area* case reveals the concern on the part of some of the Justices that existing First Amendment doctrine may be too inflexible and categorical to cope with the rapidly changing world of telecommunications and that for the interim *ad hoc* balancing may be the wisest course.

6. SPEECH IN THE ELECTORAL PROCESS

Political speech is at the core of First Amendment concerns. It is not surprising, therefore, that the Court applies strict scrutiny when a state undertakes to regulate the content of speech during an election campaign. *Brown v. Hartlage* (1982) [application of a state law against vote buying to void the election of a candidate who had promised to take a lower salary than fixed by law if elected held unconstitutional].

Application of the strict scrutiny standard to electoral process regulation does not invariably result in invalidation. A Tennessee law which prohibited the solicitation of votes and the display of campaign materials within 100 feet of the entrance to a polling place on election day was a content-based time-place-manner regulation. Noting that all 50 states had provided "for a restricted zone around the voting compartments," the Court subjected the regulation to strict scrutiny and still upheld it. The state interests advanced in support of the statute— prevention of voter intimidation and election fraud were held to be compelling. *Burson v. Freeman* (1992).

A rule of the Minnesota Supreme Court, known as the Announce Clause, which prohibited candidates for judicial election to the state courts from announcing their views on disputed legal and political issues was held, 5–4, to violate the First Amendment. Since this was a content-based regulation of core First Amendment speech, *i.e.* political speech, the Court, per Justice Scalia, applied the strict scrutiny standard of review. The rule did not serve the asserted state interest that candidates not be biased with respect to parties since the rule did not restrict discussion "against particular *parties*, but rather speech for or against particular *issues.*" Another interest asserted to support the rule was that of assuring the impartiality of judges on controversial legal issues. The latter interest was not compelling and, therefore, did not satisfy the strict scrutiny standard of review since it was neither possible, nor indeed, desirable to find or select judges who did not have preconceived opinions on disputed legal issues. The First Amendment does not permit Minnesota to provide for the election of its judges while at the same time prohibiting those same judge-candidates from "discussing what the elections are about." *Republican Party of Minnesota v. White* (2002).

When the Republican Party in Connecticut adopted a rule that permitted independent voters to vote in Republican primaries despite a state statute requiring voters in party primaries to be registered members of that party, the Court struck down the statute because it deprived the state Republican Party of the right to enter into political association with individuals of its own choice. A state statute which placed limits on the registered voters whom a political party could ask to participate in a basic party function such as selecting candidates impermissibly burdens freedom of association. *Tashjian v. Republican Party of Connecticut* (1986).

But an Oklahoma statute which permitted political parties to limit their party primary only to voters who were registered with the party or who were registered as independent voters did not burden freedom of association. The Libertarian Party complained that the Oklahoma law required voters registered with another political party to disaffiliate and register either as independents or to change their party affiliation to Libertarian in order to vote in the Libertarian primary. The Court ruled that the Oklahoma law did not violate freedom of association and placed only a minor burden on voters. *Tashjian* was not in point since the Oklahoma law, unlike the law in *Tashjian*, did not require independents to affiliate with a party in order to vote in the party's primary. Strict scrutiny will be applied when election regulations place severe burdens on associational rights but not when the regulations impose only lesser burdens. In that case, reasonable nondiscriminatory regulations will be valid if they can be justified by important state regulatory interests. The important state interests served here—maintaining political party identity and viability, encouraging party-building and electioneering and ensuring against party-raiding and "sore loser" candidacies by unsuccessful primary contenders—justified the minor burdens placed on associational rights. *Clingman v. Beaver* (2005).

Similar over-regulation of the political process was set aside by the Court when it struck down provisions of the California Electoral Code which prohibited the official governing bodies of political parties from making primary endorsements and which mandated the organization and composition of those governing bodies. Such provisions were directed at speech at the core of the electoral process, did not serve a compelling governmental interest, and could not be justified by state interests such as the stability of government and protecting voters from undue influence and confusion. The regulation of party governance was also invalid. The state had no business to tell a political party what its structure should be. *Eu v. San Francisco County Democratic Central Committee* (1989). This theme was sounded again in *California Democratic Party v. Jones* (2000) where a state law establishing a so-called "blanket" primary was struck down as a violation of a political party's right to freedom of association. In a "blanket" primary, the ballot lists each candidate regardless of party affiliation and the voter may select among them. The "blanket" primary law impermissibly opened up the candidate selection process to persons not belonging to the party. No compelling state interest justified forced association changing the message associated with a political party. The First Amendment protects the right of an association to exclude those who do not share its views.

A more generalized balancing test was used in reviewing regulations governing access to the ballot of independent and minority parties in *Anderson v. Celebrezze* (1983). *Anderson* held, 5–4, that Ohio's March filing deadline for November elections placed an unconstitutional burden on the supporters of independent presidential candidate John Anderson. Major political parties which had demonstrated vote support were assured a place on the ballot and were able to select their candidate after the March filing deadline. Justice Stevens, for the Court, focused on "the character and magnitude of the asserted injury" to the First Amendment rights of the voters (not the candidate). An early filing date was seen as severely limiting the ability of disaffected voters to coalesce around an independent candidate and as impeding the ability of voters to respond to major events. Since the major parties were not subject to the March deadline, the Ohio law had a differential impact on an identifiable class of voters, *i.e.*, those who chose not to align with the major parties; it discriminated against independent voters. While political stability would be a legitimate state objective, less burdensome means were available. Greater precision of regulation than the discriminatory Ohio law was possible.

Minnesota prohibited "fusion" candidacies. A candidate could not appear on the ballot of more than one party. States are permitted to enact reasonable election regulations and to reduce election and campaign disorder. Indeed, the law upheld in *Storer* was far more burdensome. Weighing the burden on associational rights against the state interests, the Court held that the ban on "fusion" candidacies did not violate the First Amendment associational rights of political parties. *Timmons v. Twin Cities Area New Party* (1997). But three ballot-restriction laws were stuck down in Colorado in connection with its ballot initiative process. First, a restriction that initiative and petition circulators had to be registered voters greatly limited the number of persons available to circulate petitions. The fact that the registration requirement was imposed by referendum did not insulate it from any level of judicial review since voters were no more free to violate the constitution than legislators. The contention that the restriction would aid in "policing lawbreakers among petition circulators" was rejected because each circulator was already required to submit an affidavit stating her name and address. The voter registration requirement imposed a "burden on political expression that the state had failed to justify." Second, a name badge requirement that circulators had to display their names on their badges was invalidated. This requirement chilled participation in the petition process because it deprived the circulator of anonymity at exactly the time she was most likely to be harassed because of the message identified with the petition or initiative. Any governmental interest in the identity of the circulators was satisfied by the less burdensome affidavit requirement. Third, a final report requirement which obliged sponsors of an initiative to report the names and addresses of all *paid* circulators as well as the amount paid to each was struck down as unnecessary. Other disclosure provisions already existed which disclosed the influence well-heeled interest groups had on the initiative process. The Colorado ballot initiative, which allows its citizens to enact laws directly, facilitates interactive political communication, *i.e.*, core political speech. The strict scrutiny standard of review was thus applicable. The state interests of informing the electorate, preventing fraud, and furthering efficiency failed to satisfy that rigorous standard. *Buckley v. American Constitutional Law Foundation* (1999).

Why were the ballot restriction measures in *Timmons* upheld and the ballot restriction measures in *Buckley* struck down? The answer is that the validity of state election regulation depends on the severity of the burden that the regulation places on political expression. Severe or heavy burdens on state election regulation have to be narrowly tailored and have to serve compelling government interests. The state interests advanced in *Buckley* were simply too insubstantial to be deemed compelling.

In *McIntyre v. Ohio Elections Commission* (1995), the Court, per Justice Stevens, struck down an Ohio statute prohibiting the distribution of any materials aimed at influencing voters in an election unless the name and address of a responsible person was prominently included. Relying on *Talley v. California* (1960) which extended First Amendment protection to the distribution of unsigned handbills, Justice Stevens declared: "The freedom to publish anonymously extends beyond the literary realm." Relying on *Anderson v. Celebrezze* and *Storer v. Brown*, Ohio contended that reasonable and nondiscriminatory burdens on voters were valid. But *McIntyre* distinguished *Anderson* and *Storer*. The prohibition on anonymous political speech was not a mere regulation of the election process but a regulation of speech content. The anonymous speech prohibition did not survive the exacting scrutiny which is applied to regulations of core First Amendment speech. Although the interests asserted by Ohio, avoidance of fraud and libel, were legitimate, they were not sufficiently compelling to warrant a blanket prohibition of anonymous speech.

Freedom of association includes the right of like-minded voters to join in pursuit of shared political goals and to form new political parties. State regulation restricting access to the ballot of new parties must be narrowly drawn to advance state interests of compelling importance. An Illinois state law which conditioned ballot access for a new party on securing 25,000 signatures in *each* political subdivision and which prohibited the use of the name of a party established in one political subdivision from being used in another—even with the party's permission—failed to meet this standard. Although the state has strong interests in the prevention of misrepresentation and confusion among voters, these restrictions violated the right of political association since they swept more broadly than was necessary to protect the electoral process. A more narrowly tailored law could have served the state interests as well. *Norman v. Reed* (1992).

Laws that place severe burdens on the right to vote warrant strict scrutiny. But reasonable and nondiscriminatory regulation of the right to vote is presumptively valid. For example, where state law provides for easy access to the ballot, a prohibition against write-in voting to prevent "unrestrained factionalism at the general election" is valid. *Burdick v. Takushi* (1992).

Perhaps the most controversial area of First Amendment electoral law involves the status of restrictions on campaign spending by individuals and groups. In *Buckley v. Valeo* (1976), a divided Court held, *per curiam,* that a federal law limiting individual *contributions* to candidates for office served the state's compelling interest in limiting the actuality and appearance of corruption. However, a law limiting *expenditures* by candidates, individuals, and groups was unconstitutional.

The Court's *per curiam* opinion first rejected efforts to characterize the spending law as a regulation of conduct, only incidentally burdening speech. Money is a form of speech and the law regulated speech itself. Even if the funding limits were treated as a regulation of conduct, strict scrutiny was appropriate since, although ideologically neutral, the law was directed at the harmful content of the communication, *i.e.,* it was content-based regulation. The government's interest, reasoned the Court, "arises in some measure because communication allegedly integral to the conduct is itself thought to be harmful." Unlike simple time, place and manner regulation, the dollar limitations involved "direct quantity restrictions on political communication and association."

Having concluded that speech is significantly burdened on the basis of content by spending restrictions, it might have been expected that the strict scrutiny test would be applied. Instead, in an analysis suggestive of a balancing test, a distinction was drawn between the severity of the burden imposed by contribution and expenditure limits. While close scrutiny was applicable to both contributions and expenditures, the expenditure ceilings were said to impose "significantly more severe restrictions on protected freedoms." A limit on the amount a person or group can spend "necessarily reduces the quantity of expression," impacting on the quality and diversity of political speech. Limitations on contributions, on the other hand, impose only a "marginal restriction on the contributor's ability to communicate." The Court reasoned that "[t]he quantity of communication by the contributor does not increase perceptively with the size of his contribution;" it is the symbolic act of contribution itself that is communicative. While a contribution may be used to increase the quality of a recipient's speech, this was "speech by someone other than the contributor," *i.e.,* speech by proxy.

The Court then considered the governmental interest in maintaining contribution and expenditure limitations, focusing on the interest in preventing corruption. Large contributions are often given to secure political favors and Congress should be allowed to limit the opportunity for abuse, *i.e.,* seek to prevent "political quid pro quos," or dollars for political favors. On the other hand, limitations on expenditures on behalf of a candidate were seen as less clearly serving the anti-corruption interests. The lack of control by the candidate over independent spending limited the possibility that such spending would be given as a quid pro quo for political influence.

The government's argument that the expenditure limits could be justified as serving the interest in equalizing the ability of individuals and groups to exercise electoral influence was rejected. "[T]he concept that government may restrict the speech of some elements of our society in order to enhance the relative voice of others is wholly foreign to the First Amendment, which was designed to secure the widest possible dissemination of information." Simply, the desire for greater equality could not be achieved by sacrificing the liberty interests in free speech. Justice White, dissenting, argued that First Amendment interests in free dialogue are actually promoted by spending limitations, by controlling the "overpowering advantage" of the wealthy and by "encouraging the less wealthy." In short, it is big money that distorts the electoral marketplace.

Cases following *Buckley* have struggled with the imprecision created by its dichotomy between limitations on campaign expenditures and contributions. In *California Medical Ass'n v. FEC* (1981), a federal law limiting the amount an incorporated association can contribute to a multi-candidate political committee was upheld. Such spending was viewed, not as independent political speech, but rather as "speech by proxy." Thus, the spending was deemed analogous to group contributions to a candidate which can be regulated.

FEC v. National Conservative Political Action Comm. (1985) held 6–3 that a provision of the Federal Election Campaign Fund Act prohibiting political action committees (PAC) from expending more than $1000 to further the candidacy of a candidate who chooses to receive public financing violated the First Amendment. As in *Buckley,* "the expenditures at issue in this case produce speech at the core of the First Amendment" necessitating a "rigorous" standard of review. Justice Rehnquist, for the Court, likened the restriction to allowing a speaker in a public hall to express his views while denying him use of an amplifier. Both limitations reduce the quantity and quality of expression. Nor was this simply a restriction on "speech by proxy." Although contributors do not control the particular use of their funds, "the contributors obviously like the message they are hearing from these organizations and want to add their voice to that message; otherwise they would not part with their money." Concluding that PAC expenditures are entitled to full First Amendment protection, the Court could find no governmental interest sufficiently strong to justify restricting PAC expenditures.

In *Colorado Republican Federal Campaign Committee v. Federal Election Commission* (1996) (*Colorado I*), the Court ruled that all expenditures by a political party that were independent of the political candidate's control could not be restricted under the First Amendment. However, in *Federal Election Commission v. Colorado Republican Federal Campaign Committee* (2001), (*Colorado II*) the Court amplified this holding and ruled that expenditures by a political party that are coordinated with a candidate are deemed contributions and, therefore, subject to the limits set forth in the Federal Election Campaign Act. The Court's rationale was that contribution limits could easily be evaded if the limits on donor contributions to candidates could be undone by channeling them through the political parties.

In *FEC v. Massachusetts Citizens for Life (MCFL)* (1986), the application of a provision of the Federal Election Campaign Act prohibiting direct expenditure of corporate funds to a nonprofit, voluntary political association concerned with elections to public office was struck down as inconsistent with the First Amendment. Protected political speech could not be so infringed in the absence of a compelling governmental interest—an interest clearly absent in the case of application of the provision to a small voluntary political association which refused to accept contributions from either business corporations or labor unions. Moreover, the association had no shareholders and was not engaged in business. In such circumstances, the regulation was a limitation on speech which failed to use narrowly tailored means to achieve its end.

However, the application of a Michigan statute prohibiting corporations from making campaign contributions from their general treasury funds to a nonprofit corporation was held not to violate the First Amendment. The nonprofit corporation involved, the Michigan Chamber of Commerce, lacked three of the distinctive features of the organization protected in *MCFL*: (1) The Chamber of Commerce, unlike MCFL corporation, was not formed just for the purpose of political expression; (2) The members of the Chamber of Commerce had an economic reason for remaining with it even though they might disagree with its politics; and (3) the Chamber, unlike *MCFL*, was subject to influence from business corporations which might use it as a conduit for direct spending which would pose a threat to the political marketplace. Use of the corporate form did not, of course, remove corporate speech from the scope of First Amendment protection. But the Michigan statute's burden on corporate political speech was justified by the state's compelling interest in preventing political corruption or the appearance of undue influence. Unlike the situation in *MCFL*, the statute was precisely targeted, *i.e.*, narrowly tailored, to achieve its goal. *Austin v. Michigan Chamber of Commerce* (1990).

The anti-corruption interest of the government relied on in *Buckley* to uphold spending limits on contributions is not applicable to spending limits on contributions in referenda. In *Citizens Against Rent Control v. City of Berkeley* (1981), a local ordinance placing a $250 limitation on contributions to committees formed to support or oppose ballot measures submitted to a popular vote was held unconstitutional. It violated both the right of association (*i.e.*, it limited individuals wishing to band together in advancing their views while placing no limit on individuals acting alone) and individual and collective rights of free expression (*i.e.*, it limited the quantity of expression). Since the ordinance did not advance a significant state interest sufficient to satisfy the Court's "exacting scrutiny," the law failed.

A major development in federal political campaign reform legislation occasioned a vigorous First Amendment challenge in *McConnell v. Federal Election Commission* (2003). However, the Court upheld most of the important elements of the Bipartisan Campaign Finance Reform Act of 2002, also known as the McCain–Feingold law. Basically, the law, *inter alia*, placed restrictions on so-called "soft money," *i.e.*, a term applied to funds raised and spent by political parties which were not subject to contribution limits to political candidates under the prior law. Indeed, under the prior law, individuals and corporations were free to make unlimited donations to the national political parties so long as funds were not used to specifically advocate election of a particular candidate. With respect to such donations, the parties were free to spend the funds as they wished. In practice, the limitation that these funds could not be used to advocate election of a particular candidate proved to be toothless. For example, the donations were used to fund so-called "issue ads." These ads attacked or supported a candidate's position on a particular issue but carefully refrained from urging the candidate's defeat or election. Funds were also used to urge support of the entire Republican or Democratic tickets as well as for voter registration campaigns. But these campaigns were usually directed at voters likely to vote for a particular party's candidate. The Court viewed McCain–Feingold's ban on "soft money" as a limit on contribution limits rather than a limit on expenditures. Accordingly, the Court following *Buckley v.*

Valeo applied a lesser degree of scrutiny than strict scrutiny. Thus, *McConnell* required that the contribution restrictions be "closely drawn" to serve an "important interest." Banning "soft money" plus limiting the ability of contributors to do an end run around the ban was reasonably tailored to implement the anti-corruption objectives of Congress. This standard was satisfied because contribution limits sought to "prevent corruption and the appearance of corruption."Massive "soft money" contributions otherwise tended to evoke a suggestion of corruption. Furthermore, the Court noted that very large "soft money" contributors gave to *both* Democrats and Republicans, thereby suggesting that the contributions were not expressions of ideological conviction but instead constituted an effort to buy access or to evade retribution. In these circumstances, First Amendment rights were less likely to be significantly affected. Finally, the Court stressed that limits on contributions were not limits on expenditures by the political parties themselves.

In a surprise invalidation of a limitation on campaign contributions, the Court held that a ban on campaign contributions by minors could not be justified by the concern that parents would use their children to make contributions beyond those permitted by the Bipartisan Campaign Reform Act of 2002. In the absence of evidence that such a practice existed, the right to political expression through campaign contributions protected by the First Amendment outweighed this hypothetical concern. Finally, *McConnell* rejected a First Amendment attack on a provision of the Act which prohibited "hard money" funding by corporations or unions of broadcast advertisements, *i.e.*, "electioneering communications" defined, *inter alia*, as communications that mention or otherwise identify a federal candidate's name and which are communicated within sixty days of a general election. The provision in the Act requiring that such expenditures be disclosed to the Federal Election Commission was validated as well.

7. GOVERNMENT–FUNDED SPEECH

Federal regulations governing federally funded family planning grantees explicitly barred them from providing abortion counseling or making referrals to abortion clinics. The regulations also barred the grantees from the encouragement, promotion or advocacy of abortion. Also, the grantees were required to organize themselves so that they were " 'physically and financially separate' "from abortion related activities. The regulations did not constitute impermissible viewpoint discrimination. Government had simply chosen "to fund one activity to the exclusion of the other." Just because a government decision to fund a program to accomplish certain lawful goals thereby discourages competing goals does not invalidate such government choices or subsidies. Abortion is a right but government is not obliged to fund it. Nor does the conferral of grants with such conditions violate the unconstitutional conditions doctrine. The condition runs to the program. The recipient is still free to exercise the constitutional right in question. *Rust v. Sullivan* (1991).

A critical distinction turns on whether government or private speech is involved. In 1996, Congress prohibited funding any organization representing clients that sought to amend or alter existing welfare law. When a Legal Service Corporation grantee of federal funds providing legal assistance to indigents was not permitted to continue representation in a welfare matter, the Supreme Court held, 5–4, that this limitation violated the First Amendment. *Rust* was distinguished because the expressive activity there constituted *government* speech. Congress funded LSC grantees to afford legal assistance to indigent clients in order to facilitate *private* speech not to transmit a government message. *Legal Services Corporation v. Velazquez* (2001).

The problem of indecent speech also arises in the context of government grantmaking where the government acts not as a regulator of the marketplace of ideas (as in *Sable*, *Denver Area*, and *Reno*) but as a participant. The federally-funded National Endowment for the Arts (NEA) funded exhibits which included Robert Mapplethorpe's homoerotic photographs and Andres Serrano's "Piss Christ," depicting a crucifix in urine. Congress soon enacted a law requiring the NEA to take into account "general standards of decency and respect for the diverse beliefs and values of the American people." Performance artists whose projects had been recommended for funding but were subsequently denied thereafter brought suit contending that the law was facially invalid. The Court, held, per Justice O'Connor, that those making a facial challenge to a law must "demonstrate a substantial risk that application of the provision will lead to the suppression of speech." Such a showing had not been made here. Although the plaintiffs argued that the law constituted viewpoint discrimination, the NEA responded that the law was only hortatory. The Court held that the law stopped short of restricting speech and merely added some new considerations to the selection process. *National Endowment for the Arts (NEA) v. Finley* (1998).

Plaintiffs in *NEA* relied heavily on *Rosenberger v. Rector and Visitors of the University of Virginia* (1995) where the Court set aside a state university's decision to deny funding to all student publications taking religious editorial viewpoints. But Justice O'Connor denied that *Rosenberger* was applicable. That case held that "by subsidizing the Student Activities Fund, the University had created a limited public forum, from which it impermissibly excluded all publications with religious editorial viewpoints." But the NEA's job is to make aesthetic judgments as well as content-related judgments about "excellence." These features distinguished NEA grants from the subsidy in *Rosenberger* which was available to all student groups concerned with the educational mission of the university.

Viewpoint discrimination in federal grantmaking is not constitutional the *NEA* Court ruled. But this was a facial challenge and there is no viewpoint discrimination on the face of this law. Overbreadth is used only sparingly in facial validity cases. Unless the challenged law were applied in a manner that raises concerns about the suppression of unpopular viewpoints, the First Amendment is not violated. Nor is the law unconstitutionally vague as the lower courts believed. When government acts as a patron rather than as a regulator, harms caused by imprecision are less constitutionally severe. Where selective subsidies are involved, clarity is not always possible.

In a vitriolic concurrence, Justice Scalia insisted that this was viewpoint discrimination *and* that it was perfectly appropriate in government grantmaking: "It is the very business of government to favor and disfavor points of view on innumerable subjects." Justice Souter, in dissent, said that one had only to read the law to glean its hostility to offensive messages. The law constituted viewpoint discrimination and, in his view, was thus invalid.

Rust influenced the result in a First Amendment challenge to the Child Internet Protection Act [CIPA] which provided that public libraries may not receive grants of federal funds to provide Internet access unless they install software to block images containing obscenity or child pornography. Chief Justice Rehnquist, speaking for a plurality including Justices O'Connor, Scalia and Thomas, declined to apply public forum analysis in this context. Internet access was neither a traditional nor a designated public forum. Internet access has certainly not been used "time out of mind" for communication. Thus, it was not a traditional public forum. Nor did Internet access in a public library satisfy the requirement of a designated public forum. Public libraries provide Internet access not to encourage a diversity of viewpoints from private speakers but to facilitate research, learning and recreational pursuits. Accordingly, the judgment of the public libraries to block online pornography is no different than the similar decision that libraries make with respect to the exclusion of pornography from their print collections. Heightened review does not attach to these decisions. Nor does the fact that the software used in blocking pornography may result in overblocking yield a different result. A patron who encounters an erroneously blocked site has only to ask a librarian to unblock that site or to disable the filter. CIPA's pornography restriction is content-oriented but public libraries necessarily have to make content decisions with respect to their collections and this situation is no different than that. CIPA is not imposing an unconstitutional decision on the receipt of federal assistance. Relying on *Rust v. Sullivan,* the Court denied that government was denying a benefit to anyone. Government was simply requiring, as it had in *Rust*, that public funds be spent only for the purposes which Congress had intended. CIPA imposes no penalty on public libraries that choose to provide Internet access for pornography. All CIPA does is implement the congressional decision not to subsidize pornography. The

Court held that CIPA was not facially invalid under the First Amendment.

Justice Kennedy, concurring, also agreed that CIPA was facially constitutional since a librarian on the request of an adult could unblock a site or disable a filtering device. Furthermore, he pointed out that if an adult who desired to access Internet content protected by the First Amendment was in fact substantially burdened by CIPA, an as-applied challenge would be available. In dissent, Justice Stevens objected that *Rust* was not controlling since that case only applied to government speech, *i.e.*, situations where government was communicating a specific message. Here no message favored by government was being subsidized. CIPA unconstitutionally conditioned the receipt of government funds "on the restriction of significant First Amendment rights." *United States v. American Library Association, Inc.* (2003).

CHAPTER VIII

FREEDOM OF RELIGION

The First Amendment guarantee of freedom of religion "was adopted to curtail the power of Congress to interfere with the individual's freedom to believe, to worship, and to express himself in accordance with the dictates of his own conscience." *Wallace v. Jaffree* (1985) [silent prayer law held unconstitutional]. The two components of the freedom of religion guarantee, *i.e.*, the Free Exercise Clause and the Anti–Establishment Clause, have both been applied to the states through incorporation into the Fourteenth Amendment due process guarantee of liberty. [*Cantwell v. Connecticut* (1940), free exercise; *Everson v. Board of Educ.* (1947), Anti–Establishment].

But while both components are part of our constitutional freedom of religion, the clauses often appear to conflict. Exemption from generally applicable laws when such laws burden a particular religion may serve the interests of religious freedom, but such exemptions can be perceived as government support for religion violative of the Establishment Clause. The proscription against religious establishment may bar government support for religion and religious institutions, but denial of public benefits and services (especially given the important role played by government in our lives), may impose hardships on religion presenting free exercise problems. A continuing problem is how to reconcile these potentially-conflicting constitutional demands. While some have argued for the primacy of free exercise when the two clauses conflict, the Court has not thus far clearly accepted this approach. Rather, the basic command has been that government maintain a position of "neutrality." The Rehnquist Court is much less insistent on the strictness with which government must maintain this neutrality and is much more willing to entertain government accommodation of religion. This is particularly true of the newer appointees to the Court such as Justices Kennedy and Scalia.

A. THE ESTABLISHMENT CLAUSE

The First Amendment prohibits the making of laws "respecting the establishment of religion." This has not been read simply as a prohibition against a government sponsored church [*but see Wallace v. Jaffree* (Rehnquist, J., dissenting)] or as simply a demand of equal treatment of religions (*i.e.*, an anti-discrimination guarantee) but as a broader prohibition against laws "which aid one religion, aid all religions, or prefer one religion over another." *Everson.*

What constitutes impermissible aid? At times, the Court has stated that the Clause erects a "wall of separation" between church and state. *Reynolds v. United States* (1878). At other times, the Court has referred to the wall metaphor as "not a wholly accurate description of the practical aspects of the relationship that in fact exists between church and state" [*Lynch v. Donnelly* (1984)] and has asserted that the Constitution "affirmatively mandates accommodation, not merely tolerance, of all religions and forbids hostility towards any." *Id.*

In most cases, the Court requires that each part of a three-part test be satisfied in order to withstand an Establishment Clause challenge: (1) the law must have a secular legislative purpose; (2) the principal or primary effect of the law must neither advance nor inhibit religion; and, (3) the law must not foster "an excessive government entanglement with religion." *Lemon v. Kurtzman* (1971). The *Lemon* test has been severely criticized. Further, the Court has departed from the test in upholding prayers opening legislative sessions, emphasizing instead the historical acceptance of the challenged practice making it a "part of the fabric of our society" *Marsh v. Chambers* (1983); *Walz v. Tax Com'n of New York* (1970) [emphasizing historic practices in upholding state tax exemptions for property and income of religious institutions]. *Larson v. Valente* (1982), also avoided *Lemon* in invalidating a state law imposing disclosure requirements only on religious organizations soliciting more than 50% of funds from non-members on the ground that it discriminated against non-traditional religions in violation of the Establishment Clause. *Larson* used the strict scrutiny test for laws discriminating against some religions in favor of others. Whether the tripartite *Lemon* test will survive is not clear. There are new trends that have become apparent. Increasingly, the Court is asking whether the law at issue constitutes an endorsement of religion or a particular religious belief. Justice O'Connor has indicated that she believes that this is a more useful test than *Lemon. Lynch v. Donnelly* (1984). Justice Kennedy, on the other hand, believes that endorsement is too imprecise a concept and that the appropriate inquiry is whether the state is proselytizing so that the government action is coercive. *Board of Education of Westside Community Schools v. Mergens* (1990) (Kennedy, J., concurring.) As of now, the *Lemon* test has not yet been repudiated.

1. PUBLIC AID TO RELIGION

A recurring problem in Establishment Clause jurisprudence is the extent to which government can provide financial and other assistance to religious institutions. The aid may be directly to the institution itself. Alternatively, religious institutions may benefit only indirectly through assistance to citizens using the services of the religious institution, *e.g.*, tax breaks for parents of students attending private religious schools. Disposition of such cases has produced case-by-case decisions that resist efforts to formulate generally applicable principles. But it does appear that the Court is more tolerant of aid programs providing benefits to citizens generally than those involving aid directly to the religious institutions.

Everson v. Board of Educ. (1947), upheld a local program for reimbursing parents for funds spent in transporting their children to school by public buses. The law was "a general program to help parents get their children, regardless of their religion, safely and expeditiously to and from accredited schools." The public welfare benefit was available to all students and any aid to religion was only incidental. In short, the law had a secular purpose and a secular primary effect. Similarly, state approved, secular textbooks may be loaned to private school students, including parochial school students. *Board of Educ. v. Allen* (1968). A law which imposes a general obligation on the state to provide a sign language interpreter for a deaf student can be applied to a student at a Catholic high school. The Establishment Clause is not violated just because a sectarian institution receives an "attenuated financial benefit" from a government program which neutrally distributes benefits. *Zobrest v. Catalina Foothills School District* (1993) [providing a sign language interpreter for a deaf student in a Catholic high school does not violate the Establishment Clause]; *Witters v. Washington Department of Services for the Blind* (1986) [grant by a state of vocational tuition to a blind person who will use the grant for a religious vocation does not violate the Establishment Clause]. On the other hand, loan of instructional materials, (*e.g.,* maps, magazines, tape recorders) and providing public transportation for field trips to parochial school students, have been struck down. *Wolman v. Walter* (1977). *Wolman* concluded: "In view of the impossibility of separating the secular education function from the sectarian," the state aid presented too great a danger of advancing the religious teaching mission of the parochial schools. See *Meek v. Pittenger* (1975) [state loan of non-textbook instructional material and equipment to private schools held unconstitutional].

Mueller v. Allen (1983) upheld 5–4 a Minnesota program permitting parents to deduct from their state tax certain expenses incurred in educating their children. Justice Rehnquist, for the Court, noted that the educational deduction was only one of many deductions designed to equalize tax burdens and encourage desirable expenditures. Most important, unlike an earlier tax break program for parents of private school children which the Court had invalidated [*Committee for Public Educ. v. Nyquist* (1973)], the Minnesota tax break was available to *all* parents, including those whose children attend public schools. Justice Rehnquist commented: "[A] program that neutrally provides state assistance to a broad spectrum of citizens is not readily subject to challenge under the Establishment Clause." The argument that the bulk of deductions would be claimed by parents who pay high tuition at sectarian schools was dismissed as lacking "principled standards by which such statistical evidence might be evaluated." Further, Justice Rehnquist saw no significant danger of "comprehensive discriminating, and continuing state surveillance" in the religious schools which might excessively entangle the state in religion.

Historically, programs of direct assistance to private elementary and secondary schools have produced a checkered, but essentially a negative, response from the Court. Parochial schools particularly have been characterized as being permeated with religious objectives and activities. Aid to religious schools involves young, immature students who are susceptible to religious indoctrination. Political divisiveness over aid to religious schools is common. In short, the probability that state aid will have a primary effect of advancing religion is enhanced. Increased state surveillance of the religious schools to prevent sectarian use of the funds becomes necessary and this threatens church-state entanglement. Although not abandoning these concerns, the Court now gives them much less weight where government funds benefitting religious private and elementary schools are awarded on a neutral basis and are the result of individual rather than government choice. *See, infra, Zelman v. Simmons–Harris* (2002).

Nevertheless, aid to religious elementary and secondary schools does not necessarily violate the *Lemon* test. The nature of the aid will be considered (*e.g.,* whether it affords an opportunity for ideological persuasion); whether the aid is administered by and requires personal involvement of private school personnel or whether it is state-run; and, whether the aid is provided in the private school building or on publicly-owned property. While such considerations provide no bright-line standard, they reflect concerns over the danger that the religious mission of sectarian schools will intrude into the operation of the state aid program.

Just such considerations were cited in *Lemon v. Kurtzman* (1971), in striking down state salary supplements to teachers of secular subjects at private schools. Noting that "parochial schools involve substantial religious activity and purpose" and citing the difficulty of assuring that the teachers would not engage in religious teaching, it was found unnecessary to consider the "primary effect" of aid. The need for state monitoring to assure that the aid was not used for advancing religion violated *Lemon's* third prong: "The cumulative impact of the entire relationship involves excessive entanglement between government and religion."

State programs to provide auxiliary services to private schools or to reimburse private schools for testing, record-keeping and reporting have produced a myriad of program-by-program results yielding few general principles. *Levitt v. Committee for Public Educ.* (1973), rejected state reimbursement of parochial schools on a lump sum per project basis for costs of administering tests where some of the tests were prepared by the private school teachers— there was little control to assure that funds would not be used to advance religion. But in *Committee for Public Educ. v. Regan* (1980), state payments to private schools for administering standardized tests and for other state mandated record-keeping and reporting was upheld. In this instance, the state retained control over the tests which "serves to prevent the use of the test as part of religious teaching." The state mandated services were "ministerial" and "lacking in ideological content or use." Entanglement concerns were dismissed since the services "are discrete and clearly identifiable," not requiring excessive government monitoring.

Wolman v. Walter (1977) approved furnishing of speech, hearing, and psychological diagnostic services by public employees, even though the aid was located in the private school. Diagnostic services are non-ideological, have no educational content and are not closely associated with the educational mission of the school. Further, the diagnostician has a limited relationship with the student, limiting further the "risk of the fostering of ideological views." It followed that there would be no need for excessive state surveillance, involving impermissible entanglement. On the other hand, therapeutic services, guidance counseling and remedial education, involving a greater danger of ideological persuasion, can be offered only at religiously-neutral locations off the private school premises. The danger of advancing religion arises "from the nature of the institution, not from the nature of the pupils." If the program is conducted outside of the religious school, "[i]t can hardly be said that the supervision of public employees performing public functions on public property creates an excessive entanglement between church and state." *Wolman*. See *Meek v. Pittenger* (1975), invalidating programs involving provision of such services *at the private school*.

School Dist. of Grand Rapids v. Ball (1985), invalidated a shared time and a community education program which provided classes financed by the public school system, taught by teachers hired by the public school system, held in classrooms leased from private schools. Stressing the "pervasively sectarian" nature of almost all of the private schools involved, Justice Brennan, for the Court, identified three factors as establishing that the programs had the primary effect of advancing religion. First, teachers who teach in the program may either by design or inadvertence end up indoctrinating students with particular religious beliefs. Second, impressionable children may view the program as "a crucial symbolic link between government and religion." Government would be seen as supporting the religious denomination sponsoring the school thus contravening a core purpose of the Establishment Clause, the avoidance of any message of government approval of religion. Third, the program could have the impermissible effect of direct promotion of religion by means of providing a government subsidy "to the primary religious mission" of the religiously sponsored school. The primary effect was the "direct and substantial advancement of the sectarian enterprise."

Aguilar v. Felton (1985), a companion case, invalidated a program involving the use of federal funds to pay the salaries of public school teachers who provided remedial instruction and clinical and guidance services to educationally deprived low income children in parochial schools. Efforts to distinguish *Ball* by emphasizing the use of public monitoring to prevent religious influences failed. While this might avoid the religious effects prong of *Lemon,* the Court found that the ideological nature of the aid and the religious character of the institution receiving the aid threatened excessive government entanglement in religion. "[T]he scope and duration of [the] program would require a permanent and pervasive State presence in the sectarian schools receiving aid."

More than a decade after *Aguilar* the parties to that decision sought and received relief from it. Justice O'Connor ruled for the Court that post-*Aguilar* Establishment Clause case law had changed the law in two important ways. First, *Zobrest, supra*, had abandoned the presumption that the presence of public school teachers in parochial school classrooms always led to state-sponsored religious indoctrination. Indeed, *Ball* had wrongly assumed such presence constituted a "symbolic union between government and religion." Second, *Witters, supra*, departed from the ruling in *Ball* that all government aid that directly assists the education function of religious schools is invalid. Consequently, *Aguilar* as well as that part of *Ball* that dealt with the city's Shared Time Program were no longer good law. The Court insisted that the *Lemon* principles still applied. What had changed was the Court's approach to "the criteria used to assess whether aid to religion has an impermissible effect." Even though the program at issue had been found to create an excessive entanglement of government and religion in *Aguilar*, not all entanglements between government and religion resulted in advancing or inhibiting religion. An entanglement must be excessive before it violated the Establishment Clause. In sum, the provision by the state of remedial instruction by public employees to disadvantaged children on the premises of parochial schools is not without more an impermissible endorsement of religion. *Agostini v. Felton* (1997).

A federal law established a program whereby federal aid could be granted to state educational agencies who would use the funds to lend educational materials such as computers and computer software to public and private elementary and secondary schools to implement "secular, neutral and nonideological" programs. In a plurality opinion Justice Thomas, joined by the Chief Justice, and Justices Scalia and Kennedy, declared that if the government aid was offered according to neutral criteria and was secular in content, the Establishment Clause is not violated. The crucial factor for the plurality was the government aid going to religious institutions was the result of the "genuinely independent and private choices of individuals." If "numerous private choices rather than the single choice of government" determine the distribution of government aid according to neutral eligible criteria, it is unlikely that government will grant special favors that result in a religious establishment. To the extent *Meek* and *Wolman* were inconsistent, they were overruled. Justice O'Connor, joined by Justice Breyer, agreed that the suggestion in *Meek* and *Wolman* that any government aid that *could* be diverted to religious uses was unconstitutional should be overruled. What was objectionable in her view was actual diversion. Justice Souter, joined by Justices Stevens and Ginsburg, dissenting, rejected the plurality's position that evenhanded criteria of neutrality should be the "single and sufficient test for establishment constitutionality of school aid." Justices O'Connor and Breyer rejected such a test as well. In sum, a majority of the Court adheres to the view that actual proof of diversion of government aid to religious uses violates the Establishment Clause. *Mitchell v. Helms* (2000).

In *Zelman v. Simmons Harris* (2002), the controversial "school voucher" case, the Court, 5–4, per Chief Justice Rehnquist, rejected an Establishment Clause challenge to an Ohio state program providing state aid to parents so their children in the Cleveland School District could receive tuition aid or vouchers to attend participating private schools. Or, if the parents wished, they could receive tutorial financial assistance for the children in public schools. Although parents were permitted to choose among the participating private schools, eighty-two per cent (82%) of the participating private schools had a religious affiliation. Ninety-six percent (96%) of the children in the program were enrolled in schools with a religious affiliation. As in *Agostini v. Felton* the issue was whether the Ohio program had the "purpose" or "effect" of advancing religion. If so, it violated the Establishment Clause. Clearly, the Ohio program had a secular purpose of providing needed educational aid to poor children in a failing public school system. The more difficult issue was whether the Ohio program had the prohibited "effect" of advancing or inhibiting religion. The Court concluded that the Ohio program did not have the effect of advancing religion. Parents had a secular option. Under the program they may receive state tutoring aid if they chose to have their children remain in the public schools schools. Alternatively, they could choose to have their children attend a secular private school. It is immaterial that religiously affiliated schools derive most of the benefit from this government aid. The Ohio program is a neutral private choice program which does not constitute an endorsement of religious schools. *Zelman* emphasized that here, as in *Mueller*, *Witters* and *Zobrest*, the disbursement of government benefits goes to the individual receiving them and not to a religious entity. Any incidental advancement of a "religious mission" or perception of "endorsement of a religious message" was, therefore, attributable to the individual recipient and not the government.

Justice Souter, joined by Justices Stevens, Ginsburg, and Breyer dissenting, charged that *Zelman* constituted a major break with past Establishment Clause precedent since it made no distinction between whether government aid to religion is incidental or substantial: "[T]he scale of the aid to religious schools approved today is unprecedented." The Court reduces the question of an Establishment Clause violation to two factors—-neutrality and free choice. But the Court's approach to these factors was simply verbal and nothing else. The program was not neutral because, although parents using public schools could get tutoring aid, it was available in amounts markedly less substantial than the tuition vouchers available for the mostly religious private schools. As for choice, choice does not exist just because there is some less satisfactory educational alternative to the religious one. In addition, Justice Breyer contended that publicly financed school voucher programs present a grave risk of "religiously based social conflict." Religious conflict is not avoided by providing each religion with an equal opportunity to obtain government funds or say its prayers in the public schools. Religious conflict is avoided by drawing a bright line of "*separation* between church and state." Nowhere was such a line more important than in the area of primary religious education.

Government aid programs involving construction grants for higher education have generally been upheld by the Court. For example, *Tilton v. Richardson* (1971), upheld federal construction grants for buildings to be used for secular purposes at private colleges. Chief Justice Burger, for the Court, noted that "college students are less impressionable and less susceptible to religious indoctrination." There is less likelihood "that religion will permeate the area of secular education." Since construction aid involves a one-time grant, there is minimal need for government surveillance and less danger of church-state entanglement. Even annual noncategorical grants to private colleges have been upheld if there are assurances that the funds will not be used for sectarian purposes. *Roemer v. Board of*

Public Works of Maryland (1976) [upholding annual noncategorical grants]. Such a continuing assistance program, however, does require government surveillance to assure that the conditions imposed limiting the aid to secular activities are enforced and this enhances the dangers of entanglement.

2.   RELIGION IN THE SCHOOLS

Is any breach in the wall of separation resulting from the recognition of religion and religious values by public education a violation of the Establishment Clause? Does denial of the ability to pray in the classroom, to teach creationism as an alternative to evolution, to include religious values in the curriculum and educational programs, constitute hostility to religion violative of the Free Exercise Clause and establish a religion of secularism? Such are the contours of the modern debate over the extent to which religion can be accommodated in the classroom. Once again, the uncertain application of the *Lemon* test provides the structure for analysis. And, once again, there are few bright line answers.

One of the more settled areas involves the release of students from public schools for religious instruction. If the released time for religious education occurs in the public school building, so that the state could be perceived as endorsing the religious message thereby advancing religion, the Establishment Clause is violated. *McCollum v. Board of Educ.* (1948). But if the instruction occurs outside the public school, the program is a permissible accommodation of religion. Such a program "respects the religious nature of our people and accommodates the public service to their spiritual needs." The Establishment Clause does not embody "a philosophy of hostility to religion." *Zorach v. Clauson* (1952).

A far less well-settled and more divisive issue involves the question of school prayer. *Engel v. Vitale* (1962), struck down a prayer composed by the Board of Regents on the basis of the principle that "it is no part of the business of government to compose official prayers for any group of the American people to recite as a part of a religious program carried on by government." *Abington School Dist. v. Schempp* (1963), extended *Engel* beyond officially composed prayers to prohibit Bible reading and recitation of the Lord's Prayer. Even if it were assumed that the activity was for the secular purposes of promoting mortality, combating materialism and teaching literature, "the laws require religious exercises and such exercises are being conducted in direct violation of [the Establishment Clause]." While a study of the Bible or of religion as part of the educational program is permissible, state-run "religious exercises" violate the First Amendment mandate "that the Government maintain strict neutrality, neither aiding nor opposing religion." The fact that children could be excused from participating was not determinative—"a violation of the Free Exercise Clause is predicated on coercion while the Establishment Clause violation need not be so attended." Nor would exclusion of religious exercises establish a religion of secularism violative of the majority's rights—the Free Exercise Clause "has never meant that a majority could use the machinery of the State to practice its beliefs."

With the rejection of school prayer, there has been increasing interest in moments of silent prayer or quiet meditation. *Wallace v. Jaffree* (1985), involved the validity of an Alabama law requiring a 1–minute period of silence "for meditation or voluntary prayer." Applying the first prong of the *Lemon* test, Justice Stevens, for the Court, asked "whether government's actual purpose is to endorse or disapprove of religion." The Court concluded 6–3 that the sole purpose for enacting the law was to express "the State's endorsement of prayer activities for one minute at the beginning of each school day." The State's inclusion of the prayer alternative indicated an intent "to characterize prayer as a favored practice." It followed that the State had violated the principle that government must follow a course of "complete neutrality towards religion." The Court, as well as the concurring opinions in *Jaffree,* indicated that a religiously-neutral moment of silence law, not enacted solely for sectarian purposes, might well be constitutional. Justice O'Connor, concurring, noted that, unlike the prayer cases, "a moment of silence is not inherently religious" and does not require the dissenter to compromise his or her beliefs. Such a law could serve the secular purpose of devotional activities—"It is difficult to discern a serious threat to religious liberty from a room of silent, thoughtful children."

While released time and prayer in the schools have proven to be recurring Establishment Clause issues for the Court, there have been other problem cases. The Court employed the first *Lemon* prong in holding that a state statute barring the teaching of evolution violated freedom of religion. *Epperson v. Arkansas* (1968). Excluding a particular theory or segment of a body of knowledge from the school curriculum because it conflicts with dominant religious doctrine is inconsistent with the mandate of neutrality. The posting of the Ten Commandments, even though privately funded, was determined to be for a "plainly religious" purpose and hence violative of the Establishment Clause in *Stone v. Graham* (1980). Efforts to characterize the Ten Commandments in secular terms as a part of our legal heritage failed.

On the other hand, the Court struck down an effort by a state university to avoid Establishment Clause problems by denying student groups access to university facilities "for purposes of religious worship and teaching." *Widmar v. Vincent* (1981). A policy of equal access serves the secular purpose of promoting the free exchange of ideas in the public forum. It would not have a primary effect of advancing religion since there is no symbolic state approval of the religious message and the access is available to all groups, secular and sectarian. Enforcement of a policy of excluding "religious" groups would involve an even greater threat of church-state entanglement. The thin line separating moral and religious values and the ambiguity of what constitutes a religion suggests that the subject of religion in the school curriculum will be a recurring issue.

Could *Widmar* be extended to the public high schools? Congress thought so and enacted the Equal Access Act of 1984 which prohibited discrimination against religious student speech. The Act provided that if a public high school allowed "noncurriculum related groups" to meet on school premises a "limited open forum" was created. A school would then be prohibited from denying the request of student religious groups to meet on school premises during noninstructional time. Denial of such access to school premises to a student Christian club by a public high school violated the Equal Access Act; the Act was triggered because other noncurriculum related groups were recognized by the school. Moreover, the Act's principle of equal access for religious groups to school facilities under such circumstances did not violate the Establishment Clause. *Board of Education of the Westside Community Schools v. Mergens* (1990).

The plurality opinion for the Court in *Mergens* applied the *Lemon* test. The Congressional purpose behind the Equal Access Act was "undeniably secular" since it prohibited discrimination against political or philosophical speech as well as political speech on the basis of content. The Act was neutral toward religion; it does not constitute an endorsement of religion. The Act did not have the primary effect of advancing religion. High school students were mature enough to understand that a school does not endorse speech merely because speech is allowed on a nondiscriminatory basis. The wide variety of clubs assured that no official endorsement or favoritism was present. Involvement by school officials was minimal. The limited monitoring role of school officials did not constitute an impermissible entanglement with religion. In short, high school students were not so much less mature than university students to make the precepts of *Widmar* inapplicable.

A public school board may not, consistent with the Establishment Clause, deny use of public school premises to a church group which wishes to show a film series on child rearing. Such action violates the Freedom of Speech Clause since it is viewpoint discrimination to permit school property to be used for the airing of all views about child rearing except those views on that topic which have a religious orientation. Furthermore, the exhibition of the child rearing film by the church group would not offend the Establishment Clause. The film was not shown during school hours, was not sponsored by the school and was open to the general public. Finally, the Court observed that permitting the exhibition of the film on school property in these circumstances did not constitute a violation of the Establishment Clause using the tripartite *Lemon* test. *Lamb's Chapel v. Center Moriches School District* (1993).

The University of Virginia authorized payments from mandatory student fees to outside contractors for printing costs for designated student publications so long as they disclaimed any university responsibility for them. Because university guidelines did not permit the use of mandatory student fees to fund activities primarily promoting a belief "in a deity or an ultimate reality," the university refused to pay the printing costs for a student publication called *Wide Awake: A Christian Perspective*. Although the federal court of appeals agreed with the student group's contention that this refusal violated freedom of speech, they, nonetheless, held that the university's action was justified by the compelling governmental interest in complying with the Establishment Clause.

The Supreme Court, 5–4, per Justice Kennedy, reversed. The university's action constituted viewpoint discrimination very similar to the school district discrimination held invalid in *Lamb's Chapel*. That *Lamb's Chapel* involved access to public school facilities and this case involved access to state university funds is irrelevant. *Widmar*, *Mergens* and *Lamb's Chapel* all reject the idea that the Establishment Clause "justifies, much less requires, a refusal to extend free speech rights" to religious speakers who participate in neutral government programs. The Student Activities Fund was a neutral program designed by the university to open a forum for speech. The regulation constituted viewpoint discrimination which required public officials to review student publications to ascertain their religious content. This violates free speech and runs counter to the neutrality required of the state by the Establishment Clause. The Establishment Clause is not violated when the University is obliged to obey the mandates of the Free Speech Clause. *Rosenberger v. University of Virginia* (1995). In dissent, Justice

Souter, joined by Justices Stevens, Ginsburg and Breyer contended that the use of public funds to preach religion, as *Wide Awake* does, is "categorically forbidden under the Establishment Clause." The dissenters complained that the Court's reasoning leads to the approval of direct aid to religion "beyond anything justifiable for the sake of access to speaking forums."

Inclusion of a prayer offered by a clergyman selected by a public high school for a graduation baccalaureate ceremony was held, 5–4, to violate the Establishment Clause. Justice Kennedy for the Court declined to reconsider the *Lemon* test as requested by the Bush Administration. But he didn't use it either. Instead, he used a coercion test. Peer and public pressures to attend the baccalaureate ceremony exerts coercive if subtle pressure on students particularly in view of the school's involvement in the ceremony. The high school sponsored the religious exercise and chose the clergyman. The fact that students were not required to attend did not diminish the force of that pressure. *Lee v. Weisman* (1992).

Four concurring justices in *Lee* contended that an endorsement test should be used for Establishment Clause issues—does the challenged government related practice endorse religion? An endorsement test was preferable to a coercion test since the problem of coercion is already dealt with by the Free Exercise Clause. Four justices in a dissent by Justice Scalia contended that *Lemon* should be abandoned altogether and that Justice Kennedy's use of coercion was too broad since no penalties attached to non-attendance at the ceremony. The baccalaureate ceremony was merely an aspect of a civic religion long understood to be nonsectarian in character.

A public high school in a Texas town permitted student chaplains to give a pre-game prayer over the public address system at home football games. When this policy was challenged, the school district changed its policy and permitted students to vote on whether to have an invocation. If the vote was in the affirmative (as in fact it was), there was then a vote on which student should deliver it. The new policy was successfully challenged, 6–3, as a violation of the Establishment Clause. The school district argued that *Lee v. Weisman* was distinguishable, *i.e.*, private rather than public speech was involved here since students delivered the prayers.

The Court, per Justice Stevens, rejected this argument. The invocations were authorized by government policy and took place on government property at a government-sponsored school-related activity. A student election offers no protection to minority views. On the contrary, it places the minority student at the mercy of the majority. Given the past history of invocations at football games at this public high school, the present policy continues a policy of government endorsement of the selection of a religious message. Students will inevitably view the pre-game prayer as stamped with the "school's seal of approval." The school district also argued that *Lee v. Weisman* was distinguishable because here there was no government coercion. First, the prayer was the result of student rather than government choice and, second, attendance at football games was not mandatory. The Court rejected these contentions. The student choice rationale was rejected because the election mechanism encouraged divisiveness along religious lines. The attendance rationale was rejected because, for football players, cheerleaders and band members, attendance was not really voluntary since those activities received academic credit. The state may not force students to choose between facing a religious message which they did not wish to hear or not going to a football game. A government sponsored procedure which assigns "the nongovernmental subject of religion" to a majority vote without more fails a facial challenge based on the Establishment Clause. *Santa Fe Independent School District v. Doe* (2000).

A school district authorized its residents to use a school building after school hours for a variety of educational, recreational, artistic and general community uses and activities. The school district refused to allow the sponsors of a Christian club for children, the Good News Club, to use the public school facility after school. The sponsors sued the school district contending that the school district's policy violated their free speech rights. The school district, relying on the Establishment Clause, defended its refusal because the club did not propose a discussion of secular matters such as morals or character from a religious perspective but instead planned religious instruction on public school premises. But the Court held that from the perspective of the Free Speech Clause, it is irrelevant whether a club invokes Christianity and other clubs invoke teamwork, loyalty or patriotism. Each is concerned with moral and character instruction. *Lamb's Chapel* and *Rosenberger* held that subjects otherwise permissible are not rendered excludable from a limited public forum just because the subject is approached from a "religious viewpoint." The Court, per Justice Thomas, held that the school district's action constituted "impermissible viewpoint discrimination."

But is viewpoint discrimination justified in order to avoid an Establishment Clause violation? While avoiding an Establishment Clause violation may be categorized as a compelling interest, there was no need to address this issue. The school district had no valid Establishment Clause interest in this case. The club's activities were indistinguishable from the after school activities upheld in *Lamb's Chapel* and *Widmar*. Nor was it significant that the policy here affected elementary school children. The children are not coerced since they cannot attend after school activities without the permission of their parents. The school district will not be perceived as endorsing religion if the Good News Club like other clubs is allowed to use a public school facility after school. *Good News Club v. Milford Central School* (2001).

3. ESTABLISHMENT OUTSIDE THE SCHOOLS

While the educational forum has provided a fruitful source of church-state issues, Establishment Clause jurisprudence casts a broader shadow. When the state vests "substantial governmental powers" in religious institutions, excessive church-state entanglement is present. *Larkin v. Grendel's Den, Inc.* (1982) [law barring issuance of liquor license to facilities within 500 feet of a church or school if the church or school objects held unconstitutional]. The *Larkin* Court stressed that the law provided no assurance that the system would be used in a religiously neutral way and that it provided a "significant symbolic benefit to religion" by sharing state power with religious institutions.

A New York state law creating a state school district coterminous with a village populated by Satmar Hasidim, an Orthodox Jewish sect, violated the Establishment Clause since it allocated political power on the basis of a religious criterion. The separate public school district was set up just to run a special education program for handicapped children. The other village children went to parochial schools in the village. Although *Larkin* was a rare illustration of an impermissible attempt to unite civic and religious authority, the law creating the Kiryas Joel school district still resembled it. Here the delegation was of civic power to the qualified voters of the village rather than to a church parish council. But this was a distinction that made no constitutional difference. The state law defined a political subdivision in religious terms thus creating an invalid *Larkin*-type fusion of government and religious functions. It was not clear what the next religious group seeking a separate school district from the legislature would receive. Such special favored treatment on the basis of religion violated the Establishment Clause. *Board of Education of Kiryas Joel School District v. Grumet* (1994).

Sunday Closing Laws have long been upheld against Establishment Clause challenge. *McGowan v. Maryland* (1961). *McGowan* reasoned that the laws have a secular purpose and effect in promoting a common day of rest. See *Estate of Thornton v. Caldor, Inc.* (1985) [state law affording employee with an absolute unqualified right not to work on the Sabbath of their choice "has a primary effect that impermissibly advances a particular religious practice" violative of Establishment Clause]. The law in *Thornton* did not relieve the Sabbatarian from any government imposed obligation. Instead, "[t]he employer and others must adjust their affairs to the command of the State whenever the statute is invoked by an employee." However, when Congress in Title VII prohibited discrimination in employment but provided an exemption for religion, it was held that such an exemption does not violate the Establishment Clause because it is a "mere accommodation for religion." The *Lemon* analysis permits government to alleviate "significant governmental interference with their religious missions." *Corporation of Presiding Bishop of the*

Church of Jesus Christ of Latter–Day Saints v. Amos (1987).

Lynch v. Donnelly (1984), upheld, 5–4, a municipality's erection of a creche or Nativity scene as part of an annual Christmas display. For the majority, per Chief Justice Burger, the display served the secular purpose of celebrating the holiday and of depicting the origins of the holiday. Noting the frequent government recognition of religious holidays and events, the Court focused on the increasing secularization of Christmas. Further, the religious effects were no more egregious here than in many of the public aid programs approved by the Court. The Chief Justice concluded that any benefit to religion was "indirect, remote and incidental." The absence of any ongoing day-to-day interaction between church and state made any entanglement concerns *de minimis*. Fear of political divisiveness alone could not serve to invalidate otherwise permissible municipal conduct.

Placement of a Christmas creche on the Grand Staircase, the most public and most beautiful part of the Allegheny County Courthouse violates the Establishment Clause. However, the placement at the entrance to the City–County Building of an eighteen foot Chanukah menorah next to the City's Christmas tree and a sign celebrating liberty did not violate the Establishment Clause. *Allegheny County v. ACLU* (1989). Justice Blackmun explained for the Court the seemingly anomalous result in *Allegheny County*. The creche stood by itself with no other secular symbols of the holiday season.

The County thereby "sends an unmistakable message that it supports and promotes the Christian praise to God that is the creche religious message." The teaching of *Lynch* is that "government may celebrate Christmas in some manner and form, but not in a way that endorses Christian doctrine." The menorah display, on the other hand, was permissible under the Establishment Clause because its display along with the tree and the sign simply constitutes a recognition "that both Christmas and Chanukah are part of the same winter-holiday season." This season has achieved a secular status in American society. The menorah was not an endorsement of religion but rather a secular celebration of "cultural diversity."

When the Ku Klux Klan sought to erect a ten foot cross on a public square adjoining the state Capitol building in Columbus, Ohio, state officials relying on the Establishment Clause refused to permit them to do so. The lower federal courts ordered the granting of a permit to erect the cross. Earlier, permits had been granted for the display of a Christmas tree and a menorah. The display of the cross was private religious speech and entitled to the same protection under the Free Speech Clause accorded to private secular expression. The public square was a traditional public forum. Therefore, content-based regulation of it must be evaluated under the strict scrutiny standard. Although compliance with the Establishment Clause can sometimes be deemed a compelling government interest sufficient to justify a content-based regulation, that was not the case here. The state did not sponsor or endorse the Klan's expression. This private expression was undertaken on premises owned by the government that had been opened to the public for speech. The Supreme Court held that display of the cross did not constitute an impermissible endorsement of religion and did not violate the Establishment Clause. *Capitol Square Review Board v. Pinette* (1995).

The issue of the constitutionality of the display of religious messages or symbols on public property arose again in two cases involving the Ten Commandments. In one case, the executives of two Kentucky counties placed an abridgment of the King James Bible version of the Ten Commandments on the walls of the county courthouses. After the displays were challenged as violations of the Establishment Clause, the exhibits were twice enlarged by the addition of a number of other framed documents of equivalent size. Although the counties contended that the documents in the final displays comprised a secular effort to educate the citizenry on the foundations of American law and government, the Court, 5–4, per Justice Souter, held, using the *Lemon* test, that the displays violated the Establishment Clause. The secular purpose prong of the *Lemon* test served the important function of mandating government neutrality with respect to religion: "When the government acts with the ostensible and predominant purpose of advancing religion, it violates that central Establishment Clause value of official religious neutrality." Neutrality cannot exist when the purpose of government action "is to take sides." A governmental assertion of secular purpose is entitled to deference but courts still have the duty to separate a sincere secular purpose from a sham one. *Stone v. Graham, supra,* invalidating a display of the Ten Commandments in a public school setting, was controlling; the dispositive factor is the pre-eminent purpose of the government's conduct. The inquiry can not be limited to only the most recent post-litigation courthouse display of the Ten Commandments. A reasonable observer would perceive a religious message in the evolution of the displays. This was not to suggest, however, that every integration of a sacred text in a government display violated the constitution. But the obvious religious message proclaimed in these displays was impermissible. Justice Souter concluded by saying that the "divisiveness of religion in current public life is unescapable." This was hardly the time, therefore, to stray from the mandate of the Establishment Clause that government remain neutral where religious belief is concerned. Although joining in the opinion for the Court, Justice O'Connor who often takes an acccomodationist stance, concurring, warned that "line-drawing between religions" was impermissible: The Religion Clauses of the Constitution extended "to adherents of all religions as well as to those who believe in no religion at all." *McCreary County v. ACLU* (2005).

Justice Scalia, dissenting, castigated the unprincipled manipulability of the *Lemon* test. To make matters worse, he said *Lemon* had been altered by the majority in *McCreary* in two ways. First, governmental purpose was analyzed not "as an end in itself" but on the basis of how the government's conduct appeared to an observer. Second, the secular purpose requirement was heightened by yet an additional requirement that a secular purpose must predominate over any purpose to advance religion. Denying that "government practice can not favor religion," Justice Scalia pointed out that in the United States "97.7% of all believers" adhered to three monotheistic religions—Christianity, Judaism and Islam: "If religion in the public forum has to be entirely non-denominational, there could be no religion in the public forum at all." Such a result, he argued, was in defiance of history and in fact contrary to past precedent.

At the same time the Court decided that two Kentucky county courthouses could not display the Ten Commandments, the Court decided, 5–4, that a monument, 6–feet high and 3 and 1/2 half feet wide, inscribed with the Ten Commandments, which stood on the grounds of the Texas State Capitol did not violate the Establishment Clause. In a plurality opinion, Chief Justice Rehnquist, joined by Justices Scalia, Kennedy and Thomas, agreed that while government had to maintain separation between church and state, government could not undermine the very neutrality for which the Establishment Clause stands by exhibiting a hostility to religion. The plurality declined to apply *Lemon* to evaluate the "passive [Ten Commandments] monument" on the Texas State Capitol grounds. Of course, the Ten

Commandments had religious significance but that did not invalidate every public display of the Ten Commandments: "Simply having a religious content or promoting a message consistent with a religious doctrine does nor run afoul of the Establishment Clause." *Stone v. Graham* was distinguished as a far less passive display than was the case in *Stone* where the Ten Commandments "confronted elementary students every day."

Justice Breyer, concurring in the judgment but not in the plurality opinion, declared that the Texas Ten Commandments monument conveyed a secular as well as a religious message and that the nonreligious element pre-dominated. There was nothing sacred about the siting of the Texas monument. Set in a large park of 17 monuments and 21 historical markers, these park displays were designed to celebrate the ideals of those who settled Texas and live in it now. This case was unlike the Kentucky courthouse displays whose short history disclosed "a governmental effort substantially to promote religion, not simply an effort to reflect historically, the secular impact of a religiously inspired document." The Texas Ten Commandments monument here had been unchallenged for 40 years. A contrary holding might encourage the very religious divisiveness that the Establishment Clause exists to prevent, particularly given the controversy that would arise from the removal of Ten Commandment displays from the many public buildings across the country where they are displayed. *Van Orden v. Perry* (2005).

Justices Ginsburg, O'Connor, Souter and Stevens dissented in *Van Orden*. Justice Stevens dissenting, contended that the Texas monument offended the central theme of the Establishment Clause——the neutrality principle. The Establishment Clause does not simply prohibit discrimination by government among religious sects. That Clause also prohibits "the aggregation of several orthodoxies under the state's banner." Justice Souter, dissenting, argued that *Stone* in fact was in point. Texas had displayed the Ten Commandments on the State Capitol grounds so that the citizens would see them just as the public school had impermissibly done with respect to the school children in *Stone*. In sum, separationists prevailed in *McCreary* and accomodationists in *Van Orden*. Yet the critical vote in each case was that of Justice Breyer and his analysis was so fact-specific as to give neither position a decisive edge.

Another non-academic context in which the meaning of the Establishment Clause has arisen involves the tax liability of religious organizations. Does the grant of an exemption violate the Establishment Clause? *Walz v. Tax Com'n of New York* (1970) held that a property tax exemption for places of religious worship did not violate the Establishment Clause given the historical acceptance of such exemptions. But *Texas Monthly v. Bullock* (1989) held that where a state grants exemptions from sales and use taxes only to religious periodicals, such exemptions violate the Establishment Clause. These exemptions constitute an impermissible endorsement of religious beliefs. Such an exclusive subsidy to religion lacks both the requisite secular purpose or the primary secular effect.

On the other hand, *Hernandez v. Commissioner of Internal Revenue* (1989) held that a refusal by the IRS to recognize as charitable contributions payments made by members of the Church of Scientology to that Church did not violate the Establishment Clause. The charitable contributions provisions of the Internal Revenue Code made no explicit distinction between religious and non-religious organizations. Since the provision applied to all religious entities, there was no impermissible denominational preference.

Similarly, a state sales and use tax applied to a religious organization selling religious materials in the state did not violate the Establishment Clause. Using the *Lemon* test, it was held that the tax was generally applicable and was neutral and nondiscriminatory with respect to matters of religious belief. Moreover, there was no excessive governmental entanglement either. Since the state sales and use tax was imposed without an exemption for religious organizations, the state was not required to look into the religious content of the materials sold but only with the question of whether there had been a sale or use. *Jimmy Swaggart Ministries v. Board of Equalization* (1990).

Another example of allowing for "play in the joints" between the Free Exercise Clause and the

Establishment Clause arose with regard to a challenge to a section of the Religious Land Use and Institutionalized Persons Act of 2000 which provides: "No government shall impose a substantial burden on the religious exercise of a person residing in or confined to an institution" unless the burden furthers "a compelling governmental interest," and does so by "the least restrictive means." A unanimous Court, per Justice Ginsburg, rejected a contention that the provision violated the Establishment Clause. Since institutionalized persons experience unusual government-created burdens on their private religious exercise and are dependent on government permission and accommodation to practice their religion, the law at issue simply takes account of the burdens a requested accommodation imposes on nonbeneficiaries. The Court declared that the law did not "elevate accommodation of religious observances over an institution's need to maintain order and safety." Prison officials in Ohio had objected that the law would result in subordinating prison administration to the wishes of religious practitioners celebrating Satan or white supremacy. Responding to these objections, the Court stated that if inmate requests for religious accommodation were excessive or unjustified in terms of the burdens they placed on other prisoners or prison administration and security, such accommodations could be challenged on an as-applied basis. *Cutter v. Wilkinson* (2005).

B. FREE EXERCISE OF RELIGION

Coercion of religious beliefs or conduct is the essence of a claim under the Free Exercise Clause. "The freedom to hold religious beliefs and opinions is absolute." *Braunfeld v. Brown* (1961). See *Torcaso v. Watkins* (1961) [test oath requiring profession of a belief in God for public employment held violative of free exercise]. See U.S. Const., Art. VI, proscribing use of religious tests for federal employment. When an individual is required to engage in conduct which violates his religious beliefs or opinions, he may seek refuge in the First Amendment. *West Virginia State Bd. of Educ. v. Barnette* (1943), involved a Jehovah's Witness' challenge to a law requiring him to salute the flag—a practice which he believed violated the Scriptures. In striking down the law, the Court declared that government may not prescribe what shall be orthodox in politics, nationalism, religion or other matters of opinion.

While the Court initially indicated that government could regulate religious conduct without any Free Exercise Clause constraints [*Reynolds v. United States* (1878), federal law criminalizing bigamy held constitutional], this view was quickly abandoned. Freedom to believe would be a hollow right without freedom to act pursuant to that belief. Prior to *Employment Division v. Smith* (1990), *infra*. Even religiously-neutral laws which significantly burdened religious practices had to satisfy the demands of the Free Exercise Clause. *Cantwell v.*

Connecticut (1940) [conviction for religious soliciting without a license reversed]. *Smith* declared that exemptions to accommodate religion were for the legislature not the judiciary.

Does the First Amendment require government to grant exemptions from religiously-neutral laws because conformity to the law burdens religious practices? *Cantwell* stated that while the freedom to believe is absolute, freedom to act pursuant to one's religion cannot be. "Conduct remains subject to regulation for the protection of society." Further, the grant of a religious exemption raises Establishment Clause problems—such an exemption would be granted for the purpose of aiding a particular religion.

In attempting to define standards for determining what accommodation to religion is required by the Free Exercise Clause, the Court has sometimes distinguished between direct and indirect burdens on religion. Direct burdens, *e.g.*, laws which make a religious practice unlawful, impose an especially severe burden on freedom of religion. In *Braunfeld v. Brown* (1961), in upholding Sunday Closing laws against free exercise attack, the Court distinguished laws imposing direct burdens from laws which only indirectly burden religious practices. Since the closing law imposed only an economic burden on Orthodox Jewish merchants who closed on Saturdays for religious reasons, the burden was indirect. Such a burden is constitutional, "unless the State may accomplish its [secular] purpose by means which do not impose such a burden." Granting an exemption to Sabbatarians, the Court concluded, could have undermined the States religiously-neutral purpose of promoting a uniform day of rest.

But the judicial deference manifested in *Braunfeld* to laws imposing only indirect burdens on religious practices was lost in *Sherbert v. Verner* (1963). The Court, per Justice Brennan, who had dissented in *Braunfeld,* struck down the denial of state unemployment benefits to a Seventh Day Adventist for refusing to work on Saturday, the Sabbath day of her faith. While the burden on her religion was admittedly indirect, the coercive effect of the law imposed a significant burden, a penalty, on her religious liberty: "The ruling forces her to choose between following the precepts of her religion and forfeiting benefits on the one hand, and abandoning one of the precepts of her religion in order to accept work, on the other." Government imposition of such a choice could be justified only by showing a "compelling state interest" and "that no alternative form of regulation" would suffice. The State failed to meet this burden. For Justice Brennan, this accommodation was not violative of establishment principles but only an effort to maintain neutrality between Sunday and Saturday Sabbatarians.

Sherbert was deemed controlling in *Thomas v. Review Board of the Indiana Employment Sec. Div.* (1981). The Court, per Chief Justice Burger, overturned Indiana's denial of unemployment benefits to a Jehovah's Witness who left his job producing armaments because of a sincere belief that such work violated his religion. The fact that other Jehovah's Witnesses continued to work did not defeat the free exercise claim. Thomas was coerced in his religious beliefs and that constituted a substantial burden, albeit indirect, in the free exercise of his religion. The state failed to show that it had used "the least restrictive means of achieving some compelling state interest."

A denial of state unemployment compensation benefits to a Seventh–Day Adventist who was fired by her private employer for refusing to work on Friday evenings and Saturdays violated the Free Exercise Clause. No compelling state interest was served by placing pressure on the claimant to modify her behavior and to violate her religious beliefs. It did not matter that the claimant converted to the Seventh Day Adventist faith after she commenced her employment. *Hobbie v. Unemployment Appeals Compensation Commission of Florida* (1987). However, where the government chose to use numbers in administering its social security system, a free exercise challenge based on religious opposition to the use of a social security number failed to demonstrate a significant burden on free exercise. Religious belief does not entitle a claimant to dictate the internal processes of government. *Bowen v. Roy* (1986) But where a Christian who did not belong to any specific Christian denomination was denied unemployment compensation benefits because he refused to take a job which would entail working on Sunday, eligibility for those benefits could not be conditioned on requiring him to violate his beliefs. Absent a compelling state interest an individual in such circumstances could not be forced to choose between his faith and state unemployment benefits. *Frazee v. Illinois Department of Employment Security* (1989).

However, benefits can be denied if denial is the incidental effect of a generally applicable and otherwise valid criminal law. Strict scrutiny would not be used in such circumstances. Where the general criminal law has the consequence of prohibiting a religious practice, imposing the lesser burden of denying of unemployment compensation benefits to persons violating the criminal law is constitutional. *Employment Division v. Smith* (1988) (*Smith I*).

While indirect burdens on religion are sufficient to invoke strict scrutiny review, laws which compel an individual "to perform acts undeniably at odds with fundamental tenets of their religious beliefs" (*i.e.,* direct burdens) are especially coercive of religious liberty. *Wisconsin v. Yoder* (1972). In *Yoder,* the Court invalidated application of Wisconsin's law requiring compulsory school attendance until age 16 to Amish children. The Amish refused to send their children to public schools beyond the eighth grade, based on their "deep religious convictions" about the way to live. "Only those interests of the highest order and those not otherwise served can overbalance legitimate claims to the free exercise of religion." *Braunfeld* had concluded that an exception would undermine the state's interest in a uniform day of rest. But in the case of the Amish in *Yoder,* the state's interests in promoting self-reliant and self-sufficient participants in society were not undermined by an exemption for the Amish. Most Amish children stayed in the community and were well-suited for life in their society. The state interest in including the Amish under the law was not sufficiently overriding to justify the significant burden on religious liberty.

Finding of a significant burden on religious liberty does not invariably result in invalidation of the law. *United States v. Lee* (1982), upheld the federal government's refusal to exempt an Amish employer from participating in the social security system. While accepting that the law significantly burdened a sincerely held religious belief, the government met its burden of demonstrating that denial of the exemption was "essential to accomplish an overriding governmental interest." Mandatory and continuous participation in the social security system is vital to the integrity of the system and "it would be difficult to accommodate the comprehensive social security system with myriad exceptions flowing from a wide variety of religious beliefs." Further, it would be hard to cabin such an exception to social security: "[t]he tax system could not function if denominations were allowed to challenge the tax system because tax payments were spent in a manner that violates their religious beliefs." See *Tony & Susan Alamo Found. v. Secretary of Labor* (1985) [application of Fair Labor Standards Act to commercial activities of nonprofit religious organization and employees receiving no cash salaries held not to involve a significant burden on free exercise or to violate Establishment Clause]. The Free Exercise

Clause requires an exemption from a government program only if the mandates of the program actually burdened the complainant's free exercise rights. The Fair Labor Standards Act did not require the workers in *Alamo* to accept wages nor did it prevent them from returning those wages to their religious organization. Similarly, a state sales and use tax on religious materials did not violate the Free Exercise Clause. The religious beliefs of the individuals involved did not forbid them from paying the tax. The state is not required to provide an exemption for a religious organization to a generally applicable tax when there is no significant burden imposed by the state on their free exercise rights. *Jimmy Swaggart Ministries v. Board of Equalization* (1990).

The foregoing cases have used a two step approach that dates back to Sabbatarian cases like *Sherbert v. Verner* in the 1960's. This approach makes two inquiries. First, it measures the severity of the burden the law places on the individual's free exercise. If that burden is a significant one, then the government must show that the law is narrowly tailored to achieve a compelling state interest. The less burdensome alternatives or less restrictive means test, often used in the free expression context, will be applied. The question then posed is this—Could the state's interest be accomplished by less burdensome means? In practice, the use of this test has sometimes meant that this strict scrutiny standard of review exempted individuals making a free exercise claim from compliance even with laws that are religiously neutral. This result has obtained because once this two step test is applied the effect of the law at issue has been deemed to significantly burden an individual's free exercise of religion. However, this doctrinal approach has undergone major change. In *Lyng v. Northwest Indian Cemetery Protective Association* (1988) and *Employment Division v. Smith* (1990) (*Smith II*), the Court held that the strict scrutiny approach just described did not apply to a generally applicable and otherwise valid law. This conclusion was reached despite the fact that application to the law in question in both cases incidentally imposed a substantial burden on free exercise. It was feared that these cases were the harbingers of a radical doctrinal change which would no longer use a strict scrutiny standard of review for religiously neutral laws having only an incidentally burdensome effect on free exercise.

When the federal government allowed timber harvesting and road construction in a national forest which had been used for religious purposes by Indian tribes, a free exercise challenge of the government action was rejected. The effect of the governmental action was incidental in nature. Even though the consequences of the governmental action might destroy the religious practice, such "indirect coercion or penalties" on free exercise did not invoke the use of a strict scrutiny standard. The government after all owned the land and had not directly prohibited any specific Indian religious practice. *Lyng v. Northwest Indian Cemetery Protective Association* (1988).

A state may validly deny unemployment compensation to Indian workers who were fired from their jobs because of work-related misconduct resulting from the use of the drug peyote while participating in the rites of the Native American Church. Such denial does not infringe on free exercise. Under Oregon law use of the drug peyote was a criminal violation and the Oregon unemployment compensation law forbade the payment of benefits for work-related misconduct. These laws were religiously neutral and, therefore, presumptively valid. A free exercise claim does not free an individual from compliance with a generally applicable religiously neutral criminal law which is otherwise valid. Strict scrutiny is not triggered when a free exercise challenge is directed to a generally applicable criminal prohibition. This result is not altered even if the religious practice the free exercise claim is designed to protect is central to the religious faith of which the complainant is a member. It is inappropriate for courts to investigate whether a particular religious practice is or is not central to a religious faith. Furthermore, use of strict scrutiny in this context would invite requests for the creation of "constitutionally required religious exemptions from civic obligation of almost every conceivable kind." Moreover, exemptions from legislation based on a desire to accommodate religion is a more appropriate task for the legislature than for the judiciary. *Employment Division v. Smith* (1990) (*Smith II*). The doctrinal approach of *Lyng* and *Smith II* means that incidental burdens on free exercise would be insufficient to trigger the strict scrutiny standard. Thus, the conclusion that the burden was incidental would be dispositive of the free exercise claim.

In the Religious Freedom Restoration Act of 1993 (RFRA), Congress sought to undo the holding in *Smith II* by restoring the use of the compelling governmental interest test, as set forth in *Sherbert* and *Yoder*, in cases presenting a substantial burden to the free exercise of religion. RFRA provides that government is precluded from imposing substantial burdens on free exercise even if they result from laws of general applicability unless such laws further a compelling governmental interest and are the least restrictive means of accomplishing that interest. In *City of Boerne v. Flores* (1997), the Court held RFRA to be an unconstitutional exercise of congressional power under Section 5 of the Fourteenth Amendment because of its inconsistency with *Smith II*. See, *infra*, Ch.10. Justice O'Connor, dissenting, contended that *Smith II* was wrong since it was supported "neither by precedent nor history." Justice Scalia, concurring, said the issue was whether the Court or Congress would control the outcome of concrete cases.

Not all substantial burdens on free exercise will escape invalidation even if the laws of general applicability approach of *Smith II* endures. It would still be open to show that a law was not a law of general applicability. Thus municipal ordinances which prohibited animal sacrifice but exempted non-religious animal slaughtering were held to violate the Free Exercise Clause. The ban against animal sacrifice could not be placed under the rubric of a law of general applicability because of the municipality's interest in promoting and preventing animal cruelty and protecting public health. Although these were secular objectives, they were "pursued only with respect to conduct motivated by religious beliefs." The challenged ordinances were not neutral and were aimed at the Santeria religion which practices animal sacrifice. The ordinances were invalid since they directly burdened religion. Applying strict scrutiny, it was clear—given the exemptions afforded to non-Santerian animal practices—that the municipal ordinances at issue were not narrowly tailored to serve a compelling governmental interest. *Church of the Lukumi Babalu Aye, Inc. v. Hialeah* (1993).

There is "room for play in the joints" between the Free Exercise Clause and the Establishment Clause. Some actions by the state are permitted by the Establishment Clause yet they are not required by the Free Exercise Clause. An example is seen in the Court's treatment of the Washington state Promise Scholarship Program to assist academically gifted students with post-secondary education expenses. In accordance with the state constitution, the Program precluded the use of these scholarship for degrees in devotional theology. A recipient of one of the Scholarships who sought to use it to study theology contended that the state restriction on use of the scholarship violated his free exercise rights under the federal constitution. Relying on *Church of the Lukumi Babalu Aye, Inc. v. Hialeah,* the student contended that the program was not only not facially neutral, it targeted religion. The Court, per Chief Justice Rehnquist, disagreed and ruled that the Promise Program did not violate the student's free exercise rights. While it was true that the federal Constitution would permit the use of state funds to study devotional theology, the Washington state law did not violate the Free Exercise Clause. *Lukumi* was not to the contrary; that case dealt with a law which specifically sought to prohibit a practice of the Santeria religion. This law imposed neither criminal nor civil sanction on any religious exercise. The state of Washington had merely decided not to fund a particular category of educational endeavor. *Locke v. Davey* (2004).

A fundamental problem runs throughout the field of freedom of religion: what *is* a religion? The Court has not directly answered this question. It has, however, indicated that non-theistic beliefs can qualify for constitutional protection. *Torcaso; United States v. Seeger* (1965) [conscientious objector status available to person having a sincere, meaningful belief which "occupies a place in the life of its possessor parallel to that filled by the orthodox belief in God"]. See *Welsh v. United States* (1970) [Court plurality extends C.O. status to those having strong moral or even public policy objections]. On the other hand, the Court rejected conscientious objector status for those objecting to a particular war. *Gillette v. United States* (1971). *Wisconsin v. Yoder* stressed that a person is not allowed to convert his own personal standards on matters of conduct into a religious belief requiring constitutional protection. The Amish claim, by contrast, was said to reflect "deep religious conviction, shared by an organized group, and intimately related to daily living." Yet a free exercise claim will be upheld even where the claimant is not a member of organized religion or any particular sect. All that is required is a sincerely held "religious belief." *Frazee v. Illinois Department of Employment Security* (1989). While commentators frequently suggest that religion should be given a broader definition in Free Exercise cases, the question of what constitutes a religion remains open.

In the past the two-step approach worked as follows. First, it was necessary to determine if the law significantly burdened the free exercise of religion. Then the Court had to consider the extent to which the belief was sincerely held [*Thomas*] and the importance of the practice or belief (*i.e.,* centrality) in the religion [*Yoder*]. But it declined to consider the truth or falsity of the belief or doctrine [*United States v. Ballard* (1944)] or choose between doctrinal viewpoints within a religion [*Thomas*]. See *Jones v. Wolf* (1979) [state court may decide property disputes between contending church groups if it does not require an inquiry into religious doctrine]. However, in *Employment Division v. Smith* (1990) the Court observed that it is "no more appropriate for judges to determine the 'centrality' of religious belief before applying a 'compelling interest' test in the free exercise field than it would be for them to determine the 'importance' of an idea before applying the 'compelling interest' test in the free speech field." These observations raise the question whether the inquiry into centrality in the free exercise field will soon be eliminated altogether.

Second, in the past, if religious liberty was significantly burdened then the government could justify its denial of an exemption only if it could demonstrate that comprehensive coverage was essential to achieve an overriding or compelling government interest. But see *Goldman v. Weinberger* (1986) [application of Air Force dress codes "reasonably and evenhandedly" to prevent Orthodox Jew from wearing a yarmulke as required by his religion held constitutional, citing "far more deferential" standard of review in military cases]. Apparently the Establishment Clause and the demand for government neutrality is not violated when the Free Exercise Clause does mandate the religious accommodation. *Lyng* and *Smith II*, however, do not require the state to meet a compelling state interest standard where the free exercise challenge was directed to a valid, generally applicable, religiously neutral law which only imposed an incidental burden on the free exercise of religion.

CHAPTER IX

STATE ACTION

A. INTRODUCTION

With the exception of the Thirteenth Amendment, the guarantees of the Constitution run only against the national and state governments. Absent congressional legislation extending these rights to private conduct, "state action" is required. In part, this demand for governmental involvement to make the constitutional protections work is a matter of constitutional language, *e.g.,* the First and Fourteenth Amendments specifically refer to government wrongs. But the state action doctrine also reflects the nature of the Constitution as organic law. It defines the relation of persons and citizens to their government rather than to each other. Further, the requirement of state action is perceived by many as a vital protection for personal liberty, limiting governmental interference with freedom of action and association, including the ability to freely use one's own property. Finally, the state action doctrine is argued by some to further the values of federalism by forcing recourse to state rather than federal law.

Problems arise, however, in defining when seemingly private action is truly private. Privately owned corporations today often exercise power over persons comparable to that of government agencies and much of that private power is attributable to benefits provided by government. Government may be "significantly intertwined" with nominally private individuals, groups, clubs, and associations; their conduct may be authorized or so encouraged by official action as to make the label "private action" inappropriate. Some functions these groups perform may be so public in character that the activity remains essentially governmental even when performed by a private actor. In such cases, the question arises whether the private conduct should be treated as "state action."

B. FRAMING THE STATE ACTION DOCTRINE

In the *Civil Rights Cases* (1883), the Court, per Justice Bradley, held the Civil Rights Act of 1875, proscribing racial discrimination in places of public accommodation, unconstitutional. Since the case was decided well before the commerce power reached its present expansive proportions, and since the Act was not limited to interstate commerce, the Court examined whether the enforcement clauses of the Thirteenth and Fourteenth Amendments gave Congress power to enact the law. Justice Bradley began from the premise that Sec. 1 of the Fourteenth Amendment prohibited only state action: "Individual invasion of individual rights is not the subject matter of the Amendment." What then was the scope of congressional power under Sec. 5 of the Amendment? Simply, to enforce the limited prohibition against state action: "To adopt appropriate legislation for correcting the effects of such prohibited state laws and statutes, and thus to render them effectually null, void and innocuous." The power was strictly corrective or remedial, *i.e.*, to provide remedies for what the courts determined to be substantive rights but not to define the substantive rights themselves. Congressional power was limited to correcting government misconduct. Concern for personal liberty and for federalism motivated the Court. To extend the guarantees of the Amendment further would be to allow Congress "to establish a code of municipal law regulative of all private rights between man and man in society. It would be to make Congress take the place of the state legislatures and to supersede them." Private wrongs, "not sanctioned in some way by the state, or done under state authority" should be vindicated by state law. Since the 1875 law operated directly on private actions and itself defined what was the substantive wrong, it was beyond Congress's legislative power.

For the first Justice Harlan, dissenting, the 1875 law was a valid enforcement of the Citizenship Clause set forth in the first sentence of the Fourteenth Amendment, which was "of a distinctly affirmative character." The citizenship thus conferred on Blacks by this affirmative grant, he argued, could be protected by congressional legislation "of a primary direct character." Section 5 of the Fourteenth Amendment gave Congress the power to enforce both the prohibitive and the affirmative provisions of the Amendment. What did the grant of citizenship include? It included, at least, "exemption from race discrimination in respect of any civil right belonging to citizens of the white race in the same state." The Amendment was designed to protect these privileges and immunities not only from unfriendly state legislation, but also from the hostile action of corporations and individuals. Alternatively, Justice Harlan argued that the owners of places of public accommodation are "agents of the state, because amenable, in respect of public duties and functions, to public regulation." Since the rights recognized in the 1875 Act were legal, not social rights, the Act was a valid exercise of Congress's Fourteenth Amendment power.

The Court in the *Civil Rights Cases* also rejected the claims that the Act was constitutional under the Thirteenth Amendment. Justice Bradley did accept that Sec. 1 of that Amendment abolished slavery, "established universal freedom," and was self-executing against private misconduct. Congress pursuant to Sec. 2 of the Amendment could enact "primary and direct" legislation "abolishing all badges and incidents of slavery in the United States." But these expansive premises were then undercut by the conclusion that an act of racial discrimination at a place of public accommodation "has nothing to do with slavery or involuntary servitude, and that if it is violative of any right of the party, his redress is to be sought under the laws of the State." The Court rejected the premise that Sec. 1 of the Thirteenth Amendment was violated. Again, Justice Harlan's dissent directly took issue with the Court. The Thirteenth Amendment, he asserted, was designed to protect the former slave "against the deprivation, on account of their race, of any civil rights enjoyed by other freemen in the same state." Congress correctly determined that racial discrimination by corporations and individuals in the exercise of their public or quasi-public functions, constitute a "badge of servitude"—the Act was a constitutional exercise of Congress' power under Sec. 2 to enforce the Thirteenth Amendment guarantee.

Had Justice Harlan's approach to the meaning of the Civil War Amendments been accepted, much of the confused history of the state action doctrine might have been avoided. Similarly, if the Court had been willing to accept the argument that state failure to protect the Thirteenth or Fourteenth Amendments was itself a wrong (*i.e.,* the amendments impose an affirmative duty on the states), correctable by congressional legislation, constitutional protection against a broader range of conduct might have become available. But the Court in the *Civil Rights Cases* forged a far more limited doctrine for bringing the constitutional guarantee into play. While much of the impediment to federal protection fashioned in the case has been eroded (especially that pertaining to congressional enforcement), its essential principle that, apart from the Thirteenth Amendment, governmental action is necessary to implicate constitutional rights, remains a formidable obstacle to a party seeking to claim constitutional protection against nominally private action.

C. FINDING STATE ACTION

The continuing vitality of the state action doctrine forged in the *Civil Rights Cases* has produced a mass of confusing litigation designed to avoid its strictures. It is clear that the acts of officials, federal or state, even if the acts violate the law, constitute "state action." Further, the term covers the action of all governmental subdivisions and agencies. Or, if government officials participate in the management or administration of an enterprise, the government is responsible for its activities. Indeed, even though Congress stated in its governing legislation that Amtrak was not a government agency, the judiciary is not bound by that determination. When government creates a corporation like Amtrak and reserves for itself the permanent authority to appoint a majority of its directors, such an entity is a public actor. Therefore, when Amtrak refused to let an artist display his billboard in New York City's Penn station, that decision is subject to judicial review to ascertain whether it violated the First Amendment. *Lebron v. National Railroad Passenger Corp.* (1995).

But state involvement is usually far more indirect and unclear than in these official misconduct cases. When *can* private action qualify as state action?

This is the critical question in state action cases. During the Warren Court years, the Court seemed so willing to find state action in nominally private conduct that commentators began to speak of the twilight of the state action doctrine. It seemed as if the doctrine was being merged into the issue of whether the right was violated rather than serving as a threshold issue of whether the constitutional right was even implicated. But with the coming of the Burger Court, the state action doctrine has been restored—and with a vengeance. Generally today, the state action cases resolve into three questions: (1) whether an activity is a "public function;" (2) whether the government is so significantly involved with the private actor as to make the government responsible for the private conduct; (3) whether the government may be said to have approved or authorized (or perhaps, significantly encouraged) the challenged conduct sufficiently to be responsible for it.

1. PUBLIC FUNCTIONS

The Court has never accepted the argument that the Fourteenth Amendment imposes affirmative duties on the state so that government failure to use its regulatory power to protect the guaranteed rights constitutes state action. However, the Court has accepted the proposition that a function may be so governmental in character that the state may not disclaim responsibility for its performance—the state's failure to act where it has a duty to prevent the wrong becomes a form of action.

When electoral processes such as primaries are performed by private political parties, the group's actions constitute state action under the Fourteenth and Fifteenth Amendments. *Smith v. Allwright* (1944); *Terry v. Adams* (1953) [primaries conducted in a racially discriminatory manner]. Whether the actions of political parties always constitute state action has not been decided but does seem unlikely. When privately-owned property has taken on the essential characteristics of a municipality, *e.g.,* company towns, state action is present. *Marsh v. Alabama* (1946) [use of trespass laws to prevent distribution of religious literature]. While it seemed that shopping centers might also come under this "public function" principle [*Amalgamated Food Employers Union Local 590 v. Logan Valley Plaza, Inc.* (1968), informational picketing related to activities at the shopping center constitutionally protected], later cases first circumscribed [*Lloyd Corp. v. Tanner* (1972), hand billing unrelated to shopping center activities held not protected] and then rejected the view that a privately owned shopping center is "the functional equivalent of a municipality." *Hudgens v. N.L.R.B.* (1976) [*Logan Valley* overruled; distinction based on whether the speech was related to shopping center activities would be an impermissible discrimination based on speech content]. In short, only when privately owned property is the "functional equivalent" of a municipality is there state action.

The difficulty of the public function approach is demonstrated not only by the shopping center cases but also by *Evans v. Newton* (1966). *Evans* held that racial discrimination at a park managed by private trustees violated the Fourteenth Amendment. Justice Douglas, for the Court, described the case as requiring the reconciliation of "the right of the individual to pick his own associates" and "to fashion his private life" with the constitutional ban "against state-sponsored racial inequality." While Justice Douglas might have rested the Court's decision that the government was responsible solely on the finding that the municipality remained "entwined in the management or control of the park," *i.e.,* public administration, he also relied on the public function approach, reasoning that "the service rendered even by a private park of this character is municipal in nature." Analogizing the services provided by a park to those of a fire or police department, Justice Douglas concluded that "the predominant character of the park is municipal."

While the Court continues to accept the public function theory of state action, its doctrinal scope has been severely restricted. Presently, the public function theory is limited solely to functions which are "traditionally exclusively reserved to the State." Applying this restrictive standard, the Court refused to find state action in the running of a privately-owned public utility. *Jackson v. Metropolitan Edison Co.* (1974) [the state is not obligated to furnish utility services; supplying utility service "is not traditionally the exclusive prerogative of the State"]. Nor does state approval of the sale of stored goods pursuant to a warehouseman's lien as a means of resolving a dispute delegate "an exclusive prerogative of the sovereign," given the variety of remedies available to the debtor. *Flagg Bros., Inc. v. Brooks* (1978). And the operation of a private school for maladjusted high school students is not state action for purposes of an action by a teacher challenging the constitutionality of the school's decision to discharge him. The education of the maladjusted is not the exclusive province of the state. *Rendell–Baker v. Kohn* (1982). Nor is the state responsible for decisions regarding the transfer or discharge of patients at a privately-operated nursing home. Even if the state had been obligated under its laws to provide nursing care (which it was not), "it would not follow that decisions made in the day-to-day administration of a nursing home are the kind of decisions traditionally and exclusively made by the sovereign for and on behalf of the public." *Blum v. Yaretsky* (1982).

2.   SIGNIFICANT INVOLVEMENT/JOINT PARTICIPATION

Another approach to finding state action is to look to the nature of the relationship between government and the nominally private actor. In *Burton v. Wilmington Parking Auth.* (1961), the Warren Court was asked to determine this question: Is a city constitutionally responsible for racial discrimination practiced by a privately-owned restaurant which rented space in its municipal parking garage? Justice Clark, for the Court, answered this question in the affirmative. He cited the public ownership of the facility, the financing of its operations through municipal obligations, its public upkeep and maintenance and, referring to a factor that was to assume critical future importance, he noted the "mutual benefits" derived from the operation. The public might patronize the restaurant because they had a place to park; they might park at the garage in order to dine at the restaurant: "The state has so far insinuated itself into a position of interdependence with [the restaurant] that it must be recognized as a joint participant in the challenged activity." The aggregate of all of the contacts between the state and the restaurant provided the basis for finding state action: "Addition of all these activities, obligations and responsibilities of the Authority, the benefits mutually conferred indicates that degree of state participation and involvement in discriminatory action which it was the design of the Fourteenth Amendment to condemn." While *Burton* suggested an expansive approach to the state action doctrine, subsequent cases have not fulfilled the promise. Instead of aggregating all of the State's contacts with the private actor, the Court has tended to treat each contact seriatim. Further, the Court has demanded that the State be a partner or joint venturer in the challenged activity. Finally, the Court has increasingly focused on the state's relationship to the particular conduct being challenged (*i.e.,* a "nexus" between the state and the challenged act is required).

The fact that the state licenses and pervasively regulates the private actor is insufficient for a finding of state action. *Moose Lodge No. 107 v. Irvis* (1972) [racial discrimination in services by a private club held not to involve the "symbiotic relationship" found in *Burton*]. The fact that government financial support is critical to the existence of a private entity does not make the state responsible for its actions. Thus, in *Blum v. Yaretsky* (1982), the Court stated: "That programs undertaken by the state result in substantial funding of the activities of a private entity is no more persuasive than the fact of regulation of such an entity in demonstrating that the state is responsible for decisions made by the entity in the course of its business." In *Blum,* the Court held that state subsidization of the operating costs of a nursing home and the financing of the medical expenses of 90% of its patients did not make the state responsible for the institution's decisions regarding the transfer or discharge of patients. And, in *Rendell–Baker v. Kohn* (1982), the fact that over 90% of the operating expenses of a private high school for maladjusted students was paid by government did not make the state responsible for the decision of the school to discharge teachers. Bear in mind, however, that there are some earlier decisions, involving state assistance to racially segregated private schools, that were based on a lower threshold of state responsibility. See *Norwood v. Harrison* (1973) [state financial support available to racially segregated schools for the purchase of textbooks constitutes state action]; *Gilmore v. Montgomery* (1974) [city under desegregation order held to violate equal protection by permitting exclusive use, even on a temporary basis, of recreational facilities by segregated private schools]. These decisions may be explainable as reflecting a more stringent Court attitude towards racial discrimination or as simply as a product of an earlier, more lenient attitude towards the state action mandate.

3. ENCOURAGEMENT, AUTHORIZATION AND APPROVAL

A state is also responsible for private action when it has "exercised coercive power" over the challenged action or "has provided such significant encouragement, either overt or covert, that the choice must in law be deemed that of the state." *Blum v. Yaretsky* (1982). Again, the student should be aware of the tightening of the state action mandate under the Burger Court. Often, "encouragement" of private action gives way to a requirement that the state "command" the particular decision or action being challenged.

The Court's decision in *Shelley v. Kraemer* (1948), suggested to some commentators that any state enforcement of private racial discrimination would constitute state action. *Shelley* involved the question whether state court enforcement of a racially discriminatory restrictive covenant in a deed constituted state action. The Court, per Chief Justice Vinson, held that while the private restrictive covenant itself would not violate the Fourteenth Amendment, court enforcement of the agreement did violate the Constitution. But it is important to note that the effect of the state court action in *Shelley* was to force willing white sellers to racially discriminate against willing Black buyers. Thus, the state was making available "the full coercive power of government to deny to [Black buyers], on the grounds of race or color, the enjoyment of property rights in premises which [Black buyers] are willing and financially able to acquire and which the [white sellers] are willing to sell." By invoking its common law policy to aid the covenantors in preventing the sale, the state had used its coercive powers to enforce racial discrimination.

State action is present, then, when government forces unwilling parties to racially discriminate. On the other hand, neutral state enforcement of its laws in a way that does not force or coerce persons to discriminate does not constitute state action. The fact that enforcement of the laws may aid a person seeking to racially discriminate is unlikely, without more, to constitute state action. Thus in *Evans v. Abney* (1970), a state's application of its trust laws to allow a testamentary grant of land to revert to the estate when the terms of the bequest (*i.e.,* that the land be used as a park "for whites only") could not be implemented, was not unconstitutional state action.

But when government actively "significantly encourages" private racial discrimination, the Court has, at least in the past, found the requisite state action. In the sit-in cases of the 1960s, actions by city officials instigating private restaurant owners to refuse service to Blacks made the state responsible for the discrimination. *Lombard v. Louisiana* (1963). And, in *Reitman v. Mulkey* (1967), the high point of this "encouragement approach" to state action, the Court held 5–4 that a referendum amendment (Proposition 14) of the California Constitution prohibiting governmental interference with a person's right to racially discriminate in the sale or rental of housing constituted state action. Justice White, for the Court in *Reitman,* rejected the dissent's position that Proposition 14 was simply an assertion of official neutrality regarding private discrimination; that the law was "simply permissive in purpose and effect, and inoffensive on its face." Instead, the Court deferred to the finding of the California Supreme Court that the "design and effect" of Proposition 14 was to overturn the state's fair housing laws and to authorize private racial discrimination—it would "significantly encourage and involve the State in private discrimination." This was no policy of state neutrality or simply a repeal of existing fair housing laws or merely a state failure to prevent private racial discrimination. The effect of Proposition 14 was to embody a "right to discriminate" on racial grounds in the State's basic Charter. Private racial discrimination could now operate "free from censure or interference of any kind from official sources." Private discrimination had been given constitutional status. The dissent in *Reitman* warned that, in relying on "encouragement," the Court was "forging a slippery and unfortunate criterion." Whatever the merits of this evaluation, the "encouragement" thesis has not really been employed in later cases. While lip service is still paid to "significant encouragement" as a basis for finding state action, the Court is increasingly demanding a showing of "authorization and approval" of the challenged private action.

By the early 1970's, however, it became clear that the generous interpretation of the state action concept which had characterized Warren Court era cases like *Reitman* was coming to a close. A series of cases in the early seventies made it clear that it was going to be much more difficult to reach private conduct through judicial expansion of state action. This approach begun in the era of the Burger Court, and ascendant now under the Rehnquist Court, requires a significant increase in the degree of government involvement in private conduct to justify the conclusion that state action is present. Litigants are now required to show that a close nexus exists between the private action at issue and government. From the state action perspective, the domain of the private sector is now significantly increased.

For example, in *Jackson v. Metropolitan Edison Co.* (1974), the Court considered a procedural due process challenge to termination of services for non-payment by a privately-owned utility company. Even though the state had reviewed the utility's tariff schedule providing for the challenged termination, the Court found no state action. While there was state "failure to overturn the practice," the state "has not put its own weight on the side of the proposed practice by ordering it." State toleration of a practice does not place the state's imprimatur on it. In *Flagg Bros. Inc. v. Brooks* (1978), the Court rejected "mere acquiescence" or "inaction" by the state in a warehouseman's sale of goods without notice or hearing to the debtor as sufficient to constitute state action. Even though the state's UCC law specifically *permitted* such a sale, the state had "merely announced the circumstances under which its courts will not interfere with a private sale." In *Rendell–Baker v. Kohn* (1982), the Court found no evidence that the private school's challenged discharge of employees was "compelled or influenced by any state regulation." And in *Blum v. Yaretsky* (1982), there was insufficient evidence that state regulations "dictate the decision to discharge or transfer [the nursing home patients] in a particular case." While there was pervasive state regulation, including adjustment of state financial benefits based on the nursing home's decisions, this did not "constitute approval or enforcement of that decision."

In each of these above cases, there was inadequate showing of official involvement in the particular challenged action—the state had not sanctioned it. However, when a deprivation of a federal right is caused by the exercise of some right or privilege created by the state or by a rule of conduct imposed by the state, *and* where the party charged with the deprivation may fairly be said to be a state actor, state action will be found. Or, at least, this is what the Court held 5–4 in *Lugar v. Edmondson Oil Co.* (1982). Acting pursuant to state law, Edmondson had obtained, *ex parte,* a prejudgment attachment of some of debtor Lugar's property. The writ of attachment was issued by a court clerk and executed by the sheriff. The Court held both requirements for state action were present. Lugar was claiming that the statute, which defined a "rule of conduct" for prejudgment attachment, was depriving him of due process. The second element, *i.e.,* involvement of a state actor, resulted from the "joint participation," by the state officials with the private party. For the dissent, this official action was simply neutral state action since invocation of state law, without more, does not make the state a partner to the crime.

State responsibility for the particular private action being challenged has become a critical focus. And the factual predicates for finding state responsibility are increasingly limited. But race-based peremptory challenges by private litigants constitutes state action. Such challenges meet the two-part *Lugar* test. First, such challenges were authorized by state law. Second, a government official, a judge, conducts the *voir dire* and administers the use of such challenges. Therefore, the requisite joint participation between state and private actors is satisfied. *Edmonson v. Leesville Concrete Co.* (1991).

Lugar was a narrow crack in the formidable wall to constitutional litigation created by the modern state action doctrine. *American Manufacturers Mutual Insurance Co. v. Sullivan* (1999) illustrates how narrow that crack was. The state workers' compensation law permitted an insurer to suspend benefits without notice or opportunity to be heard pending a review as to whether the treatment was reasonable or necessary. A private insurer's decision to withhold payment for disputed medical treatment under this law was unsuccessfully challenged by insurance claimants who contended that this provision violated Fourteenth Amendment due process.

The Supreme Court, per Chief Justice Rehnquist, held that the private insurer's decision to withhold payment and seek review of the medical treatment issue was not "fairly attributable to the State so as to subject insurers to the constraints of the Fourteenth Amendment." *Jackson v. Metropolitan Edison, supra,* established that the mere fact that a business was regulated by the state did not thereby convert that private action into state action. A nexus of "sufficient closeness" between the state and the challenged private activity is required. The state did not encourage or coerce the protested private activity. The state law allowing withholding payment can be viewed as "state inaction"—-a state decision not to interfere in a dispute between an insurer and an employee. Nor is state action present because the state had delegated to private actors, *i.e.,*the insurers, power traditionally exclusively reserved to the State. State law did not require the state to provide either medical treatment or worker's compensation benefits to injured workers. Private employers, not the state, are required to provide medical treatment or workers' compensation benefits to injured workers. All the state did was to authorize what the insurance company would have done anyway——-withhold payment of a disputed medical treatment until its necessity and reasonableness could be reviewed. The *Burton v. Wilmington Parking Authority* "joint participation" doctrine was not applicable. *Blum v. Yaretsky,, supra,* and *Jackson* make clear that private businesses which provide services that the state would not necessarily provide do not fall under this doctrine even though the businesses may be subject to extensive state regulation.

Even a close working relationship between the public action and the private party will sometimes on close examination be found insufficient to show the requisite joint action. When the National Collegiate Athletic Association (NCAA) threatened the University of Nevada–Las Vegas(UNLV), a state university, with sanctions unless it took disciplinary action against its basketball coach, Jerry Tarkanian, the NCAA conduct was held not to constitute state action. *National Collegiate Athletic Association v. Tarkanian* (1988). The *Tarkanian* case was the "mirror image" of *Burton v. Wilmington Parking Authority, supra. Burton* had involved state encouragement of private action. *Tarkanian* involved private encouragement of state action. It turned out to be a significant difference. The NCAA did not act as an agent of the state university but in response to its obligation to its other members to enforce its rules. UNLV was under no compulsion to stay in the NCAA. No power had been delegated by the state to the NCAA to discipline a state university employee, the basketball coach. The NCAA sanctions were not created or required by Nevada law. The Court noted that UNLV had resisted the effort by the NCAA to have it impose sanctions. A crucial point was that the state university and the NCAA were not willing joint actors but adversaries.

A private high school brought a Sec. 1983 action against a statewide non-profit private athletic association, which regulated interscholastic sports for the state's public and private high schools, to prevent enforcement of the association's rules. The private high school contended that the association was violating its First and Fourteenth Amendment rights. The private high school would have had no case unless it was found that the action of the non-profit state athletic association constituted state action. Surprisingly, that is exactly what the Court found. Justice Souter, held, 5–4, that there was such a pervasive entwinement of the public officials of a single state in the private association's activities that state action was present. *Brentwood Academy v. Tennessee Secondary School Athletic Association* (2001). *Tarkanian* was distinguished because there the NCAA's policies were not just developed by the state University of Nevada but by hundreds of member institutions outside Nevada "exhibiting no color of Nevada law." Here the affected schools were located within a single state. The fact that the overwhelming majority of the association's member schools were public showed that entwinement was present from the "bottom up." The fact that the association's rules were subject to review and approval by a state board showed that entwinement was also present from the "top down." Justice Thomas for the dissenters protested the reach of the Court's undefined entwinement test. He feared that any organization involving public institutions and public officials in its activities might now be subject to being viewed as state action.

CHAPTER X

CONGRESSIONAL LEGISLATION IN AID OF CIVIL RIGHTS AND LIBERTIES

A. SOURCES OF CONGRESSIONAL POWER

Congress can draw on a variety of constitutional provisions when it seeks to legislate in aid of civil rights and liberties. For example, Congress has used its commerce power to provide remedies against racial discrimination in places of public accommodation. *Heart of Atlanta Motel, Inc. v. United States* (1964); *Katzenbach v. McClung* (1964). In Title VI of the 1964 Civil Rights Act, Congress employed its spending power to prohibit racial discrimination by grantees of federal funds and it has used that same power to require the use of minority businesses in public works projects funded with federal monies. *Fullilove v. Klutznick* (1980). Congress may also legislate to protect "federal rights" arising from the relationship of citizens to the national government as it did in providing remedies against private interference with the right of interstate movement [*Griffin v. Breckenridge* (1971)] and in its prohibition of the use of residency requirements in presidential and vice presidential elections which similarly inter-

fered with the right to interstate movement. *Oregon
v. Mitchell* (1970). In legislating under these various
constitutional sources of power, Congress may legislate against even private misconduct.

Various constitutional amendments also recognize congressional legislative power to implement
their guarantees. The Thirteenth, Fourteenth, Fifteenth, Nineteenth [women's right to vote], Twen-
ty-third [vote for the District of Columbia in presidential elections], Twenty-fourth [abolishing the
poll tax], and Twenty-sixth [eighteen year old vote]
Amendments all have provisions authorizing Congress to enforce their guarantees by appropriate
legislation. In construing the congressional power
under these constitutional grants, the Court has
adopted the same broad perspective of congressional
power that characterizes its treatment of the commerce and spending powers. So long as Congress
could reasonably conclude that the legislation is in
furtherance of the constitutional guarantee, Congress has power to legislate. *McCulloch v. Maryland*
(1819).

B. ENFORCING THE THIRTEENTH
AMENDMENT

The Thirteenth Amendment, Sec. 2, provides that
Congress shall have power to enforce the Amendment's prohibition against slavery or involuntary
servitude by "appropriate legislation." While the
Court has taken a highly restrictive view of its own
power to remedy private and state misconduct as

violative of the Thirteenth Amendment, Sec. 1, it has read the Thirteenth Amendment, Sec. 2, to give Congress broad power to enact legislation necessary and proper for eradicating all "badges and incidents of slavery in the United States." Since the Thirteenth Amendment, Sec. 1, proscribes even private action violative of the right guaranteed, Congress can enact legislation reaching private imposition of badges of slavery.

Jones v. Mayer (1968), upheld an 1866 federal law which was read to prohibit even private discrimination in the sale or rental of real and personal property. In addressing the issue of Congress' constitutional power, Justice Stewart, for the Court, held that the enabling clause of the Thirteenth Amendment "clothed 'Congress with power to pass all laws necessary and proper for abolishing all badges and incidents of slavery in the United States.' "Since Congress could rationally conclude that the burden and disabilities of slavery include restraints upon the essence of civil freedom, *i.e.,* the right to purchase and lease property, the law was constitutional. "When racial discrimination herds men into ghettos and makes their ability to buy property turn on the color of their skin, then it is a relic of slavery." The dissent limited itself to challenging the Court's interpretation of the 1866 civil rights law to reach private discrimination, not the Court's exegesis on the constitutional grant of power.

Again, in *Runyon v. McCrary* (1976), the Court upheld congressional power under Sec. 2 of the

Thirteenth Amendment to prohibit discrimination against blacks in their ability to "contract" on the same basis as white citizens. The legislation was interpreted to prohibit discrimination against blacks by private, commercially operated, non-sectarian schools. While the dissent challenged the Court's interpretation of the federal law to reach private racially motivated refusals to contract rather than state legal rules disabling persons from making or enforcing contracts, it did not challenge the Court's interpretation of the Thirteenth Amendment to sanction Congress' proscription of racial discrimination. *Runyon* also rejected arguments that the federal law violated freedom of association. Parents retained the freedom to send their children to schools that teach racial segregation but the Constitution did not protect the school's practice of excluding racial minorities. *Runyon* left open the question whether Congress could prohibit racial discrimination based on religious grounds. The Court similarly rejected the contention that the law infringed privacy rights. While the right of privacy might extend to a genuinely private social club, it did not insulate private schools advertising and offering their services to members of the general public from appropriate federal legislation.

However, in *Memphis v. Greene* (1981), the Court rejected a challenge based on the Thirteenth Amendment and federal legislation to a decision by Memphis to close a road which traversed a white residential community from outside traffic coming from black neighborhoods. First, the Thirteenth

Amendment was not violated because the disparate impact of the closing on black citizens "could not be fairly characterized as a badge or incident of slavery." There was no showing of racially discriminatory motivation and the adverse impact on blacks was not deemed sufficient to offend the Thirteenth Amendment since such a holding "would trivialize the great purpose of that great charter of freedom. Proper respect for the dignity of the residents of any neighborhood requires that they accept the same burdens as well as the same benefits of citizenship regardless of their racial or ethnic origin." Turning to the congressional enactment, the Court simply found that the actions of Memphis did not involve any discrimination impairing the kind of property interests that the legislation was designed to proscribe. There was no showing that Memphis officials had granted benefits to white citizens that would have been refused to black citizens or that the official action significantly depreciated the value of property owned by black citizens.

C. ENFORCING THE FOURTEENTH AMENDMENT

1. CONGRESS' REMEDIAL POWERS

Sec. 5 of the Fourteenth Amendment provides that Congress can enact appropriate legislation to enforce the guarantees of that Amendment. Pursuant to this enabling clause, Congress can provide remedies for violations of Fourteenth Amendment rights as they have been defined by the courts.

In Sec. 4(e) of the Voting Rights Act of 1965, Congress provided that no state could deny the franchise because of an inability to read or write English to a person who had successfully completed the sixth grade in a Puerto Rican school. In upholding the constitutionality of this provision on the basis of the Fourteenth Amendment, Sec. 5, *Katzenbach v. Morgan* (1966), invoked the broad standards of *McCulloch v. Maryland*: "Correctly viewed, Sec. 5 is a positive grant of legislative power authorizing Congress to exercise its discretion in determining whether and what legislation is needed to secure the guarantees of the Fourteenth Amendment." Sec. 4(e) could be regarded as a reasonable means to secure non-discriminatory treatment by government in basic public services. It was for Congress to weigh the enhanced political power for the Puerto Rican community against the intrusion on the constitutionally based state power to set voter qualifications. "It is not for [the Court] to review the congressional resolution of these factors. It is enough that the [the Court is] able to perceive a basis upon which Congress might resolve the conflict as it did."

2.   CONGRESS' SUBSTANTIVE POWERS

But Justice Brennan, writing for the Court in *Morgan,* did not stop merely with an affirmation of Congress' power to provide remedies for judicially recognized Fourteenth Amendment rights. Instead, the opinion could be read to indicate that Congress could itself make the substantive determination that state literacy requirements violate the equal protection guarantee, even though the Court previously had held that such voting qualifications did not violate the Amendment. Sec. 4(e) could be upheld as legislation aimed at eliminating invidious discrimination in state voter qualifications. Congress had applied its "specially informed legislative competence." For Justice Harlan, joined by Justice Stewart, dissenting, the Court's premise that the Sec. 5 power extended beyond remedies to defining substantive rights was an unacceptable abdication of the judicial role. It was for the judicial branch to determine if New York's application of its literacy test violated equal protection. While Congress might inform the judicial judgment, it could not substitute its interpretation of the Constitution for that of the Court.

Another construction of *Morgan* gives less far reaching legislative power to Congress under the Fourteenth Amendment. In this view, *Morgan* means only that when Congress exercises its remedial power under Sec. 5 of the Fourteenth Amendment, it may on the basis of an examination of the facts conclude that a state lacks sufficient justification for the action which Congress has chosen to correct by legislation. For example, New York state in *Morgan* lacked sufficient justification for the voting discrimination practiced by the literacy test; therefore, Congress has legislative power under Sec. 5 to take corrective action through the Voting Rights Act.

Justice Harlan also argued in his *Morgan* dissent that the Court's reading of Sec. 5 would allow Congress "to exercise its Sec. 5 'discretion' [to enact] statutes so as in effect to dilute equal protection and due process decisions of [the] Court." But Justice Brennan, in a footnote, rejected any congressional power to dilute the constitutional guarantees. "We emphasize that Congress' power under Sec. 5 is limited to adopting measures to enforce the guarantees of the Amendment; Sec. 5 grants Congress no power to restrict, abrogate, or dilute these guarantees." This is the "ratchet theory"—Congress' Sec. 5 powers operate in only one direction, *i.e.,* it is a power "to enforce" or extend rights, not to dilute Fourteenth Amendment rights. Congressional legislation authorizing state use of racially segregated schools, suggested Justice Brennan, would not be a reasonable means for enforcing the equal protection guarantee.

Oregon v. Mitchell (1970), established that congressional power under the enabling clauses is not unlimited. A badly-fragmented Court held unconstitutional, 5–4, a provision of the 1970 Voting Rights Act lowering the voting age in state elections to age 18. But no opinion commanded majority support. At most, the case stands for the limited principle that Congress cannot use its Sec. 5 powers to violate other constitutional provisions, *i.e.,* Art. 1, Sec. 2, gives the states the power to define the qualifications of voters for state officers and thus limits Congress' power to override state age requirements for state elections.

When local zoning authorities denied the request by a Catholic church, located in an area designated a historic district, for a building permit to enlarge its building, the church, relying on the Religious Freedom Restoration Act of 1993 (RFRA), brought suit. RFRA was a Congressional response to *Employment Division v. Smith* (1990) holding that "neutral, generally applicable law may be applied to religious practices even when not supported by a compelling governmental interest." *Smith* was a departure from *Sherbert v. Verner* (1963) which had asked whether a government restraint "substantially burdened a religious practice and, if it did, whether the burden was justified by a compelling governmental interest." RFRA stated that its purpose was "to restore the compelling interest test as set forth in *Sherbert*" and "to guarantee its application in all case where free exercise of religion is substantially burdened." The Court, per Justice Kennedy, held that Congress could not predicate its enactment of RFRA on its Fourteenth Amendment enforcement powers. Congress could not declare "the *substance* of the Fourteenth Amendment's restrictions on the States." Congress may enforce a provision of the Constitution such as the Free Exercise Clause but it may not alter its meaning: "Congress does not enforce a constitutional right by changing what the right is." The Fourteenth Amendment gives Congress power to remedy unconstitutional actions but not "to make a substantive change in the governing law." *City of Boerne v. Flores* (1997).

Boerne rejected an expansive view of Congressional Sec. 5 powers based on *Katzenbach v. Morgan*. The history of the Fourteenth Amendment reveals that Sec. 5, the Enforcement Clause, is of a remedial rather than a substantive nature. Fourteenth Amendment case law also rejects the idea that "Congress has a substantive, non-remedial power under the Fourteenth Amendment." *Morgan* is not to the contrary. Although *Morgan* might be read as attributing to Congress the power "to enact legislation that expands the rights contained in Sec. 1, of the Fourteenth Amendment," this is not its necessary or even its best reading. *Morgan* had two rationales, one designed to combat discrimination in government services, the other to combat discrimination in setting voter qualifications. A more expansive interpretation would impermissibly allow Congress to "define its own powers by altering the Fourteenth Amendment." Such an interpretation would reduce the constitution to the level of ordinary legislative acts. *Boerne* did not address the *Morgan* ratchet theory. But since the *Boerne* Court denied the power of Congress to substantively define constitutional rights under the Enforcement Clause of the Fourteenth Amendment, it is questionable whether the ratchet theory has continuing vitality.

RFRA could not be validated as a remedial measure either. RFRA came to the Court with no record demonstrating a need to remedy past discrimination as in the voting rights cases. The appropriateness of a remedial measure must be evaluated in the light of the harm to be prevented. RFRA was a response out of proportion to any remedial objective. RFRA was a sweeping measure applicable "at every level of government," not limited by any termination date, and subject to invocation by anyone asserting a substantial burden on free exercise rights. By contrast, in *South Carolina v. Katzenbach*, the challenged provisions were confined only to those parts of the country where voting discrimination had been flagrant and then only to state voting laws. *Boerne* applied a congruence test: Whether enforcement measures are remedial under Sec. 5 is determined by their "proportionality or congruence between the means adopted and the legitimate ends to be achieved." Finally, there is a relationship between the design of the Fourteenth Amendment and the doctrine of separation of powers. When the political branches of the government act contrary to a "judicial interpretation of the Constitution already issued," they trespass upon the responsibilities of the federal judiciary. *Marbury v. Madison* has long established that it is the Judicial Branch which has the responsibility to say what the law is. Therefore, Congress exceeded its powers *vis-a-vis* the states under the Enforcement Clause of the Fourteenth Amendment and acted contrary to the separation of powers. The issue of whether RFRA is valid against the federal government remains.

In 1992 Congress enacted the Patent Remedy Act which expressly abrogated the sovereign immunity of the states in patent infringement cases. College Savings, a New Jersey bank, sued Florida Prepaid, a

Florida state entity, for patent infringement contending that in administering its tuition prepay-
ment program Florida Prepaid infringed College
Savings' patent for its educational financing method. College Savings further contended that the Patent Remedy Act was authorized by Sec. 5 of the
Fourteenth Amendment. Congress sought to protect
against deprivations of property without due process of law. The Court held 5–4, per Chief Justice
Rehnquist, that Congress had failed to identify any
pattern of patent infringement by the states which
would constitute due process violations that were
proportionate to the Patent Remedy Act's abrogation of state sovereign immunity in patent infringement cases. *Florida Prepaid Postsecondary Education Expense Board v. College Savings Bank*
(1999). Legislation enacted under Section 5, the
Enforcement Clause of the Fourteenth Amendment,
must be congruent to the wrong Congress was
seeking to remedy. Evidence of this kind of congruence was simply lacking here.

*College Savings Bank v. Florida Prepaid Postsec-
ondary Expense Education Board* (1999) sets forth a
further limitation on Congressional power under
Section 5 of the Fourteenth Amendment. The
Trademark Remedy Clarification Act (TRCA) subjected the states to suit for false and misleading
advertising. Constitutional authority for the TRCA
was predicated on Section 5 of the Fourteenth
Amendment. But the Court held, 5–4, per Justice
Scalia, that the TRCA was not authorized under
Section 5. The right to be free from false advertis-

ing or to be secure in one's business activities is not property within the meaning of the Fourteenth Amendment. Hence Congress has no authority under Sec. 5 to legislate to protect such interests and, therefore, no authority to abrogate state sovereign immunity with respect to such matters.

By a clear and plain statement, the federal Age Discrimination in Employment Act (ADEA) prohibits employers including the states from engaging in age discrimination. Furthermore, Congress has authority under *Fitzpatrick v. Bitzer, supra,* to abrogate the sovereign immunity of the states. But the Court held, per Justice O'Connor, that the ADEA was not appropriate legislation under Sec. 5 of the Fourteenth Amendment. The ultimate interpreter of the substantive meaning of the Fourteenth Amendment is the responsibility of the judicial branch of government. On the basis of the "congruence and proportionality" tests applied in *Boerne* and *Florida Prepaid,* the ADEA prohibits "substantially more state employment decisions and practices than would likely be held unconstitutional under the applicable equal protection, rational basis standard." Congress may, of course, enact legislation that is "reasonably prophylactic." But Congress failed to identify any pattern of age discrimination on the part of the States that did not meet the rational basis standard of review used to evaluate to age discrimination on the part of the States. *Kimel v. Florida Board of Regents* (2000).

In *Board of Trustees of the University of Alabama v. Garrett* (2001), employees sued their state employers for money damages under Title I of the Americans with Disabilities Act (ADA). But the state employers successfully contended that the ADA was not a valid exercise of Congressional power under Sec. 5 of the Fourteenth Amendment. The Court held, 5–4, per Chief Justice Rehnquist, that the predicate required for suits for money damages against unconsenting states authorized by federal legislation enacted under Sec. 5 of the Fourteenth Amendment is "documentation of patterns of constitutional violations committed by the state in its official capacity." There had been no showing by Congress that there was a pattern of state discrimination against the disabled which violated the Fourteenth Amendment. Consequently, the remedy imposed by the ADA on the states was not congruent or proportional to any asserted violation. As in *Kimel*, the relevant standard of review for legislation affecting disabled persons is whether the actions of the states concerning them satisfy the rational basis standard of review. The states may decline to make special accommodation for disabled persons as long as their decisions are not irrational.

The Court's recent aversion to abrogation of state immunity to suit even with respect to Congressional legislation based on Sec. 5 has some significant exceptions. For example, Congress in the Family Medical and Leave Act authorized eligible employees, including state employees, to take up to twelve weeks of unpaid leave on grounds such as taking care of an employee's spouse. This benefit extended to men as well as women. The Act gave state employees the right to recover damages if a state failed to comply with the Act's provisions. Did Congress have authority under Sec. 5 to abrogate state immunity under the Act in order to remedy and deter gender-based discrimination?

Chief Justice Rehnquist, for the Court, held that the record of state "unconstitutional participation in, and fostering of, gender based discrimination in the administration of leave benefits [was] was weighty enough to justify the enactment of prophylactic Sec. 5 legislation." There was significant evidence of widespread gender-based discrimination by the states with respect to leave benefits. Under equal protection law, gender based discrimination that is intentional is subject to heightened review, *Garrett* and *Kimel* were distinguished on the ground that discrimination based on age or disability was subject only to a rational basis standard of review. In those cases, Congress had to show [and had failed to so] that there had been "irrational reliance" by the states with respect to the use of these criteria. However, where heightened review was applicable as in the case of gender discrimination, the congressional task in showing a pattern of state constitutional violations was easier. Congress had sought to remedy the cycle of discrimination that bound women to serve as primary care-givers and which reinforced employer stereotypes about "women's commitment to work and their value as employees." Therefore, the Family and Medical Leave Act was " 'congruent and proportionate to the targeted violation.' " *Nevada Department of Human Resources v. Hibbs* (2003).

The Court distinguished *Garrett* and *Kimel* on the basis that a heightened rather than a rational basis standard of review was applicable in yet another Sec. 5 case. Title II of the Americans with Disabilities Act forbade discrimination against individuals with disabilities with respect to benefits from public services, programs or activities. Two paraplegics who used wheelchairs claimed they were denied access to state courts by reason of their disabilities. One of these individuals had to crawl up two flights of stairs in a county courthouse to answer criminal charges. Congress had found by way of an extensive record that there was disability discrimination in access to judicial services that had not been otherwise remedied. This discrimination implicated rights under the Due Process Clause, the First Amendment and the Sixth Amendment which, unlike the laws reviewed in *Garrett* and *Kimel*, were subject to heightened review. Relying on *Hibbs*, the Court, per Justice Stevens, ruled that the the Act was appropriate prophylactic legislation. Title II remedied a pattern of exclusion and discrimination against the disabled and was congruent and proportionate to the Congressional objective of implementing the fundamental right of access to the courts. Title II, therefore, as it applies to that class of cases, was a valid exercise of congressional authority under Section 5. *Tennessee v. Lane* (2004).

3. REACHING PRIVATE CONDUCT

In the *Civil Rights Cases* (1883), the Court held that Congress' enforcement power under the Civil War Amendments was limited to providing remedies against conduct proscribed by the amendments. Congress was authorized only "to provide modes of redress against the operation of state laws, and the actions of state officers, executive or judicial." Private rights were secured by the Amendment only to the extent that Congress could provide legislative remedies to correct state wrongs against private persons. To allow Congress to legislate directly against private action would allow that body "to establish a code of new municipal law regulative of all private rights between man and man in society. It would be to make Congress take the place of the state legislatures and to supersede them."

But this seemingly absolute prohibition against congressional use of Sec. 5 of the Fourteenth Amendment to reach private conduct was at least brought into question in *United States v. Guest* (1966). Justice Stewart's opinion for the Court rested on the premise that the indictments alleging violation of federal civil rights laws contained an allegation of state involvement or alleged an interference with the right of interstate travel, a fundamental constitutional right which is not limited to state action. However, six justices concurring in *Guest,* indicated that Congress had power under Sec. 5 to legislate against private interference with the Fourteenth Amendment right to use state-owned facilities free from racial discrimination. Justice Brennan, joined by Chief Justice Warren and Justice Douglas, for example, asserted that Sec. 5 authorizes Congress to protect rights under the Fourteenth Amendment: "Congress is thus fully empowered to determine that punishment of private conspiracies interfering with the exercise of such a right is necessary to its full protection." He specifically disapproved of the premise that Congress' power was limited to enacting corrective legislation against state action. The *Guest dicta* that Sec. 5 could be used to reach private action was repudiated in *United States v. Morrison,* Ch. II, *supra.* Sec. 5 could be used to enact laws prohibiting discrimination by state officials but not, as in the Violence Against Women Act, for laws aimed at discrimination by private individuals.

The scope of congressional power to protect civil rights through the Commerce Clause, the Spending Power, and the Thirteenth Amendment, has made it unnecessary to determine the full scope of congressional power to reach private action under Fourteenth Amendment, Sec. 5. See *Griffin v. Breckenridge* (1971), upholding application of a federal civil rights statute authorizing damages against private individuals interfering with various constitutional rights on the basis of the Thirteenth Amendment and the right of interstate movement. The Court specifically noted that the allegations of the complaint did not require consideration of the scope of congressional power under Sec. 5 of the Fourteenth Amendment.

D. ENFORCING THE FIFTEENTH AMENDMENT

Like the other Civil War amendments, Sec. 2 of the Fifteenth Amendment gives Congress the power to enforce the guarantees of the article by appropriate legislation. In interpreting this grant of power, the Court again has applied the mandate of *McCulloch v. Maryland.* So long as Congress could reasonably conclude that the legislation will effectuate the constitutional prohibitions against racial discrimination in voting, the legislation is constitutional. Thus in *South Carolina v. Katzenbach* (1966), the Court upheld the 1965 Voting Rights Act prohibiting voter registration requirements which Congress had determined to be racially discriminatory. The Court stated: "As against the reserved powers of the States, Congress may use any rational means to effectuate the Constitutional prohibition of racial discrimination in voting." Congress could reasonably conclude that the unique remedial devices fashioned in the Voting Rights Act were justified because of the failure of case-by-case litigation to combat wide-spread and persistent voting discrimination. Again, in *Oregon v. Mitchell* (1970), the Court upheld provisions of the 1970 Voting Rights Act prohibiting the use of literacy tests noting that Congress had before it a long history of the discriminatory use of literacy tests to disenfranchise voters on account of their race.

In *City of Rome v. United States* (1980), the Court upheld provisions of the 1965 Voting Rights Act as applied by the Attorney General in disapproving electoral changes made by the City of Rome, Georgia, on grounds that the changes would have had a discriminatory effect. The City of Rome argued that, since the Fifteenth Amendment, Sec. 1, prohibited only purposeful racial discrimination in voting, Congress was similarly limited in fashioning remedial provisions under the Fifteenth Amendment, Sec. 2. But the Court stated: "It is clear that under Sec. 2 of the Fifteenth Amendment Congress may prohibit practices that in and of themselves do not violate Sec. 1 of the Amendment, so long as the prohibitions attacking racial discrimination in voting are 'appropriate,' as that term is defined in *McCulloch v. Maryland.*" Congress could have rationally concluded that, "because electoral changes by jurisdictions with a demonstrable history of intentional racial discrimination in voting create the risk of purposeful discrimination, it was proper to prohibit changes that have a discriminatory impact."

An opportunity for reaffirmation of *City of Rome* was provided when a North Carolina apportionment scheme for its state legislature using multi-member districts was challenged. Black voters contended that the scheme gave them less opportunity than white voters to elect representatives of their choice. They challenged the multi-member district scheme under the 1982 amendments to the Voting Rights Act. The Act established "the 'results' test" as "the relevant legal standard." Sec. 2, as amended, of the Act directed that this standard should be applied through a "totality of the circumstances" approach.

This approach inquires into whether the voting scheme in question impairs the opportunity of members of racial minorities to participate in the political process. The Court interpreted the Act, as amended, to reach discriminatory effects, accepting that the Act, so interpreted, was a constitutional exercise of Congressional power under Sec. 2 of the Fifteenth Amendment regardless of whether Sec. 1 of the Fifteenth Amendment requires a showing of discriminatory purpose or not. *Thornburg v. Gingles* (1986).

INDEX

References are to Pages

CONSCIENTIOUS OBJECTORS
Free exercise of religion, 593–594

CONSENT OR APPROVAL
Abortion, 226
State, consent to suit in federal court, 19

CONSTITUTIONAL PRINCIPLES
Generally, 1–3
Amendments, generally, 3
Bill of Rights, generally, 3
Checks and balances, 2
Congressional Power, this index
Due Process of Law, this index
Equal Protection, this index
Executive Power and Congress, this index
Expression, Freedom of, this index
Federalism, 2
Judicial Review, this index
Limited government principle, 2–3
Religion, Freedom of, this index
Separation of powers, generally, 1
State Action, this index
State Power in American Federalism, this index

CONTRACEPTION LAWS
Minors, limiting access to contraceptives, 229–230
Privacy, right of, 215 et seq.

COUNSEL, RIGHT TO
Enemy combatants, 272

COURTS
Access to, 362–368
Article III courts, 10 et seq.
Judicial Review, this index

CRIMINAL LAW AND PROCEEDINGS
Commerce clause, use to federalize criminal law, 82
Indigent defendants, rights of, 362 et seq.
Media access, 511–513

CROSS–BURNING
Expression, freedom of, 432–433

CUMULATIVE EFFECTS PRINCIPLE
Congressional power to regulate commerce, 79, 82, 89

DUE PROCESS OF LAW—Cont'd
Prisoners—Cont'd
    Liberty interests, 258–259
Privacy rights, 215 et seq.
Procedural due process
      Generally, 253–273
    Arbitrariness, avoiding, 264
    Balancing of interests, 265–266
    Conclusive presumption doctrine, 263
    Enemy combatants, 270–273
    Fundamental fairness, 262
    Institutional due process, 268–269
    Liberty interests, 257–262
    Life, liberty and property interests, generally, 254–262
    Process that is due, generally, 262–273
    Property interests, 255–257
    Seizure of property, 270
    Sex offenders' registry (Megan's Law), 264
    Teachers' rights, 255–256
Property interests, 255–257
Protection, right to, 245–248
Punitive damages, standard of review, 199–201
Putative natural father, rights of, 241
Rational basis test, economic due process, 198–201
Regulatory takings, 204
Reputational interests, 261–262
Right to die, 249–250
Roe vs. Wade, 220–222
School procedures, 267
Seizure of property, procedural due process rights, 270
Selective incorporation approach, 190–191
Sex offenders
    Civil commitment, 248–249
    Registry (Megan's Law), 264–265
Sodomy laws, 233–238
Strict scrutiny standard
    Abortion rights, 221, 227
    Fundamental personal rights, generally, 211–215
    Privacy rights, 218
    Undue burden test compared, 227
Substantive due process
      Generally, 192–253
    Abortion laws, 215 et seq.
    Alien juveniles in custody, 242–243
    Assisted suicide rights, 250–252

†